Cognitive Analytic Supervision

Cognitive Analytic Supervision is the first book to present a cognitive analytic perspective on psychotherapy supervision. This edited collection of original chapters reflects the ways in which CAT therapists and supervisors have developed the model and used it in diverse settings. It is a significant contribution to the literature on relational psychotherapy supervision, written by established CAT supervisors, trainers and therapists who, together, have an enormous amount of professional and clinical experience.

The book covers important areas such as:

- the relational theory and practice of CAT supervision
- a cognitive analytic conceptualisation of narcissistic difficulties
- intercultural issues in supervision
- ethical and clinical dilemmas in supervision
- supervision of consultancy work

Cognitive Analytic Supervision will be of interest to CAT supervisors, therapists and trainee supervisors, as well as supervisors and therapists working in other therapeutic models, in particular those with a relational approach.

Deborah Pickvance is a UKCP registered cognitive analytic psychotherapist, an accredited supervisor and trainer in cognitive analytic therapy. Her experience of psychotherapy supervision spans thirty years; this includes supervising therapists and supervisors practising in many different settings at trainee and post-qualification level. She has worked in NHS psychotherapy and psychology departments, primary care and women's therapy services.

'CAT emerged from many years of practice and supervision but not from the intention of founding the new model which eventually emerged. In this book experienced CAT supervisors and teachers reflect upon their practice and consider the relation of what they do to other models. They show how CAT has continued to grow through reflection based on extensive supervised practice and reassure me that the model, drawing on the participation of therapists and patients, generates continuing development.'
– **Anthony Ryle**, founder of Cognitive Analytic Therapy

'This superb volume, edited by Deborah Pickvance, makes a major contribution to the development of Cognitive Analytic Therapy (CAT) and to the field of psychotherapy supervision in general. Although, as Pickvance makes clear, both CAT and CAT supervision have always been implicitly relational in nature, this book explicitly highlights the relational features of CAT supervision including: the centrality of the supervisory alliance, the recognition that learning takes place in a relational context, the emphasis on the supervisor's (and therapist's) use of the self, and the importance of maintaining an ongoing awareness of relational patterns being enacted by both supervisee and supervisor. Chapters present masterful overviews of a range of important areas including: mindfulness in CAT supervision, the CAT supervisory relationship, the health of the CAT supervisor, and supervision of CAT therapists working with borderline personality disorder. This book will be appreciated by CAT therapists, CAT supervisors, and both therapists and supervisors practicing a wide range of other therapeutic modalities as well.'
– **Jeremy D. Safran**, Ph.D., Chair & Professor of Psychology, The New School for Social Research

'This book makes a very useful contribution to the field of supervision, showing how the integrative and relational approach of Cognitive Analytic Therapy can be applied to supervision. Supervisors of all traditions will find value in many of the thoughtful and reflective chapters in this book.'
– **Professor Peter Hawkins**, lead author of *Supervision in the Helping Professions* and many other books (www.renewalassociates.co.uk)

'*Cognitive Analytic Supervision* makes a significant contribution to the literature on supervision. The first book to be written about supervision from a Cognitive Analytic Therapy (CAT) perspective, it brings the reader the most contemporary information about working with relational processes in supervision. With multi-professional contributions from experienced therapists, trainers, researchers, supervisors and supervisees, this is an invaluable resource for CAT practitioners and trainees as well as for those working within other models of psychotherapy. Use of clinical and supervision examples from a wide range of settings makes the material highly accessible in a way that readily can be applied.'
– **Linda Steen**, Clinical Director, Clinical Psychology Doctoral Programme, The University of Manchester, co-author of Fleming, I. and Steen, L. eds., 2013, *Supervision and Clinical Psychology: Theory, Practice and Perspectives* (Routledge)

Cognitive Analytic Supervision

A relational approach

Edited by Deborah Pickvance

LONDON AND NEW YORK

First published 2017
by Routledge
2 Park Square, Milton Park, Abingdon, Oxon OX14 4RN

and by Routledge
711 Third Avenue, New York, NY 10017

*Routledge is an imprint of the Taylor & Francis Group,
an informa business*

© 2017 selection and editorial matter, Deborah Pickvance; individual chapters, the contributors

The right of the editor to be identified as the author of the editorial material, and of the authors for their individual chapters, has been asserted in accordance with sections 77 and 78 of the Copyright, Designs and Patents Act 1988.

All rights reserved. No part of this book may be reprinted or reproduced or utilised in any form or by any electronic, mechanical, or other means, now known or hereafter invented, including photocopying and recording, or in any information storage or retrieval system, without permission in writing from the publishers.

Trademark notice: Product or corporate names may be trademarks or registered trademarks, and are used only for identification and explanation without intent to infringe.

British Library Cataloguing in Publication Data
A catalogue record for this book is available from the British Library

Library of Congress Cataloging-in-Publication Data
Names: Pickvance, Deborah, editor.
Title: Cognitive analytic supervision : a relational approach / edited by Deborah Pickvance.
Description: Abingdon, Oxon ; New York, NY : Routledge, 2017. | Includes bibliographical references.
Identifiers: LCCN 2016003815 | ISBN 9781138837782 (hardback) | ISBN 9781138837799 (pbk.) | ISBN 9781315716145 (ebook)
Subjects: | MESH: Cognitive Therapy – organization & administration | Interprofessional Relations | Psychiatry | Mentors
Classification: LCC RC489.C63 | NLM WM 425.5.C6 | DDC 616.89/1425—dc23
LC record available at http://lccn.loc.gov/2016003815

ISBN: 978-1-138-83778-2 (hbk)
ISBN: 978-1-138-83779-9 (pbk)
ISBN: 978-1-315-71614-5 (ebk)

Typeset in Times New Roman
by Apex CoVantage, LLC

This book is dedicated with gratitude to the creator and pioneer of Cognitive Analytic Therapy, Dr Anthony Ryle – always an inspiration as thinker, therapist and supervisor.

Contents

Preface x
Acknowledgements xiii
List of contributors xiv
Glossary of CAT terms xvii

SECTION 1
CAT supervision: Theory, process and evidence 1

1 CAT supervision: A relational model 3
   DEBORAH PICKVANCE

2 The healthy supervisor: A CAT understanding of the
   process of psychotherapy supervision 19
   ANNIE NEHMAD

3 The CAT model and the practice of CAT supervision 37
   EVA BURNS-LUNDGREN

4 What makes supervision helpful? A review of research 53
   CAROLYN LAWSON

SECTION 2
Challenges in relational supervision 69

5 Clinical and ethical challenges in relational supervision 71
   DEBORAH PICKVANCE AND GLENYS PARRY

6 The use of the CAT model in the supervision of CAT
   therapists working with borderline personality disorder 83
   LIZ FAWKES AND VAL FRETTEN

viii Contents

7	Are narcissists a special case? Narcissism and supervision ANNIE NEHMAD	95
8	Intercultural supervision: Acknowledging cultural differences in supervision without compromise or complacency JESSIE EMILION AND HILARY BROWN	109

SECTION 3
Methods and tools of supervision   123

9	CAT group supervision: The social model in action JANE BLUNDEN AND HILARY BEARD	125
10	Using CAT mapping in relational supervision STEVE POTTER *(WITH A CONTRIBUTION BY CHERYL DELISSER)*	137
11	Integration of competency assessment into CAT supervision: A practical guide STEPHEN KELLETT AND DAWN BENNETT *(WITH A CONTRIBUTION BY FIONA PURDIE, BEN HAGUE AND NICK FIRTH)*	149
12	The value of mindfulness in CAT supervision ELIZABETH WILDE McCORMICK *(WITH CONTRIBUTIONS BY RENE BOSMAN, SYDNEY BAYLEY AND LIZ HALL)*	163
13	The microcosm in CAT supervision JASON HEPPLE	174

SECTION 4
Supervision in different contexts   185

14	The supervision relationship in a training context YVONNE STEVENS *(WITH A CONTRIBUTION BY SUE YABSLEY)*	187
15	Supervising non-CAT therapists MARK WESTACOTT	198
16	Supervising CAT consultancy in mental health teams ANGELA CARRADICE *(WITH A CONTRIBUTION BY MEGAN BLACK)*	209

17	**Supervising CAT with young people**	**222**
	LOUISE K. McCUTCHEON, LEE CROTHERS AND STEVE HALPERIN	
18	**Dilemmas in relational supervision in intellectual disability services**	**234**
	JULIE LLOYD *(WITH A CONTRIBUTION BY JACKIE DROHAN)*	
19	**CAT supervision in forensic practice: Working with complexity and risk**	**248**
	KAREN SHANNON	

Appendix 1: Resources	261
Appendix 2: ACAT Code of Ethics and Practice for Training and Supervision	263
Appendix 3: The CCAT – A measure of competence in Cognitive Analytic Therapy (CAT), by Dawn Bennett and Glenys Parry	271
Index	285

Preface

Cognitive Analytic Therapy (CAT) has grown greatly since Anthony Ryle started developing it in the 1970s, and it is now practised in many countries. The strength and originality of the model, its effectiveness and its unique integration of object relations, cognitive, and dialogical theory have made it a popular choice among mental health professionals. Supervision has always been an essential element of the model, and training in supervision has been provided in the UK, Finland, Australia and Spain. However, until now there has not been a book about supervision from a specifically CAT perspective.

This book invites supervisors – and supervisees – to draw on a range of tools, methods, perspectives, evidence and clinical experience, all presented within the framework of CAT's relational understanding. It will be a primary resource for CAT trainee supervisors and also useful for CAT supervisors and therapists. As supervisors we have a natural tendency 'to do as we have been done to' and to reproduce our own experience as supervisees in the supervision we ourselves do. This book will enable supervisors to develop their practice further by looking at supervision through the lens of the CAT model and other ideas.

CAT concepts and ways of working with relational processes in supervision, described in the book, can be applied within supervision in other psychotherapy models. They will be useful for supervisors working in models which are not explicitly relational, who want to know more about, or incorporate, a relational approach to supervision. Supervisors who already work relationally can draw on the CAT model, the exploration of complex supervisory issues and the accounts of supervising in different settings and using different supervisory methods.

The book will also be useful to supervisees, helping them to make better use of supervision, e.g. by understanding the group dynamics of their supervision group or having the courage to name parallel processes if they suspect them.

This book's CAT perspective is intended to supplement such invaluable texts as Hawkins and Shohet's (2012) *Supervision in the Helping Professions* (Open University Press), Gilbert and Evans' (2000) *Psychotherapy Supervision* (Open University Press) and Page and Wosket's (2015) *Supervising the Counsellor and Psychotherapist* (Routledge).

In keeping with CAT's dialogical perspective, this book gives voice to supervisees, by including contributions about their experience of CAT supervision. It also illustrates many points with clinical examples. Most of these are fictionalised, and the remainder are published with the consent of supervisees or clients. The book mirrors the multi-voiced CAT community rather than presenting an artificial uniformity. For example, it uses both terms 'client' and 'patient', reflecting the diverse clinical settings, professional backgrounds and preferences of the contributors.

Readers unfamiliar with CAT are invited to read the introduction to the CAT model in Chapter 3, the definition of some key concepts in Chapter 2 and to refer to the glossary.

The book is divided into four sections:

Section 1, CAT supervision: Theory, process and evidence, introduces the theoretical roots and the practice of CAT supervision, CAT as a therapy, and relevant research evidence. Just as CAT has a strong theoretical base, formed by an integration of other theories and informed by research, so too has CAT supervision. It is a fundamentally relational approach, consistent with the CAT model, while also drawing on other theories and research. In Chapter 1 I review relational models of supervision and situate CAT supervision among them. In Chapter 2 Annie Nehmad uses CAT concepts, along with ideas drawn from Hawkins and Shohet, Heron, and Siegel, to describe the characteristics and role of the 'healthy supervisor'. In Chapter 3 Eva Burns-Lundgren introduces the CAT model and presents the practice of CAT supervision at each stage of therapy. In Chapter 4 Carolyn Lawson provides a review of empirical research evidence about the elements of supervision which make it helpful or unhelpful.

Section 2, Challenges in relational supervision, covers some of the ethical, clinical, cultural and relationship challenges that supervisors may face. In Chapter 5 Glenys Parry and I use clinical vignettes to show how a CAT-based understanding of the relational processes of supervision can help supervisors and therapists find a way through ethical and clinical difficulties. Chapters 6 and 7 look at two of the complex presentations which CAT therapists frequently work with. Liz Fawkes and Val Fretten describe the powerful relational enactments in therapy with borderline personality disorder and the role of supervision, illustrating their points by following one therapy. Annie Nehmad presents a development in the CAT understanding of narcissism, with suggestions for subtly modifying how CAT is delivered, and considers narcissistic procedures in therapists and supervisors. Chapter 8, by Jessie Emilion and Hilary Brown, looks at a different sort of challenge, describing an approach to intercultural supervision developed through experience of training and supervision in India and the UK.

Section 3, Methods and tools of supervision, describes the use of several different methods within supervision. The emphasis on both conceptual and practical tools in learning is a key part of the CAT model and applies to supervision as well as to therapy. In Chapter 9 Jane Blunden and Hilary Beard write about group supervision, using group theory, the CAT model and practical ideas drawn from experience, to show how supervisors can help the group itself to be a resource for its members. In Chapter 10 Steve Potter describes mapping (or making diagrams), an integral part of CAT, and explains how supervisors can assist therapists in this process and use mapping within supervision. In Chapter 11 Stephen Kellett and Dawn Bennett present the measure for assessing competence in CAT (CCAT) and offer guidance on how supervisors and supervisees can integrate competency assessment into supervision. In Chapter 12 Elizabeth Wilde McCormick describes mindfulness and its use in supervision to support concentration and deepen awareness. Jason Hepple in Chapter 13 uses the idea of the microcosm and the use of metaphor to explore enactments in supervision.

Section 4, Supervision in different contexts, starts by looking at the role of the supervisor in a training setting in Chapter 14. Here Yvonne Stevens considers how the supervisor can address the needs and anxieties of trainees at different stages of training. The remaining chapters reflect the diverse uses and applications of CAT and CAT supervision. In Chapter 15 Mark Westacott describes the issues involved in offering CAT supervision to therapists who work in other models and are not trained in CAT. Angela Carradice in Chapter 16 provides an overview of CAT consultancy approaches and describes common processes in the supervision of these. In Chapter 17 Louise K. McCutcheon, Lee Crothers and Steve Halperin use their experience of CAT with young people to outline themes in the supervision of this work and ways of addressing them. In Chapter 18 Julie Lloyd discusses supervision of CAT within a learning disability context (an area often regarded as beyond the reach of all but the most behavioural therapies), and offers guidance for CAT supervisors whose expertise is mainly within learning disabilities on supervising outside this field. Chapter 19, by Karen Shannon, describes the challenges posed in forensic settings and describes how supervision can support therapists working in this area.

Deborah Pickvance
November 2015

Acknowledgements

This book has been a truly collaborative effort and I would like to thank everyone who has played a part in its development, foremost all the contributors for their commitment, effort and enthusiasm, in particular Annie Nehmad and Glenys Parry for their additional work on the index and proofreading, Eva Burns-Lundgren, Elizabeth Wilde McCormick and Jason Hepple. I would like to thank Anna Pethen for her patient work on the illustrations, ACAT Trustees for providing funding for them, and also Anna Jellema, Annalee Curran, Jane Ryan, Marisol Cavieres, Anthony Ryle, Laura Hill, Janet Eddlestone, Susie Godsil, Sarah Blandy, Steve Kennedy, Chris Pickvance, Richard Pickvance and John Kirby.

Contributors would like to thank: Cherry Boa, Jay Dudley, Alexandra Fairfull, Timothy Keen, Tim Sheard, Ashley Simons, the late Gerry Kent, Gillian Hardy, Steve Bamford, Anne Rees, Susie Black, Tirril Harris, Anna Jellema, Nicola Kemp, Julia Large, Anthony Ryle, Barbara Williams, Patsy Holly, Rebecca Mort, Melany Ball, Prof. Tony Sam George, Elizabeth Thomas and Alison Macdonald.

We all owe gratitude to our supervisors and our supervisees, past and present, from whom and with whom we have learnt so much.

Contributors

Hilary Beard is a consultant adult psychotherapist, CAT psychotherapist, supervisor and trainer, and course director for the inter-regional residential ACAT psychotherapy training and St Thomas' CAT practitioner training, London.

Dawn Bennett is a consultant clinical psychologist and CAT psychotherapist, trainer and supervisor; her doctoral research was on formulation, alliance threats and therapist competence in CAT and her subsequent research developed the CAT competency measure.

Jane Blunden is a consultant psychiatrist in psychotherapy with over 20 years' experience working in the NHS. She is a CAT psychotherapist, supervisor and trainer and a group analyst.

Hilary Brown is emeritus professor of social care at Canterbury Christ Church University, a social worker specialising in safeguarding vulnerable adults and an accredited CAT psychotherapist and supervisor.

Eva Burns-Lundgren is a CAT psychotherapist, supervisor and trainer, who ran the Oxford CAT Practitioner Course for 10 years before retiring in 2012; she contributed to the training and supervision of the first CAT therapists and supervisors in Australia.

Angela Carradice is a consultant clinical psychologist, CAT therapist, supervisor and trainer who works in mental health services in the NHS and provides supervision and training in private practice.

Lee Crothers is an occupational therapist, CAT practitioner, supervisor and trainer who works in the HYPE programme (an early intervention service for young people with borderline personality disorder in Melbourne, Australia), and in private practice.

Jessie Emilion is a BACP accredited counsellor, UKCP registered CAT psychotherapist, supervisor and trainer in the NHS and private sector with a particular interest in bi-lingualism, culture, language and race and the impact of these factors on mental health.

Liz Fawkes is Head of Psychological Services, Somerset Partnership NHS Foundation Trust, and a CAT psychotherapist, supervisor and trainer.

Val Fretten is a CAT practitioner and supervisor, working in Dorset Healthcare University Foundation Trust and in private practice.

Steve Halperin is a clinical psychologist, CAT practitioner and supervisor who uses CAT with young people and as a model for consultation.

Jason Hepple is a consultant psychiatrist for Somerset Partnership NHS Foundation Trust and a CAT psychotherapist and trainer.

Stephen Kellett is an organisational psychologist and consultant clinical psychologist in the NHS where he practises and supervises CAT. He is also the IAPT programme director at the University of Sheffield, where he coordinates various CAT research streams.

Carolyn Lawson, after many years working as a clinical psychologist in the NHS, is an independent CAT practitioner. Her doctorate research examined the process of helpfulness in supervision.

Julie Lloyd supervises in both clinical psychology and CAT and has worked in learning disability services for 37 years.

Elizabeth Wilde McCormick is a mindfulness based CAT psychotherapist, supervisor, trainer and writer, a founder member and trustee of ACAT.

Louise K. McCutcheon is a clinical psychologist, CAT therapist, supervisor and trainer who jointly founded a CAT based early intervention programme for borderline personality disorder (Helping Young People Early, HYPE) in Melbourne, Australia.

Annie Nehmad, a founder member of ACAT, was Clinical Lead for CAT in a secondary care psychotherapy department until 2013 and now works in private practice as therapist, supervisor and trainer.

Glenys Parry is Emeritus Professor of Psychological Therapies at the University of Sheffield and a CAT psychotherapist, trainer and supervisor. She was a founder member of ACAT and has undertaken research in CAT.

Deborah Pickvance is a CAT psychotherapist, supervisor and trainer. She has worked in various NHS settings, is a former Chair of ACAT Training Committee and a moderator on several ACAT training courses.

Steve Potter is a CAT psychotherapist, supervisor and trainer based in London. He teaches the uses of CAT mapping contextually with teams and organisations as well as with individuals.

Karen Shannon is a clinical psychologist, CAT therapist, supervisor, trainer and trustee of ACAT. Her experience is in NHS forensic services; now in private practice, she provides training and supervision for CAT therapists and non-therapists, who work with complexity.

Yvonne Stevens is a CAT psychotherapist, supervisor and lecturer, and practises CAT in the NHS and in private practice in Bristol; she supervises and teaches CAT trainees and therapists throughout the South West of England.

Mark Westacott is a consultant clinical psychologist and CAT practitioner, trainer and supervisor. He is a past Chair of ACAT and works in private practice in Cambridge.

Glossary of CAT terms

Countertransference Feelings, thoughts or actions of the therapist, which are either *elicited* in response to the reciprocal role procedures of the client, or *personal*, reflecting the therapist's own reciprocal role procedures.
  Identifying countertransference The therapist thinks, feels or acts in a way which echoes, or over-identifies with, one of the client's reciprocal role procedures, often one which a client is unaware of (e.g. the therapist feels hopeless, just as the client does).
  Reciprocating countertransference The therapist thinks, feels or acts in a reciprocal response to one of the client's roles (e.g. a client is critical of the therapist and the therapist feels inadequate and incompetent).
Dilemma A 'black or white' or 'all or nothing' pattern of thinking, in which only two opposite alternatives seem possible, neither of them good (e.g. *It's as if I can only be either a bulldozer or a lump of jelly*).
Exit (or Aim) A way out of a target problem procedure. An exit may be a way of relating to others differently, or a way of improving self-care or managing difficult feelings or thoughts.
Goodbye letter Letters written by the therapist and client and exchanged at the end of therapy, reflecting on how each experienced the therapy process, what therapy has achieved, the meaning of the ending and outlining areas still to be worked on.
Procedure or procedural sequence* A sequence of aims, assumptions, beliefs, actions and consequences. It is originally developed through, and later reinforced by, relational experience, e.g. *I want to avoid rejection* (aim), *I feel bad about myself, so expect other people not to like me (*assumption*). I think people will accept me if I try to please them* (belief)*, so I do things for others and bury my own needs and wishes* (action)*. People take me for granted and I end up feeling resentful and depressed, which makes me feel bad again* (consequences).
Psychotherapy file A CAT tool used at the beginning of therapy, consisting of descriptions of common problem procedures (traps, snags and dilemmas) and states, which helps clients to reflect on themselves quickly and recognise and monitor patterns underlying the difficulties they have brought to therapy.

Reciprocal role (RR) A role which involves thoughts, subjective experience, feelings, behaviour and the expectation of a reciprocating response by another person. A RR is one of a pair of complementary roles (e.g. *loving and caring* in relation to *loved and secure*, or *threatening and domineering* in relation to *intimidated and overpowered*). Both poles of the RR pair are internalised. This occurs most powerfully in relationships in childhood but also later in life. A person may enact either pole of the pair and anticipates, or tries to elicit (not necessarily consciously), a complementary response from another person. The term is developed from Object Relations Theory.

Reciprocal role procedure (RRP)* A pattern of interaction in interpersonal relationships or in relation to the self, which arises from, and is an enactment of, a reciprocal role. The example of a procedure, described above, is an attempt to avoid the painful *rejected* role (in relation to an internalised 'rejecting' other).

Reciprocal role repertoire The range of paired roles which each person has internalised and so is able to enact in relationships with other people and also in relation to the self. It is often restricted and inflexible.

Reformulation A narrative, offering the client a new and validating understanding of current difficulties, in terms of strategies adopted to cope with negative experiences in earlier life which persist and are dysfunctional. It is developed collaboratively with the client and offered in the form of a letter (the 'prose reformulation') early in therapy. It will normally identify a focus for therapy and suggest how problem procedures may affect the therapy.

Scaffolding The strategies and support used by a therapist to help a client learn, linked closely to the client's need and capacity to learn.

Self-state A pair of reciprocal roles which may be partially or completely dissociated (split off) from the rest of the self.

Sequential diagrammatic reformulation (SDR) A diagram, or map, which depicts how a client's reciprocal roles and target problem procedures are linked to one another.

Snag (Subtle Negative Aspects of Goals) A procedure which undermines or sabotages goals or aims, because of conscious or unconscious fear of the reactions of others (e.g. envy) or feelings about the self (e.g. feeling undeserving).

State A state of mind or state of being, which is the subjective experience of being in, and enacting, a reciprocal role.

Target problem (TP) A problem which therapy aims to address. It may be the presenting problem or a problem which emerges during therapy. It is agreed by the therapist and client during the early sessions of therapy.

Target problem procedure (TPP)* A dysfunctional procedure, which is the focus of therapy. Traps, dilemmas and snags are examples of TPPs. TPPs underlie and maintain target problems. The therapist helps the client to recognise the TPP in outside events and within the therapy relationship, and to revise the TPP. The client and therapist work out aims or exits from the TPP.

Glossary of CAT terms   xix

Transference   Feelings, thoughts or action which a client experiences or enacts towards the therapist. They may be based on roles learned in early relationships and/or responses to a role enacted by the therapist. Transference is a psychoanalytic concept describing the transfer of feelings from early relationships to the therapist. In CAT it is seen as an enactment of a reciprocal role.

Trap   A circular procedure which consists of trying to avoid painful feelings or experiences, but which ends up confirming or reinforcing those feelings or experiences.

Zone of proximal development (ZPD)   A Vygotskian term. The gap between what someone can do on their own and what they can do with the help of a competent other. The therapist gauges the client's ZPD and aims to work within it.

---

* Note for readers unfamiliar with CAT: Procedure, problem procedure, role procedure, reciprocal role procedure (RRP) and target problem procedure (TPP) have very similar meanings and are used almost interchangeably.

Section I

CAT supervision
Theory, process and evidence

Chapter 1

CAT supervision
A relational model

Deborah Pickvance

CAT supervision has been practised for many years, but it was not until 2011 that the first attempt to describe a theoretical framework for it was published. Marx (2011) showed how CAT supervision could be understood in terms of CAT concepts. This chapter offers a further, new perspective on CAT supervision, presenting it as a relational approach to psychotherapy supervision, which incorporates the relational principles of the CAT model. The chapter also looks at three other approaches to relational supervision – psychoanalytic, integrative and cognitive – and compares these with CAT supervision. Lastly it considers *'parallel process'*, a supremely relational process in supervision, and recasts this concept in CAT terms.

Relational models of psychotherapy and supervision

The word 'relational' has been used so widely in psychotherapy that it risks losing meaning. In a helpful attempt at clarification Paul and Charura (2014) propose that three principles underlie relational approaches to psychotherapy: social and individual life are understood using relational concepts; relationships are central to the development of personality, the sense of self and the problems which bring people into therapy; and the therapy relationship is fundamental to the therapeutic process. Models differ in the emphasis they give to each of these principles, for example some focus on therapeutic process and say little about relational factors in the development of personality. However, most relational models of psychotherapy agree on some key features of therapy: the co-creation of meaning and experience, the importance of the intersubjective space between therapist and client, the increased engagement of the psychotherapist in the therapeutic dialogue, and the importance of affect (Gilbert and Evans 2000).

Similarly, relational approaches to supervision share an emphasis on the importance of the supervisor – supervisee relationship and on experiential processing and learning in supervision. However, they differ in their view of other aspects of supervision, for example the use of self-disclosure by the supervisor and the extent to which supervision has a therapeutic dimension.

It is important to note that explicitly relational models of supervision are not the only ones to focus on relational aspects of supervision; pan-theoretical models of supervision also do this. Developmental models of supervision, for example, often describe how the supervision relationship changes at different stages in the development of the supervisee from novice to experienced clinician. Hawkins and Shohet's (2012) seven-eyed process model, while not named a relational model, focuses closely on the supervisory relationship and the therapeutic relationship and they see a good supervisory relationship as central to supervision.

CAT as a relational therapy

CAT is an explicitly relational model of psychotherapy which was developed in the 1970s and 1980s by Dr Anthony Ryle. Psychoanalytic object relations ideas, in particular those of Guntrip, Fairbairn and Winnicott, and cognitive approaches, in particular personal construct theory, were important influences in its early development. Ryle rejected the classical psychoanalytic idea of innate conflicting drives and drew on the findings of infant development studies, which demonstrated the active engagement and collaborative playfulness of infants with significant others (Ryle and Kerr 2002). These findings confirmed the Vygotskian ideas of the child's active collaboration in the learning process and the important role in a child's learning of a competent other, who is able to 'teach' at a pace appropriate to the child's development. Integrating Vygotskian activity theory and the Bakhtinian view of the dialogical self, the cognitive analytic model has a concept of a self which forms through interaction with others in an intersubjective environment. The nature of the therapeutic relationship in CAT reflects these ideas: it is a collaborative relationship in which the therapist engages actively and responds flexibly in the unfolding dialogue with the client. The client learns and changes through the experience of working collaboratively with another and by internalising benign reciprocal roles. The focus of therapy is on developing a reformulation of the client's problems in terms of dysfunctional interpersonal patterns, learnt in childhood and repeated in adulthood, and then on recognising how these are enacted in current relationships, including the therapy relationship, and in relation to the self. The exploration of such enactments within the therapy relationship is an important aspect of CAT. The therapist offers the client an opportunity to change by not reciprocating the client's dysfunctional patterns, instead facilitating the client to recognise and reflect on these patterns and to develop new ones.

The beginning of CAT relational supervision

Supervision has always been an integral part of the CAT model. While no model of supervision was explicitly articulated in the early days of CAT, the practice was implicitly relational. In the 1980s Anthony Ryle ran two large supervision groups for therapists who came from a wide range of backgrounds. Ryle's approach was to empower supervisees, to encourage them and to convey his characteristic trust and belief in the potential of others. In this and in other ways the supervision process was congruent with the CAT model. The group was a place for learning, it was busy, members had to make the best use of the limited time available in it and it was characterised by an honest, pragmatic, down-to-earth, non-hierarchical approach.

These first supervision groups, along with meetings about the developing approach, formed a crucible for the model. Ryle led members of the groups in introducing, and experimenting with, new tools such as the goodbye letter and the prose reformulation, always emphasising the need to use the client's language. Annalee Curran (personal communication) remembers the moment in a supervision group in the 1980s when he reached for an old envelope and drew a procedure on it – the first step in the evolution of the diagram which would later become a central feature of CAT.

The recognition of enactments, in which therapists unwittingly become caught up in their clients' problematic patterns, was a key element of supervision, and Ryle knew the value of supervision in alerting therapists to this process. He was aware of the impact of the work on therapists, concerned for their well-being and modelled a '*caring and nurturing*' to '*cared for and nurtured*' reciprocal role procedure towards them. He was willing to recount anecdotes from his own experience as a therapist, which was helpful and anxiety-reducing for his supervisees. Ryle's attitude to his supervisees and his attention to the interpersonal dynamics of therapy demonstrated the relational understanding that has always been intrinsic to CAT. In time, the more experienced therapists began to run supervision groups, providing some initial experience in the model to the many health and social workers who expressed interest in it. As in most other psychotherapy models at that time, there was no training in supervision, so the practice of supervision reflected supervisors' own experience of receiving supervision.

CAT supervision as a relational model

CAT supervision reflects many of the relational aspects of CAT therapy. Six features of CAT supervision mark it out as a relational approach, all of which are elaborated further elsewhere in this book.

1   **The use of CAT relational theory** The supervisor draws on the relational theory underpinning the CAT model to guide the supervisee in developing the reformulation of the client's difficulties, to help the supervisee build the therapeutic relationship and work with enactments, to assist the supervisee to work appropriately at each stage of a CAT therapy, and to understand the supervisory relationship.
2   **The supervisory alliance** In CAT therapy there is an emphasis on building a strong working alliance, on the early establishment of a collaborative

relationship and on the therapist's open, explicit approach to explaining the therapist role and discussing the boundaries and expectations of therapy. Similarly, the CAT supervisor aims to develop a strong working alliance with each supervisee and with the supervision group, as it is only within this relational context that a supervisee can learn fully from the combination of support and challenge offered in supervision. Thus a supervisor will, from the outset, discuss the aims and scope of supervision, address any apprehensions felt by supervisees and encourage supervisees to be honest and say if they do not understand. The supervisor strengthens the alliance further by being flexible and responsive to the supervisee's particular learning needs and being willing to talk about past experience relevant to the supervisee's concerns. In ongoing supervision the supervisor reinforces the supervisory alliance by checking understanding and encouraging feedback from the supervisee and also by being alert to threats or ruptures in the supervisory alliance. If a rupture appears in the supervisory alliance this is an immediate focus of attention. The supervisor takes account of the evaluative aspect of supervision, aware that it can affect the development of a safe, trusting alliance. As CAT supervision usually takes place in groups, the way that a supervisor facilitates the group influences the supervisory alliances among supervisees as well as with the supervisor.

3   **Learning in an interpersonal context** The Vygotskian view of learning as an active interpersonal process underpins both CAT supervision and CAT therapy. The supervisor 'scaffolds' the supervisee's learning, adjusting interventions to the supervisee's stage of development (Marx 2011, Ryle and Kerr 2002). The supervisor has an explicit teaching role, conveying the values and methods of the model (Ryle 1990, Ryle and Kerr 2002), particularly in the early stages of learning the model, but this is undertaken in a way that is highly responsive to what supervisees can absorb at each point in their development. The active use of the group context of most CAT supervision provides a rich opportunity for learning from others and in interaction with others.

4   **Use of self** CAT supervisors, like CAT therapists, need to be aware of personal responses in supervision, including feelings, images, memories, embodied sensations, seemingly stray thoughts or other associations. The supervisor reflects on whether they are manifestations of personal countertransference, countertransference elicited in response to the supervisee or parallel process. The supervisor may choose to share them with the supervisee, aware that such disclosures can strengthen the supervisory alliance and enrich understanding, but should only be made in order to serve the supervisee's learning needs. The supervisor also encourages the supervisee's experiential awareness and self-reflection, as these can help access countertransference and shed light on unrecognised aspects of the therapy.

5   **Attention to the relational patterns of both supervisee and supervisor** As the supervisor gets to know a supervisee, some of the latter's relational

patterns are likely to emerge within the therapy relationship, the relationship with the supervisor or with other group members. The supervisor's role is to help the supervisee recognise the extent to which these patterns may affect them in the role of therapist. This is not the same as therapy, but it provides a useful opportunity for supervisees to become aware of how their relational patterns influence them – in a positive or negative way – in their professional role. In a trusting supervision relationship a supervisee may volunteer such reflections. The CAT concept of reciprocal role procedures provides an accessible language for describing such patterns in a demystifying, non-blaming and straightforward way.

> Example: *The supervisor referred to a pattern within Amy's practice, namely her reluctance to explore enactments in the therapy relationship. Amy replied, 'I know, I know I don't like doing this . . . I know I am over-protective . . . It came up in my therapy'. The supervisor and Amy talked about the effect on the client of her over-protectiveness and identified an* over-protective – disempowered *relational pattern. Sharing this personal source of her countertransference and understanding its potential impact on her client seemed to galvanise Amy into addressing it, and two weeks later she brought a recording to supervision, showing how she had attempted to deal with an enactment.*

CAT supervisors need a good understanding of how their own reciprocal role patterns may impinge on their role, in particular any negative patterns which could affect supervision. For example, an unconfident supervisor who needs to be liked may be unwilling or unable to challenge supervisees.

6 **Attention to context** CAT has a well-developed perspective on the impact of social and political context on the self, and it views relationships as embedded in a matrix of cultural, social and political influences. Both the supervisor–supervisee relationship and the therapist–client relationship exist within a complex sociocultural context. The CAT supervisor is mindful that these influences may affect the supervision in a range of ways. Influences may be evident in perceived or actual sociocultural differences, such as ethnic origin or class, between the supervisor and supervisee or among supervisees in a group. Such differences can be inhibiting, particularly if not acknowledged; when recognised, they can lead to an enriched learning experience. The pressure of organisational influences on the provision of therapy may be apparent in supervision, for example supervisees may feel insecure, over-stretched or demoralised in their work setting. Again, it is important that the supervisor and supervisee talk about the possible impact of these influences on both the therapy relationship and the supervisory relationship.

Relational psychoanalytic supervision

It is useful to understand the ideas of relational psychoanalysis in order to see the important contribution they have made to current thinking and practice in relational supervision.

The relational turn in psychoanalysis

The origins of these ideas lie in an important development in psychoanalysis, which began in the 1980s in the US. In this development the word 'relational' signified a crucial shift in perspective, which influenced psychoanalytic theory and practice. Greenberg and Mitchell (1983) first articulated the 'relational turn' as a move away from the emphasis in classical psychoanalysis on biological drives as fundamental to human development to a view of individual development as depending primarily on experience within human relationships. Holmes (2011: 305) described the key defining feature of relational psychoanalysis as 'its radical interpersonal stance, insisting that there is no such thing as a mind on its own, only a mind-in-relationship'.

The relational turn has implications not only for ways of thinking about individual development and the origin of psychological difficulties, but also for psychotherapeutic interventions. It has led to a shift away from the neutral, abstinent position of the classical psychoanalyst towards an emphasis on the analyst's personal responsiveness, creativity and spontaneity (Aron and Harris 2012, Mills 2005). The relational psychoanalyst is more authentic, vulnerable and humane, while maintaining professional restraint and analytic discipline in a relationship which is still asymmetric and unequal (Aron 1996, Aron and Harris 2012). Rather than seeing psychoanalysis as the one-way influence of the analyst on the patient, the relational view is of a two-way process, in which the patient and analyst mutually and reciprocally influence each other (Aron 1996). Mitchell (in Imber 2000: 623) describes the relational analytic process as a 'dialogic, intersubjective exchange wherein the patient and analyst act on each other in ways that at least partially shape, and even determine, what they will find'. The relational movement has resulted in a transformation from the view of the analytic process as occurring in the individual mind to one taking place between two subjects (Benjamin 1995).

Intersubjectivity

Relational psychoanalysis is not a single school, but more a movement incorporating a range of traditions, within which analysts have developed overlapping but distinct perspectives (Aron and Harris 2012). The theory of intersubjectivity is the most prominent of these perspectives and was defined by Stolorow and Atwood (1996: 182) as a field or systems theory which understands 'psychological phenomena not as products of isolated intrapsychic mechanisms, but as forming at the interface of reciprocally interacting worlds of experience'. The 'inter' part of 'intersubjectivity' refers to the interpersonal field between two interacting people, and 'subjective' refers to the personal experience of each one (Altman 2005). In deliberate contrast to the Western idea of subject and object and to the view that the influence in therapy is one-way (from the therapist to the client), intersubjectivity refers to two interacting subjects (Benjamin 1995), who influence each other in a continuous, mutual, reciprocal process. Research on infant development and communication supports the central role of intersubjectivity in human development (Trevarthen 2001).

The conceptualisation of psychoanalysis as an intersubjective process is in sharp contrast to the idea of an isolated psyche being observed by an objective observer. It also contrasts with the archaeological model of psychoanalysis as a process of uncovering objective, static, historical truths (Coburn 1999). Instead, therapy takes place in an interactional field created by the interplay between the two subjective worlds of therapist and client (Stolorow and Atwood in Mills 2005). Both therapist and patient are subject to 'mutual reciprocal influence', which is an inevitable part of intimate relationships (Wallin 2007: 168). They are engaged in co-creating meaning in a continuous process and the role of therapist is as a co-participant in a relationship between two subjectivities (Hirsch 2015).

Intersubjectivity emphasises the therapist's contribution to the client's experience and the impact of the therapist's person on the client. Intersubjective therapists have to maintain a constant awareness of their own internal processes in order to respond in an attuned way (Buirski and Haglund 2009). Ogden (1994), influenced by Bion's idea of reverie, advocates that analysts use reverie to access intersubjective experience. Rather than dismissing pre-reflective reveries and somatic experiencing, he thinks they can give the analyst access to the unarticulated experiences of the patient.

Like CAT, intersubjective theory places a high value on enactments during therapy as potential opportunities for change. Bromberg (2008: 332) views an enactment as a 'shared dissociative event' or unconscious communication process, which is common in therapy and does not have to be dramatic. The analyst must be sensitive to shifts in the states of analyst and patient and also prepared to let the boundary between personal and professional during enactments be permeable, in order for deep and lasting change to occur. Schore (2007) advocates that the therapist stops trying to understand or interpret at these times; if instead the therapist attempts to know the patient through the ongoing subjective field they share, 'an act of recognition, not understanding, takes place' (Schore 2007: 763).

Stern et al. (1998) describe 'moments of meeting' in therapy as powerful vehicles of change. Their ideas are based on research studies of mother-infant interaction which show that infants develop new capacities through engagement with caregivers in an interactive intersubjective field. They describe 'now moments' as moments in therapy which the therapist and the patient experience as unfamiliar, perhaps confusing or anxiety-provoking. The familiar intersubjective environment has changed and there is a sense of either an impasse or an opportunity. The therapist needs to respond in a novel, attuned, authentic, personal way. If a now moment can be therapeutically seized, if both partners can engage with it and explore it, the now moment can become a moment of meeting.

Psychoanalysis in the UK

Samuels (2015) sees the psychoanalysts who advocated the ideas of the relational turn as reflecting the ideas of their era. They were keen to incorporate the values they had grown up with – of radical social theory, feminism, civil rights and student politics – into their psychoanalytic practice. It is no accident that the relational turn took place, and had greatest impact, in the USA where classical Freudian theory prevailed. By contrast, in the UK, where object relations theory was the predominant model of psychoanalysis, there was already a more relational perspective on psychoanalytic theory and practice. There was a reluctance to engage with the ideas of the relational turn, as these were seen as not necessary (Samuels 2015). In Scotland in the 1950s Fairbairn developed the view that the analyst's actual personality and behaviour were crucial factors in the patient's experience of the therapeutic process (Bacal and Newman 1990). Winnicott thought that the therapist should be sensitive, involved and caring rather than analytic and drew a parallel between the good enough mother and the good enough analyst, while Guntrip emphasised the importance of the therapist feeling and communicating a 'sense of genuine personal relatedness' (Bacal and Newman 1990: 181).

Psychoanalysis and the development of CAT

These were the analysts whose object relations ideas Ryle drew on when he was developing CAT. He began creating the model before the relational turn occurred and before the term 'relational' acquired its current meaning. Nevertheless the CAT model has always been profoundly relational in theory and in practice. It can be seen as a model of its time, which continued to develop in parallel with other relational approaches. While drawing on object relations theory to understand transference and countertransference and the development of the individual, CAT has a type of therapeutic dialogue which is radically different from the traditional psychoanalytic emphasis on the power of the interpretation – a psychotherapeutic intervention which Ryle regarded as unverifiable and opaque. Using the ideas of activity theory, he advocated instead a more equal exchange between therapist and client, in which both were collaboratively engaged in a joint search for meaning. CAT shares with intersubjectivity the idea of co-creating meaning within a mutual relationship, but adds to this the important concept of scaffolding, whereby the therapist helps the client to learn by supplying tools and support specific to the client's capability and need at that time.

Applying relational psychoanalytic ideas to supervision

Following the development of the relational approach within psychoanalysis, several writers have applied these ideas to supervision. This entails a move away from the traditional view of supervision as the didactic transmission of knowledge about the patient by an all-knowing, authoritative, objective supervisor to a relatively less powerful and naïve supervisee (Berman 2000, Kaufman 2006, Yerushalmi 1999). The new approach involves a conception of supervision as an ongoing process of sharing power and mutually constructing knowledge, in which the focus is not only on the patient, or the patient and therapist, but also on enactments in the supervisory dyad (Itzhaky and Chopra 2005). This view recognises the importance of working with the emotional responsiveness and individual subjectivity of both the supervisor and supervisee (Berman 2000).

The most prominent model of supervision within the psychoanalytic relational tradition is that of Frawley-O'Dea and Sarnat (2001). Using the ideas of relationality and intersubjectivity they propose a model of relational psychodynamic supervision, which they define in terms of three dimensions: the nature of the supervisor's authority, the relevant data for processing in supervision and the supervisor's mode of participation. Relational supervision is seen as 'an analytic endeavour in and of itself' (Frawley O'Dea and Sarnat 2001: 69). In this model the supervisor and supervisee share power and authority and negotiate and co-construct meaning. While the relationship is asymmetrical it has more flexible boundaries than a therapy relationship. They suggest the metaphor of an apprenticeship to a craftsperson as an apt description of the supervisory relationship. The supervisor focuses not only on the patient's dynamics and the supervisee's countertransference to the patient, as in a traditional approach to supervision, but also on the supervision relationship. Interest in the relational processes of supervision is highlighted from the beginning of supervision, so that the supervisee is aware of this focus and encouraged to engage in such exploration. The relational supervisor is interested in such influences on the supervisory relationship as the transference and countertransference between supervisor and supervisee, the supervisee's personal therapy, parallels from therapy and enactments of organisational factors by either member of the dyad. Supervision is characterised by mutuality and negotiation. The supervisor, by being willing to share with the supervisee personal experience of the supervisory relationship and responses to the clinical material, models a demystified, collaborative role.

Relational approaches to psychoanalytic supervision have received some critical commentary. Yerushalmi (1999) suggests that a number of factors may inhibit the co-creation of meaning and playfulness advocated in relational psychoanalytic supervision, for example, the supervisor's role in evaluation and assessment, the time-limits of psychotherapy training and the differences in status and perspective of the two participants, reflecting their different positions in the profession. Black (2003) points out that psychoanalytic and supervisory processes are distinct from one another and comments that some supervisees would not feel able to respond flexibly and playfully to an examination of the dynamics of power in the supervisory relationship. Matthews and Treacher (in Howard 2007) comment on the relative lack of attention given to establishing a contract in psychoanalytic relational models and emphasise the importance of this in developing a constructive supervisory alliance.

Integrative relational supervision

In humanistic therapies in the UK there has been a strong relational element. The quality of the relationship between therapist and client has long been viewed as crucial, and early research focused on the core facilitative conditions offered by the therapist and their correlation with therapy outcome (Truax and Carkhuff 1967). Within this tradition Evans and Gilbert (2005) developed an integrative approach to therapy which emphasised the importance of the intersubjective space in therapy as a holding environment in which growth can occur. Of most relevance to this book is their important contribution to relational supervision, *Psychotherapy Supervision: An Integrative Relational Approach to Psychotherapy Supervision* (Gilbert and Evans 2000), in which they take an intersubjective view of the relational processes in supervision. Drawing on Sullivan's concept of the participant observer, they describe a relational process which involves trying to 'enter into the nature of the person's own subjective experience, whilst still being an observer of that experience' (Gilbert and Evans 2000: 9). A key concept in their model is Martin Buber's idea of 'inclusion', which involves 'the back and forth movement of being able to go over to the other side and yet remain centred in my own experience' (Hycner, in Gilbert and Evans 2000: 10). The supervisee therefore needs to keep an awareness of his or her own and the client's experience while also reflecting on the interaction between the two of them. For the supervisor the practice of inclusion means being aware of internal, countertransference responses to the supervisee while also observing the supervisee's behaviour and reflecting on the relational dynamics underpinning it.

Gilbert and Evans (2000) see a warm, collaborative working alliance between supervisor and supervisee as essential for effective supervision and they advocate active steps to develop and maintain this. These include developing a supervision contract which outlines the agreed goals of supervision and also a contract about the relational process of supervision, in which the supervisor and supervisee agree to discuss any barriers to the supervisory alliance. A process contract may become more focused on specific aspects of the relational process, as the supervisor and supervisee become aware of particular difficulties between them. In addition they stress the importance of creating an effective learning environment and make the point that this will often involve actively countering the effects of shaming experiences in previous educational settings. Supervisors need to understand that these may result in anxiety about exposure in a learning setting and they can address them by affirming supervisees, dispelling the idea of right and wrong approaches in psychotherapy, focusing instead on what leads to effective therapeutic outcomes and encouraging supervisees to ask what may feel to them like naïve questions.

In a discussion of the supervisor's personal style, Gilbert and Evans (2000) advocate a flexible, supportive approach with jointly agreed goals and some structure, and they stress the importance of honest, clear, direct feedback. They consider several frequently cited features of relational supervision: self-disclosure by the supervisor, use of the supervisor's countertransference and the place of psychotherapy in supervision. They regard self-disclosure as useful when it entails sharing examples from a supervisor's clinical experience or professional development. This can reduce the sense of hierarchy and supervisees appreciate feeling less alone and hearing that people seen as authorities have also experienced uncertainty. However they advise sparing and careful use of self-disclosure, with due regard for the sensitivity and needs of supervisees. They view the supervisor's countertransference responses as a potentially rich source of understanding which the supervisor can share sensitively and explore in a curious way with the supervisee. They support exploring whether a supervisee's countertransference responses reflect a familiar personal pattern, but caution against the supervisor being intrusive. Instead they advise that this is undertaken only with the agreement of the supervisee and with the supervisee reflecting, from an adult position, on the origin of the responses.

Relational supervision of cognitive therapy

Early versions of cognitive behaviour therapy neither emphasised the contribution of interpersonal factors to emotional disorders nor treated the therapy relationship as an important ingredient in therapeutic change (Safran 1990a). This changed as an increasing number of authors emphasised the importance of interpersonal context, with Safran (1990a, 1990b) pre-eminent among them in proposing an integration of interpersonal concepts into cognitive theory and practice. He intended this to result in a refinement of both, rather than a new theory or model of change (Safran 1990a). Initially he applied the concept of the interpersonal context in Sullivan's interpersonal psychotherapy to cognitive therapy and described a cognitive-interpersonal cycle, in which 'cognitive activity, interpersonal behaviours and repetitive interactional or me-you patterns are linked together and maintain one another in an unbroken causal loop' (Safran 1984: 342). Central to his view is the concept of the interpersonal schema, a 'generic cognitive representation of interpersonal events' which he likens to a programme for maintaining interpersonal relatedness (Safran 1990a: 89). Interpersonal schemas develop as a result of interaction with attachment figures, and individuals use them to predict interactions with others.

In Safran's view the therapeutic relationship is itself an important mechanism of therapeutic change (Safran 1990b). This has significant implications for the role of the cognitive therapist. The therapist must recognise personal feelings and reactions to the client's dysfunctional interpersonal behaviour and communication, and resist reacting to the client in a complementary fashion. The therapist engages in collaborative exploration of the client's interpersonal schemas as they emerge in therapy, looking at how they may link to the client's problems outside therapy.

Safran and Muran's relational approach to supervising cognitive therapy (Safran and Muran 2001, Safran et al. 2007) emphasises the importance of two key elements in supervision: its relational context and its experiential nature. In their view it is important to develop the supervisory alliance by negotiating the tasks and goals of supervision and the supervisor must monitor the nature and quality of it. It is important for supervisees to feel able to say if they do not find supervision helpful. When the supervisory alliance is adequate the relationship can move into the background, but if there are any tensions or strains within it, the supervisor must prioritise exploring these with the supervisee, looking at the contribution of both parties to any rupture. They make the point that exploration of such issues can itself form useful experiential learning for the supervisee. They warn of reification and the risks of therapists holding onto fixed concepts and formulations about the client or the therapy relationship, as these can take the therapist's attention away from the all-important perceptual and experiential level to a more conceptual abstract one. They advocate that supervisors help supervisees gain understanding in an experiential way and at a bodily felt level. To facilitate this process they use mindfulness exercises and explore problems brought to supervision through role play, often involving other members of the supervision group.

Parallel process

Parallel process is a psychoanalytic concept which describes a truly interpersonal process in supervision and it therefore belongs in any discussion of relational supervision. In a useful review of the literature on parallel process Miller and Twomey (1999) define it as 'the unconscious replication in supervision of conflicts and difficulties that have arisen in the therapy relationship and have not been fully understood in this situation'.

The origins of the concept of parallel process lie in Searles' (1955: 159) description of the 'reflection process', in which relational processes operating between therapist and patient are reflected in the supervisory relationship. The therapist unconsciously brings difficulties in the therapy relationship, which have not been fully processed, to supervision, and the supervisor's emotional experience offers a clue that this is happening. Searles thought that this process, while comprising only a small part of the material of supervision, could be useful for understanding difficulties in the therapy relationship. The concept of parallel process was first used to describe this phenomenon by Ekstein and Wallerstein (McKinney 2000). In contrast to Searles, who located the difficulties in the patient, they thought the problems typically lay with the therapist, whose intrapsychic conflicts led to problems both in therapy and in supervision (McKinney 2000).

Parallel process is usually seen as a symmetrical process in which the same relational dynamics are played out in both the supervision and therapy dyads.

However, some authors refer to asymmetric parallel process. Frawley-O'Dea and Sarnat (2001), for example, describe how a supervisor and supervisee may enact an aspect of the transference and countertransference which is significant but not currently evident in the therapy relationship, and this is more likely to occur when the patient has dissociative experiences.

Miller and Twomey (1999) note that the significance of parallel process has been questioned, as the awareness of other influences on the supervisory relationship has grown. Frawley-O'Dea and Sarnat (2001) propose a contemporary relational view which sees parallel process as starting with either dyad (supervisor–supervisee or therapist–client) and influencing the other dyad. As a member of both dyads the supervisee is the conduit for this relational material. They caution against making assumptions about parallel process, suggesting that the two dyads may enact similar dynamics for independent reasons. They also point out that a supervisor might be more receptive to some parallel process enactments than others and they suggest that supervisors might use the concept of parallel process to avoid looking at their personal responses to a supervisee. So they recommend that the supervisor and supervisee explore the many potential meanings of transference and countertransference that arise between them, only one of which is the phenomenon of parallel process.

A CAT understanding of parallel process

In cognitive analytic terms parallel process is the enactment in the supervisor-supervisee relationship, or within the supervision group, of relational patterns ('reciprocal role procedures') which originate in the therapist-client relationship. The therapist unwittingly conveys her unprocessed countertransference to the client's relational patterns by enacting this within the supervision group. Group members (including the supervisor) may respond to (or reciprocate) these patterns. Within CAT it is usually considered that parallel process can go in either direction. For example, a therapist's undigested experience of an over-controlling supervisor may be re-enacted in the therapy by the therapist becoming over-controlling towards the client. CAT supervision groups provide rich opportunities for members to comment on both symmetric and asymmetric parallel processes.

The CAT model provides an additional dimension to the concept, as it views the process as occurring not only within, and between, relationships, but also intrapersonally within the client, in a 'self to self' enactment of the interpersonal procedure. Parallel process can offer useful information for the supervisee, who may then explore whether the client enacts the pattern, which has appeared as a parallel process in supervision, internally towards herself.

> Example: *The supervisee, Martin, talked in an uncharacteristically pressured way about his new client, trying to convey her complex problems to the supervisor. While listening to Martin the supervisor felt bombarded and unable to think. Aware of her reaction, she commented on it to Martin and*

they considered whether this could be a parallel process. Martin said the client spoke volubly about her multiple problems, switching from one to the next without pause, and he felt overwhelmed by her and struggled to think or intervene. Together Martin and the supervisor identified an overwhelming, pressurising *in relation to* overwhelmed, helpless and stuck *reciprocal role procedure. This pattern was being enacted in therapy and also in the supervision relationship. The recognition of this reciprocal role procedure helped Martin to re-gain a sense of agency. The supervisor wondered whether the client enacted the same procedure towards herself. Martin decided he would explore with the client whether she overwhelmed herself with her frenetic worrying and then ended up stuck and unable to reflect on her problems.*

Ryle and Kerr (2002) see the value of recognising parallel process, as the supervisor and supervisee can use it to consider feelings and patterns which may not have been articulated before. However, like Frawley-O'Dea and Sarnat (2001), they advise that such phenomena are 'treated as a prompt to enquiry rather than as representing any exact mirroring or re-enactment' (Ryle and Kerr 2002: 130).

Conclusion

There is common ground among the approaches described – notably the importance attached to the quality and use of the supervisory relationship. At the same time, each approach emphasises different features. For example, relational psychoanalytic approaches to supervision have expanded usefully on the original understanding of the concept of parallel process. Integrative relational supervision prioritises the creation of the conditions for an honest and trusting supervisory relationship, for example, highlighting the value of contracting and the recognition of the influence of past negative experiences of learning. Relational cognitive supervision emphasises working with enactments and repairing ruptures in the supervisory relationship and incorporates mindfulness exercises to facilitate experiential awareness in supervision.

While CAT supervision shares much with other relational approaches, it also has its own distinctive characteristics. For example, the CAT supervisor helps supervisees to consider the impact of interpersonal patterns on an individual's relationship with the self ('self to self procedures'), and uses scaffolding to support supervisees' learning, in particular diagrammatic representations of the relational patterns which occur in the supervisory and therapy relationships. CAT supervision therefore occupies a distinct position alongside other relational approaches to supervision. Like most psychotherapy supervision, CAT supervision was practised before it was theorised. By considering relational approaches to supervision, CAT supervision in particular, this chapter aims to make explicit what has been implicit: that CAT supervision is and always has been relational.

References

Altman, N. (2005) 'Relational perspectives on the therapeutic action of psychoanalysis', in J. Ryan (ed) *How Does Psychotherapy Work?*, London: Karnac.
Aron, L. (1996) *A Meeting of Minds: Mutuality in Psychoanalysis*, Hillside, NJ: Analytic Press.
Aron, L. and Harris, A. (eds) (2012) *Relational Psychoanalysis, Volume 5*, New York: Routledge.
Bacal, H.A. and Newman, K.M. (1990) *Theories of Object Relations: Bridges to Self Psychology*, New York: Columbia University Press.
Benjamin, J. (1995) *Like Subjects, Love Objects: Essays on Recognition and Sexual Difference*, New Haven: Yale University Press.
Berman, E. (2000) 'Psychoanalytic supervision: The intersubjective development', *International Journal of Psychoanalysis*, 81: 273–290.
Black, M.J. (2003) 'Enactment: Analytic musings on energy, language, and personal growth', *Psychoanalytic Dialogues*, 13, 5: 633–655.
Bromberg, P. (2008) 'Shrinking the tsunami: Affect regulation, dissociation and the shadow of the flood', *Contemporary Psychoanalysis*, 44, 3: 329–350.
Buirski, P. and Haglund, P. (2009) *Making Sense Together, the Intersubjective Approach to Psychotherapy*, Lanham, MD: Rowman and Littlefield.
Coburn, W.J. (1999) 'Attitudes of embeddedness and transcendence in psychoanalysis', *Journal of the American Academy of Psychoanalysis*, 27: 101–119.
Evans, K. and Gilbert, M. (2005) *An Introduction to Integrative Psychotherapy*, Basingstoke: Palgrave Macmillan.
Frawley-O'Dea, M.G. and Sarnat, J.E. (2001) *The Supervisory Relationship*, New York: Guildford Press.
Gilbert, M.C. and Evans, K. (2000) *Psychotherapy Supervision*, Buckingham: Open University Press.
Greenberg, J.R. and Mitchell, S.A. (1983) *Object Relations in Psychoanalytic Theory*, Cambridge, MA: Harvard University Press.
Hawkins, P. and Shohet, R. (2012) *Supervision in the Helping Professions*, Buckingham: Open University Press.
Hirsch, I. (2015) *The Interpersonal Tradition: The Origins of Psychoanalytic Subjectivity*, Hove: Routledge.
Holmes, J. (2011) 'Donnel Stern and relational psychoanalysis', *British Journal of Psychotherapy*, 27: 305–315.
Howard, S. (2007) 'Models of supervision', in A. Petts and B. Shapley (eds) *On Supervision: Psychoanalytic and Jungian Analytic Perspectives*, London: Karnac Books.
Imber, R.R. (2000) 'The dilemma of relational authority', *Contemporary Psychoanalysis*, 36: 619–638.
Itzhaky, H. and Chopra, M. (2005) 'Hope in the supervision of therapy of patients with psychotic disorders', *Psychoanalytic Social Work*, 12: 63–82.
Kaufman, J. (2006) 'Candidates' anxiety in supervision: A discussion', *Psychoanalytic Perspectives*, 3: 147–157.
Marx, R. (2011) 'Relational supervision: Drawing on cognitive-analytic frameworks', *Psychology and Psychotherapy: Theory, Research and Practice*, 84: 406–424.
McKinney, M. (2000) 'Relational perspectives and the supervisory triad', *Psychoanalytic Psychology*, 17, 3: 565–584.
Miller, L. and Twomey, J.E. (1999) 'A parallel without a process: A relational view of a supervisory experience', *Contemporary Psychoanalysis*, 35: 557–580.

Mills, J. (2005) 'A critique of relational psychoanalysis', *Psychoanalytic Psychology*, 22, 2: 155–188.
Ogden, T.H. (1994) 'The analytical third: Working with intersubjective clinical facts', *International Journal of Psychoanalysis*, 75, 1: 3–20.
Paul, S. and Charura, D. (2014) *An Introduction to the Therapeutic Relationship in Counselling and Psychotherapy*, London: Sage.
Ryle, A. (1990) *Cognitive-analytic Therapy: Active Participation in Change*, Chichester: Wiley.
Ryle, A. and Kerr, I. (2002) *Introducing Cognitive Analytic Therapy*, Chichester: Wiley.
Safran, J.D. (1984) 'Assessing the cognitive-interpersonal cycle', *Cognitive Therapy and Research*, 8, 4: 333–348.
Safran, J.D. (1990a) 'Towards a refinement of cognitive therapy in light of interpersonal theory: 1. Theory', *Clinical Psychology Review*, 10: 87–105.
Safran, J.D. (1990b) 'Towards a refinement of cognitive therapy in light of interpersonal theory: 2. Practice', *Clinical Psychology Review*, 10: 107–121.
Safran, J.D. and Muran, J.C. (2001) 'A relational approach to training and supervision in cognitive psychotherapy', *Journal of Cognitive Psychotherapy: An International Quarterly*, 15, 1: 3–15.
Safran, J.D., Muran, J.C., Stevens, C. and Rothman, M. (2007) 'A relational approach to supervision: addressing ruptures in the alliance', in C.A. Falender and E.P. Shafranske (eds) *Casebook for Clinical Supervision: A Competency-based Approach*, Washington, DC: American Psychological Association.
Samuels, A. 'Relational psychoanalysis in the USA and Britain: Past, present and future', *Advances in Relational Psychotherapy*, Online module, Confer. Available HTTP: <http://www.confer.uk.com/modules/relational/index.html> (accessed 27 November 2015).
Schore, A. (2007) 'Review of "Awakening the Dreamer: Clinical Journeys" by P.M. Bromberg', *Psychoanalytic Dialogues*, 17, 5: 753–767.
Searles, H. (1955) 'The informational value of the supervisor's emotional experiences', in H. Searles (ed) (1965) *Collected Papers on Schizophrenia and Related Subjects*, London: Karnac.
Stern, D.N., Sander, L.W., Nahum, J.P., Harrison, A.M., Lyons-Ruth, K., Morgan, A.C., Bruschweiler-Stern, N. and Tronick, E.Z. (1998) 'Non-interpretive mechanisms in psychoanalytic therapy: The "something more" than interpretation', *International Journal of Psychoanalysis*, 79: 903–921.
Stolorow, R.D. and Atwood, G.E. (1996) 'The intersubjective perspective', *Psychoanalytic Review*, 83: 181–194.
Trevarthen, C. (2001) 'Intrinsic motives for companionship in understanding: Their origin, development, and significance for infant mental health', *Infant Mental Health Journal*, 22, 1–2: 95–131.
Truax, C.B. and Carkhuff, R.R. (1967) *Toward Effective Counselling and Psychotherapy*, Chicago: Aldine.
Wallin, D.J. (2007) *Attachment in Psychotherapy*, New York: Guilford Press.
Yerushalmi, H. (1999) 'Mutual influences in supervision', *Contemporary Psychoanalysis*, 35, 3: 415–436.

Chapter 2

The healthy supervisor
A CAT understanding of the process of psychotherapy supervision

Annie Nehmad

This chapter uses CAT theory to help us think about the quality and helpfulness of supervision – and, just as importantly, the problems and obstacles which may make our supervision less effective, or even unhelpful.

I summarise relevant aspects of the CAT model, and I also draw on:

- the *seven-eyed model of supervision*, and other ideas and concepts in *Supervision in the Helping Professions* (Hawkins and Shohet 2012)
- *Six Category Intervention Analysis* (Heron 1975, 2001)
- Interpersonal neurobiology (IPNB) (Siegel 2010a, 2010b).

Some of these authors' concepts and ideas overlap with those of CAT. Others expand, or shed new light, on a CAT understanding. By spelling out the wisdom implicit in the CAT model, and integrating other authors' contributions, I offer a new framework for thinking about the supervision we give, and receive.

The CAT model

Reciprocal role procedures, self-states and state shifts

The child learns and incorporates (mainly from key caregivers) procedures for organising relationships (ways of being with another). Each parental *role* results in one or more *reciprocal roles* in the child. Two examples are in Figure 2.1:

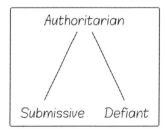

Figure 2.1 Examples of reciprocal roles

The child internalises both the parent-derived and the child-derived roles, and these pairs of reciprocal roles become aspects of the self, known as *self-states* in CAT. Self-states may be more or less dissociated from the rest of the self. Each self-state includes behaviours, thoughts, feelings, body posture, voice, vocabulary and memories.

Procedures arising from reciprocal roles are known as *reciprocal role procedures* (RRPs). Procedures tend to be self-reinforcing. They may be healthy and adaptive (e.g. I am supportive to colleagues, they appreciate me, I feel good, so I continue to be supportive), or maladaptive and self-defeating (e.g. lacking self-confidence, and fearing rejection by others, I avoid eye contact, so people think I am unfriendly, so I remain friendless, which lowers my self-confidence).

RRPs also include ways of relating to oneself (e.g. self-nurturing, harshly self-critical). Though internalisation of reciprocal roles is most powerful in early childhood, it continues throughout life, so that even as adults we may develop new reciprocal role procedures, for example as a result of abuse – or as a result of effective psychotherapy.

People with 'neurotic' difficulties often lack a broad enough repertoire of reciprocal role procedures (especially those associated with secure attachment, and being attuned to in childhood) and/or they may be stuck in polarised responses, e.g. 'either defiant or submissive.'

People who have suffered trauma and/or serious emotional neglect in childhood (e.g. those with a diagnosis of borderline personality disorder) have similar difficulties. In addition, because trauma (including significant neglect) tends to lead to dissociation, they fail to integrate their various self-states, which are each experienced very intensely, split-off from and unmodulated by contact with the rest of the self. There are often sudden 'switches' from one self-state to another – for example from *idealising–idealised* to *devaluing–devalued*. These are known as state shifts.

This may happen, for example, in relation to a partner or a therapist. While idealising, only the other person's good qualities and behaviours are 'registered'; then when the other person disappoints, even in a small way, they may be suddenly perceived as 'all bad', as even recent memories of their goodness become temporarily inaccessible. This poorly integrated way of functioning can make such people very confusing and difficult to help. They are themselves also confused by their sudden switches, and usually find CAT explanations and diagrams very containing.

People expect others to respond in familiar reciprocal roles and may seek (usually unconsciously) to elicit these responses from others, for example behaving in a dependent way, eliciting overprotective responses. When a therapist is 'recruited' by a client into a reciprocating role, the therapy becomes counterproductive and anti-therapeutic. By responding to the client's invitation to enact a role familiar to, and expected by, the client, the latter's 'mental map' of 'ways of being with another' is confirmed, rather than undermined, challenged and broadened. Of course if the therapist realises what has happened, and feeds this back to the client, it becomes a therapeutic learning experience, which may in fact be truly transformative.

Level 1, level 2 and level 3 procedures

In most of his books and articles, Anthony Ryle (founder of CAT) focuses only on what is unhealthy, maladaptive or problematic. The main exception is an article in which he introduces the concept of level 1, level 2 and level 3 procedures.

Level 1 procedures are reciprocal role procedures (both adaptive and maladaptive).

Level 2 procedures are higher order procedures which enable us to access, mobilise, and sequence appropriate level 1 procedures from our repertoire.

> For example, a child at breakfast might effortlessly combine, by means of level 2 functions, three level 1 procedures: (a) silent obedience to an irritable father, (b) nurturant affection to a depressed mother, and (c) cheerful mutuality with a sister.
>
> (Ryle 1997: 83)

Though Ryle does not use the word 'healthy', this child clearly has well-developed level 2 functions, and appropriately deploys different RRPs 'effortlessly' because, unlike poorly integrated people, he has simultaneous access to all (or most of) his RRP repertoire.

Level 3 procedures entail reflection about oneself and about other people – and enable us to make changes, if necessary, to the level 1 procedures deployed.

Though it is helpful conceptually to think about level 2 and level 3 procedures separately, in practice they 'travel together'; when one of them is under-developed, so is the other. They also improve in parallel. The key text on CAT refers to 'metaprocedures', without explaining that this means *level 2* and *level 3 procedures* (Ryle and Kerr 2002: 10, 60, 179).

Metashifts

In addition to state shifts (i.e. shifts from one self-state to another), we undergo *metashifts*, i.e. *shifts between degrees of integration* (Nehmad 1997).

In Figure 2.2, the circle on the left represents an ideally well-integrated person (or a person at a well-integrated moment). There is a clear boundary between the person and others; the person is clear about what they are feeling and thinking, with no need to project unacceptable parts of themselves onto others, and with partial access to all parts of themselves (hence the dotted lines between different parts of the self). There are no split-off self-states. The 'child at breakfast' would be near the left of Figure 2.2.

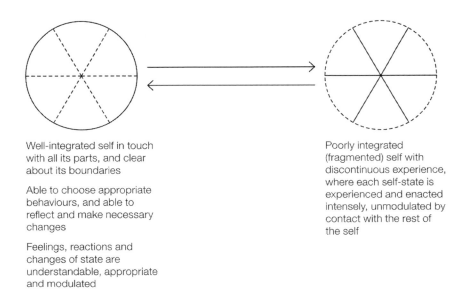

Well-integrated self in touch with all its parts, and clear about its boundaries

Able to choose appropriate behaviours, and able to reflect and make necessary changes

Feelings, reactions and changes of state are understandable, appropriate and modulated

Poorly integrated (fragmented) self with discontinuous experience, where each self-state is experienced and enacted intensely, unmodulated by contact with the rest of the self

Figure 2.2 The 'Universal Diagram' showing a metashift (a shift between degrees of integration)

The circle on the right represents a fragmented person (or a well-integrated person during a temporary shift into poorly integrated functioning). The dotted lines around the person represent a 'leaky boundary' to the self – with projection onto others, and excessive 'absorption' of others' moods, wishes, etc. The solid lines represent 'high walls' between aspects of the self – so that when the person is, for example, 'angry at a betraying other', they have no access to their own compassion, good memories, professional skill, sense of humour, etc. Each self-state is split off from the rest of the self.

A metashift (change in our degree of integration) may be:

- Gradual: e.g. a client comes to a psychotherapy session in a fragmented state; an hour later they are feeling somewhat more integrated.
- Sudden: the colloquial English expression, 'I lost it!' refers to temporarily 'losing' one's reason, or composure, or usual way of being or doing. It could be restated as 'I lost access to most of my self – so that I operated temporarily from just one split-off self-state'. In CAT terms it could also be stated as 'I temporarily lost access to my level 2 and level 3 procedures'.

It is important to emphasise that each 'wedge' in Figure 2.2 could be a self-state, but it could also be, for example, professional knowledge and skill (which we may temporarily 'lose' when under stress), the ability to think creatively, the capacity to reflect (i.e. Level 3 procedure), ethical values, awareness of one's own body.

Other people may 'recruit' us into a particular role (for example, we may try to be the ideal carer to our needy and dependent client). Crucially, other people may also 'recruit' us into a particular *degree of integration* – in other words, they may trigger a metashift in us. When we are with a poorly-integrated/fragmented person, they may recruit us into a similarly fragmented state. On the other hand, if we are able to stay integrated, they are likely to become more integrated (Nehmad 1997).

Scaffolding and the zone of proximal development

An important element of the CAT model is the concept of *scaffolding* (Bruner 1986: 77), which describes what a good teacher (or parent, or therapist) provides to a learner: support while they are learning a new skill or task which they cannot yet do independently. It may include help, encouragement, hints, leading questions, etc. Scaffolding is what is required in the learner's *zone of proximal development* or ZPD (Vygotsky 1980; see Chapter 3, this volume). All good teaching – and psychotherapy – should take place within the ZPD. The teacher acts as an 'external mental function' for the learner, who has not yet developed certain mental functions sufficiently.

How may the *healthy supervisor* be conceptualised in CAT terms?

Using CAT concepts the healthy supervisor can be thought of:

- In terms of level 1, level 2 and level 3 procedures
- In terms of integration/fragmentation
- In terms of ability to gauge and work within the supervisee's ZPD

In terms of level 1, level 2 and level 3 procedures

Having healthy level 1 roles

e.g. *generous, compassionate, empathic, respectful, flexible, inclusive, open to learning from others, boundaried, encouraging, acknowledging own mistakes and limitations, skilled and competent but not perfectionist.*

This is likely to create a reciprocal state in supervisees of:

valued, understood, included, safe, able to disclose difficulties and doubts.

As stated above, reciprocal roles are internalised throughout life. The supervisor's healthy level 1 procedures enable supervisees to learn or consolidate healthy and appropriate ways of relating to others and to themselves, by enacting the healthy supervisor-derived roles. For example, if the supervisor is able to tell the therapist, 'I don't know – let's think about it together', the therapist is more likely to be able to say that to the client.

On the other hand, a supervisor who does not express uncertainty may well lead therapists to feel they must show certainty when dealing with the client – and when presenting in supervision. In the words of Pawl and St John (quoted in Siegel and Shahmoon-Shanok 2010: 9), good supervisors are able to 'do unto others as they would have them do unto others'.

Having a wide range of level 1 procedures

e.g. able to be strict and boundaried, as well as open and flexible.

Having well-developed level 2 procedures

i.e. the ability to choose appropriately and flexibly from their repertoire of reciprocal role procedures. For example, they have the ability to confront, but do not feel compelled to confront. They can validate, listen and empathise, before, or instead of, confronting.

Having well-developed level 3 procedures

i.e. the ability to reflect on oneself and on the supervision group and process, and to make changes if necessary in the procedures deployed.

In terms of levels of integration/fragmentation

Being in touch with all (or most) aspects of themselves

i.e. near the left side of the diagram in Figure 2.2.
  Thus, the *healthy supervisor:*

1   enacts role procedures which are complex and modulated, with relatively smooth and understandable movements between them
2   is able to connect to her own anger, sadness or other emotions. (If a supervisor is cut off from her own feelings of sadness, she is less likely to pick up unexpressed sadness in a patient's or therapist's account)
3   is connected to her own bodily sensations, and therefore better able to attune to that of her supervisees (picking up countertransference, discomfort, etc.)
4   is able to be a 'safe container' for therapists, who may well come to supervision in a relatively fragmented state – at least in relation to the patient being discussed. As explained above, if the supervisor (and/or group members) are able to remain well-integrated, the therapist is likely to regain his level of integration during supervision. In terms of Figure 2.2, the therapist will then be able to 'move to the left', regaining access to his repertoire of RRPs, professional skill, capacity to reflect, etc.

In terms of ability to gauge, and work within, the supervisee's ZPD

One could say this is a form of attunement to the supervisee's current state of development (healthy level 1 procedure: *attuned* to *understood*). For example, at some stages of the supervisee's development it may be appropriate to tell the supervisee what to do, or to draw a diagram for him, as he is unlikely to manage it himself, and really needs to be 'held' and guided by the supervisor. At later stages in the supervisee's development, such interventions by the supervisor may be unnecessary, and may even get in the way of the supervisee's acquisition of skills and confidence.

The ability to work within the supervisee's ZPD requires well-developed level 2 and level 3 functions. Level 2 enables the supervisor to choose appropriately from her repertoire of role procedures, and/or skills (Tell him what to do? Ask the group what they think? Encourage him to figure it out?). Level 3 enables the supervisor to reflect on whether this is working well, and change course if necessary.

Having explained in CAT terms what is required for good enough (healthy) supervision, I will now consider other important sources of understanding of the process of psychotherapy supervision.

Hawkins and Shohet's contribution

Supervision in the Helping Professions (Hawkins and Shohet 2012) is a wonderful, rich and thought-provoking book which I believe every supervisor should read. Supervisees also benefit from it, as it enables them to think critically about the supervision process – after all, supervision is not something 'done to' the therapist. Rather, it is a relationship engaged in by supervisor and supervisees.

Their book draws on various authors' approaches and models of supervision, (and other useful ideas), and details their own *seven-eyed model of supervision*. They had observed that each experienced supervisor had a preferred 'mode'. For example, some focused mainly on the material brought by the client, while others focused mainly on their own countertransference, or on the client-therapist dynamic. Hawkins and Shohet argue that supervisors should not supervise in just one or two preferred modes. Instead, they should seek to become competent in, and comfortable with, all seven modes (summarised in Box 2.1). I have added an eighth mode, group dynamics, as most CAT supervision happens in group settings.

Hawkins and Shohet speak of '*helicopter ability*' – the ability to switch focus between different modes, and say that this is 'the most difficult new skill that supervision requires' (2012: 53). I would say that 'helicopter ability' is a 'metaskill', similar to the CAT concept of metaprocedures (i.e. level 2 and level 3 procedures). Skill at supervising in each 'mode' is important, but it is just as important for supervisors to be able to choose appropriately from their repertoire of types of intervention. For example, a mode 1 comment (about the patient's story) may well be useful and interesting, but it may not be the most important focus when the therapist is

> **BOX 2.1 Seven-eyed model of supervision**
>
> The supervision process involves two interlocking systems or matrices: *Client–Therapist* and *Therapist–Supervisor*, each of which includes three levels on which the supervisor may focus. These in turn exist within a *Context* which also needs considering, as it influences both matrices.
>
> The *Client–Therapist matrix* includes:
>
> 1. **Client** – how they present, what they present → increase therapist's ability to attend to client.
> 2. **Strategies and interventions by therapist** – which were used, when, how, why. Discuss alternative strategies → broaden therapist's repertoire of skills and interventions.
> 3. **Relationship between client and therapist**, conscious and unconscious → help therapist notice relationship dynamics.
>
> The *Therapist–Supervisor matrix* includes:
>
> 4. **Therapist** – how therapist is consciously and unconsciously affected by the client; therapist's development (reflecting, relating, resilience) → increase therapist's capacity to engage with clients and to use their own responses more effectively.
> 5. **Supervisor–therapist relationship** – quality of alliance; possible paralleling of dynamic with client.
> 6. **Supervisor's own here-and-now experience** – what thoughts, feelings, images, physical sensations arise in supervisor, in response to what therapist is bringing, and how therapist is bringing it.
>
> Both matrices are affected by, and encompassed by:
>
> 7. The contexts within which therapy and supervision are taking place. These may include professional codes and ethics, family, organisational expectations, training requirements, departmental policies, political and economic situation, etc.
> 8. Attention to group dynamics [not part of the *Seven-Eyed Model*, but an equally important aspect for supervisors to pay attention to].
>
> (Adapted from Hawkins and Shohet (2012); eighth mode is my own addition)

having difficulty grasping the dynamic between himself and the client (mode 3), or if the therapist's management of the case has just been contemptuously criticised by another group member – group dynamics (mode 8, which I have added to Hawkins and Shohet's seven levels, as most CAT supervision happens in group settings).

A given supervisor-supervisee relationship may restrict itself to one or two modes, even if the supervisor is usually flexible. As long as the supervisor is aware of this, it may be appropriate to do this at certain stages or in certain cases.

Darongkamas et al. (2014) offer a useful discussion of the *seven-eyed model* from a CAT perspective. They propose a different 'eighth mode' – the 'observing us', a collaborative expression of the CAT 'observing eye/I' (see Chapter 3), jointly exercised by supervisor and supervisee(s). They see this as similar to 'helicopter ability'. I agree, though I would argue that the 'observing us', like helicopter ability and Level 2 and Level 3 procedures, is in fact a meta-level, or meta-skill, rather than simply an extra 'mode'.

How do we learn 'helicopter ability'?

Sometimes, of course, we just learn through experience, which involves a lot of getting it wrong. To quote Oscar Wilde, 'Experience . . . was merely the name men gave to their mistakes' (Wilde 2001: 48).

In fact, most trainee CAT supervisors spend at least six months in a supervision group with an experienced supervisor. It is possible to use this time creatively, so that both the supervisor-mentor and the trainee supervisor benefit from having somebody observe and comment on their practice. This is how I have done it:

Typically, four cases are brought to the group. I supervise two cases, while the trainee supervisor observes. The other two cases are supervised by the trainee supervisor, while I observe. I ask the trainee not to comment on 'my' cases at all (unless I am missing something really important), and to concentrate instead on the supervision process itself – noticing the dynamics between me and the supervisees; thinking about which of Hawkins and Shohet's 'modes' my interventions are in, and so on. Freed from the pressure of having to offer interventions, the trainee supervisor is able to consider mine – how they are received, what I might have said or done instead, whether I was omitting or over-using one of the 'modes', etc.

I then do the same for them – i.e. I refrain from commenting on their cases, and concentrate on the process of supervision. In the 30 minutes after the supervision group, the trainee supervisor and I discuss how the supervision went, including what other interventions each of us might have made within each 'mode'. In this way the trainee supervisor can develop and practise using helicopter ability – and the supervisor-mentor gets valuable feedback.

Heron's contribution

Heron's seminal 23-page document, 'Six Category Intervention Analysis' (Heron 1975), was later expanded into a book, *Helping the Client* (Heron 2001). His analysis applies to anybody offering any kind of 'enabling service and skill' to a person, group or organisation. Because it has such wide application, he refers to the 'practitioner' offering interventions to his 'client'. In our case, the 'practitioner' is the supervisor, and the 'client' is the supervisee or supervision group.

Heron defines an intervention as 'an identifiable piece of verbal and/or non-verbal behaviour that is part of the practitioner's service to the client' (Heron 2001: 3). He classifies interventions according to their function and intention (see Box 2.2). He points out that no category is intrinsically better or worse than the others. All of them are important and useful, when deployed appropriately. He argues that competence in all six types of intervention should be cultivated, and his book offers many examples.

Heron points out that the categories are not exclusive of each other, and are not always in 'pure form'.

> Thus an effective confrontation . . . is rooted in a fundamentally supportive attitude.
>
> (Heron 1975: 3)

Heron is particularly useful for helping us think about unhelpful interventions. He points out that any category of intervention may be used inappropriately, and discusses in great detail the various types of inappropriateness.

BOX 2.2 Six categories of intervention

Authoritative – Supervisor takes an overtly dominant or assertive role; emphasis is on what therapist is doing.

1 **Prescriptive**: advises; is judgmental, critical, evaluative; explicitly seeks to direct the behaviour of the supervisee ('you should inform the GP')
2 **Informative**: Didactic; imparts new knowledge ('here's a good article on it'; 'this usually works')
3 **Confronting**: challenging, especially of therapist's restrictive attitude, belief or behaviour ('how come you didn't bring this issue to supervision?')

Facilitative – Supervisor seeks to elicit a state of being in the therapist.

4 **Cathartic**: seeks to enable therapist to release emotion ('what do you feel like saying or doing when your client becomes so contemptuous?')
5 **Catalytic**: encourages self-directed problem-solving by therapist ('what do you think you might do the next time your client is late?')
6 **Supportive**: validating, approving ('you dealt really well with a tough situation')

(Adapted from Heron (2001); examples are my own)

Interventions within each of the six categories may be:

> *Valid* – appropriate to the situation, and to the therapist's stage of development. Content and use of language are fitting, and the intervention is delivered with good timing.
> *Degenerate* – fails in at least one of the attributes of a valid intervention, because the supervisor lacks skill, experience or awareness.
> *Perverted* – deliberately malicious.

I am not sure one can always distinguish degenerate from perverted – how does one really know an intervention was intentionally unhelpful? I would prefer the term 'unhelpful' – instead of the emotionally charged 'degenerate' and 'perverted'.

Heron points out that some intervention categories may be engaged in 'compulsively', while others may be avoided. Some examples: a supervisor unable or unwilling to use confrontation, because she needs to be liked; a supervisor using mainly prescriptive and confronting interventions, as a way of asserting her power; a supervisor avoiding cathartic interventions, as she would be uncomfortable with 'too much feeling' in the supervision group. In CAT terms, such difficulties and shortcomings relate to a restricted repertoire of reciprocal role procedures, and/or the avoidance of feared roles. A healthy supervisor needs to become aware of, and develop, 'missing' (or underdeveloped) RRPs relevant to supervision.

One could also speak of 'helicopter ability' or 'level 2 procedure' when considering Heron's six categories of intervention. It is important to be skilled at using all six categories of intervention, and it is also fundamental to be able to choose the most appropriate intervention, and deliver it appropriately. So, the skilled supervisor ('practitioner' in Heron's terms):

> a) is equally proficient in a wide range of interventions in each of the categories;
> b) can move elegantly, flexibly and cleanly from one intervention to another and one category to another . . .;
> c) is aware . . . of what intervention they are using and why;
> d) knows when to lead . . . and when to follow . . .;
> e) has a creative balance between power over the [supervisee], power shared with the [supervisee], and the facilitation of power within the [supervisee].
>
> (Heron 2001: 9)

The above description may be translated into CAT terms:

> (a) refers to skills, and a broad repertoire of Level 1 procedures
> (b) (d) and (e) are evidence of level 2 procedures or capability. 'Elegantly, flexibly and cleanly' evokes Ryle's 'effortlessly' when describing the child at breakfast

(c) is a Level 3 procedure or capability
(d) and (e) refer to the supervisor's ability to work within the supervisee's ZPD.

The supervisor described by Heron in the above quote would be in the well-integrated place illustrated on the left side of Figure 2.2.

Fluctuating levels of integration and of access to skills

In CAT terms, supervisors need a broad repertoire of reciprocal role procedures, and well-developed level 2 and level 3 procedures, as well as skills such as self-awareness and helicopter ability.

However, it is not enough for healthy supervisors to be skilled and reasonably well-integrated. They need to be well-integrated, with access to their skills, their full repertoire of level 1 procedures, and their level 2 and level 3 procedures, *in the moment.*

A supervisor (like any human being) does not have a fixed level of integration. The latter can increase gradually over time with maturity, or as a result of psychotherapy, mindfulness practice, etc. It can also decrease in the short term because of stress, illness, etc. If a supervisor is upset and/or preoccupied, she may well become temporarily less integrated.

> *I certainly found this to be the case when my redundancy was announced by my NHS Trust. I was devastated, and intensely preoccupied with writing documents arguing for the preservation of the CAT team. I was therefore functioning less well, both as therapist and as supervisor. As all my supervisees, and almost all my patients, were familiar with the diagram in Figure 2.2, I was able to use it to let them know that I was feeling less integrated than usual. I was able to tell them the actual reason why I was in that state: my impending probable redundancy.*
>
> *If the issue had been about my life outside work, I could have used the same wordless diagram to let them know I was feeling significantly less well integrated that day, without having to disclose any actual details. I believe this simple statement is more containing for a supervisee (or client) than for us to try and 'be professional,' by pretending to be normal, while our supervisee experiences us very differently (e.g. less 'present' and attuned) but with no acknowledgement or explanation. This unacknowledged disparity between how we are feeling and how we are pretending to be might echo similar disparities in their childhood, so it might be unsettling, especially since the disparity is likely to be 'felt in the body' rather than put into words.*

A supervisor may become less integrated during supervision. This might be as a reaction to the material reported by a supervisee, or due to 'recruitment' by a supervisee into a particular self-state and/or into a lower level of integration. For example, when a supervisee repeatedly fails to 'hear', or take on board, feedback, the supervisor may become increasingly tense and frustrated, so that supervisor and supervisee may get stuck in unhelpful reciprocal roles, in an escalating spiral, where each 'role' keeps the other person in its reciprocal:

frustrated, despairing, repetitive, nagging, ineffectual to *unhearing, defensive.*

Parallel process

This is another means by which supervisors may temporarily lose access to their skills, and level of integration. This is an immensely valuable concept in supervision (see Chapter 1) and is a key part of the toolbox of CAT supervisors, who restate this psychoanalytic concept in CAT terms.

When a therapist is unaware that he has been 'recruited' into a split-off role by the client, it is likely that he will come to supervision in this state, and parallel process is likely to ensue, i.e. the reciprocal role procedures between client and therapist will get re-enacted within supervision. For example, if the client could not take on board what the therapist was saying (or vice versa), the supervisor may well not take on board what the therapist is saying (or vice versa).

Experienced supervisors tend to notice parallel process, but of course they may miss it, precisely because in the moment, while they are 'recruited', they are not as well integrated as usual. For this reason, it is a good idea to tell all supervisees, including absolute beginners, about parallel process, and to ask them to look out for it, and comment on it if they think it might be happening. This is especially relevant when treating patients with a diagnosis of borderline personality disorder, and others who function in a fragmented way, because they are more likely to recruit therapists into split-off roles, and/or into a lower level of integration.

Scaffolding in supervision

As explained earlier in the chapter, scaffolding is needed to aid learning within the ZPD. Scaffolding within supervision is also necessary when a therapist (experienced or inexperienced) temporarily loses access to his skills, level of integration, or reflective capacity, e.g. when he has been recruited by a client into a fragmented state (on the right of Figure 2.2). He may seem 'out of character.' The supervisor or group may recognise this either directly, or indirectly through parallel process. The therapist's level 2 and level 3 functions are temporarily 'out of action' or inaccessible.

A skilled and experienced supervisee, who is usually creative and receptive to feedback and suggestions, is feeling stuck, paralysed and unable to take on board any suggestions.

The supervision group can provide 'external level 2 and level 3 functions,' offering scaffolding to the therapist until he can regain his own ability to reflect (level 3), and to choose appropriately from a repertoire of responses (level 2). This scaffolding will be similar to that which a therapist offers a patient:

- commenting on what he does not seem able to notice for himself ('you seem upset and paralysed by this patient', 'it feels as if you can't access your creativity in this case')
- eliciting level 3 through questions ('why do you think you haven't yet produced a diagram for this patient?')
- commenting on the reciprocal roles and possible parallel process in the room ('you seem unable to hear our feedback', 'you seem as stuck as your patient and I am feeling somewhat stuck too – not sure how to best help you')
- helping with tasks at which the supervisee is usually competent ('would you like us to do a diagram together now?')
- offering specific advice on what to do, if he seems unable to figure this out, even when catalytic interventions (see Box 2.2) are deployed.

Once the therapist feels relatively integrated again, he can continue the therapy, often including providing 'external level 2 and level 3 functions' for his client.

> Winnicott points out that it is very hard for any mother to be 'good enough' unless she herself is also held and supported, either by the child's father, or by another supportive adult.
>
> (Hawkins and Shohet 2012: 4)

Hawkins and Shohet see this as an analogy for supervision. I agree and would add that the 'holding' needed by both mothers and therapists includes external support for their level 2 and level 3 functions (or level of integration), which they may temporarily lose access to.

Minimising the effects of supervisors' shortcomings

No supervisor is perfect; some of us are not very good at certain aspects of the role. We have deficiencies, avoided roles and preferred (or even compulsive) ones. Some of us may need to be 'the nice guy', or 'always right'. In Ekstein's pithy words (quoted in Hawkins and Shohet 2012: 74), we may have *dumb spots, blind spots* and *deaf spots:*

> *Dumb spots* are areas of ignorance about the other's experience (e.g. not knowing what it is like to do psychotherapy within a learning disability context.)
> *Blind spots* are aspects of ourselves we cannot see (e.g. not realizing that we talk too much, so our supervisees do not have time to think things out for themselves.)

Deaf spots are when we cannot 'hear' (i.e. take on board) what others are telling us.

So how can we minimise the effects of our shortcomings on our supervisees?

Firstly, create an ethos and atmosphere of relaxed tolerance, mutual learning and good humour, in which we convey that we seek, and can take, constructive criticism, and that we are open to learning from our supervisees, who often have a wealth of knowledge and experience of different lives, different therapeutic models and different work contexts. It is useful to seek feedback both formally (e.g. through questionnaires and reviews) and informally, and to act on it.

Just as importantly, supervisors should *actively use* the group (rather than merely 'deal with group dynamics'). We can encourage supervisees to give feedback to each other, not only on reformulation letters or diagrams, but on every aspect, such as their therapeutic relationship with the patient or their *dumb spots*, *blind spots* and *deaf spots*. Even beginners can be part of the 'observing us' (see page 27). Unhelpful and stuck reciprocal roles between supervisor and supervisee, such as those described on page 31, may respond more readily to an intervention by other group members.

A neurobiological perspective on supervision

Dan Siegel's work brings together findings from mathematics, physics, neuroscience, psychotherapy, attachment theory, mindfulness and more. His interpersonal neurobiology (IPNB) is profoundly relational. He is critical of 'single skull/single person psychology' which considers that 'mind equals brain' – because human beings are relational and responsive to context. IPNB emphasises the findings of contemporary neuroscience regarding neuroplasticity – the ability of brain cells and connections to grow throughout life rather than only in early childhood.

Siegel is a prolific author but to date has not written a book on psychotherapy supervision, so what follows is an extrapolation from selected works (Siegel 2010a, 2010b, Siegel and Shahmoon-Shanok 2010).

Siegel has coined a number of useful terms and concepts, and ways of thinking about the mind and about relationships.

- *Mindsight* refers to the ability to have insight and empathy for the mental experience of self and others. It enables us to be aware of our mental processes without being swept away by them; it lets us 'name and tame' the emotions we are experiencing, rather than being overwhelmed by them. Crucially, as we develop mindsight we actually re-sculpt our neural pathways, stimulating the growth of areas of the brain that are crucial to mental health (and which may have been underdeveloped as a result of deficiencies in parent–child attunement in early childhood).
- *'Health is integration'* For Siegel, this applies at every level of the brain, mind and relationships. This fits very well with a CAT understanding.

- *River of integration,* within which there is a sense of harmony, as we function in ways which are flexible, adaptive, coherent, energised and stable. This river flows between two dangerous 'banks': on one side chaos, on the other rigidity. For Siegel, almost every psychiatric diagnosis can be restated in terms of rigidity and/or chaos.

Siegel considers that a psychotherapist, in order to be truly therapeutic, needs above all to offer presence, attunement and resonance. These three elements enable 12 other elements he considers important in the therapeutic relationship, including trust, transformation and tranquillity (Siegel 2010b).

- *Presence:* a state of receptivity and awareness, without too much distortion by our filters of prior learning. It enables us to be flexible, and open to possibilities (of relationship, of action, of interpretation of the other's behaviour, etc.). It is 'the harmonious flow of a receptive state where we feel joined with others, and ourselves. Integration is at the heart of presence' (Siegel 2010b: 32).
- *Attunement:* the capacity to 'focus our attention on the other person and take their essence into our own inner world' (Siegel 2010b: 34). For attunement we need presence – because attunement may be limited by our wanting or perceiving 'what should be' rather than being open to what is. Attunement leads to secure attachment, a sense of well-being and resilience. Crucially, it requires interoception (perceiving, with our cerebral cortex, the interior of our body, e.g. heart rate, muscle tension).
- *Resonance:* When we register the other person's attunement to us, and feel that we are 'held in mind', our own state can change.

> The observed takes in the observer having taken her in, and the two become joined . . . Beginning with a genuine sense of care and interest by the focus of the other's careful attention, resonance extends this positive interaction into a fuller dimension of the other being changed because of who we are. This is how we feel 'felt'.
>
> (Siegel 2010b: 54–55)

Siegel's ideas greatly enrich our understanding of the healthy, 'good enough', integrated supervisor. Presence, attunement and resonance are helpful within any human relationship. They are particularly important when someone needs us to provide an integrating function for them, as their own is deficient. This is the case with young children, and with clients who, because of an adverse childhood, are not well integrated. It is also the case with therapists who become temporarily fragmented when they have been recruited by a client into a lower level of integration. The well-integrated supervisor is able to offer presence, attunement and resonance to their supervisees.

Chaos and rigidity, the twin dangers to integration, are a potential pitfall for supervisors, who might oscillate between (or fear) the chaos of 'anything goes' and the rigidity of inflexible adherence to a narrow view of 'the therapy model'. (In CAT terms, this would be a dilemma, where only two polarised undesirable alternatives seem possible).

Finally, neurobiology adds to our understanding about the importance of supervisees feeling safe within supervision. We know that if supervisees feel unsafe, they may not disclose information or feelings which expose their vulnerability or fallibility. Neurobiology adds something else: when people feel unsafe, their threat systems are activated, an excess of cortisol is produced, and there is increased blood flow to the amygdala (threat centre, responsible for fight, flight, freeze reactions), and reduced blood flow to the medial pre-frontal cortex. The latter is the specifically human part of the brain, responsible for reasoning, planning, moral judgments, creativity, empathy, etc. – presumably where level 2 and level 3 procedures reside.

So, when our supervisees feel stressed and unsafe, they are likely to be on 'automatic pilot,' driven by the amygdala and primitive parts of the brain where habitual procedures reside; their focus will be narrow and defensive, and they will have little capacity for choice or for creative thinking. They are likely to become reactive rather than responsive and reflective – and they are unlikely to find new and creative solutions because, in that state, openness to possibilities closes down. Considering different options, or brainstorming imaginatively to resolve therapeutic problems, becomes difficult or impossible.

In summary, what takes place in effective supervision?

The healthy ('good enough', well-integrated) supervisor, thanks to her well-developed level 2 and level 3 functions, is able to focus on the various modes detailed in the *seven-eyed model of supervision*, plus the eighth mode of group process. She offers a wide range of interventions appropriately, within the six categories described by Heron. She can deploy 'helicopter ability' and generate an 'observing us' with her supervisee(s).

For all therapists, supervision enables reflection on practice, and the regaining (when necessary) of level 2 and level 3 functions which may have been temporarily 'lost' – at least in relation to a particular patient.

Crucially, supervision is a 'place' and a relationship within which:

- supervisees are 'put back together again' (i.e. helped to re-integrate when temporarily fragmented) by the supervisor and/or other group members.
- supervisees may contribute to the supervisor's growth and learning (e.g. when the supervisor has *dumb spots* which supervisees can help with) and to the supervisor's re-integration, e.g. when the supervisor is caught in parallel process and has not noticed.

A nurturing relationship is 'one that helps the growth of one or more members of the relationship' (Siegel and Shahmoon-Shanok 2010: 8). As supervisors, we should be aware of skills and techniques (and of our own deficiencies, which we should try and remedy). But just as important is our capacity to remain integrated (and to be aware of when we are not), because, when we are not integrated, we lose access to our reflective capacity, and even to our skills. When we are integrated in the moment, we can offer presence and attunement. Resonance may follow, enabling positive change and growth in one or more people within the nurturing relationship that supervision can and should be.

References

Bruner, J. (1986) *Actual Minds, Possible Worlds*, Cambridge, MA: Harvard University Press.

Darongkamas, J., John, C. and Walker, M.J. (2014) 'An eight-eyed version of Hawkins and Shohet's clinical supervision model: The addition of the cognitive analytic therapy concept of the "observing eye/I" as the "observing us"', *British Journal of Guidance & Counselling*, 42, 3: 261–270.

Hawkins, P. and Shohet, R. (2012) *Supervision in the Helping Professions, (fourth edition)*, Maidenhead: Open University Press.

Heron, J. (1975) *Six Category Intervention Analysis*, mimeographed handout. Human Potential Research Group, University of Surrey.

Heron, J. (2001) *Helping the Client: A Creative Practical Guide, (fifth edition)*, London: Sage Publications.

Nehmad, A. (1997) 'Beyond state shifts – "Metashifts"', *ACAT Newsletter*, 8: 8–14. Online. Available HTTP: <http://www.acat.me.uk/reformulation.php?issue_id=37&article_id=374> (accessed 23 October 2015).

Ryle, A. (1997) 'The structure and development of borderline personality disorder: A proposed model', *British Journal of Psychiatry*, 170: 82–87.

Ryle, A. and Kerr, I.B. (2002) *Introducing Cognitive Analytic Therapy*, Chichester: Wiley.

Siegel, D.J. (2010a) *Mindsight*, Oxford: Oneworld Publications.

Siegel, D.J. (2010b) *The Mindful Therapist*, London: Norton.

Siegel, D.J. and Shahmoon-Shanok, R. (2010) 'Reflective communication: Cultivating mindsight through nurturing relationships', *Zero to Three (J)*, 31, 2: 6–14.

Vygotsky, L.S. (1980) *Mind in Society: The Development of Higher Psychological Processes,* Cambridge, MA: Harvard University Press.

Wilde, O. (2001) *The Picture of Dorian Gray*, Ware: Wordsworth Classics.

Chapter 3

The CAT model and the practice of CAT supervision

Eva Burns-Lundgren

This chapter begins with an introduction to the essential theory and practice of Cognitive Analytic Therapy (CAT). It then describes the practice of CAT supervision, showing how it integrates CAT's philosophical and theoretical stance with general clinical practice.

The theoretical foundations of CAT

As the name indicates, CAT is an integrated model, theoretically as well as clinically, and one early aim of Anthony Ryle, its originator, was to create a common language for the psychotherapies. It combines psychoanalytic understandings, especially those of Object Relations Theory, with cognitive processing theories, with their focus on negative beliefs and assumptions. Ryle's early research use of Repertory Grids from Kelly's Personal Construct Theory explored the active role humans play in creating understanding and meaning in their interpersonal world (Ryle and Kerr 2002). It also confirmed the importance of therapists working alongside patients to establish *accurate descriptions* of relational patterns, rather than in the role of experts with privileged access to interpretations.

CAT therefore actively works on the joint creation of a new narrative, to provide an improved understanding of the interpersonal roots and maintenance of unhelpful relationship and self-management procedures. Core to CAT is its identification of these in the form of *reciprocal roles* (RRs), interpersonal roles experienced and internalised in early life, and maintained in the present through *reciprocal role procedures* (RRPs). These shape expectations of and engagement with others, including in the therapy via transference and countertransference, and the attitude to and treatment of one's self. Later developments in CAT saw the incorporation of a dialogic perspective (Holquist 1990, Leiman 1997) on human development and change. Central to this is the social and cultural formation of mind. External voices acquired 'in activity and conversation with others' (Ryle and Kerr 2002: 14) are internalised to create a 'dialogic self', in continuous and ongoing engagement with others in the world – i.e. the interpersonal is seen to precede the intrapersonal. Observational research on early development increasingly supports the CAT view of the significance of social interaction and relationships in the development of the self (Reddy 2008).

CAT draws on Vygotsky's four central concepts about interpersonal learning, which apply equally in therapy and in supervision:

- All learning takes place within the *zone of proximal development* (ZPD). In therapy this is the gap between what the patient can do on his own and what he can learn to do with the help of a more competent other, i.e. the therapist.

> The zone of proximal development defines those functions that have not yet matured but are in the process of maturation, functions that . . . are currently in an embryonic state.
>
> (Vygotsky 1980: 86)

Vygotsky's statement, 'what the child does with an adult today, she will do on her own tomorrow' (Ryle and Kerr 2002: 41) becomes in supervision what the therapist 'can think through and work on with the help of the supervisor today', he will do on his own tomorrow.

(Marx 2011: 415)

- 'The *social formation of mind'*. Learning takes place in relation to others, and 'our activity and the acquisition of facts and their meaning are inseparable' (Ryle and Kerr 2002: 40).
- Learning is seen to be mediated via the *joint creation of signs*, such as language and CAT tools (or the signs that emerge within the supervision relationship itself).
- *Internalisation* Individuals' conceptual development occurs through the internalization of dialogues with others. Thus, in therapy the therapist's voice becomes internalised, recognisable in comments like 'I struggled to know what to do, and then I heard your voice.'

Joint activity and reflection within the person's zone of proximal development, which then becomes internalised (Vygotsky 1980), is therefore central to CAT's view of human development and to the therapeutic change process alike. CAT is of its essence a relational approach which aims to create and maintain a safe and structured space within which patient and therapist together reflect on interpersonal patterns and their consequences. Its consistent interpersonal and dialogic stance ensures that the therapy relationship, a central factor for good outcome (Lambert 2007, Safran 1993), is actively explored and used in the therapy. As well as exploring interpersonal procedures outside therapy, close attention is paid to potential enactments of reciprocal role procedures within the therapy relationship. Via the active use of CAT-specific tools unique opportunities are created for the lived experience of joint reflection in the moment, and thereby for a gradual breaking of unhelpful patterns. The therapist will be aware of any invitations into the 'relational dance', and will actively use herself and her reactions as vital information in this process.

From a cognitive perspective, time is spent in therapy clarifying the main *Target Problems* (TPs) that cause people to seek therapy. These are often found to be different from either symptoms or the 'presenting problem' a patient or referrer might have focused on, and they are invariably relational in nature. In addition patient and therapist together identify and track the *Target Problem Procedures* (TPPs), which represent the person's attempts at dealing with their difficulties, attempts which often inadvertently maintain and confirm them.

CAT normally lasts for 16 or 24 sessions, but rather than describe it as a brief therapy, it is seen as a time-limited model, and for carefully considered reasons. The belief is that actively engaging the patient in collaborative, early identification of higher-order descriptions of unhelpful or damaging procedures reduces resistance and enables rapid challenges to these. CAT builds a solid structure and boundaries to the therapeutic work, via its clear phases of Reformulation, Recognition and Revision, and the tools used within each stage provide the scaffolding for the learning and change process, as described by Wood et al. (1976). As the number of sessions is agreed from the start of therapy, the end of therapy is kept actively in mind throughout the work, with careful attention paid to issues of separation and loss. At least one follow-up session is offered as part of the therapeutic contract.

The relational tools of CAT

Within this structure CAT-specific therapeutic tools are used and jointly created within the therapy relationship. These are of a written or schematic nature, which adds visual impact, aiding memorising and internalisation.

- The *Psychotherapy File* is a tick-box self-report form, which patients are usually given at the end of the first therapy session and asked to return completed for session two. It outlines common unhelpful procedures or TPPs which have over time thwarted the patient's attempts to address their difficulties or Target Problems. The most common TPPs are *Traps* (vicious circles), e.g. tendencies to please and placate others in order to improve a sense of worth or acceptability, *Dilemmas* (false dichotomies or black-and-white thinking) and *Snags* (self-sabotaging patterns). The file also identifies the presence of recurring, often dissociated self-states, which are commonly part of the more complex presentations in personality disorders.
- After roughly the first four sessions the therapist writes a *Reformulation Letter* to the patient, and reads it out aloud in the next session The letter provides a draft summary of the understanding that they have gained together of the person's experiences in life and, crucially, of the conclusions he has drawn from them about his personal value, about relationships, and how to deal with the feelings and conflicts that arise from these. It draws out the Target Problems and interpersonal and self-management patterns (TPPs) along with tentative suggestions for a focus for the remainder of the work. It will commonly identify ways in which the TPPs might be activated in the work and in the therapy relationship, such as a tendency to sabotage gains or to please the therapist at a cost to personal fulfilment. The letter is open for revision

and amendment until a consensus is reached, and then forms a solid, shared underpinning for the rest of the therapy. As well as gaining a clearer personal narrative (Holmes 1993) and more continuous sense of self, patients usually feel attuned to (Stern 2004) and validated through this process, and that their sufferings have been witnessed (Bakhtin, in Hepple 2012).

- The *Sequential Diagrammatic Reformulation* or SDR. This is a visual representation of the most common reciprocal roles, usually between two and four, which recur and dominate the person's life, both inter- and intra-personally. It also outlines the emotional and behavioural enactments (Reciprocal Role Procedures) which emerge from these self-states, usually with the aim of relief or escape, but invariably leading to their confirmation. The therapist and patient normally create the diagram (or map) live and collaboratively in sessions. It plays a crucial part in the recognition and active use of transference phenomena, and in avoiding or recovering from re-enactments, where a therapist has been invited or recruited into familiar reciprocal role(s). It is a descriptive and non-blaming tool, highly valued by most patients, and plays a unique and powerful role in the creation of a perspective or an 'observing eye (I)' on the patient's habitual ways of relating. Figure 3.1 is an example of a simple diagram, showing core RRs (in boxes) and the inter- and intra-personal patterns these give rise to. It demonstrates how both parent- and child-derived roles are learned and enacted.

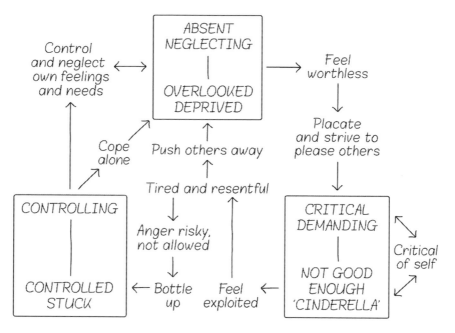

Figure 3.1 CAT diagram (SDR)

- *Goodbye Letters* These are written by patient and therapist alike, and read out aloud, normally in the final session. They provide an opportunity for each, from their perspective, to summarise and draw out gains from the therapy, but also to make a realistic appraisal of it, including opportunities missed and challenges ahead. It helps each patient to assume responsibility for changing and to make their own evaluation of what has worked in therapy and how to continue to use it. It also provides an opportunity to express feelings related to the ending and to say a 'farewell'.

An important aspect of the therapy is the transparency with which these relational tools are co-created, stripping them of mystique, reducing power imbalances, and re-affirming Socratic questioning and dialogue (Ryle and Kerr 2002).

Relational supervision in CAT

Psychotherapy supervision is an intense and intimate activity, 'built on a mutuality of trust and of sharing' (Reggiori 1992: 8), where the supervisory working alliance significantly 'influences supervision process and outcome in crucial ways' (Ladany 2004: 5). In the same way that the quality of the therapeutic alliance and relationship influences therapy outcome, so the supervisory relationship is key to supervisees' experience of supervision and to the success of the process of supervision (Marx 2011). As the core focus in CAT theory and practice is on relationships, external and internal, the same naturally applies in CAT supervision, which is characterised by 'collaboration and mutual discovery' (Marx 2011: 418).

CAT supervisors similarly pay close attention to the relationships within the supervision group, some of which reflect the reciprocal roles of individual supervisees, some those of the supervisor herself, and this is of special importance when relationships change or relational issues get in the way of the therapeutic process or the learning. At these points it is essential for the supervisor to name and attend to reciprocal role procedures and to use herself and her reactions in this process.

What do we do when supervisees do not see or do not want to look at their own potential contribution to alliance ruptures or reciprocations of reciprocal role procedures? As supervisors we need to find ways of offering feedback, and to maintain a sense of 'optimal conflict', where supervisees are 'neither overwhelmed by the conflict nor able to escape or diffuse it' (Kegan in Hicks 2011: 154). That is where the CAT model truly comes into its own, with supervisors called upon to model its core tenets of 'accurate description', naming and opening up troubling matters for joint reflection.

An example of this occurred when a supervisee in the later stage of his CAT training responded to suggestions I made, (which he experienced as criticism), with irritation and dismissiveness – 'I've already done/ thought of that'. In spite of my encouragement for simplification, a plethora of SDRs were in use, blurring the focus of the work. When this had happened more than once, giving rise to frustration in me, I took the opportunity of a quieter moment in supervision to describe what I felt to be happening, including my emotional reaction. I wondered aloud whether he recognized my description of events, and whether we could think together about what might be occurring. The open, descriptive, non-blaming stance and invitation to jointly reflect immediately jelled, and we were able to identify the reciprocal roles we had entered into. The supervisee acknowledged his annoyance at my seeming interference when he was a nearly qualified practitioner. He recognized his own reasons for this specific reaction, and I could acknowledge that my suggestions might have felt like that. The atmosphere became relaxed, and we were then able to return to the patient and recognize a parallel process also occurring, with many of her reciprocal roles re-enacted between us. As well as enhancing the understanding of the patient, the supervisee found this a real turning point in his development, providing him with a lived experience of how uncomfortable issues can safely be named and explored together, using CAT understanding and tools. He was quickly able to put this into practice with his patient, using one SDR only and addressing an issue, which had previously been avoided. He had already emerged from an early stage of Dependence in supervision, but now returned from self-sufficient Independence to accept the reality of our Interdependence.

(stages described in Hicks 2011: 155–156)

It is important to carefully tease out in supervision whether the feelings and role patterns which emerge originate in the therapist-patient relationship, reflect a supervisee's own reciprocal roles (i.e. personal countertransference) or in fact belong in the supervisory relationship. Issues need to be identified as early as possible, and as with all feedback, it is important that it is offered in a timely and reciprocal manner that can be clearly understood.

Supervision in CAT is a multifaceted, complex and demanding venture. The supervisor has to enable the supervisee to link CAT theory to practice and to undertake CAT specific tasks, as well as attend to the normal business of psychotherapy supervision, such as creating a learning environment, attending to patient and trainee development needs, and dealing with ruptures and threats to the therapy alliance and relationship (Bennett and Parry 2003, Safran 1993). Not surprisingly, supervisors can therefore at times feel pressurised, overseeing many tasks within a limited time frame and in the intensity of a supervision group. But using the CAT tools, and especially the diagram, in the supervision process itself, offers clarity and containment, and learning in supervision thereby echoes the process of learning in therapy.

Setting up supervision

With each new supervision group or supervisee, we will enter a new interactive 'arena', whatever our experience as supervisors. Whether its members are all CAT trainees on courses, or it is a mixed group with trainees, honorary therapists or medical/psychology trainees on placements, its members will bring individual as well as shared aspirations and anxieties. As supervisors we also bring our own, be that apprehension at a new venture, excitement at developing and providing good therapy for more patients, hope for shared joy at the attainment of new skills and psychotherapeutic ease, or feeling fatigue in a pressured NHS role.

It is therefore essential to create space and time at the start of a new supervision group for all participants to introduce themselves to one another, including their experience of therapy and CAT and their hopes for supervision. It is helpful to hear what people enjoy and find rewarding as therapists, as well as what they are less confident about. Areas to explore could include cultural backgrounds, as well as underlying ethical and professional stances. It is important to use open and inclusive language, as this resonates with CAT's stance of therapy as a shared undertaking, which addresses core human and interpersonal struggles of identity and relatedness – 'the we of me' (McCullers 2001: 52).

This kind of conversation also models CAT's inclusive mode of interacting, which is curious about and values people with different backgrounds and ways of thinking, and about how these have been formed. We need to create a welcoming atmosphere which cultivates 'intelligent kindness' (Ballatt and Campling 2011) and builds SOS, 'Sharing and Openness in Supervision,' (Claire Tanner, ACAT conference workshop, March 2013, Reading, Berkshire). These are needed to create in each participant a state of receptivity to learning, captured by Siegel (2012) in the helpful acronym COAL: Curious, Open, Accepting and Loving.

The first meeting, like that in any therapy, will be important in terms of setting the scene and establishing the tone, frame and context for the shared work ahead. Paying attention to good groundwork at this stage, can help encourage rich growth later, to echo Elizabeth Wilde McCormick's (2012) metaphor in her self-help CAT book, *Change for the Better*. One aspect of this first meeting involves establishing ground rules, drawing up a 'contract' for the supervision and agreeing its objectives. Some supervisors may agree a contract verbally or in writing, while many NHS services will have a pro-forma to use. Basic information will include times, punctuality, venue and notification of changes or absences. Equally important is discussing the relational aspects of supervision – e.g. encouraging openness, and the giving and receiving of feedback.

Langs (1994) writes extensively about the importance of structure and boundaries, which are needed to create scaffolding for therapy and learning, and to create safety around the creative space – a safe space in which to do risky things. He maintains that we all continuously and unconsciously monitor interactions for potential boundary breaches, and that every breach gives rise to powerful feelings which can make the work unsafe, especially without clear procedures for how to raise issues or reflect on them. Supervisors therefore need to be clear about the expectations agreed in a contract – and remember to apply them consistently.

It is crucial for supervisors to create an atmosphere which encourages supervisees to be open to exploring personal reactions and struggles in the therapy – and supervision – process, and to frame this as a strength, without which the work becomes limited (Safran et al. 2008) Feedback needs to be offered in timely, constructive and respectful ways, and members of the group encouraged to use their position as an 'observing eye' or place of 'otherness' (Bakhtin, in Holquist 1990) in the group, to reflect on overall patterns that might not be immediately obvious to either the supervisee who presents or to the supervisor. It is important to stress the value of the joint reflection, the shared commentary which supervision groups offer, and how different members of a group might pick up painful or avoided reciprocal roles and be able to 'voice' feelings or experiences hitherto hidden in a person's 'inner speechlessness' (Sutton 1999: 5). It also reflects CAT's emphasis on active participation in the process of learning and the internalisation of self-reflective skills.

It is useful to agree how to divide time in supervision sessions – per trainee or case, and in which order and how supervisees bring their work. It is useful to emphasise that supervisees need to present their work as succinctly as possible and, with limited time, to be clear about what they want or need from the group in any particular session.

It is important to clarify how to raise and address unhappiness or complaints with the supervision process, the supervisor or the group. Regular reviews, when such issues can be addressed as part of a normal process, relieve supervisees of any sense of being 'trouble-makers' or of carrying the responsibility for raising difficulties. Supervisees can raise issues as part of checking-in at the beginning of each supervision session, and for supervisees on training courses reviews naturally fit in with bi-annual appraisals.

Specifically for CAT, and especially in early stages of learning the model, the supervisor will explain that supervisees need to bring and discuss drafts of reformulation and goodbye letters to supervision, prior to reading them out in therapy.

The Reformulation stage

At this stage, the level of CAT experience of supervisees will greatly influence the task of supervision. Trainees new to the model often experience great anxiety over 'getting it right'. The supervisor therefore has to provide a calm presence, helping supervisees to connect with skills they already possess and to draw on their natural observations, in addition to using the specific CAT tools and approach. We need to offer a combination of encouragement and support while holding the time boundary and structure of the model and helping supervisees not to get lost in detail. The capacity of CAT to quickly reach a higher-order understanding of patterns is a core strength of the model, although a skill which takes time to learn.

It is essential for supervisors to encourage supervisees to form strong, empathic relationships with their patients, and to be alert to the potential for CAT tools to get in the way of this process, rather than be helpful devices for creating shared understanding. Ryle and Kerr put it thus (2002: 5), 'Practice embedded in theoretical clarity must be combined with accurate empathy if therapists are to be able to reach and maintain an understanding of their patients' experiences'.

As supervisors we need to be careful not to appear critical or judgemental, but rather model a CAT stance of being intrigued or curious about interactions, and finding ways of thinking about them together.

In supervision, just as in therapy, it is important to 'push where it moves' (Ryle and Kerr 2002) and not stick too rigidly to set ways of doing things, but try and build on supervisees' own knowledge and tools. Someone from a family therapy background might, for example, naturally gain useful information via a family tree, or a cognitive therapist via identification of individual and family assumptions and negative beliefs.

Most supervisors are faced with questions about how to phrase comments in therapy sessions, including how to introduce and use CAT tools. We can encourage supervisees, with the help of the group, to think of ways and phrases which they can make their own, and which are therefore more likely to emerge naturally in a session. If people become stuck, we might suggest wordings we ourselves have found helpful, and ask people to reflect on their pros and cons, prefacing it with Yalom's (2002: 35) statement, 'Do not try this in your next session, but in your situation I might have said something like. . .'. At other times the teaching or supervision might be more indirect or by way of modelling joint activity. Casement (1985) is helpful as regards identifying interpersonal patterns (RRs), and supervisees usually see these once they are encouraged, as he suggests, to remove names and pronouns from the verbal content of what the patient brings. The supervisor can summarise it thus; 'I seem to hear you describe interactions where one person says or does A or B to another, who then in turn says or does the following . . . Does this ring any bells, is this something you recognise?' This opens issues up for joint reflection, and also provides a model of collaborative exploration, which the supervisee can use with their patient.

Writing the reformulation letter can be challenging, especially when it comes to 'seeing the wood for the trees' and not getting lost in detail. It is important to help supervisees not just to write a 'history' of events, but to draw out with their patients the *conclusions* the person has drawn from their experiences, about themselves and their value, about how to be in relationships and how to deal with conflicts within them. This will be of crucial importance when identifying in the letter a provisional focus for the remainder of the work – the TPs (Target Problems) and TPPs (Target Problem Procedures). There are variations in supervision practice and between supervisors regarding how strictly this practice is adhered to, and the trend is towards focusing more on reciprocal role procedures rather than the TPs/TPPs of the early days of CAT. There are, however, some good reasons for asking supervisees to continue to identify TPs/TPPs:

- It helps them to think clearly and offer a clear rationale for the work. So, for the target problem, what is the problem that the person keeps struggling with and fails to revise, and how is this different to the presenting problem or symptoms? What are the procedures or TPPs that maintain the problem rather than solve it?

- Putting the target problem in terms of 'I don't know how to . . .' is helpful for the patient in clarifying that they are not at fault, personally flawed or 'bad', but rather that they have not had opportunities to learn how to do certain things. This in turn can help supervisees maintain an empathic stance and create opportunities for learning.
- It helps prevent 'therapeutic heroics', where both patient and supervisee might aim to change core reciprocal roles, which represent essential aspects of the person's sense of self, and which might therefore be outside their zone of proximal development, at least in the early stages of therapy or with a novice therapist.

Regarding the actual wording of the letter, it is important that it reflects the collaborative stance of CAT, so supervisees need to consider using phrases such as 'together we have come to understand that. . .' and 'you have told me how. . .' or 'we have explored how this led you to. . .', rather than the more dogmatic 'you must have felt. . .', which might reflect the therapist's feelings rather than an attuned understanding of the patient's actual experience. This is a joint RE-formulation of the stuck 'formulation', which has brought the patient to therapy, and it needs to be worded as such and expressed tentatively, if this is to be a truly collaborative undertaking.

To help supervisees write in an empathic and attuned way, the supervisor might encourage use of Casement's (1985: 34) 'trial identification' to consider what it might feel like hearing this letter read out to them. Alternatively the supervisor might use role play or encourage feedback from group members. It is also helpful for supervisees to read the letter out to themselves after writing it.

Grasping the concepts of RRs and RRPs, and then sketching them out on paper, can again feel like a daunting prospect to those new to the model, but once accomplished, they become an obvious and great resource and a container for the work. There are many ways of helping supervisees to identify them, e.g. using Casement's (1985) model, engaging the group in a playful manner, using mini role plays or chair work in supervision sessions. One useful place to start is to explore what the supervisee felt at various points in the therapy session, including bodily manifestations, and what this might tell them about the roles they had been invited into. Often group observations are invaluable in this process, members noting disavowed feelings, and picking up on contradictions and non-verbal expressions.

Many supervisees feel – or perceive – pressure to get everything 'right' by themselves, to come up with 'answers' and carry full responsibility for the change process. It is therefore important as a supervisor to continually stress the collaborative nature of the work, and to enable supervisees to bring things into therapy sessions in a tentative manner, emphasising the provisional nature of the letter or diagram. This is especially so when the supervision session takes place shortly before therapy sessions, as the supervisee may take 'advice' from the supervision straight to therapy, 'undigested'. When supervisees feel overly responsible or anxious about not knowing or having 'the' answer, they often find it a great relief to be asked gently 'Have you thought of asking N (i.e. the patient)?'

The recognition and revision stages

As part of the Reformulation phase patients will normally have started the process of recognising unhelpful patterns, either spontaneously or with the therapists' guidance. This can take the form of keeping a diary, which is brought to therapy sessions, or more formally through completing rating sheets of TPPs.

An important task for this phase of therapy is to help supervisees create the *Sequential Diagrammatic Reformulation* or SDR of the patient's patterns or 'procedures', often building on early partial maps created during the reformulation phase of a CAT therapy. A word of warning; the tools or techniques of CAT therapy are only as good as the therapy relationship within which they are used, and so we should always prize the latter above the former. Unless we help supervisees do this, diagrams and letters risk becoming formulaic and mechanical in nature, which is contrary to the spirit of CAT and prevents us from 'creating a new therapy for each patient' (Yalom 2002: 34). We therefore need to pay attention to how the drawing of diagrams and its rationale is introduced into therapy, enabling supervisees to attune to the patient's language and ZPD, if necessary practising in supervision. Trainees can find it helpful to see drafts or more complete versions of the supervisor's own diagrams, to reduce anxiety and recognise the process as messy and organic. This process crucially depends on active collaboration with the patient in order to be meaningful. Mapping interactions in the supervision session itself can provide a 'lived' experience of the usefulness of a diagram.

Although revision of a TPP might already have begun, once a final version of a diagram has been established, the stage is set for more consistent attention to the revision or change phase. This is a gear-change, especially when a new supervisee has relaxed after writing the letter and getting a useable SDR in place and thinks, 'Help! What do I do now? How will we fill the rest of the sessions?' They may find it hard to trust that an organic process will naturally emerge, and that there will be no shortage of opportunities to identify, reflect on and challenge unhelpful procedures – especially as they invariably occur in the therapy relationship itself.

I always ensure that each patient's diagram is put on the table in supervision. It enables the supervision group to know immediately who we are talking about (e.g. 'explosive Mog' or 'controlling John'). With one supervisee, whose patient's absent pilot father had tended to 'hover' in the wings and just occasionally drop in, we only needed to raise our arms a fraction towards flying level, for smiles of recognition to spread. The clear depiction of RRs and RRPs in the SDR also helps in quickly identifying when transference or countertransference might occur via RR reciprocations or recruitment.

As in therapy sessions, the diagram makes it easy to invite reflections, in an uncritical, non-persecutory manner, especially at stuck points; 'Where do you think you (or the patient) might have been on the map in last week's session?'

This becomes a powerful means of developing the 'Observing Eye/I', a position of growing self-awareness or observation, often represented on the diagram via the drawing of an actual eye.

The Ending Stage of CAT

Supervision must always keep the ending in CAT in mind and refer to it when appropriate. Two issues repeatedly emerge in relation to the ending: keeping to the frame of the agreed number of sessions and the writing and sharing of the goodbye letters.

We have to help supervisees hold the boundary of the therapy and thereby enable them to keep the therapeutic space safe. We can do this by reminding them that symptoms or TPs often recur towards the end of therapy, to help them calmly state this as a normal occurrence when with their patients. We need to hold our nerve so they can hold theirs, and other group members are often crucial in this process, reminding them of changes and good work done. In this phase supervisees with personal issues relating to loss may need encouragement to identify which feelings belong to them – and may need to be taken to their own therapy – and which the patient needs help in facing. An accurate SDR will prove invaluable at this stage, and supervisees can fruitfully return to the reformulation letter, which will usually have predicted enactments of procedures relating to ending. This supports supervisees in exploring them with the patient as understandable and foreseen issues, which they can hold and manage together, rather than resort to anxious reactions like offering extra sessions or making external referrals.

The goodbye letter can again bring out the striving perfectionist in supervisees, or else turn into something that borders on a detached discharge letter. The task for the supervisor is to help supervisees find their own authentic voice when reflecting on the process of therapy, tracing changes as well as missed opportunities and regrets. As in therapy sessions, we have to help supervisees name what actually was/is, rather than resort to the 'Tyranny of Niceness' (Sommers 2007) or wishful thinking. A good test is to make sure that all draft letters are read out aloud in supervision. A supervisee will quickly pick up on a wrong 'note', or the group can hear discrepancies, say between written content and tone of voice.

Whatever the level of supervision, it is good practice to encourage supervisees to draw out the main issues and learning points from each completed therapy. Supervisees are then better able to take responsibility for their learning, becoming aware of gaps in their knowledge and of personal issues, which might impact on their work. 'Being responsible means that we hold ourselves accountable for our actions, especially those that are hurtful to others' (Hicks 2011: 113).

Note-keeping

At the beginning and end of therapies, a supervisor will need to ensure that supervisees adhere to the administrative requirements of the clinical setting. If supervisees are not familiar with expectations of the agency, the supervisor can ask, at least initially, to see correspondence in draft, and they may also need to help supervisees learn how to write in the role of psychotherapist.

Similarly, in an environment of increasing demands for computerised record-keeping, careful thought has to be given to how therapists' and supervisors' notes are kept and who can access them. While it is important to have a record which, for example, demonstrates that risk issues have been addressed, it is often neither necessary nor helpful to record matters relating to a supervisee's learning process, e.g. personal or countertransference issues. A guiding principle for both supervisors' and supervisees' notes would be to consider the minimum record required for others' 'need to know'. Supervisors can record themes raised and discussed relating to the therapy, along with agreed conclusions and action points, and these will often be enough to act as prompts to attend to in ensuing supervision sessions. This is a complex area, and supervisors clearly have to be aware of the requirements of their organisations.

Supervising experienced therapists

Supervision of experienced practitioners adds new dimensions, which can often enrich the work. When core principles and practice can be taken for granted, there is scope to incorporate or develop more in-depth or specialist approaches. It can be valuable for experienced supervisees to identify specific areas they want to focus on as part of their ongoing professional development. As participants will have had their own personal therapy, countertransference or other personal reactions are approached with more ease or openness, and often with humour. Experienced CAT therapists are however also often the ones who see patients with the most complex and challenging presentations, and it is important to create a safe and nurturing place to support this work.

Supervising experienced colleagues, where the power dynamics are different, also carries other complexities. Set habits might be hard to challenge, especially if clinical CAT practice has been learned during an earlier stage of the development of the CAT model, for example, concerning how the therapist works with TPPs or develops diagrams. Challenging such a practitioner's own unresolved procedures, without being experienced as undermining, demands sensitivity and judgement. Again the CAT model can be relied on to address the most delicate impasses, with its use of accurate description rather than interpretation, its relational approach to interactions and its dialogic stance which encourages joint reflection. Although our supervision input offers the 'Surplus of Seeing' (Bakhtin, in Holquist 1990: 36) afforded from our external position, 'a dialogic world is one in which I can never have my own way completely, and therefore I find myself in constant interaction with others – and with myself' (Holquist 1990: 39). It is only through this struggle to create meaning together, with experienced others from whom we can also learn, that we avoid growing stale or remaining in fixed positions.

Distance supervision

The CAT approach has expanded well beyond the UK, and supervision has made good use of digital and online tools in this process, including internet software. Key issues here are ethical ones pertaining to the preservation of patient anonymity and confidentiality, for example, checking the safety of the service used, replacing patient names, changing identifying information, and using encryption. When supervision takes place in people's home environment, privacy of communication needs to be ensured, both physically, and regarding access to the computer and its documents (see Rousmaniere [2014] for a discussion of using technology in supervision).

Quite apart from technical issues such as computer skills, internet speed and intermittent loss of connection, there are additional challenges to do with creating and maintaining the supervision relationship and group cohesion. For example, things might happen off camera that the supervisor cannot see but other group members can, and these need to be explicitly named and described. It is also more difficult to read body language, for example, to remember that if someone looks down, they may simply be reading notes. Where there are cultural differences and participants have different mother tongues, special care needs to be taken to understand these and check them out so that misunderstandings do not occur. It is also important to be clear about who carries clinical responsibility, and to make this part of an early contract. Given these safeguards, suitably anonymised SDRs and letters can be sent as encrypted attachments or by post, and be read out and referred to – even held up to the camera – in supervision. Combined with the dialogue of supervision, this provides a similar immediacy of experience, even when supervisor and supervisee are on different continents. Much of the early development of CAT in Australia was undertaken in this manner, combined with reciprocal personal visits to ensure a solid relational base for the work. Interpersonal 'voices' are clearly heard and internalised, whatever the distance.

Supervisors' self-care

Finally, a few words about our duty to ourselves as supervisors. As this chapter shows, CAT can be a busy therapy, and CAT supervision even busier. We owe it to ourselves, our supervisees and our agencies to keep an eye on the level of pressure and to remember our obligation to ensure our 'survival-with-enjoyment' (Coltart 1993: 3). If we take on too much – and agencies usually happily allow us to do so – the responsibility for safe service delivery of therapy is removed from where it belongs, and we, our supervisees and their patients can only suffer. We must maintain open dialogue with our colleagues and managers, regularly review our supervision workload and make sure there is space for laughter and fun in supervision. If we do not do this, people will feel that CAT 'is too much like hard work'. But if we do, and use the CAT model to its full, working with even the most challenging supervision issues will bring great rewards.

References

Ballatt, J. and Campling, P. (2011) *Intelligent Kindness: Reforming the Culture of Healthcare*, London: RCPsych Publications.

Bennett, D. and Parry, G. (2003) 'Maintaining the therapeutic alliance: resolving alliance-threatening interactions related to the transference', in D.P. Charman (ed) *Core Processes in Brief Psychodynamic Psychotherapy*, London: Routledge.

Casement, P. (1985) *On Learning from the Patient*, London: Tavistock Publications.

Coltart, N. (1993) *How to Survive as a Psychotherapist*, London: Sheldon Press.

Hepple, J. (2012) 'Cognitive analytic therapy in a group: Reflections on a dialogic approach', *British Journal of Psychotherapy*, 28: 474–495.

Hicks, D. (2011) *Dignity: The Essential Role It Plays in Resolving Conflict*, New Haven: Yale University Press.

Holmes, J. (1993) *John Bowlby and Attachment Theory (Makers of Modern Psychotherapy)*, London: Routledge.

Holquist, M. (1990) *Dialogism*, London: Routledge.

Ladany, N. (2004) 'Psychotherapy supervision: What lies beneath', *Psychotherapy Research*, 14: 1–19.

Lambert, M. (2007) 'Presidential address: What we have learned from a decade of research aimed at improving psychotherapy outcome in routine care', *Psychotherapy Research*, 17: 1–14.

Langs, R. (1994) *Doing Supervision and Being Supervised*, London: Karnac Books.

Leiman, M. (1997) 'Procedures as dialogical sequences: A revised version of the fundamental concept in cognitive analytic therapy', *British Journal of Medical Psychology*, 70: 193–207.

Marx, R. (2011) 'Relational supervision: Drawing on cognitive-analytic frameworks', *Psychology and Psychotherapy: Theory, Research and Practice*, 84: 406–424.

McCormick, E.W. (2012) *Change for the Better: Self-Help through Practical Psychotherapy*, London: Sage.

McCullers, C. (2001) *The Member of the Wedding*, London: Penguin.

Reddy, V. (2008) *How Infants Know Minds*, Cambridge, MA: Harvard University Press.

Reggiori, J. (1992) 'The practice of supervision: style or method', in *The Practice of Supervision: Some Contributions*, Papers from the Public Conference, Jungian Postgraduate Committee of the British Association of Psychotherapists, Monograph, 4: 8–14.

Rousmaniere, T. (2014) 'Using technology to enhance clinical supervision and training', in C.E. Watkins Jr. and D.L. Milne (eds) *Wiley-Blackwell International Handbook of Clinical Supervision*, Chichester: Wiley.

Ryle, A. and Kerr, I.B. (2002) *Introducing Cognitive Analytic Therapy*, Chichester: Wiley.

Safran, J.D. (1993) 'Breaches in the therapeutic alliance: An arena for negotiating authentic relatedness', *Psychotherapy: Theory, Research and Practice,* 30: 11–24.

Safran, J.D., Muran, J.C., Stevens, C. and Rothman, M. (2008) 'A relational approach to supervision: addressing ruptures in the alliance', in C.A. Falender and E.P. Shafranske (eds) *Casebook for Clinical Supervision: A Competency-based Approach*, Washington: American Psychological Association.

Siegel, D. (2012) *Pocket Guide to Interpersonal Neurobiology: An Integrative Handbook of the Mind*, New York: W.W. Norton & Company.

Sommers, E. (2007) *Tyranny of Niceness: A Psychotherapeutic Challenge*. Online. Available HTTP: <https://www.psychotherapy.net/article/Niceness> (accessed 4 November 2015).

Stern, D. (2004) *The Present Moment in Psychotherapy and Everyday Life (Norton Series on Interpersonal Neurobiology)*, New York: W.W. Norton & Company.
Sutton, L. (1999) 'CAT in later life: Becoming a historian of the self', *ACAT News*, Summer: 4–6.
Vygotsky, L.S. (1980) *Mind in Society: The Development of Higher Psychological Processes*, Cambridge, MA: Harvard University Press.
Wood, D., Bruner, J.S. and Ross, G. (1976) 'The role of tutoring in problem solving', *Journal of Child Psychology and Psychiatry*, 17: 89–100.
Yalom, I. (2002) *The Gift of Therapy: Reflections on Being a Therapist*, London: Piatkus Books.

Chapter 4

What makes supervision helpful? A review of research

Carolyn Lawson

Introduction

Most supervisors are highly committed to providing effective supervision and will therefore ask themselves: How can I best help my supervisees to help their patients? This chapter looks at empirical research studies to answer this question. It reviews research about the supervisory relationship and practice, specific supervisor behaviours and the content of supervision sessions, as well as evidence regarding the impact of supervision on client outcomes.

It is important to acknowledge that the value of research to clinicians has been questioned (see Marzillier 2004). As clinicians we tend not to turn to journals to find answers, and there are concerns that studies do not reflect our work practices. In Lucock et al.'s (2006) study, theory-based journal articles were rated lowest among factors influencing clinical practice. In contrast, supervision was highly rated by the 96 qualified and the 69 trainee clinicians, and was placed first for both groups, alongside professional training for the unqualified group. In addition the quality of supervision studies has been questioned, notably by Ellis et al. (1996) and Ellis and Ladany (1997) who made an extensive critique of the supervision research literature. Their concerns were small sample sizes, lack of statistical power, infrequent use of standardised measures, ambiguous research hypotheses, reliance on self-reports and poor definitions.

Since the mid-1990s, however, there have been significant improvements in the research: greater specificity, clearer models, better measures, and authors have often addressed the criticisms of Ellis and his colleagues in the design of their studies. These improvements mean that results have greater validity and deserve the attention of any supervisors who are concerned with developing their practice. This chapter is not a systematic review of the literature, but a brief overview of studies published in the two decades following the mid-1990s, which are most relevant to the question about how supervisors can best help their supervisees. Wheeler and Richards (2007) is a good start for those wanting a systematic review.

Defining supervision

Supervision can be a 'catch-all' phrase, being used to cover a range of work including caseload management or micro-skills teaching in mental health settings. Defining supervision is essential to ensure that we know what is being investigated and that studies can be compared.

The most quoted and familiar definition of psychotherapy supervision is from Bernard and Goodyear (2004: 8), who say that 'supervision is an intervention provided by a more senior member of a profession to a more junior member of that same profession. This relationship is evaluative, extends over time and has the simultaneous purposes of enhancing the professional functioning of the more junior person, monitoring the quality of professional services offered the clients seen and serving as a gatekeeper for those who are to enter the particular profession'.

Milne (2007) produced an elaboration of Bernard and Goodyear's (2004) definition, using a logical analysis to draft the definition and then producing a best evidence synthesis from a systematic review of 24 studies of clinical supervision. The resulting definition can be used as a standard to compare the activity described as supervision in different studies. Operationalising supervision in this way is a step forward in meeting the critique of Ellis (1996) regarding the heterogeneity of definitions and has potential to improve supervision research.

An alternative definition is provided by Hawkins and Shohet (2012: 5), 'Supervision is a joint endeavour in which a practitioner with the help of a supervisor, attends to their clients, themselves as part of their client practitioner relationships and the wider systemic context, and by so doing improves the quality of their work, transforms their client relationships, continuously develops themselves, their practice and the wider profession'. This definition takes supervision beyond the training arena, and emphasises the stakeholders involved in supervision, including the employing organisation and professional body.

As Roth et al. (2015: 4) point out, 'defining supervision is challenging, largely because the content and structure of supervision varies with professional grouping, therapeutic orientation and clinical context'. No definition has been so specific as to give details of supervisor training, frequency and time given to supervision. This is left to training organisations and professional associations to determine, and the spectrum of practice ranges from no training to substantial accredited training courses, and from a weekly hour for trainees to more ad hoc arrangements for senior clinicians. So despite the efforts of Milne (2007), the variability in defining supervision remains a difficulty when comparing research studies.

The impact of supervision on client outcomes

The general consensus has been that proving the value of supervision depends on showing that it has a positive impact on the outcome for the client. Ellis and Ladany (1997: 485) called this the 'acid test' of supervision but the number of variables involved has made the evidence elusive.

Reviews in both the US and UK (Watkins 2011, Wheeler and Richards 2007) identify a few studies that provide limited evidence that supervision has a beneficial effect on supervisees, the client and outcome of therapy. Wheeler and Richards (2007) in their review of the impact of supervision on counsellors/therapists, their practice and their clients, screened over 8000 studies and found 25 studies that met the review's inclusion criteria. Only one study (Bambling et al. 2006) looked at client outcome. This showed that supervised therapists achieved better client outcomes than unsupervised therapists. All of the 127 patients had a diagnosis of major depression, and were offered eight sessions of problem-solving treatment. The 127 therapists were in three supervisory conditions: no supervision; alliance skill-focused; or alliance process-focused supervision. Eight sessions of supervision were provided to each therapist. Both groups which received supervision achieved positive results for symptom reduction, client-rated working alliance, treatment retention and client evaluation of therapy.

Callahan et al. (2009) addressed previous review recommendations by using a cross-tabulation methodological design and found that client outcome was significantly related to supervisor. They reported that 'supervisors may account for approximately 16% of the variance in outcome beyond that accounted for by the client's initial severity and the treating therapists' attributes', and note that this 'exceeds the amount of variance commonly associated with specific treatment interventions' (Callahan et al. 2009: 75). The differences between the nine supervisors in the study were attributed to their skill set and experience as a supervisor.

It is not only the everyday clinician who values supervision, but researchers do as well. Roth et al. (2010) analysed 27 studies for the reporting of the amount of supervision provided in clinical trials. They were concerned that research trial outcomes are not replicated in everyday practice. Though supervision was not well described in the papers, they found that 'almost universally, trials report that therapists received regular model-specific supervision throughout the trial . . . (and) sixteen trials reported on supervision frequency' (Roth et al. 2010: 295). Twelve of the studies were providing weekly individual supervision. The suggestion is that good outcomes in research trials are supported by frequent supervision.

Watkins' (2011) review includes two studies from mental health nursing (Bradshaw et al. 2007, White and Winstanley 2010). Bradshaw et al.'s (2007) study showed that supervision reduced positive symptoms and improved function for patients with a diagnosis of schizophrenia. The study by White and Winstanley (2010) found that although there were benefits for the staff (reduced burnout and increased staff retention) there was no difference between a year-long supervision group and the no supervision control group, in terms of client outcomes. White and Winstanley's (2010) study provided supervision in a group format for six to nine people once a month. This is in contrast to the evidence from Roth et al.'s (2010) analysis of good therapy outcomes where supervision was more likely to be individual weekly supervision. In addition, Roth et al. (2010) found that senior clinicians provided the supervision in successful therapy research trials, whereas Bradshaw et al.'s (2007) supervisors had a matter of hours training in supervision.

This highlights the need for clarity about interventions defined as supervision. Despite the difficulty of researching client outcomes as a consequence of supervision, the evidence is that supervision has a positive impact on client outcomes.

How do I help my supervisees help their clients? A research study of CAT supervision

To answer this question, I will discuss the idea of helpfulness, give a brief account of a study of CAT supervision, and then discuss the wider empirical research about the different elements of supervision.

The concept of helpfulness has a history in psychotherapy research, both in therapy sessions (Elliott 1985, Paulson et al. 1999) and in the context of supervision (Cushway and Knibbs 2004, Strozier et al. 1993). To be helped is a common experience. We recognise situations when, through the assistance or intervention of another, we are helped. This is particularly true when learning a new skill, task or technique. In psychotherapy supervision, the help comes through dialogue which allows for a new perspective of the work in hand. The helpfulness can take various forms but the momentum of learning is maintained. What is happening in supervision when a supervisee identifies something that is helpful to their learning? A CAT supervision process study by the author (Lawson 2003) was designed to answer that question.

The study examined the most and least helpful events as experienced by supervisees in the context of supervision provided in the usual small group format of CAT supervision. The groups had been meeting weekly for a year at the time of the research. The supervisees were half way through their two year CAT practitioner training course and were all experienced mental health professionals.

Three measures were used: first, demographic information (age, gender, professional training, clinical and supervision experience) was requested from supervisees and supervisors. In addition two standardised measures were used. The Helpful Aspects of Supervision scale (HAS) was used to identify helpful events. This is an amended version of the Helpful Aspects of Therapy form first used in psychotherapy research by Llewellyn et al. (1988). This has a nine point scale from 'extremely hindering' (1); through 'neutral' (5); to 'extremely helpful' (9) and asks participants to identify a significant event in the preceding supervision session and then rate its helpfulness. In addition the Supervisory Working Alliance Inventory (SWAI) (Efstation et al. 1990) was completed at the beginning and end of the project, to assess the supervisory alliance. It has two versions; one for supervisors (23 items) and one for supervisees (19 items).

The research method had three stages. In stage one, five supervisees in three supervision groups tape-recorded 10 supervision sessions with their clients' consent, and completed a HAS form after each session. In stage two, the supervisees were interviewed (and audio-taped), using the Brief Stimulated Recall (BSR) interview method (Elliott and Shapiro 1988) to explore two events, those scored most and least helpful on the HAS. The interview was used to focus on the 'peak statement', a single speaking turn, identified by the supervisee as the core of the identified helpful event.

Stage three consisted of a Comprehensive Process Analysis (CPA). This is an interpretive, qualitative research method for describing and understanding the significant process, context and impact of clinical events (Elliott 1993). It relies on 'explication', a consensual method of identifying the different levels of meaning in what is being said by the supervisee or supervisor. A group of four observers were recruited to do the analysis, in addition to the main researcher. The first step of the analysis involved explication of each HAS statement, and the event 'peak'. The peak was generally a single speaking turn. The subsequent dialogue between supervisee and supervisor was considered and the meaning expanded, focusing on the supervisee experience. This is the process pathway. The context and the impact of the event on supervision and the supervisee were analysed, using information from the BSR interview. The second step was a comparison of the 10 events (2 for each supervisee), looking at common and differentiating themes between the most and least helpful events.

The quantitative results from the SWAI for supervisors and supervisees were comparable to the normative data from Efstation et al.'s (1990) study of the supervisory alliance. This suggests that there was a similar level of moderate working alliance. The HAS mean event score showed that identified events were rated as moderately helpful, with the most and least helpful events being rated as distinctly different. It would appear that this was typical supervision: supervisees were engaged in a process of learning which was valued, though sometimes a struggle.

The implication from the most helpful events was that supervision was experienced as most helpful when supervisees acquired a meta-perspective of the clinical work and had a sense of working collaboratively with a supervisor who directly addressed their concern. Supervisees then felt more involved in supervision and had greater clarity about therapy problems and how to solve them. The implications from least helpful events were that supervision which underestimated and did not address intense emotion in therapy (whether felt by the client or the therapist) was experienced as least helpful, and led to supervisees feeling criticised, and disengaging from the supervisory process. Lack of supervisory time compounded their experience of supervision as less helpful (see Table 4.1). Nevertheless, the least helpful events did allow supervisees to develop their own solutions to therapeutic difficulties, become more confident and learn something about themselves.

It is beyond the scope of this chapter to provide more than a glimpse of the details of the most and least helpful events in supervision, their context and the dialogue, and the learning outcomes for the supervisees. This study was highly specific, but not perfect, in particular because the sample size was small. It is in the nature of qualitative research that it is not good at revealing differences or making generalisations because of small numbers. The strength of the study lies in its clear aims and use of standardised measures, and in the fact that it was a study of real supervision, following the course of sessions, rather than asking

Table 4.1 Summary of discriminating themes from the comprehensive process analysis domains for most and least helpful events

Discriminating themes	Most helpful events	Least helpful events
Central theme from HAS statement	Supervisee struggling to complete a task with client Supervisee anxious about getting it right for the client	Negative impact of client-therapist relationship on supervisee Intense feelings in supervisee or client
Context	Supervision helpful (pre-session) Supervisee task to overcome feeling stuck (episode) Supervisee asks directly for guidance (local cue)	Lack of time (pre-session) Supervisee sensitive to criticism (pre-session) Restatement of previous concern (local cue)
Process Pathway	Introduction of focus on technique Focus on specific issue Supervisor offers new explanation: supervisee agrees Supervisor develops the understanding: supervisee agrees and values the work Ending: sense of natural closure	Conditional agreement at start, mismatch in supervisor / supervisee focus Supervisor offers alternative / opposite understanding Implicitly / explicitly trainee is doing it wrong Supervisor gives another focus Ending: discontinuity, change of subject, sense of unfinished business
Supervisee experience	Confused, stuck, worried, unconfident Reassured, listened to, understood Actively involved, has insight and understanding Feels validated/supported: relief Ending: takes something useful away	Disengagement, frustrated Reluctant to talk in supervision Misunderstood, criticised, disappointed Ending: tries to restore the positive feeling to supervision

supervisees to self-report about experiences in supervision at an unspecified time afterwards. The comparison of most and least helpful results shows clear differences, which will be discussed in relation to other empirical studies.

Characteristics of helpful and unhelpful supervision

Further evidence about what is helpful and unhelpful in supervision comes from several research studies which have attempted to identify the factors that differentiate good and bad supervision. Research on supervision quality has tended to use surveys to focus on satisfaction or preferences of supervisees. However surveys have inherent limitations: they often have low return rates, use a self-selected sample which may not be representative of the general population of supervisees or supervisors and rely on retrospective recall of supervisory experiences.

The following two studies stand out for their use of a different methodology, namely prospective recording of supervision sessions. Shanfield and colleagues (Shanfield et al. 1993, Shanfield et al. 2001) looked at excellent supervision. Shanfield et al. (1993) used videotapes recorded for an earlier study and selected 15 videotaped supervision sessions from a total of 53. The 15 tapes were of the nine highest-rated sessions, three sessions assigned mid-level ratings and three assigned low ratings. Transcripts were analysed by experts (the authors). They found supervisors who were rated as excellent allowed the supervisee story to develop, tracked the most immediate concerns of the supervisee and made comments that were specific to the material being presented. In the second study, Shanfield et al. (2001) found excellent supervisors were also calmly accepting of supervisees' concerns and provided guidance about highly charged clinical dilemmas, as well as acknowledging the supervisees' worries about the impact of the supervisee's personal experiences on the clinical encounter.

Not all supervision goes well and research on poor or harmful supervision is useful for showing the type of practices that supervisors must avoid. The work of Ellis et al. (2014), Nelson and Friedlander (2001) and Gray et al. (2001) suggests that there is a continuum of supervision: at one end there are mistakes or ruptures in the supervisory relationship, which are usually unintentional and quickly and easily resolved, in the middle is inadequate supervision, where the needs of the supervisees are not met, and at the other end, there is harmful supervision where a supervisor is acting inappropriately or with malice, negligence or violating accepted ethical standards.

Ellis et al. (2014), in a two-stage study, first defined two levels of poor supervision, namely inadequate and harmful, which were refined by expert consensus. Then a sample of 363 supervisees was asked about their experiences. Inadequate supervision, when the supervisor was unable or unwilling to meet the primary needs of the supervisee, was defined by 16 statements. The minimum for inadequate supervision to be identified was: less than an hour of supervision a week, failure to use a contract or consent form for supervision and the supervisor did not directly oversee the supervisee's sessions. Harmful supervision was defined by 21 statements but the minimum for identification was: for the supervisee to be physically threatened or sexually intimate or in a sexual relationship with the supervisor. Only one truly bad session or incident was required to count as inadequate or harmful supervision; 24.6% of supervisees had a current experience of inadequate supervision and 12.4% were currently experiencing harmful supervision. Inclusion of experiences with previous supervisors elevates the reporting to an aggregate figure of 93% of supervisees experiencing inadequate supervision and 35.3% experiencing harmful supervision.

There is scope for both under- and over-reporting of events in supervision that contribute to inadequate or harmful supervision. Participants in Ellis et al.'s (2014) study were self-selected, so likely to be a biased sample. The bar has been set quite low for a measure of inadequate supervision given that it is a single incident or session that determines inadequacy. There is a great difference between a single incident and an ongoing situation that cannot be resolved. Nevertheless inadequate or harmful supervision is not always easy to report given the inherent vulnerability of supervisees, particularly when on training courses.

The small-sample-size qualitative studies of Gray et al. (2001) and Nelson and Friedlander (2001) give more detail of the negative impact of the supervisory relationship. Both studies conducted interviews with 13 supervisees. Four types of events were described by Gray et al. (2001): (1) when a supervisor denied a trainee a request, (2) misunderstood a trainee, (3) directed a trainee to be different with a client, and, most frequently, (4) when a supervisor dismissed a trainee's thoughts or feelings and was unempathic. Nelson and Friedlander's (2001) study looked at conflictual supervisory relationships and reported that a typical experience was of a power struggle which began with the supervisee feeling unsupported from the start of the supervisory relationship. The supervisee perceived the supervisor to be angry with them, to deny any responsibility for the situation, or felt that the supervisor behaved irresponsibly. Both these studies reported early difficulties in the supervisory relationship which led the supervisee to lose trust, feel unsafe and withdraw from the relationship.

The supervisory relationship

A relational approach to supervision sees the supervisory relationship as a central element in the experience of helpful supervision. Safran and Muran (2000: 213) stated that 'in training, as in therapy, the relational context is of utmost importance: it is impossible for the supervisor to convey information to the supervisee that has meaning independent of the relational context in which is it is conveyed'. Worthen and McNeill (1996: 29) in their phenomenological study of 'good' supervision events from eight supervisees, found that the 'most pivotal and crucial component of good supervision experiences . . . was the quality of the supervisory relationship.'

Different aspects of the supervisory relationship have been the subject of many studies. For example, Weaks' (2002) qualitative study of nine experienced counsellors found that equality (in terms of the relationship), safety (secure to talk about any aspect of the work) and challenge were the three core conditions of the supervisory relationship, which were key to a good experience of supervision.

Efstation et al. (1990) developed a scale to measure the working alliance in supervision. Through factor analysis they defined the alliance from the supervisor's perspective as client focus, rapport and identification and, from the supervisee's perspective, client focus and rapport. They compared scores with scales from two standardised measures, the Supervisory Styles Inventory and the Self-efficacy Inventory. They found that the quality of the working alliance was linked to supervisor style (attractiveness, interpersonal sensitivity and task orientation) and supervisees' self-efficacy.

Many studies look at changes in the supervisory alliance in relation to other aspects of supervision, such as role conflict and ambiguity (Ladany and Friedlander 1995), concepts taken from the organisational psychology literature. A supervisee may experience incompatible demands being made of them (role conflict) or have uncertainty about what is expected of them (role ambiguity). Ladany and Friedlander (1995) found a correlation between experiences of role conflict and ambiguity and the quality of the alliance. As might be expected, less conflict and ambiguity correlated positively with a better alliance in the 123 counsellors surveyed. A second study (Ladany et al. 1999) found that the supervisor's nonadherence to ethical guidelines was linked to lower reported supervisee satisfaction and a weaker alliance.

In Beinart's (2004) grounded theory study of the supervisory relationship, she proposed a framework for the supervisory relationship. The main element was a 'boundaried relationship', meaning both structural (time, place and frequency) and personal/professional boundaries. Another aspect of the framework was a mutually respectful, supportive and open relationship. A collaborative relationship was a stated preference by the supervisees, some of whom were still in training, and hence being evaluated. A supervisor's commitment to supervision and sensitivity to the supervisees' needs were key factors which aided the educative and evaluative tasks of supervision.

Foster et al. (2007) used attachment theory to investigate the supervisory relationship. In the sample of 90 distinct supervisor-supervisee dyads, they found that supervisees developed the same attachment relationship with their supervisor as they did in more personal, close relationships. Trainees who had an insecure attachment pattern reported low levels of professional development, whereas their supervisors' reports indicated higher levels of development.

Bambling and King (2014) found that the social skills of supervisors were an important factor in the development of a positive supervisory alliance and learning outcomes. In their study, 40 supervisors and 50 supervisees completed a standardised measure, the SWAI, three times over the course of eight supervision sessions. In addition, supervisors completed a social skills inventory and supervisees evaluated supervision using a supervision evaluation scale.

Roth and Pilling (2015) pointed out that the quality of the supervisory relationship may influence the assessment of a supervisee in training, particularly if the learning outcomes are poorly defined. They refer to research, which shows that when the supervisor and supervisee are getting on well, it is difficult for the supervisor to 'separate out the influence of context and complexity from the capacity of the trainee' (Roth and Pilling 2015: 7). Foster et al. (2007) supported this finding from the supervisees' perspective. Considering the discrepancy between supervisor and supervisee ratings of supervisees' professional development, they commented that 'supervisee ratings of development may be a function of the support, nurturance and availability the supervisor provides rather than actual professional development...(and) it may also prevent the fledgling supervisee from full awareness of skill deficits and areas of weakness' (Foster et al. 2007: 348). This suggests that it is important for the supervisor to balance support with a willingness to address weak aspects of a supervisee's practice. Cushway and Knibbs (2004) reported that a level of rapport and safety is needed for the supervisee to use supervision well, but client focus and challenge are also needed to maintain the learning.

Dealing with difficulties in supervision and therapy

In everyday supervision there will inevitably be times when the supervisee describes a rupture in therapy or when there is a rupture in the supervisory relationship. These delicate moments offer the potential for learning as well as risk of perpetuating poor practice, and so the way a supervisor deals with them is crucial, if supervision is to be helpful. Daniels (2000), in a qualitative empirical study, interviewed supervisors about their understanding of supervisees' mistakes. She asked supervisors to draw a distinction between minor and serious mistakes. All supervisors interviewed saw mistakes as inevitable but there were widely differing views, with some supervisors seeing certain behaviours as unethical, for example hugging a client at a client's request, whilst others saw it as a minor mistake. She suggested three concepts as a continuum framework: how intentional was the behaviour, how 'clumsy' (could it be quickly resolved with the client) and *where* the mistake happened in relation to the stage of development of the therapeutic relationship. An unintentional, quickly resolved mistake happening late on in therapy was less serious than an intentional, unresolved problem happening early on in therapy. Supervisors, when interviewed, talked about exploring in supervision where the mistake came from, and the need for a positive supervisory relationship that is open to the discussion of issues sensitive to the supervisee.

Nelson et al. (2008) interviewed 12 highly competent supervisors about how they dealt with conflict in supervision. They were asked about their definitions and beliefs about conflict in supervision as well as their strategies and learning from conflict with past supervisees. A synthesis of grounded theory and consensual qualitative research methods was used to analyse the data. The core theme was openness to conflict, both parties acknowledging their part in it and a willingness to learn from mistakes. Building a positive collaborative supervisory alliance and modelling an openness to discussion of conflict, whilst communicating clear expectations and giving feedback early on, helped these supervisors deal with conflict. Although most of the supervisors viewed conflict as necessary and beneficial, they disliked it and found it extremely stressful to address.

Grant et al. (2012) also interviewed supervisors about managing difficulties in supervision. Using a consensual qualitative research method they identified four key approaches that the 16 supervisors used: relational, reflective, confrontative and avoidant. Naming the difficulties, validating and normalising them, as well as attuning to the supervisee's needs, were the typical relational interventions used, while common reflective strategies included remaining mindful, transparent and patient whilst monitoring the situation and facilitating reflexivity. When these approaches failed, confrontative approaches were often the last resort, even after avoidant strategies had been tried.

The supervisory dialogue

Supervisee non-disclosure

Helpful supervision relies on good open communication between supervisor and supervisee. Studies in the 1990s highlighted nondisclosure by supervisees in psychotherapy supervision (Ladany et al. 1996, Webb and Wheeler 1998, Yourman and Farber 1996). It was found to be almost universal. Ladany et al. (1996) reported 97% of their cohort withheld information in supervision. Each study asked different questions, so the significance of what was being withheld was hard to determine. Information about both clients and therapy sessions was withheld, but more often a negative personal reaction to supervision remained unspoken. Mehr et al. (2010) completed a further study, looking at non-disclosure in supervision among trainee psychologists. Within the single supervision session on which they reported, 84.3% of trainees withheld information from their supervisors. Trainees reported an average of 2.68 nondisclosures in the session, with the most common nondisclosure involving a negative supervision experience. Trainee perception of a better supervisory working alliance was related to less nondisclosure and greater overall willingness to disclose in supervision. Higher trainee anxiety was related to greater nondisclosure and lower overall willingness to disclose in supervision.

Supervisor self-disclosure

Ladany and his co-workers have done several studies that have shown the importance of supervisor self-disclosure in effective supervision (Ladany and Lehrman-Waterman 1999, Ladany et al. 2013). In the first study 105 supervisees reported on their supervisors' self-disclosure. The more supervisors self-disclosed, the more the supervisee perceived there to be a strong emotional bond with the supervisor. The most frequent supervisor self-disclosures were of personal issues (73%), neutral counselling experiences (55%) and struggles in counselling (51%). Ladany and Lehrman-Waterman (1999: 152) comment on the variable impact that these self-disclosures have on supervisees and that 'supervisors should consider their intentions when they disclose personal information'. Their study of effective supervision (Ladany et al. 2013: 41) found that supervisor self-disclosure was an effective supervisory skill when the supervisor was able to 'self-disclose clinical information that was relevant to the supervisees' presenting concerns and was in the service of the supervisee'. Knox et al. (2008) interviewed 16 supervisors about their use of self-disclosure and found they used self-disclosure to enhance supervisee development and normalise their experiences. It was frequently a response to supervisees struggling, often with their reaction to their clients.

Although it can be helpful for a supervisor to disclose a similar experience, if it is not relevant to the supervisee's own concern, it can leave the supervisee feeling 'patronized, frustrated and disappointed' (Lawson 2003: 64), further disengaging from supervision. One supervisee said, when interviewed, 'sometimes you get a feeling, you go in with the problem, and they (the supervisor) say something and you think that's not what I needed, so you say it again and if you get more of the same, (you think) I'll go somewhere else to get help with this' (Lawson 2003: 65).

Skjerve et al. (2009) looked at non-disclosure by supervisors. Thirty supervisors completed a questionnaire about the experience of providing group supervision, what they might not disclose and the reasons for this. The responses were then analysed using a consensual qualitative research method. The results showed that almost all supervisors were careful both about the feedback they gave to trainees and the way they gave it, in order not to interrupt the learning process by arousing negative feelings in the supervisees.

Making best use of supervision

Supervision time is often limited and this can be an issue in CAT supervision groups where several cases are discussed in a relatively short time. Time allocation is important within groups, particularly if it is perceived to be unfair or insufficient or if supervisees feel not attended to. Although there have been studies of small group supervision, the issue of time was not specifically addressed (Boethius et al. 2006). It may be helpful for the supervisor to use checklists of priorities (Mills and Chasler 2012), and to encourage the supervisee to formulate their difficulty as a question (Lawson 2003).

Another technique which helps focus supervision time is the use of feedback from clients. Two papers (Grossl et al. 2014, Reese et al. 2009) highlight the value of client feedback about therapy in supervision. Clients were asked to complete a four item self-report scale at the start of therapy sessions to monitor their progress, which was then used in supervision. The first study followed 28 trainees who were randomly assigned to a continuous feedback or no feedback condition for a year. Both conditions demonstrated better client outcomes at the end of their training than at the beginning, but the feedback condition improved more. The repeat study by Grossl et al. (2014) assigned 44 trainees to the same conditions and found that supervisees were more satisfied with supervision when using clients' feedback, but supervisory alliance scores and client outcomes were not significantly different.

Conclusion

The answer to the question of how supervisors can help supervisees to help their clients is essentially bound to the supervisory relationship. The evidence is that good-quality supervision has a positive impact on client outcomes and repeatedly the research comes back to the quality of the supervisory relationship. It emphasises the importance of a boundaried, collaborative relationship, characterised by support and mutual respect. A good supervisory alliance depends on establishing clear, unambiguous roles. The supervisor's role involves creating open dialogue, providing guidance, encouraging supervisees' autonomy, having good social skills and practising ethically. Supervisors should use self-disclosure sensitively and only when relevant to the supervisees' concerns. Supervisors need to be committed to supervision, clear about their role, aware of the need to attune to supervisees' concerns, able to attend to complex clinical dilemmas, prepared to challenge, skilled in addressing conflict and ruptures and willing to use different methods to increase focus in supervision. In the absence of a good relationship, or when the needs of the supervisee are not the primary concern of the supervisor, supervision can become unhelpful, inadequate and potentially harmful.

The research literature on supervision is extensive, but there remain numerous general and CAT specific supervision questions that have not been addressed, such as: What is helpful or unhelpful in CAT supervision? Is group supervision better, worse or just different from individual supervision? Is there an optimum time for discussing a case in supervision?

The research confirms that supervision is a difficult task to do well and highlights its complexity. It also offers invaluable guidance about the qualities of the role, the dialogue and the type of relationship that supervisors need to establish in order to make supervision helpful.

References

Bambling, M.L. and King, R. (2014) 'Supervisor social skills and supervision outcome', *Counselling and Psychotherapy Research*, 14: 256–262.

Bambling, M.L., King, R., Raue, P., Schweitzer, R. and Lambert, W. (2006) 'Clinical supervision: Its impact on working alliance an outcome in the treatment of major depression', *Psychotherapy Research*, 16: 317–331.

Beinart, H. (2004) 'Models of supervision and the supervisory relationship and their evidence base', in I. Fleming and L. Steen (eds) *Supervision and Clinical Psychology, Theory, Practice and Perspectives*, Hove: Brunner-Routledge.

Bernard, J.M. and Goodyear, R.K. (2004) *Fundamentals of Clinical Supervision, (third edition)*, Boston: Pearson/Allyn and Bacon.

Boethius, S.B., Sundin, E. and Ogren, M.L. (2006) 'Group supervision from a small group perspective', *Nordic Psychology*, 58: 22–42.

Bradshaw, T., Butterworth, A. and Mairs, H. (2007) 'Does structured clinical supervision during psychosocial intervention education enhance outcome for mental health nurses and the service users they work with?', *Journal of Psychiatric and Mental Health Nursing*, 14: 4–12.

Callahan, J.L., Almstrom, C.M., Swift, J.K., Borja, S.E. and Heath, C.J. (2009) 'Exploring the contribution of supervisors to intervention outcomes', *Training and Education in Professional Psychology*, 3: 72–77.

Cushway, D. and Knibbs, J. (2004) 'Trainees' and supervisors' perceptions of supervision', in I. Fleming and L. Steen (eds) *Supervision and Clinical Psychology, Theory, Practice and Perspectives*, Hove: Brunner-Routledge.

Daniels, J. (2000) 'Whispers in the corridor and kangaroo courts: the supervisory role in mistakes and complaints', in B. Lawton and C. Feltham (eds) *Taking Supervision Forward*, London: Sage.

Efstation, J.F., Patton, M.J. and Kardash, C.M. (1990) 'Measuring the working alliance in counselor supervision', *Journal of Counseling Psychology*, 37: 322–329.

Elliott, R. (1985) 'Helpful and nonhelpful events in brief counseling interviews: An empirical taxonomy', *Journal of Counseling Psychology*, 32: 307–322.

Elliott, R. (1993) *Comprehensive Process Analysis: Mapping the Change Process in Psychotherapy*, unpublished research manual. Available from the author, School of Psychological Sciences and Health, University of Strathclyde, Glasgow, G1 1QE.

Elliott, R. and Shapiro, D.A. (1988) 'Brief structured recall: A more efficient method for identifying and describing significant therapy events', *British Journal of Medical Psychology*, 61: 141–153.

Ellis, M.V., Berger, L., Hanus, A.E., Ayala, E.E., Swords, B.A. and Siembor, M. (2014) 'Inadequate and harmful clinical supervision: Testing a revised framework and assessing occurrence', *The Counseling Psychologist*, 42: 434–472.

Ellis, M.V., Krengal, M., Ladany, N. and Schult, D. (1996) 'Clinical supervision research from 1981 to 1993: A methodological critique', *Journal of Counseling Psychology*, 43: 35–50.

Ellis, M.V. and Ladany, N. (1997) 'Inferences concerning supervisees and clients in clinical supervision: an integrative review', in C.E. Watkins (ed) *Handbook of Psychotherapy Supervision*, New York: Wiley.

Foster, J.T., Lichtenberg, J.W. and Peyton, V. (2007) 'The supervisory attachment relationship as a predictor of the professional development of the supervised', *Psychotherapy Research*, 17: 343–350.

Grant, J., Schofield, M.J. and Crawford, S. (2012) 'Managing difficulties in supervision: Supervisors' perspectives', *Journal of Counseling Psychology*, 59: 528–541.

Gray, L.A., Ladany, N., Walker, J.A. and Ancis, J.R. (2001) 'Psychotherapy trainees' experience of counter-productive-events in supervision', *Journal of Counseling Psychology*, 48: 371–383.

Grossl, A.B., Reese, R.J., Norsworthy, L.A. and Hopkins, N.B. (2014) 'Client feedback data in supervision: Effects on supervision and outcome', *Training and Education in Professional Psychology*, 8: 182–188.

Hawkins, P. and Shohet, R. (2012) *Supervision in the Helping Professions, (fourth edition)*, Maidenhead: Open University Press.

Knox, S., Burkard, A.W., Edwards, L.M., Smith, J.J. and Schlosser, L.Z. (2008) 'Supervisors' reports on the effects of supervisor self-disclosure on supervisees', *Psychotherapy Research*, 18: 543–559.

Ladany, N. and Friedlander, M.L. (1995) 'The relationship between the supervisory working alliance and trainees experience of role conflict and role ambiguity', *Counselor Education and Supervision*, 34: 220–231.

Ladany, N., Hill, C.E., Corbett, M.M. and Nutt, E.A. (1996) 'Nature, extent and importance of what psychotherapy trainees do not disclose to their supervisors', *Journal of Counseling Psychology*, 43: 10–24.

Ladany, N. and Lehrman-Waterman, D.E. (1999) 'The content and frequency of supervisor self-disclosures and their relationship to supervisor style and the supervisory working alliance', *Counselor Education and Supervision*, 38: 143–160.

Ladany, N., Lehrman-Waterman, D., Molinaro, M. and Wolgast, B. (1999) 'Psychotherapy supervisor ethical practices, adherence to guidelines, supervisory working alliance and supervisee satisfaction', *The Counseling Psychologist*, 27: 442–475.

Ladany, N., Mori, Y. and Mehr, K.E. (2013) 'Effective and ineffective supervision', *The Counseling Psychologist*, 41: 28–47.

Lawson, C.J. (2003) 'Difficult experiences and helpful events in psychotherapy supervision', unpublished Doctorate of Clinical Psychology thesis, University of Sheffield.

Llewellyn, S.P., Elliott, R., Shapiro, D.A., Firth, J. and Hardy, G. (1988) 'Client perceptions of significant events in prescriptive and exploratory methods of individual therapy', *British Journal of Clinical Psychology*, 27: 105–114.

Lucock, M.P., Hall, P. and Noble, R. (2006) 'A survey of influences on the practice of psychotherapists and clinical psychologists in training in the UK', *Clinical Psychology and Psychotherapy*, 13: 123–130.

Marzillier, J. (2004) 'The myth of evidence-based psychotherapy', *The Psychologist*, 17: 392–395.

Mehr, K.E., Ladany, N. and Caskie, G.I.L. (2010) 'Trainee nondisclosure in supervision: What are they not telling you?', *Counselling and Psychotherapy Research*, 10: 103–113.

Mills, J.A. and Chasler, J.K. (2012) 'Establishing priorities in the supervision hour', *Training and Education in Professional Psychology*, 6: 160–166.

Milne, D.L. (2007) 'An empirical definition of clinical supervision', *British Journal of Clinical Psychology*, 46: 437–447.

Nelson, M.L., Barnes, K.L., Evans, A.L. and Triggiano, P.J. (2008) 'Working with conflict in clinical supervision: Wise supervisors' perspectives', *Journal of Counselling Psychology*, 55: 172–184.

Nelson, M.L. and Friedlander, M.L. (2001) 'A close look at conflictual supervisory relationships: The trainee's perspective', *Journal of Counseling Psychology*, 48: 384–395.

Paulson, B.L., Truscott, D. and Stuart, J. (1999) 'Clients' perceptions of helpful events in counseling', *Journal of Counseling Psychology*, 46: 317–324.

Reese, R.J., Usher, E.L., Bowman, D.C., Norsworthy, L.A., Halstead, J.L., Rowlands, S.R. and Chisholm, R.R. (2009) 'Using client feedback in psychotherapy training: An analysis of its influence on supervision and counsellor self-efficacy', *Training and Education in Professional Psychology*, 3: 157–168.

Roth, A.D. and Pilling, S. (2015) *A Competence Framework for Supervision of Psychological Therapies*. Online. Available HTTP: <https://www.ucl.ac.uk/pals/research/cehp/research-groups/core/competence-frameworks/Supervision_of_Psychological_Therapies> (accessed 15 October 2015).

Roth, A., Pilling, S. and Turner, J. (2010) 'Therapist training and supervision in clinical trials: Implications for clinical practice', *Behavioural and Cognitive Psychotherapy*, 38: 291–302.

Safran, J.D. and Muran, J.C. (2000) *Negotiating the Therapeutic Alliance*, New York: Guilford Press.

Shanfield, S.B., Hetherly, V.V. and Matthews, K.L. (2001) 'Excellent supervision: The residents' perspective', *Journal of Psychotherapy, Practice and Research*, 10: 23–27.

Shanfield, S.B., Matthews, K.L. and Hetherly, V.V. (1993) 'What do excellent psychotherapy supervisors do?', *American Journal of Psychiatry*, 150: 1081–1084.

Skjerve, J., Nielsen, G.H., Jacobsen, C.H., Gullestad, S.E., Hansen, B.R., Reichelt, S., Ronnestad, M.H. and Torgersen, A.M. (2009) 'Non-disclosure in psychotherapy group supervision: The supervisor perspective', *Nordic Psychology*, 61: 28–48.

Strozier, A.L., Kivlighan, D.M. and Thoreson, R.W. (1993) 'Supervisor intentions, supervisee reactions, and helpfulness: A case study of the process of supervision', *Professional Psychology: Research and Practice*, 24: 13–19.

Watkins, C.E., Jr. (2011) 'Does psychotherapy supervision contribute to patient outcomes? Considering thirty years of research', *The Clinical Supervisor*, 30: 235–256.

Weaks, D. (2002) 'Unlocking the secrets of "good supervision": A phenomenological exploration of experienced counsellors' perceptions of good supervision', *Counselling and Psychotherapy Research*, 2, 1: 33–39.

Webb, A. and Wheeler, S. (1998) 'How honest do counsellors dare to be in the supervisory relationship?: An exploratory study', *British Journal of Guidance and Counselling*, 26, 4: 509–524.

Wheeler, S. and Richards, K. (2007) 'The impact of clinical supervision on counsellors and therapists, their practice and their clients: A systematic review of the literature', *Counselling and Psychotherapy Research*, 37: 296–316.

White, E. and Winstanley, J. (2010) 'A randomised controlled trial of clinical supervision: Selected findings from a novel Australian attempt to establish the evidence base for causal relationships with quality of care and patient outcomes, as an informed contribution to mental health nursing practice development', *Journal of Research in Nursing*, 15, 2: 151–167.

Worthen, V. and McNeill, B.W. (1996) 'A phenomenological investigation of "good" supervision events', *Journal of Counseling Psychology*, 43: 25–34.

Yourman, D.B. and Farber, B.A. (1996) 'Non-disclosure and distortion in psychotherapy supervision', *Psychotherapy*, 33: 567–575.

Section 2

Challenges in relational supervision

Chapter 5

Clinical and ethical challenges in relational supervision

Deborah Pickvance and Glenys Parry

Introduction

Whilst the function of supervision is to foster learning, provide a space for thinking, facilitate good practice and ultimately to improve the quality, safety and outcomes of psychotherapy, research shows that it does not always succeed in these aims (see Chapter 4, research on ineffective supervision). One reason for this is that supervisors are inevitably faced with situations which pose tricky ethical questions or raise fears for the effectiveness of therapy. Codes of ethics, such as the Association of Cognitive Analytic Therapy's Code of Ethics and Practice for Training and Supervision (ACAT 2014, see Appendix 2), describe the broad principles underpinning good supervision and provide an important guide for supervisors. However, the application of these principles is not always straightforward and sometimes needs particularly careful reflection in order to avoid colluding with unhelpful or unsafe practice. Codes of ethics cannot give answers of the fine-grained, delicately balanced type needed by supervisors who are struggling with complex supervisory situations. For these, supervisors need to reflect, use their own supervision and at times consult with experienced colleagues. Of course some situations require a quick response, for which there is no time to consult, and supervisors have to offer guidance in the moment relying on their own experience, judgement and insight.

Difficulties are common and inevitable in supervision and can be stressful and worrying for both the supervisee and supervisor. Some situations which challenge supervisors involve finding a balance between conflicting ethical principles. Others require a supervisor to address problematic aspects of a supervisee's practice and to move from a benignly supportive role to a more challenging one. Nowhere is a relational approach to supervision more important than when such clinical and ethical challenges arise. This chapter shows how a CAT-based understanding of the relational processes of supervision can help supervisors and therapists find a way through ethical and clinical difficulties.

72 Deborah Pickvance and Glenys Parry

Examples

In this section we introduce four illustrations of supervisory challenges: clinical or ethical dilemmas typically faced by a psychotherapy supervisor. We shall use them later in the chapter to demonstrate that there is rarely a simple 'right answer' to complex difficulties and to explore how the CAT relational method would approach them.

1. Risk to other – safe-guarding

Adam, a junior psychiatrist training in CAT, was working with Seema, a Bangladeshi woman in her mid-thirties who had been diagnosed with a borderline personality problem, and had attended 7 sessions of a 24 session therapy. Adam came from Malaysia, had trained in the UK and spoke fluent English. Seema told him her friend, another Bangladeshi woman, was caring for a three year old boy whose mother had gone abroad for a few weeks. Her friend then left the child with Seema, just for the weekend. However, after three days Seema's friend had not returned as promised and Seema was getting anxious because she could not contact her and the boy's mother did not know where he was. The supervisor, from a white British background, was aware that there was a safeguarding issue here, and that his employer's policy required disclosure, but also that the therapeutic alliance could be irreparably damaged if social services were alerted immediately, and the child might still not be protected.

2. Risk to client – threat to therapy boundary

Robert was an accredited psychotherapist in a private group practice, who was receiving individual CAT-informed supervision. He discussed his sessions with a young woman client in rather vague and joking terms, mentioning how she was seductively dressed and seemed to be flirting with him, which on one occasion he said he had quite enjoyed. His female supervisor was concerned that he was brushing this off and becoming evasive. He showed resentment when his supervisor raised issues about the eroticised transference, saying he and his client understood each other perfectly well and telling her not to worry about it. From a chance meeting with the practice receptionist, Robert's supervisor hears that he was seeing this young woman as his last client of the day and often stayed late with her in his room after other staff had left the building. The supervisor was concerned at the therapist's dismissive attitude, feeling the client might be at risk of harm, but unable to decide how to address the problem.

3. Risk to therapist – balancing competing ethical principles

Lorna, a skilled CAT practitioner, was six months pregnant and seeing a male client who had begun to ask intrusive questions about her pregnancy. They had worked with the reciprocal role procedure of 'overpowering – powerless' *and*

Lorna did not want to let him intrude on her. At session 12 he told Lorna he had been having intense violent fantasies about her baby; this left her feeling threatened and anxious. She talked tearfully in supervision of feeling scared and dreading seeing him again. The supervisor felt worried and protective about Lorna, and was uncertain whether she should continue the therapy.

4. Concern about performance

Jenny, a psychologist with 15 years' experience, was under severe pressure at work, afraid of losing her job in an impending re-organisation. She had become erratic, arriving late and unprepared for supervision and seeming unable to concentrate. Two of her clients had dropped out recently and she did not address the ambivalence of one, nor follow up the other when she cancelled. The supervisor was increasingly concerned, having tried to deal with each issue as it arose, but aware that Jenny was functioning less and less well.

Addressing problems in supervision

Managing difficulties productively and appropriately depends on the supervisor's ability to create and maintain an open, collaborative supervisory alliance. Supervisor skills and the quality of the supervisory alliance are crucial influences on the supervisee's experience of supervision and the quality of their practice (Ladany 2013). Supervisors can pre-empt difficulties by preparing the ground, so that, if problems do arise, supervisees can discuss difficulties in supervision honestly and at an early stage. Supervisors may assume that an alliance will develop naturally, and underestimate or disregard the anxieties that supervisees bring. It is worth fostering the alliance actively, for example, by explicitly encouraging honesty and openness at the initial contracting stage of supervision, asking about a supervisee's concerns and needs, and agreeing the tasks, goals and boundaries of supervision. Supervisors need to encourage supervisees from the beginning to bring issues which may signify difficulties, for example, changes to therapeutic boundaries (Page and Wosket 2015), difficult or ego-dystonic countertransference feelings, or perceived mistakes. It is helpful for the supervisor to emphasise that this work is often difficult, that all therapists make mistakes, and that being able to recognise, talk about and reflect on errors and setbacks are hallmarks of a good therapist. Supervisees find it helpful when supervisors give personal examples of mistakes they have made and what they learned from them. The engaged, transparent, enabling stance of the CAT therapist is equally important in the CAT supervisor's role; and supervisors must be as reliable, committed and present in supervision as they would be in therapy. Periodic reviews of supervision, in long-standing as well as newer supervision relationships, provide an opportunity to raise any difficulties and help to renew and refocus supervision.

In CAT terms, a good supervisory alliance involves the supervisor enacting an '*empathic, facilitative, encouraging*' reciprocal role in relation to a '*safely exploring, curious, learning*' supervisee. This enhances a supervisee's procedure of recognising difficulties, trying new solutions, practising skills and reflecting honestly on process. To this necessary basis, other nuanced roles may be appropriate at different stages of therapist development. For example, earlier in training therapists require more support from their supervisors and more experienced therapists benefit from skills training, greater independence and challenge (Guest and Beutler 1988).

Unfortunately, these benign reciprocal role procedures are not universally achieved; instead the supervisor can enact a *judgemental, unempathic, ignoring, controlling* or even *persecutory* role in relation to a *shamed and incompetent (*or *defiantly defensive)* supervisee. If there is an unresolved rupture in the supervisory alliance, or when the supervisor is concerned about the supervisee's performance, it may be useful to follow some of the principles outlined in the model developed by Bennett et al. (2006) for resolving threats to the alliance in the therapy relationship. Applying this model to the supervisory alliance involves, above all, the ability of the supervisor to recognise when the relationship has gone 'off track' and to pull back from routine supervision to initiate a conversation about what is going on. One is aiming for an honest and open exploration of both participants' experience and perception of the supervision and attempting, collaboratively, to link this to possible reciprocal roles. Where the supervisory use of the model differs from the therapeutic use is that it is not the supervisor's job to 'play the therapist' in relation to the supervisee, i.e. offering a formulation of their problem procedures and linking the supervisory problem to it. However, if the supervisor takes an open, non-blaming approach, supervisees are often spontaneously willing to consider which aspects of their own experience and reciprocal role repertoire are influencing the situation.

Common enactments in supervision

We have found that there are two common reciprocal role enactments in supervision relationships which can have a particularly negative effect when difficulties need addressing in supervision. Both result in the supervisor and supervisee becoming out of dialogue.

Avoidant, ignoring *in relation to* unheard, ignored *reciprocal role procedure*

Either the supervisor or the supervisee may initiate this procedure. The supervisor is most likely to enact it in relation to monitoring and evaluating a supervisee's performance. The tensions of combining evaluation within supervision are well recognised. For example, Shaw (2013: 302) asks, 'How does one carry out a monitoring function that generates anxiety, when trying to maintain a respectful, collaborative arrangement? Is this some kind of impossible paradox?' The supervisor is aware of an issue but is reluctant to challenge, to step out of the more comfortable supportive role and risk conflict with the supervisee, and hopes that the issue will resolve itself without intervention. The result is that the supervisee continues to practise in a way which may be ineffective, or even damaging for clients, or that the supervisory alliance is strained, which inhibits dialogue and limits the supervisee's learning and development. However in some situations it is only by talking about potentially conflictual issues, by taking the risk of moving into uncomfortable territory, that the supervisor can ensure the safety and efficacy of the therapist's practice.

A supervisee may also avoid bringing challenging issues to supervision, and there is evidence that supervisees do not disclose important aspects of their clinical work (Ladany et al. 1996), because they do not trust the supervisor enough, fear being criticised or feeling shamed.

Over-controlling, critical *in relation to* controlled, silenced, criticised *reciprocal role procedure*

A supervisor may enact this procedure when feeling anxious about a situation which a supervisee presents. The supervisor assumes too much authority, becomes directive and reactive, instead of allowing space for joint thinking about a situation. Packwood (in Page and Wosket 2015) suggests this reaction is linked to the narcissistic buzz which a supervisor gains from giving smart advice. When this happens, supervision does not offer a place for joint reflection, nor yield a mutually agreed way forward. Instead the supervisee feels either bound to act in a way determined by the supervisor or inclined to rebel quietly against the imposition of the supervisor's view. Exposing one's psychotherapy practice to supervision commonly places therapists in a narcissistically vulnerable position, so if the supervisor's role includes a superior, criticising stance, the supervisee's narcissistic injury usually leads to a closed, defensive stance, either experiencing or warding off shame. The supervisory alliance will be weaker as a result and supervisees may use the supervisor's voice in therapy rather than speaking authentically with their own. Alternatively, supervisees may be unable to take in and use any of the supervisor's thoughts, reflections or suggestions and instead become preoccupied by anxiety over their performance, further inhibiting the authenticity that is the *sine qua non* of good practice.

Examples

We now return to the earlier examples to show some ways of working with competing ethical principles and challenges in supervision without recourse to the above enactments.

1. Risk to other – safeguarding

Adam's supervisor started to reflect on the ethical conflict between therapeutic confidentiality and a duty to prevent harm to the child. Adam confessed that he was made so anxious about the situation with his patient, Seema, that he had phoned the Trust manager responsible for safeguarding, who told him he must report the child's situation to social services, which he then did. His supervisor expressed surprise that he did not delay this decision until after the supervision session, and encouraged him to consider the impact on Seema of breaking confidentiality without warning her. Adam began to feel judged and criticised, but was able to express this and the supervisor responded by being more empathic about the intensity of his anxiety and more accepting of his actions. Adam thought Seema would feel angry and betrayed by him, and was fearful of her reaction in the next session. Supervision then focused on how his fear of Seema's anger also echoed many aspects of her experiences of abuse, and on how Adam could manage his own emotions in order to allow Seema to feel and express her own.

There are at least four thorny issues embedded in this example. First, there is the degree to which a supervisee in therapy training is empowered to make their own autonomous clinical decisions, even when the supervisor disagrees with them. With therapy trainees who are already fully qualified in their core profession (in this case psychiatry), it is arguable that it is not the supervisor's role to direct them in what to do. They have to exercise their own professional judgement as they are accountable to their own professional body.

There is also a tension here between the professional's absolute duty to respect their client's confidentiality (and to warn them if they feel impelled to breach it) and the NHS employer's policy in relation to safeguarding. Although the therapist only phoned the safeguarding manager for advice, once he was informed he 'must' report the issue, not to do so would have put him in breach of his employment contract and could have led to disciplinary action. This is not an uncommon problem. It often occurs, for example, where a risk-averse employer insists that every suicidal threat is reported to management and a safeguarding protocol implemented. This can be in conflict with a therapist's desire to enable someone to confide their deepest thoughts, fears and fantasies and learn to contain, tolerate and manage them, without the threat of this triggering an intrusive and controlling process which would disrupt the therapy relationship and rob the client of autonomy.

A third issue is the role of the cultural differences between the client, therapist and supervisor which can influence their actions. The people in this example hailed from three different cultures. The therapist may have misunderstood how culturally normative it was for the Bangladeshi women to care for each other's children. His own cultural background may have made him deferential to the 'authority' of the employer and the need to follow rules and protocols to the letter. The supervisor's white British cultural background may have made him misjudge the therapist as unable to contain his anxiety rather than as a good doctor adhering to best practice. All these misunderstandings demonstrate the need for cultural awareness and sensitivity in supervision.

Finally, the example shows how there is often no 'right answer' to an ethical dilemma; it is a matter of judgement and supervisors have to act without the benefit of hindsight. Sometimes their decisions prove inadequate, but could not be seen as such at the time. In the event, the client was, as predicted, angry at the breach of confidentiality and refused to disclose any further details about the child. Social services felt unable to take any action as they did not have the child's name, the parent's name nor even know the child's current whereabouts. The client did not attend any further sessions, and therapy ended prematurely.

2. Risk to client – threat to therapy boundary

Robert did not attend his supervision group for the next two weeks, sending apologies but not giving an explanation. The supervisor believed he was avoiding her, and began by emailing him, asking if they could meet outside the group to discuss the supervision. When he did not respond, she called him and left a message. After another week, he returned her call and reluctantly agreed to meet. At this meeting the supervisor told Robert she was concerned about his lack of concern over the sexualised transference and countertransference. Robert became very irritated, saying that he was an experienced therapist and he knew what he was doing, and that she was being rigid, over-controlling and heavy-handed. The supervisor suddenly felt very angry and said that she was astounded he could say that; perhaps he had problems with women in authority, women he couldn't flirt with? Robert said 'Oh shut up!' and left the room.

After he left, his supervisor felt very distressed. She realised she had failed, in her own terms, to maintain a professional attitude and that she had become drawn into a very personal, emotional reaction. She asked an experienced colleague for peer supervision, during which she was able to link her rage to a much earlier experience of being flirted with and almost seduced by a senior male colleague, who later treated her dismissively and tried to block her promotion when she would not go to bed with him. After this consultation, she felt able to contact Robert and invite him to discuss what had happened now they were both calmer. Robert emailed back and also apologised for his behaviour saying 'I felt very angry, but I shouldn't have said what I did'.

When they met again, the supervisor tried to avoid playing into the critically contemptuous *to* humiliated and angry *reciprocal role. Instead, she apologised that she was coming across as critical and controlling, and acknowledged she had personal reasons why she had reacted so strongly, without going into detail. Robert admitted he 'had a problem with headmistress types'. The supervisor felt a twinge of annoyance at being portrayed in this way, and felt an impulse to contradict him, but managed not to act on it. Instead, she calmly reiterated that she was genuinely concerned that he was not listening to her valid point about the nature of the therapy relationship being potentially harmful for the client. She reminded him about a reciprocal role procedure in the client's childhood, when she had had a sexualised abusive relationship with her father, which she had experienced as her only source of affection and attention, because her relationship with her mother was poor. It was difficult for the therapist not to respond to her behaviour as if it was a 'normal' part of an attachment relationship. However, this would be untherapeutic and could be damaging, because it re-enacted a problem pattern and ignored the client's actual unmet emotional needs.*

Robert seemed to respond less defensively to this approach, saying he was aware of the client as a 'lost little girl' as well as the 'sexy woman' she portrayed. He just didn't know how to raise the issue of her sexualised behaviour without seeming to reject her or criticise her. The supervisor then realised he was trying to maintain a good alliance, but thought this meant keeping the therapy relationship comfortable and warm instead of addressing the enactment between them. She was still unsure of the extent to which Robert was able to work with these issues. However, she realised it had been a big step for him to admit there was something he didn't know, and for the first time she felt that they were having a genuine conversation about the client's needs and the therapist's anxieties.

The *superior, contemptuous* to *inferior, contemptible* reciprocal role procedure can often be enacted by trainees, who are moving from 'unconscious incompetence' to 'conscious incompetence'. Although this is good progress in skill acquisition, it often feels the opposite to the trainee, and so it is helpful to warn them in advance that it is likely to happen.

Sometimes the supervisee resists supervision, or even shows dismissive contempt for the supervisor's suggestions, and sometimes it is not possible to avoid giving a 'knee-jerk' response, acting into the reciprocal role. It is useful to consult one's supervisor colleagues (i.e. seek 'supervision of supervision'), so that the enactment does not continue beyond the point of repair.

Robert's story illustrates another problem: How can a supervisor know whether the therapist is going beyond poor technique into frankly transgressive behaviour? One important method is to use direct observation, or 'microsupervision' of samples of the therapy interaction, through audio or video recordings of the session. Many therapists who have never experienced it feel really anxious about the direct observation of their practice, and require careful preparation. However, it is the most effective way to cut through the evasions and avoidance. It is also essential if one has any suspicion that the client is at risk of harm.

Ideally, the supervisor tries to explore with the supervisee the rupture in their relationship, and they reach some shared understanding. Often ruptures may be repaired in this way and when repaired can lead to a strengthened supervisory alliance (Watkins and Scaturo 2014), but some remain unresolved and supervisees may decide to change supervisor. In this situation, Robert's feeling that the supervisor was acting like a punitive headmistress might make it impossible for him to benefit from microsupervision with her, so a properly negotiated change of supervisor, to someone who would undertake direct observation, might be a possibility. However, if Robert had remained unwilling to discuss this issue or had dropped out of supervision altogether, the supervisor could decide to signal her concerns about the ethics of his practice to his professional body.

Breakdowns in supervision relationships, while uncommon, do occur occasionally, and qualitative research studies have identified factors which lead to negative experiences of supervision (Ellis 2010, Nelson and Friedlander 2001). It is essential when addressing a rupture to consider whether cultural or other differences play a part. A supervisor needs to reflect on and learn from supervisees' negative comments. Each supervisor, though supervising the same model of therapy, brings different personal qualities and experience to the role, and some supervisory relationships inevitably work better than others. It is important to explore supervisees' reasons for wanting to make a change and to respect their choices without undermining their autonomy.

3. Risk to therapist – balancing competing ethical principles

Lorna's supervisor recognised her own urge to advise Lorna to stop the therapy, but instead asked Lorna whether she felt able to help her client when she felt so anxious, and whether she felt she was looking after herself. Lorna acknowledged that her personal procedures of refusing to be intimidated by other people, pushing herself to face her fears and feeling she must not let people down could sometimes over-ride her anxiety and need for self-care. Nevertheless, after reflection, Lorna decided she wanted to continue and her supervisor suggested discussing her elicited countertransference of anxiety and fear with the client.

In the following therapy session Lorna told her client she felt vulnerable in relation to his words and that she owned some of her anxiety as a new mother, but said she was curious as she had not noticed these feelings with other clients and wondered if there were any negative feelings which it was hard for him to tell her about. He replied saying he thought she had been distracted since she had told him she was pregnant. He did not feel that she was bothered about him or that therapy was helping and this made him really annoyed. He added that therapy was going to end soon, then she would forget all about him. She acknowledged his need for help, his disappointment about therapy and his sense of rejection and anger, and they looked at how he had tried to express his anger and exert power through questioning her and telling her about his fantasies. They were able to complete the therapy.

This example shows how the supervisor avoids acting on the strong countertransference pull to become over-controlling or over-protective, and instead helps the therapist to explore her feelings about the situation. They thereby find a resolution. It also demonstrates the importance of a trusting supervisory alliance, as without this the supervisee might not have been so open. Occasionally a therapist may feel intensely threatened or intimidated by a client, and supervision is crucial in helping the therapist cope with this challenge. Clients may be physically threatening, verbally attacking, make vexatious complaints, attempt to stalk the therapist or instil fear in the therapist in other ways. The supervisor's role involves helping the supervisee to find a balance between her ethical obligation to honour the therapy contract with the client and her right to protection and self-care. Supervision may include a discussion of whether therapy should continue and, if not, how the supervisee can draw it to a close. A supervisor must also ensure that the therapist tells their manager about any threat which might require managerial action.

This vignette focuses on a situation in which a pregnant therapist felt under attack. A pregnant therapist may feel especially vulnerable, coping with the personal impact of being pregnant (especially in a first pregnancy). She may feel exposed, as an important part of her identity and personal life is visible to all, and so one of the usual boundaries of therapy is effectively breached. She may struggle to balance her feelings about her pregnancy and protectiveness towards her baby with a commitment to be present for her clients. (And Lorna's pregnancy may have indeed led to her being less 'present' for her client, as he suspected). The supervisor may also feel particularly protective towards the therapist. A therapist's pregnancy can evoke powerful feelings and fantasies for clients, which may relate to attachment history, specific reciprocal role patterns towards women, personal experiences of pregnancy or infertility, or envy and competitiveness towards the therapist's baby. The supervisor's role is to recognise potential enactments of reciprocal role patterns for all three – therapist, client and supervisor – and to help the therapist work with those in the therapy relationship.

4. Concern about performance

> The supervisor did not want to talk about Jenny's situation in group supervision, so he arranged a separate meeting with her. He explained he was concerned that she seemed not to be coping with her work in her former competent way. Jenny seemed relieved to speak about her anxieties. She said she was worried about losing her job in the impending re-structuring of her department. Her partner had recently taken ill-health retirement so her income now had to maintain their family of three children. She was sleeping badly and ruminating about these concerns. The supervisor acknowledged the pressure she was under and validated her understandable worries. He asked her how her anxiety and exhaustion were affecting her work. Jenny revealed that she had double-booked several appointments recently and had twice been out of the department when clients had arrived for appointments. She knew the receptionists were aware of these incidents, but did not think anyone else had noticed. Jenny had told her manager about her partner's situation but not about her emotional state, nor her difficulties in work, because her manager would be on the interview panel and she did not want to jeopardise her chances of being recruited.
>
> The supervisor felt more concerned at what he heard and thought Jenny could benefit from reducing her clinical work-load or having time off work, but guessed she would be unwilling to take those steps. He asked her how she thought she could deal with the situation. She sounded stuck, feeling she must keep going, could not risk speaking to her manager and would not entertain

the idea of taking time off. He told her directly about his view of the changes he had seen in her and his concern for both her and her clients. Using the language of CAT they mapped out the anxiously preoccupied, emotionally unavailable – not heard, abandoned, overlooked *reciprocal role procedure, which Jenny had been enacting, not only towards clients but also towards herself. The supervisor said he wanted to balance his twin responsibilities of care for her and for her clients, and expressed his opinion that she needed to make some changes. She agreed and they discussed how she could regain a focus on her clinical work, manage her diary better, create some space to reflect on her clinical work by not attending some meetings and take some annual leave. At subsequent supervision sessions Jenny was more focused and she told her supervisor that she was sleeping better and was being more mindful about her clinical work and her own well-being. She was still anxious about losing her job and the supervisor remained concerned, but both felt encouraged that they could now discuss her difficulties openly and honestly.*

Supervisors can experience great concern when they become aware that a supervisee's clinical work is poor or even harmful. They sometimes find themselves addressing performance issues which managers, themselves often under pressure, are unaware of or have overlooked. 'Presenteeism' (i.e. going to work when sick) and its accompanying procedure of soldiering on under significant stress are common among health service staff (Aronsson et al. 2000). When therapists work in an insecure environment under managers to whom they cannot talk openly, supervision may be an important outlet for them, but the supervisor has to be careful about the boundaries of the relationship and encourage the supervisee to raise problems where they can be resolved. The supervisor may have to be more active or directive in situations when a supervisee is less responsive than Jenny.

Conclusion

Difficulties, problems and challenges in supervision may be clinical or ethical. In CAT they are always seen as relational. Understanding supervisor and supervisee reciprocal roles and procedures helps to formulate these difficulties and create opportunities to resolve them. There are inevitably ethical dilemmas which are difficult to resolve and clinical situations where even skilled supervisors struggle. However, a thoughtful application of CAT principles is, in our experience, invaluable in meeting these challenges and resolving these difficulties.

References

ACAT Code of Ethics and Practice for Training and Supervision. (2014) *Association of Cognitive Analytic Therapy*. Online. Available HTTP: <http://www.acat.me.uk/page/code+of+ethics+and+practice+for+training+and+supervision> (accessed 11 December 2015)

Aronsson, G., Gustafsson, K. and Dallner, M. (2000) 'Sick but yet at work: An empirical study of sickness presenteeism', *Journal of Epidemiology and Community Health*, 54, 7: 502–509.

Bennett, D., Parry, G. and Ryle, A. (2006) 'Resolving threats to the therapeutic alliance in cognitive analytic therapy of borderline personality disorder: A task analysis', *Psychology and Psychotherapy: Theory, Research and Practice*, 79: 395–418.

Ellis, M.V. (2010) 'Bridging the science and practice of clinical supervision: Some discoveries, some misconceptions', *The Clinical Supervisor*, 29, 1: 95–116.

Guest, P.D. and Beutler, L.E. (1988) 'Impact of psychotherapy supervision on therapist orientation and values', *Journal of Consulting and Clinical Psychology*, 56, 5: 653.

Ladany, N., Hill, C.E., Corbett, M.M. and Nutt, E.A. (1996) 'Nature, extent, and importance of what psychotherapy trainees do not disclose to their supervisors', *Journal of Counseling Psychology*, 43, 1: 10.

Ladany, N., Mori, Y. and Mehr, K.E. (2013) 'Effective and ineffective supervision', *The Counseling Psychologist*, 41, 1: 28–47.

Nelson, M.L. and Friedlander, M.L. (2001) 'A close look at conflictual supervisory relationships: The trainee's perspective', *Journal of Counseling Psychology*, 48, 4: 384.

Page, S. and Wosket, V. (2015) *Supervising the Counsellor and Psychotherapist: A Cyclical Model*, Hove: Routledge.

Shaw, E. (2013) 'Mentoring or monitoring: Formulating a balance in systemic supervision', *Australian and New Zealand Journal of Family Therapy*, 34, 4: 296–310.

Watkins, C.E., Jr. and Scaturo, D.J. (2014) 'Proposal for a common language, educationally-informed model of psychoanalytic supervision', *Psychoanalytic Inquiry*, 34, 6: 619–633.

Chapter 6

The use of the CAT model in the supervision of CAT therapists working with borderline personality disorder

Liz Fawkes and Val Fretten

From the outset, we would both like to echo Anthony Ryle's words, and 'confess . . . that, in general, [we] *like* borderline patients; [we] have learnt a great deal from them, and [we] have found that, once [we] come to know their stories, [we] have usually felt moved and filled with respect for what they have endured and achieved. To be able to like them it is necessary to understand them and this demands that one has a way of making sense of their often painfully destructive experiences and acts' (Ryle 1997: xii).

This chapter explores the key aspects of supervising CAT therapists working with people who present with borderline personality disorder (BPD) and illustrates these with examples from a therapy. The disorder itself is outlined, using the criteria of the *Diagnostic and Statistical Manual of Mental Disorders*, fifth edition (American Psychiatric Association 2013, DSM-5) as a basis. The chapter looks at the skills needed by CAT supervisors and at how CAT supervision addresses common problems arising from this work, such as 'splitting' in supervision groups, managing risky behaviours, and working through powerful transference and countertransference reactions.

The CAT model lends itself well to helping therapists work with people with a personality disorder, providing the essential focus, structure and collaboration (National Institute for Health and Care Excellence [NICE] Guidelines 2009 and 2015). It provides a conceptual framework which enables therapists to step back from the relational intensity of working with a borderline patient, to spot and step out of the enactments happening between them, and to recognise and seek to repair the almost inevitable relational ruptures.

Borderline personality disorder

CAT supervisors need to have an understanding of BPD alongside a thorough understanding of the CAT model of borderline pathology. DSM-5 (APA 2013) describes BPD as being marked by significant impairments in self-functioning (identity and/or self-direction) and interpersonal function (empathy and/or intimacy). Those with BPD also show pathological personality traits in terms of negative affectivity (emotional lability, anxiousness, separation anxiety and depressivity), disinhibition (characterised by impulsivity and risk taking) and antagonism (characterised by hostility).

The diagnosis itself presents challenges to services, staff and service users. The NICE quality standard for personality disorders (NICE 2015: 7) states that the 'care people receive is often fragmented', and that sometimes people with BPD are 'excluded from health or social care services because of their diagnosis'.

One of the common features often underlying the distressing difficulties described above is a childhood marked by relational trauma, abuse, abandonment and /or neglect, in which people have felt unloved and rejected. 'A hostile early world has left in its wake an extensive and various array of psychological damage. The sense of self is fragmented and the predominance of angry or distancing stances or unrealistic hopes serves to maintain deprivation' (Ryle 1997: 38).

> *When Charlie presented for CAT she had gained a reputation amongst staff in the community mental health team and local inpatient ward. She would forcefully demand that her needs be met, often interacting in an angry confrontational manner, talking at speed, with no apparent need to draw breath and certainly with no desire to listen to another perspective on the things that made her angry. Her self-harm was highly risky, and staff struggled to contain her many phone calls demanding immediate responses, which would quickly turn into a contemptuous tirade about the inadequacies of the system, the team and /or a particular staff member. Many staff offered 'care' reluctantly or resentfully, understandably protecting themselves emotionally, and not wishing to have any more contact with her than they absolutely had to have.*

CAT and borderline personality disorder

CAT has a small body of evidence demonstrating its effectiveness with people with personality disorders. Chanen et al. (2008) compared the effectiveness of up to 24 sessions of CAT with structured good clinical care. This randomised controlled trial 'substantially enhances the evidence base for this psychotherapy' (Chanen et al. 2008: 481), showing that early intervention is possible for young people developing BPD, and that participants in both groups demonstrated 'significant and clinically substantial improvement, with cognitive analytic therapy showing some evidence of more rapid onset of benefit'. A second study, published in 2012, provides evidence that CAT can be an 'effective therapeutic intervention for the self-management and interpersonal difficulties associated with a broad range of personality disorders' (Clarke et al. 2013: 132). Following the CAT model for treatment of borderline personality disorder, participants were offered 24 sessions of CAT and 3 follow-up sessions 3, 6 and 12 months later. Those who received CAT 'showed significant improvements in interpersonal functioning and significant reductions in symptomatic distress' (Clarke et al. 2013: 132).

The importance of supervision

The NICE guidelines for BPD (NICE 2009: 8) state that when offering psychological treatment providers must ensure that there is 'provision for therapist supervision'. The development of a trusting, open, honest and real relationship between the supervisor and supervisee is central. It is important particularly when working with people with BPD, because of their great difficulty with intimacy: they have 'intense, unstable and conflicted close relationships, marked by mistrust, neediness and anxious preoccupation with real or imagined abandonment; [*and they have*] close relationships [*which are*] often viewed in extremes of idealization and devaluation and alternating between over-involvement and withdrawal' (APA 2013, DSM-5: 664).

CAT supervision provides a space in which therapists are held to the model – not at the expense of their flexibility and responsiveness to their clients' individuality, but in order to keep the therapeutic relationship within safe boundaries and to help extend the therapeutic relationship beyond the limitations arising from the patients' pathology. We would suggest that it is the CAT model and the use of CAT supervision that enables CAT therapists to negotiate the swirling chaos and the relational challenges inherent in working with borderline patients. CAT therapy, like many forms of therapy, invites patients into a kind of intimacy, specific to therapy, where the therapist helps bring to the fore many intensely painful, distressing and confusing issues, memories, thoughts, actions and feelings. The very process of therapy is likely to trigger the difficulties around intimacy. As Ryle (1997: 71) says, 'given that unstable and extreme interpersonal behaviours are a central characteristic of borderline patients, it is not surprising that the main challenge they represent to psychotherapists and other clinicians is how to establish and maintain a working relationship'.

> *Despite her reputation, when I met Charlie in the waiting room she looked anxious and tentative, asking me to take her arm to help her walk to the therapy room, her other arm using a crutch for further support. She seemed anxious and wary. Inside the room she quickly switched to be more like the Charlie I had heard about during referral. Fiercely bright, she spoke loudly, quickly, with no pauses, describing the 'mental quick fire' in her head, full of tangents and blind-alley stories, asking streams of questions but allowing no answers – 'I'll have forgotten the question anyway'. The early sessions were marked by a contemptuous, angry rejection of CAT, therapy, me and mental health services in general, alternating with an expressed desire for intense fused closeness in which I would fill the 'void of need' within her.*

Supervising a therapeutic relationship that is under such intense pressure requires empathy to contain the therapist, helping them to remain firm about the limitations and boundaries of therapy in the face of idealisation, and yet valuing what can be offered and achieved in the face of forceful denigration and rejection.

The supervisor invites the therapist into a reflective space to counterbalance the intense emotionality of the therapy relationship, which, when working with borderline patients, very often renders the therapist unable to think clearly. The CAT supervisor needs to accept and understand the emotionality, and to *feel* the intensity of it, but to remain outside it, in order to help the therapist start to think through what is happening in the room.

The CAT model describes this reflective stance in terms of using an observing eye. With their 'excess of seeing' (Bakhtin 1990: 23), it is often the supervisor's observing eye which facilitates the process of beginning to sequence the patterns of relating and understand the consequences of how patients are relating to themselves and others. It is often the supervisor's role in the early phase of therapy to slow things down, to hold the capacity to think and reflect. Using supervision to map out which reciprocal roles may be playing out can begin to bring some order to a chaotic session, but sometimes the supervisor's task may be simply to describe the chaos and its impact in the supervision room.

In Charlie's case the supervisor would *'press the pause button'* regularly – stopping the therapist's account of the session to invite the therapist to consider what might be going on, and encouraging the therapist to hold onto basic phrases (*'Hang on, can we just think about that for a moment?'*), to use when 'under the cosh' of the countertransference. Containing the therapist, grounding the process through considered observation, facilitating 'volume control' emotionally and literally, can be vital in enabling the therapist to remain truly present for the patient, so that she can be helpful to her, but also so that she can create enough safety for the patient to share something of herself that lies beneath the contempt and idealisation. The relationship challenges inherent in BPD make it difficult for people to use and value what therapists can give them, whilst having to tolerate what they cannot give. Therapists need the security of a trusting supervisory relationship to hold on to that understanding in the therapy room whilst under sustained emotional pressure, in order to offer the patient the chance to learn that there is value in not necessarily getting what they *want* but in getting something that is *real*.

Alongside offering the therapist an empathic, grounding presence, the supervisor also needs to attend actively to the patient whose story will usually emerge through the early reformulation sessions. The supervisor, just as much as the therapist, seeks to build and hold a sense of empathy for the patient, as this will often be a significant factor in enabling the therapeutic dyad to create a safe, trusting enough relationship and working alliance to undertake the tasks of therapy. It is this emerging understanding of what lies behind the extreme relational stances that helps therapists to recognise and withstand the invitations to collude, reciprocate or retaliate.

> *Charlie's story began to emerge in a piecemeal fashion in the early sessions of CAT. She was born to an alcoholic mother, and as a baby her basic needs were badly neglected. Social services once found her in her cot at 18 months old with nappy rash so severe it was clear nobody had changed her for many days. She was eventually placed into foster care with her older brother, but the foster*

CAT with borderline personality disorder   87

family found her too challenging, and, although they felt able to bring up her brother, she was moved to another placement, and then back to her mother's care when she was five years old. She often had to seek out her own food from neighbours and friends, and learnt very quickly that unless she demanded what she needed, she would get nothing at all. She made sure she was the child sitting on the teacher's lap during story time, she made sure she was known and noticed and she was able in this way to elicit some care for herself from some of those around her, although nothing was consistent. At the same time, she was sexually abused by her mother's boyfriend over the course of her childhood, until she was finally placed back in a series of foster families. She had learnt from the start that others cannot be trusted, that she had to fight to get even her basic needs met, that unless she was tough she would get hurt and that within her was a burning desire for close intimacy in which her every need would be met.

Charlie's story emerged gradually in amongst her contempt for therapy and her increasingly vociferous need for merger, born of a deep-seated unmet need for safe, containing care. This fragmented process of story-telling interwoven with powerful re-enactments of the restricted reciprocal role repertoire is a common feature of work with borderline patients. It is for supervisors to ensure that space is created in which they and the therapist can begin to understand the origins of this restricted repertoire in the light of the emerging story, dominated in Charlie's case by themes of rejection, abuse and a fantasy of idealised perfect care. Her reciprocal roles were described as: *contemptuous, rejecting, abandoning* in relation to *rejected, rubbished and alone; intrusive, abusive, controlling* in relation to *invaded, abused, crushed* OR *angry and revengeful; ideally caring* in relation to *fused and ideally cared for.*

Creating space where thinking can happen is a crucial element of therapy when working with BPD. CAT supervisors might be described as inviting the therapist into a stance of curious enquiry (see Figure 6.1).

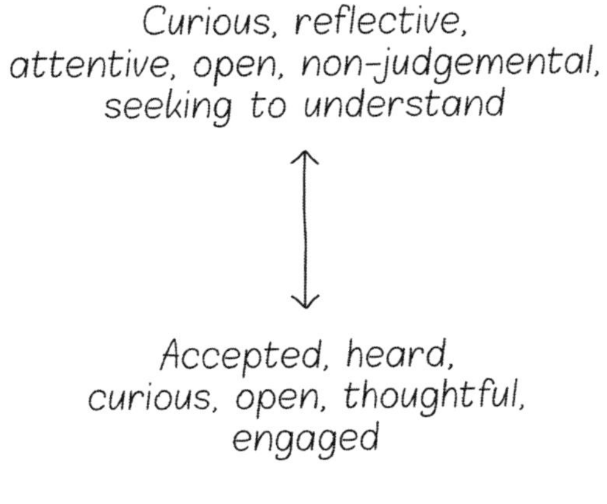

Curious, reflective, attentive, open, non-judgemental, seeking to understand

↑↓

Accepted, heard, curious, open, thoughtful, engaged

Figure 6.1 The stance of curious enquiry

This offers a place for the therapist to step aside for a time from the compelling invitations emanating from the patient to rescue or reject them. Inhabiting this reciprocal role in the supervision helps the therapist to invite the patient into the same stance within the therapy room. For borderline patients this may be the first time that they have the chance to learn how to relate within such a reciprocal role, and it is therefore likely to be a challenge to establish it in the therapy dyad. Supervision thus acts as a parallel process to the therapy, ultimately inviting the patient to take the risk of giving voice to what might normally evoke disavowal, dissociation, disapproval, avoidance or silencing.

The supervision group

Other members in a supervision group often play a key part in understanding the various reciprocal roles a patient may inhabit. Group members may well respond differently to the account of the patient's presentation, between them holding multiple aspects of the patient's personality. It could be said that the supervision group lends itself to mirroring the fragmentation of the borderline patient and that process, which can lead to 'splitting' amongst professionals, can also lead to a much richer understanding when harnessed creatively. The therapist is able to listen to the different perspectives being voiced and to join in the conversation. When wisely contained and guided by the supervisor, this can parallel the increased internal dialogue in the patient, which emerges through greater awareness of these different parts of the self, and aid the vital process of integration.

Using the CAT model in supervision

States and self-states

The different parts of the self are described in CAT in terms of single poles of each reciprocal role. Each pole is described as a 'state', which is really a 'state of being . . . defined in terms of mood, access to and control of emotion, and the reciprocal role pattern of which they are one pole' (Ryle 1997: 27). Borderline patients frequently switch from state to state, causing themselves and others a great deal of confusion, but this confusion is much reduced when it can be understood as the 'alternate dominance of a limited range of contrasting role patterns, each of which have stable and recognizable characteristics' (Ryle 1997: 26).

Self-states are split off aspects of experiences, feelings, thoughts and behaviours, as if complete in themselves, with no link to other self-states or states the person inhabits. In BPD the person is often frightened of the lack of control they feel over the 'flip' into the different ways of being, and this can drive a wish to understand and integrate this into a better sense of self. Describing these self-states and state shifts and capturing them in diagrammatic form is a key part of helping borderline patients to make sense of their changeable moods, the instability in their sense of self and their conflicting experiences within relationships. The supervisor's task is to help the therapist identify the triggers behind the 'flips', holding in mind, and on paper, the knowledge of all the identified states and self-states.

Three levels of disturbance

Ryle suggests that borderline pathology can best be understood in terms of three levels of damage. *Level 1* is defined as 'the restriction or distortion of the reciprocal role repertoire' (Ryle 1997: 34). The shared naming of the self-states and the shifts between them is central to capturing this restricted repertoire on paper. In mapping together how these are played out in the therapy relationship, and the sequences in which they occur, the patient may see, often for the first time, the distorted range of roles they inhabit.

This in turn addresses what Ryle describes as *Level 2* disturbance; namely, the 'incomplete development or disruption of higher order procedures responsible for mobilizing, connecting and sequencing reciprocal role procedures' (Ryle 1997: 34). Here the patient's various self-states are pulled together in one place, both literally on paper in the form of written reciprocal role procedures, and figuratively in the therapeutic relationship.

The third level of disturbance Ryle describes is the incomplete development or disruption of self-reflection. In CAT the task is seen as developing an *'observing eye that becomes an I'* – a phrase in common parlance in CAT, which links the self-reflective capacity with a more stable sense of self, a larger range of responses within relationships and an expanded reciprocal role repertoire.

Supervisors need to ensure that the therapy addresses each of these levels of disturbance. Encouraging the use of mapping from the first session onwards in the therapy room by continually doing so within supervision, the CAT supervisor helps the therapist create a 'Self-states Sequential Diagram' (Ryle 1997), which is a variation of the traditional basic Sequential Diagrammatic Reformulation. This diagram allows the triggers for state switches to be named and then monitored. Explicitly focusing on this experience of emotional turmoil is often grounding for the patient and the therapist, making sense of a changeability that has usually been bewildering. This process of sense-making that offers the patient the opportunity to build a capacity for self-reflection often originates with the CAT supervisors' ability to reflect on the therapist–patient dyad from outside and to name what they see in an accessible yet robust manner.

> Charlie had an ambivalent relationship with her map, but it provided a description of the key self-states and the links between them. See Figure 6.2.

Target problems and reformulation

Alongside these relational negotiations the therapist's task is to agree the *Target Problems* (TPs), a shared understanding of the issues the therapy will focus on. With borderline patients who may 'lack . . . self-direction' (APA 2013,

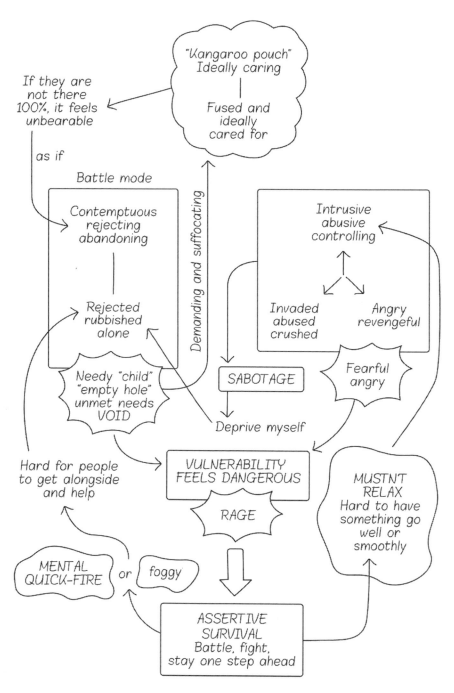

Figure 6.2 Charlie's map

DSM-5: 665) naming the TPs can be enormously challenging and the supervisor may need to ensure this task is done, and that the multiplicity of dramas that often accompany borderline patients into therapy does not seduce the therapist away from being clear about the focus of the work.

The supervisor's task of helping the therapist to capture in writing the target problems, the patient's history and their ways of coping with their experiences and feelings actively involves them in the therapy process. The reformulation letter is a sign, or tool, jointly created by therapist and patient, but it is also a tool that has been shaped at least in part in the supervision setting. The strength of borderline patients' feelings, the extreme yet restricted number of reciprocal roles, and the chaos of both the patients' presentations and their stories, makes writing reformulation letters particularly hazardous. Supervisors will often need to take a proactive role, even with experienced CAT therapists, to ensure letters are written within the stance of curious enquiry described above rather than from within the patient's reciprocal role repertoire.

When Charlie's reformulation letter was written, the supervisor had to challenge the therapist to write about her history in a way that evoked her vulnerability and her fear of abandonment, rather than disavowing this part of her, as Charlie did. The letter needed re-drafting a number of times to achieve this. One of the key skills for the CAT supervisor is to hold the reformulation in mind throughout the rest of the therapy, and the physical presence of the letter and the map serves as an anchor point in supervision as well as in therapy.

Working with enactments

Working with 'enactments' (the split off acting out of one or more of the restricted number of reciprocal roles available to the patients) is key in the CAT model. The active use of the CAT map can become particularly important when the therapy dyad experiences a rupture, something that is very common with borderline patients.

> *Halfway through the therapy, Charlie sent me an email telling me that she knew where I lived and that she had sat near my car in my village for some time the previous evening whilst in a dissociated state. I was furious with her for this invasion and outraged that she had violated my space outside the therapy room, something I had also felt within the therapy room at times. I took the incident to supervision.*

This is a description of a seminal moment in therapy, and the therapist felt it as an enactment of the *intrusive, abusive controlling* to *abused, invaded* reciprocal role procedure, clearly identified on the map. She feared the danger of being stalked, as others had before with Charlie, and she felt both *crushed* and intermittently *furiously angry*. The supervisor's response was multi-layered. He empathised strongly with the therapist, acknowledging just how hard it is when boundaries are infringed. But his key task was to help the therapist step out of the enactment – to move from the victim role back into the therapist role. He made some definitive statements, not a normal stance for the supervisory work he did with this therapist. This was 'not a deliberate infringement' he stated quite categorically, but a 'fugue in response to a symbolic parting'. Charlie was 'dealing by proxy with people who go away'. The supervisor had to help the therapist to help Charlie with some really painful feelings that she had not had the opportunity to confront, share and process before. To do this he needed to contain the therapist's outrage and fear, to move back into the therapeutic space and to have some compassion for where the enactment had originated. Charlie's unmanageable despair had been evoked by the therapist's impending leave, and her traditional response to being left had been to dissociate or to cling hard to whoever was leaving.

The supervisor helped the therapist to step outside the invasion, pulling her out of the enactment (oscillating between feeling outraged and scared) to stand metaphorically by his side to see what was going on between the patient and her. Then she was able to go back into the therapy room and work through the enactment with the patient in a real way. The therapist made it clear just how angry she felt, but also how she understood where this act had come from. Placing clear boundaries around the therapy, she made it clear that if it happened again she would not be able to continue. Later the patient said that it was the first time she had really *felt* the therapist's feelings – it was as if the anger had prompted a real encounter between the two of them that enabled her for the first time to understand the impact and possible consequences of her response to her own distress on other people. She never visited the therapist's village again, but more importantly she was able to understand more fully the extent of her 'dissolution of self', where the possibility of real emotional connectedness, such as she felt with her therapist, prompted dissociation and a wish to merge with the other; she understood how she needed to hold on to herself in order to remain in relationship whilst feeling close, understood and accepted, rather than yearn to fuse into the 'kangaroo pouch' of ideal care. Bennett et al. (2006: 414) showed that the successful resolution of alliance threats often 'involved facilitating the patient to process previously avoided feelings and memories.' By spotting and openly acknowledging the enactment and focusing on the therapeutic interaction, the potential rupture in the relationship was repaired, and this process is one that has become deeply embedded in CAT practice.

This illustrates three layers of skill required of a CAT supervisor that are of heightened salience when working under intense relational and emotional pressures. Firstly, this supervisor demonstrated the ability to gauge accurately the therapist's capacity to understand what had prompted the patient's flight into her procedures and to move off the patient's map relatively quickly. Getting to know the therapist's zone of proximal development (Vygotsky 1978), based on the level of training, experience and skill, is one of the supervisor's tasks with any supervisee. Secondly, he had to know when this particular therapist needed him to be firm and quite concrete about how to manage the situation, in order to help her to do the same. Finally, he showed a finely honed instinct for assessing risk, gauging when it was safe to take positive risks, such as in this instance, and when other action might be required. He knew enough about both the therapist and the patient to guide the dyad safely through this rupture.

Ending therapy

As the CAT model has endings on the agenda from the start and a defined number of sessions agreed early in the work, it is a task shared by supervisor and therapist to track how many sessions are left and to be aware of what ending may elicit for the patient, based upon the reformulation and maps built through the therapy. This is particularly pertinent with borderline patients, who usually struggle with abandonment issues, and for whom the ending of therapy is likely to re-activate these fears. This may be accompanied by a re-emergence of the old hostile procedures and the enactments of earlier phases of therapy. For many, an ending can either be felt but not thought about, or thought about but not felt. Having a deliberate, conscious, acknowledged process of ending can entail learning how to manage disappointment for the first time.

There may be an increase in risk, which can challenge the work that still needs to be done. The supervisor often needs to hold their nerve and help manage risk positively (whilst not being blinded to the changes that indicate the need for a different approach), holding the therapist to the task of addressing the underlying feelings that drive these risky behaviours and procedures. It may fall to the supervisor to hold onto the therapeutic optimism that 'all is not lost' and that endings can be survived. Once again the construction of the goodbye letter, this time also invited from the patient, helps to make explicit what has been achieved by the patient, what work still needs to be done, and what cannot be achieved. While many CAT therapists find writing the goodbye letter easier than the reformulation letter, the supervisor may need to help guard against an idealised ending, which avoids disappointment and avoids the pain of loss.

Finally

A good enough CAT supervisor needs to be experienced in the classic dilemmas posed by borderline patients, unafraid to deal with risk, hostile enactments, chaotic accounts, strong emotions and extreme relational stances accompanied by progress that may be slow and gradual and disappointing at times. CAT supervisors in this setting need to be able to contain, advise, guide, observe, reflect and give voice to what may be unseen or unacknowledged, and sometimes they need to be able to just listen. Under the benign eye of the supervisor who follows the CAT model there is hope that the therapist can safely navigate the pitfalls and blind alleyways. From this position we believe she will have the resources to face the often daunting but ultimately satisfying encounter with the patient with borderline personality disorder.

References

American Psychiatric Association. (2013) *Diagnostic and Statistical Manual of Mental Disorders (DSM-5), (fifth edition)*, Washington, DC: American Psychiatric Association.

Bakhtin, M.M. (1990) 'Author and hero in aesthetic activity', in M.M. Bakhtin, M. Holquist and V. Liapunov (eds) *Art and Answerability: Early Philosophical Essays* (No. 9), Austin: University of Texas Press.

Bennett, D., Parry, G. and Ryle, A. (2006) 'Resolving threats to the therapeutic alliance in cognitive analytic therapy of borderline personality disorder: A task analysis', *Psychology and Psychotherapy: Theory, Research and Practice*, 79: 395–418.

Chanen, A., Jackson, H.J., McCutcheon, L.K., Jovev, M., Dudgeon, P., Pan Yuen, H., Germano, D., Nistico, H., McDougall, E., Weinstein, C., Clarkson, V. and McGorry, P.D. (2008) 'Early intervention for adolescents with borderline personality disorder using cognitive analytic therapy: Randomised controlled trial', *British Journal of Psychiatry*, 193: 477–484.

Clarke, S., Thomas, P. and James, K. (2013) 'Cognitive analytic therapy for personality disorder: Randomised controlled trial', *British Journal of Psychiatry*, 202: 129–134. doi: 10.1192/bjp.bp.112.108670.

National Institute for Health and Care Excellence. (2009) 'Borderline personality disorder: Treatment and management', NICE Clinical Guideline, 78, NICE.

National Institute for Health and Care Excellence. (2015) 'Personality disorders: Borderline and antisocial', NICE Quality Standard, 88, NICE.

Ryle, A. (1997) *Cognitive Analytic Therapy and Borderline Personality Disorder: The Model and the Method*, Chichester: Wiley.

Vygotsky, L.S. (1978) *Mind and Society*, Cambridge, MA: Harvard University Press.

Chapter 7

Are narcissists a special case? Narcissism and supervision

Annie Nehmad

CAT is almost unique in its ability to make a real difference within 16 sessions to 'narcissistic' people, especially when the therapist or supervisor has the necessary understanding, experience, skill, compassion and optimism. Even inexperienced therapists can offer significant help, if their supervisor is able to support them, point out the pitfalls, and suggest useful modifications to 'standard' CAT.

The term 'narcissist' is a useful verbal shorthand, but it is imprecise and has pejorative overtones, so I will refer instead to people with a predominantly narcissistic dynamic (PPNDs). PPNDs are on a continuum with people who attract a diagnosis of emotionally unstable/borderline personality disorder. Both groups are poorly integrated, mainly as a result of difficult childhood experiences. When in crisis, PPNDs may show more 'borderline' behaviour. PPNDs are also on a continuum with relatively well integrated personalities, i.e. 'neurotics' and 'normal' people. None of us has experienced perfect parenting, so we may all at times resort to narcissistic procedures, or react to narcissistic wounding.

However, the experience of treating a PPND is very different to that of treating someone who is relatively well integrated, or who has borderline personality disorder. There are also particular challenges and pitfalls within supervision. So this chapter will discuss people with a predominantly narcissistic dynamic *as if* they were a separate group. It will explore:

1. my elaboration of the CAT understanding of narcissism
2. different presentations, and problems of 'diagnosis'
3. difficulties and pitfalls within therapy and supervision; suggested modifications to 'standard' CAT
4. narcissistic procedures within supervision

Early 'diagnosis' is important because modifications to 'standard CAT' make therapeutic success more likely, and because, unless the narcissistic dynamic is understood and addressed, therapy usually achieves little, even if the therapeutic relationship is good and the reformulation, TPPs and diagram are apparently adequate. In such cases, extending the duration of therapy is tempting, but does not help. The 'diagnosis' may be missed if the patient is not overtly grandiose or arrogant, and it may well be up to the supervisor to notice it.

Readers unfamiliar with the CAT model should read pages 19–23 of Chapter 2, and pages 37–41 of Chapter 3, before proceeding.

The CAT understanding of narcissism

This discussion will not limit itself to Narcissistic Personality Disorder (NPD) as defined in the *Diagnostic and Statistical Manual of Mental Disorders,* fifth edition (American Psychiatric Association 2013, DSM-5) and its predecessors. Their criteria prioritise overt grandiosity and miss the vulnerability and the painful 'contemptible underbelly'.

For a brief review of some of the cognitive and psychoanalytic literature and a detailed CAT understanding of narcissism see Nehmad (1997); for a thoughtful comparison of Kohut, Kernberg and Rosenfeld with CAT see Pollard (1997).

The CAT understanding of the narcissistic dynamic, and of the tasks of therapy, is simpler and more optimistic than that of psychoanalytic or schema-focused authors.

The *key defining features* of a predominantly narcissistic dynamic are:

1   the absolute centrality of the twin self-states in Figure 7.1
2   the absence, weakness or precariousness of the self-state in Figure 7.2
3   the terror of being 'average, ordinary'

Thus, the main or only way for PPNDs to feel OK is to feel admirable and special – or at least superior to others.

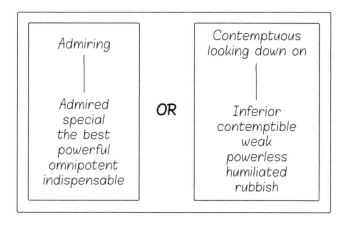

Figure 7.1 The twin self-states key to PPNDs

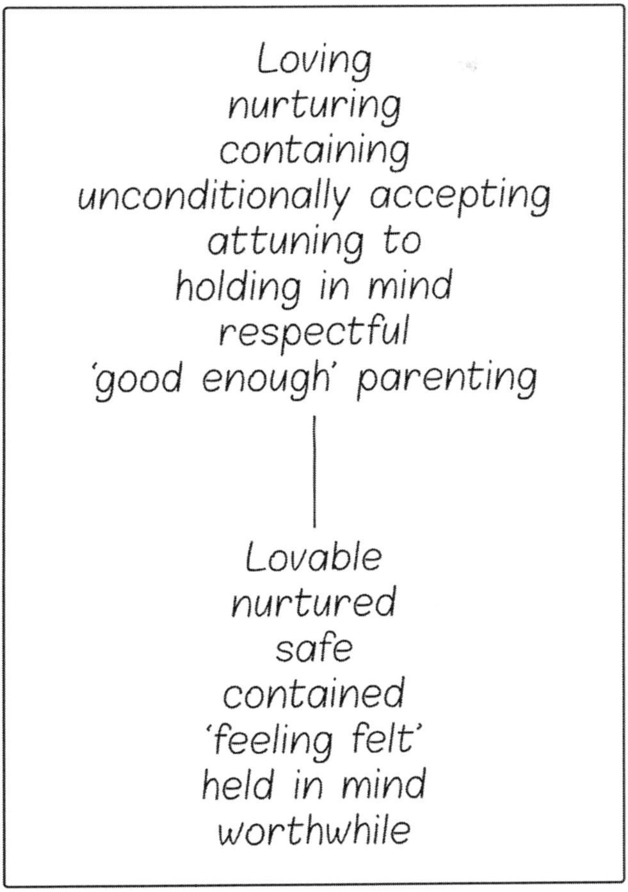

Loving
nurturing
containing
unconditionally accepting
attuning to
holding in mind
respectful
'good enough' parenting

|

Lovable
nurtured
safe
contained
'feeling felt'
held in mind
worthwhile

Figure 7.2 The healthy self-state which is absent, weak or precarious in PPNDs

Their key set of dilemmas is traditionally expressed as,

Either I'm sustained by admiration or I feel exposed. If exposed, I'm either contemptuous or contemptible.

It is easier and clearer for patients to express this as a three-cornered choice:

Either special and admired, or *contemptuous of inferior others,* or *contemptible (which is unbearable)*

Crucially, being (or being perceived as) *average, ordinary, normal, one of the crowd,* feels to PPNDs essentially the same as being *contemptible/inferior*, and is part of their unbearable core pain. In many cases, the *contemptible* pole is not merely about inferiority or inadequacy – it can feel like annihilation, non-existence. (e.g. 'For my mother, if she couldn't show off about you, you were nothing'.) Therefore, avoidance of this pole is their most important endeavour: much of what they do – and even think – is a desperate (often not conscious) attempt to avoid it.

The task of therapy is to create or strengthen a healthy self-state such as the one in Figure 7.2, and to weaken the hold of the twin self-states in Figure 7.1. In CAT, we do not offer lengthy re-parenting, though we do hope that our patients will internalise or strengthen a self-state of *caring, respectful, compassionate acceptance* to *worthwhile, cared for, 'I am OK,'* which they can then enact towards others and towards themselves.

'Healthy' narcissism?

Some therapists use this term to mean 'self-esteem,' or the ability to prioritise one's own needs. This leads to unnecessary confusion, and is incompatible with a CAT understanding. Individuals who have internalised a strong and stable healthy self-state (Figure 7.2) have genuine self-esteem, and can care for their own needs and those of others. They do not need to constantly shine, nor to put others down, in order to feel good about themselves.

In contrast, the narcissistic constellation arises from very different experiences.

Common relational factors in PPNDs

The presence of particular reciprocal roles, and the absence or weakness of others, is due to what the person has experienced (and lacked), especially in childhood.

PPNDs usually describe their childhood as 'normal'. However, one or more of the following factors may have been present (reciprocal roles are in italics):

1   *Lack of 'loving gleam in mother's eye,'* so the child feels *inadequate/defective*.
2   Parent *has high expectations* which the child cannot meet, or can meet only precariously, so the child has *low self-esteem, feels worthless (unless admirably achieving.)*
3   Parent *needs the child to be 'special'*, to bask in the child's glory. So for the child, *'ordinary, average' means of no consequence, invisible, even annihilated*.
4   Parent *treats the child as an object or extension of self*, so the child has *poor boundaries and/or little sense of self, requires approval and definition from other people*.
5   *Unrealistically over-praising* parent may lead to the child *feeling like a fraud who could be found out*.

6   *Over-indulgent* parent may produce an *entitled and self-centred* child.
7   Parent is *unattuned and unable to mirror* (because she is ill, in pain, depressed, narcissistic, needy, alcoholic, etc.), so the child may become *cut off from his own feelings and need for connection,* and *lacks emotional 'vocabulary and grammar'*. (The need for other people may well form part of the dreaded *contemptible* pole).
8   Parent whose main way of avoiding the contemptible pole is to be *contemptuous* (even of their own children), so the child feels, or fears being, *contemptible*. These individuals are often in a double bind: *If I succeed, I am envied and resented; if I fail I am looked down on.*
9   Significant abuse and/or neglect usually lead to borderline/emotionally unstable personalities. However, individuals who can derive self-worth from being *special and admired* for attractiveness or achievements may instead develop a predominantly narcissistic personality.

Presentations; problems of diagnosis; narcissism as a syndrome

It is easy enough to 'diagnose' a predominantly narcissistic dynamic in the presence of grandiosity, contemptuousness and arrogant body language. However, grandiosity may be covert or even absent, and feelings of superiority may not be expressed, even when discussing the Psychotherapy File.

People with a predominantly narcissistic dynamic are not all alike. Inherited temperament, the existence of healthier reciprocal roles, culture, actual talents and achievements, etc. all influence how they present, which procedures they engage in, and the components of each pole in the twin self-states. For example, the *admirable/special* pole may (but need not) include being depended upon and 'irreplaceable' within a work environment.

Some are shamelessly unscrupulous, while others pride themselves on their integrity. Some are in the forensic population; others have successful careers; yet others are not in employment because they consider most jobs as 'beneath them', or because of conflicts with authority. Some demand that their emotional needs be met and cannot bear these being thwarted, while others deny having any emotional needs. Some may have both insight and a genuine sense of humour. Yet others (with a greater variety of reciprocal roles) may be warm and loving and capable of attunement – as long as they are not triggered into their narcissistic self-state.

It is helpful to think of narcissism as a syndrome, i.e. a set of symptoms and signs, or 'dimensions', each of which might be present in varying degrees of intensity. Some are included in DSM-5 (APA 2013) criteria for NPD. Some are mentioned elsewhere in this chapter. Others include:

• superficial accounts of childhood and parents
• self-righteousness
• chronic dysthymia

- difficulty feeling joy or sadness
- lack of a genuine sense of humour, especially about themselves (though biting sarcasm may well be present)
- disconnection from feelings (when asked what they feel, or felt in childhood, they tend to reply with thoughts, opinions or anecdotes)
- emptiness, boredom, so may need constant stimulation (substances, extreme sports, promiscuity)

The presence of these 'dimensions' can alert therapists and supervisors to the possibility of a predominantly narcissistic dynamic. However, their presence is neither necessary nor sufficient for 'diagnosis.' The only three absolutely defining characteristics of PPNDs are: the central importance of the twin self-states (Figure 7.1), the weakness of the healthy self-state (Figure 7.2), and terror of being average, ordinary, 'one of the crowd'.

In the examples below 'Iris' and 'Arthur' showed no grandiosity or contemptuousness.

> *Iris, an unassuming woman with longstanding dysthymia, had worked in the same middle management post for twelve years. Her emotional vocabulary was poor; she had few memories of childhood, and could only describe her parents as 'normal'. She had no close friendships. She developed disabling anxiety and depression when her firm was restructured and her post disappeared, though she was given another of similar status. It emerged that she had told herself for years that her job was actually the most important one in her firm, and absolutely vital to its success. When she could no longer sustain this belief, she felt utterly contemptible, inferior, paralysed with anxiety, and unable to function at work.*

'Reacts to criticism with feelings of rage, shame, or humiliation (even if not expressed)', was a criterion for NPD in DSM-III (APA 1980) but removed from later editions due to 'lack of specificity'. I think it is useful to bear this 'dimension' in mind; it may be obvious in relation to the therapist, or in accounts of other relationships. A similar level of rage and humiliation may happen in response to perceived rejection.

> *Arthur felt devastated and furious when a friend did not choose him as his son's godfather. He strongly considered ending the long friendship, and/or not attending the christening. This dilemma was expressed as,* 'It's as if I can only *either* have pride of place, *or* feel rejected, humiliated and angry'.

I have encountered PPNDs whose difficulties had been diagnosed as depression, anxiety, panic disorder, social anxiety, dysthymia, cyclothymia, bipolar II disorder, borderline personality disorder and adult ADHD. People with eating disorders, addictions and 'anger management' issues often have an underlying narcissistic dynamic. Chronic dysthymia among PPNDs results from dissatisfaction with their life or career, compared to their expectations ('potential not achieved'), and their difficulty with feeling true enjoyment and connection to others. Cyclothymia and bipolar II may reflect the elation of feeling *special/admirable*, and the depression of feeling *inferior/contemptible*. Bipolar disorder may co-exist with a narcissistic dynamic – failure to stay in the *special* role may trigger (hypo)manic or depressed episodes.

Difficulties and pitfalls; suggested modifications to standard CAT; are 'narcissists' (PPNDs) a 'special case'?

Many PPNDs (especially if rich, famous, brilliant, attractive or adored) remain stable in the *admirable* pole if they receive enough attention, adulation and admiration. While they are symptomless, they cannot engage meaningfully with therapy. But if their narcissistic supplies are reduced (e.g. partner leaves them, business fails), they may develop depression, anxiety or other symptoms. In my experience, PPNDs who are symptomatic can change significantly through CAT, even if their goal is externally focused (e.g. 'to prevent my wife leaving').

Most PPNDs pose particular problems in therapy:

- Need to feel self-sufficient; fear of experiencing or showing neediness or vulnerability (these are often part of the dreaded *contemptible* pole)
- Grandiosity, arrogance, entitlement, contempt (which may lead to negative feelings in the therapist and even in the supervisor)
- Difficulty connecting with feelings

Some therapists consider them very difficult, as they 'can't engage', or 'can't collaborate'. In fact, it is up to therapists to find ways of collaborating with them, on their terms. Many have had to attune to their parents, rather than experiencing their parents attuning to them. We as therapists (and as supervisors) should endeavour to understand them and attune to them, and to what they can manage, rather than expect them to fit into our expectations of what therapy should be about.

To maximise the chances of an effective therapy, the supervisor can help therapists keep in mind that the therapy of a PPND should be *both* similar to that of other patients, *and* in some respects a 'special case', i.e. with some modifications to 'standard CAT'.

Similarities to 'standard CAT'

'Push where it moves,' meet the patient's agenda, and go at his pace

CAT's practice of description, collaborative mapping, joint discovery and reformulation rather than interpretation is particularly useful, as interpretation is usually counterproductive for PPNDs. Also, we help patients address their presenting problems (not what *we* think their 'real problem' is). We then co-discover the underlying problem procedures. CAT understands people's difficulties as stemming from a lack of integration, and from the self-reinforcing nature of damaging procedures (including narcissistic ones). Once people can literally see this (drawn out on paper), they are more likely to be able to make changes.

We need to start from where they are, and 'push where it moves'. Thus, if our aim is for them to accept 'a happy medium', they may feel misunderstood or even attacked, resulting in a poor therapeutic alliance. If it is hard for a PPND to access feelings (and he is not requesting help with this), we should not make this an aim of therapy (though it may become a by-product of it). This is not collusion – it is working within the zone of proximal development (see Chapter 3), staying attuned, and offering our collaboration to them, rather than expecting them to collaborate with what we think their therapy should be about.

> There is nothing intrinsically wrong with being admired-admiring. The problem is its *precariousness* – and the fact that the only perceived alternative is despicable and intensely painful contemptibility (so it becomes part of a depression and despair loop). There is nothing intrinsically wrong with feeling superior to others. The problem is that if we convey this to others (making them feel inferior) we are likely to sabotage our goals . . . There is nothing wrong with putting your own needs first – it's only a problem if, as a result of it, your girlfriends keep leaving you (so it becomes part of an abandonment, loneliness and despair loop). Unless we pose things in this way, the narcissist may well feel criticised and attacked by the therapist, and hang on ever more tenaciously to tried and trusted procedures, especially contemptuous ones.
>
> (Nehmad 1997: 8)

Be aware of reciprocal roles, and the possibility of 'recruitment'

The supervisor can warn the therapist that, given the centrality of the twin self-states, the patient may offer and/or expect admiration within therapy; he may also become contemptuous, or feel humiliated and crushed if he experiences the therapist as disapproving. However, not all PPNDs do this. 'Iris' and 'Arthur' (see above) neither invited nor offered admiration or contempt within therapy.

Furthermore, a patient's admiration need not be an attempt to recruit the therapist into an *admiring* to *admired* state. He may genuinely admire the therapist's ability to 'bring it all together' in an empathic reformulation. The supervisor can enable the therapist to accept (and enjoy) a compliment, while remaining alert to its possible function (is this a genuine compliment 'with no strings attached', or does the patient need admiration in return, and will he become annoyed and/or contemptuous if it is not forthcoming?).

Problem procedures from the psychotherapy file

The supervisor should encourage the therapist to discuss these carefully rather than take them at face value – for example, '*trying to please*' may in fact be '*trying to impress*,' e.g. with grand gestures.

Stay empathic

This can be difficult with PPNDs, especially when they display arrogance. Even when they do not, their coldness and disconnection from feelings often produce a lack of empathy in their therapists. Their contempt for us (or for our diagrams or reformulations) may wound our own narcissism. The supervisor's role is crucial in helping the therapist to stay empathic, by validating the therapist's negative feelings while reminding him of the aetiology of narcissism. This can elicit compassion in the therapist for the emotional deficits suffered by the patient (which the latter often cannot even name). It will also help explain some of the roles enacted by the patient (e.g. he treats people as objects because that is probably how he was treated).

> It is not easy to avoid sounding critical when describing narcissistic role procedures. We are more likely to succeed if we try to connect with our own narcissism, and if we ask ourselves . . . 'When I feel despair about the possibility of collaborating or truly connecting with him, what is he likely to be feeling – beyond the fleeting triumphalism of having 'won' this particular encounter?' . . . 'If we seem unable to collaborate, could it be that we have different agendas or goals, and this needs to be made explicit, and perhaps re-negotiated?'
> (Nehmad 1997: 8)

Modifications to 'standard CAT'

Prose reformulation

The supervisor should advise postponing the reformulation letter until the therapist can feel empathy for the client, as an accurate but cold letter could reflect the parenting received by the patient, and/or could be experienced as attacking.

Empathy and compassion need to be present in the therapist and in the reformulation. However, too much empathy or compassion too soon (verbally or in writing) could be counterproductive for a PPND who cannot yet face their own vulnerability. Compassion, alas, is often experienced by them as pity, which is part of the unbearable *contemptible* pole.

Mapping

Therapists may need guidance in keeping their interventions appropriate to what the patient can 'digest' at any given moment. Though we usually encourage therapists to map reciprocal roles as early as possible, and point out their occurrence within the therapeutic relationship as often as possible, when working with PPNDs caution may need to prevail. The supervisor needs to help the therapist develop sensitive timing for each intervention – in effect encouraging the therapist to attune to the patient, rather than 'deliver a therapy package' (which could happen if the therapist thinks he has to do CAT 'by the book'). A therapeutic relationship within which the patient feels relatively safe, and not too exposed, needs to be established before descriptions or explanations are proffered. This is true with any patient, but is especially true in the presence of hidden fragility.

While every PPND should have a standard CAT diagram containing all their key reciprocal roles, they also need a diagram which 'zooms in on' the narcissistic dynamic. The traditional 'split egg' CAT diagram for narcissism is unsatisfactory. Each half-egg contains one of the twin self-states; a 'healthy island' containing words like 'ordinary' or 'happy medium' is sometimes added between the two halves of the egg. Ryle and Kerr (2002: 186–187) consider that the 'split egg' descriptions are 'unflattering' and problematic.

Triangular 'cage' diagram

Figure 7.3 shows the patient as imprisoned within a cage with only two places: one precarious, the other unbearable (Nehmad 2010: 44). It is a significant advance on the 'split egg'. It can be used even at the assessment, if it fits the patient's account.

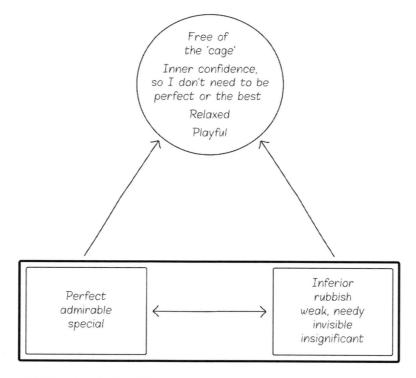

Figure 7.3 The triangular 'cage' diagram

It contains no unflattering language: I include only the *admirable* and *contemptible* poles, which PPNDs readily identify with. (I may add their reciprocals much later.)

Figure 7.3 is only a guide. The diagram should be personalised for each patient. It is important to make each pole quite rich, full of the patient's language (*'better off dead'*, *'a speck of dust'*, *'a worm'*, etc.), avoiding words they dislike (e.g. *contemptible*). The *admirable* pole may include fantasies (*'Egyptian pharaoh'*), achievements (*'top of the class'*) and aspirations (*'totally original'*).

It is usually best to draw the cage initially without the healthy place above, to depict the permanent source of their distress starkly. PPNDs often find it impossible to imagine a place 'outside the cage.' Discovering or creating this will be an important part of the therapeutic work. Patient and therapist (and supervisor) can notice instances of when the patient is not 'in the cage', e.g. 'playing with my nephews' (if he really manages to be playful without having to impress them), 'singing in the choir' (not having to sing louder or better than anyone else, but enjoying the feeling of unison with the other tenors, and harmony with the choir as a whole.) The healthy place above the cage can gradually be filled with words which are meaningful to the patient. This has an important visual impact: the new place is *free* of the cage, and *above* the cage (whereas in the 'split egg' the 'healthy island' is drawn between the problematic states, which makes little sense).

Should narcissism be named?

Supervisees may ask their supervisor whether to use the term 'narcissism'. In my view, we should not initiate its use, as the term is pejorative, unhelpful and unnecessary. If a patient has been told that he is narcissistic, and wants to know what we think, we should ask what led someone to say this. If it sounds as if he has a predominantly narcissistic dynamic, we can explain that these patterns (or 'cage thinking') are the result of his experiences – and he may change his patterns, if he wants to.

I may also explain the major emotion regulation systems (Gilbert 2009: 23–30), stating that he may have an underdeveloped oxytocin ('affiliative', belonging, contentment, soothing, compassion) system; and has learned to over-rely instead on the dopamine ('reward-focused', excitement, achievement) system instead. This explanation is not always relevant – it did not apply to 'Iris' or 'Arthur' (see above). I might add that some people also achieve dopamine-like effects with drugs such as cocaine – this is a non-judgemental comment which may aid disclosure of their substance use. One of the tasks of therapy can be to strengthen the 'affiliative' system – adding the new behaviours and feelings to the 'cage-free space', e.g. 'able to feel sadness and joy'; 'loving to my cat'.

Narcissistic procedures within supervision

The twin self-states, expressed for example as *admiring* to *admired* and *looking down on* to *inferior*, have been internalised by every supervisor and supervisee (if only because of the competitive culture we inhabit). We are all 'recruitable' by patients into any of the four roles, and we are all vulnerable to enacting these roles due to 'parallel process' (see Chapter 1 pages 14–16 and Chapter 2 page 31). Sometimes the latter is the first sign of a predominantly narcissistic dynamic in the patient.

At times, the supervisor and supervision group may 'join' the therapist in feeling bored, impatient or unempathic – and grandiosity may elicit hilarity.

> *The therapist reported that Peter, a musician, had 'no respect for musicians who aren't totally original.' The supervisor and the whole group broke into peals of laughter, with comments such as, 'Well, so much for Beethoven and the Beatles. . .'*

While shared laughter may have promoted group bonding, it was important for the supervisor to later re-integrate and remind herself, and the group, about the vulnerability behind grandiosity, and the emotional deprivation suffered. It was also important to realise that the group had become *contemptuous*, like the patient (an instance of parallel process).

The supervisor should be alert to excessive admiration from supervisees, but she can also allow herself and her supervisees to express and accept admiration. There is nothing wrong with admiring one's supervisor or supervisee (or anyone else) – as long as it is not part of the twin self-states, i.e. as long as the admiration is an optional and enjoyable extra, rather than essential in order to avoid feeling inferior and worthless, or a demand for reciprocation in a collusive 'mutual admiration society'.

The supervisor can help supervisees acknowledge their own narcissistic aspects, and narcissistic wounding (of which there is likely to be plenty when working with a PPND). This is best done through anecdotes and humour, and through the supervisor modelling this by referring to her own feelings or procedures.

The patient may trigger 'narcissistic' defensive responses in the therapist and even in the supervisor, who can collude with each other in declaring the patient 'resistant' or 'untreatable'. The supervisor needs to remind the therapist that in CAT the onus is on the therapist to adapt to their patient's problems, needs and zone of proximal development.

Narcissistic procedures in supervisees

Some examples:

- 'always right'; 'self-sufficient' (he has nothing to learn from supervision); 'the best in the supervision group' (so she cannot take any criticism, and/or she may put other group members down)

- unable to empathise with patients or predict their likely responses
- dogmatic (rather than tentative and curious) with patients
- bringing to supervision only positive aspects of his cases
- over-reacting to mild criticism ('I am useless, it's hopeless')
- defensive at any criticism or challenge
- needing to be 'indispensable' to his patient (who supposedly cannot manage without him, so he fosters dependence)
- unwilling or unable to contradict the supervisor, or express doubts about her suggestions (because he fears disapproval, and/or because he attributes to the supervisor the same level of distress at being contradicted as he would feel)

Overt manifestations of a predominantly narcissistic dynamic are uncommon within the caring professions, where PPND presentations are often subtle, as there is ample scope for socially sanctioned ways of feeling superior (e.g. power differentials with patients, and within hierarchies).

There may be instances when the supervisor feels so concerned by the supervisee's narcissistic dynamic that she needs to address this directly with him, in private. Usually, however, the supervisor can address these procedures in more indirect ways, e.g.:

- If plausible, attribute them to parallel process, e.g. 'I wonder whether your patient's intolerance of any criticism is being paralleled here'. Make general points about the purpose of therapy, such as the need to foster independence in our patients ('our job is to "make ourselves redundant" as therapists – by enabling our patients to internalise our benign reciprocal roles').
- Remind supervisees to offer positive feedback to each other before embarking on criticisms.
- Tell supervisees that we learn most by bringing to supervision the most difficult aspects or moments of a therapy (whether or not we dealt with these well).
- Reassure supervisees that it is OK to disagree with the supervisor.
- Ask yourself (and the group) whether supervision feels safe enough to bring one's difficulties or confusion. If necessary, make it safer.

Narcissistic procedures in supervisors

A supervisor who is 'always right' will not learn from her supervisees about her own 'dumb spots' (see Chapter 2). Her attitude will not foster curiosity and exploration in her supervisees, but rather a compliant attitude, and/or unspoken disobedience. She will not model openness and co-discovery, and her supervisees (in a reverse parallel process – see Chapter 2 and Chapter 1) may enact the same 'I'm always right' with their patients.

A supervisor who boasts about her own therapeutic interventions may elicit similar bragging by supervisees or fearful silence about their own doubts, mistakes and confusion. On the other hand, a supervisor who is able to share her mistakes and failures, past and present, will model a healthier set of roles, where imperfection is acceptable, normal, and part of the 'growth edge of learning'.

In conclusion

Supervisors can explain that while PPNDs pose particular difficulties they can make significant changes during CAT, thanks to its 'tools' and its 'stance' (respectful curiosity, remembering that the onus is on the therapist to overcome 'resistance', 'pushing where it moves' within the patient's zone of proximal development). The supervisor can both validate the therapist's negative feelings and remind him of the patient's hidden distress, emotional deprivation and vulnerability.

Supervisors who are comfortable with their own narcissistic aspects may enable therapists to accept their own, enabling them to be more empathic and effective therapists. Though the CAT understanding of narcissism began in the 1990s, we are still developing our theory, tools and techniques. The ideas and understanding in this chapter are a contribution to this quest.

References

American Psychiatric Association. (1980) *Diagnostic and Statistical Manual of Mental Disorders (DSM-III), (third edition)*, Washington, DC: American Psychiatric Association.

American Psychiatric Association. (2013) *Diagnostic and Statistical Manual of Mental Disorders (DSM-5), (fifth edition)*, Washington, DC: American Psychiatric Association.

Gilbert, P. (2009) *The Compassionate Mind*, London: Constable.

Nehmad, A. (1997) 'Narcissism and CAT: The missing chapter', *ACAT Newsletter*, 7: 3–9. Online. Available HTTP: <http://www.acat.me.uk/reformulation.php?issue_id=36&article_id=373> (accessed 23 October 2015).

Nehmad, A. (2010) 'A suggested new diagrammatic formulation for narcissists', *Reformulation*, 35: 44.

Pollard, C. (1997) 'Narcissism: From Kohut to CAT', *ACAT Newsletter*, 7: 10–15. Online. Available HTTP: <http://www.acat.me.uk/reformulation.php?issue_id=36&article_id=376> (accessed 23 October 2015).

Ryle, A. and Kerr, I.B. (2002) *Introducing Cognitive Analytic Therapy*, Chichester: Wiley.

Chapter 8

Intercultural supervision
Acknowledging cultural differences in supervision without compromise or complacency

Jessie Emilion and Hilary Brown

This chapter draws on our experience of teaching and supervising in India and in the UK.

In 2011 we accepted an invitation to teach a condensed CAT practitioner course within the psychology department of a small university in Bangalore. Our input comes towards the end of the two year Masters programme in Clinical and Counselling Psychology and covers broadly the same topics as the UK practitioner courses in four five-day modules. We also offer Skype-based supervision in small groups to graduates of these programmes who want to become accredited by the Indian Association of Cognitive Analytic Therapy (IACAT) as fully-fledged practitioners. We regard the distinction between 'teaching' and 'supervision' as somewhat artificial as we place a lot of emphasis on case based learning throughout the 'teaching'.

We hope to share what we have learned, separately and together, about working, not only *with* cultural differences but *across* cultures. We model openness by explicitly naming and acknowledging issues of race, religion, gender and class/caste throughout the course, even when it feels uncomfortable to do so. A great deal of the chapter represents our shared learning, and using 'we' in that context is no problem, but sometimes this 'we-ness' breaks down because the issues impact us in very different ways, so we have tried to show that where it is salient. So instead of politely evading difference, we explicitly position ourselves in relation to culturally sensitive issues such as gender-based violence, punishment of children, inclusion of sexual minorities and wealth inequality; not to do so would take away our authenticity and leave these and other cultural stereotypes undisturbed.

Msebele and Brown (2011) cite studies suggesting that the 'norm' for therapists is to skirt around, rather than to draw attention to, difference in the outside world and in the therapy room, but that this strategy fails to challenge privilege or to illuminate the impact of inequalities. We start from a position that we could not teach our students without discussing the impact of racial and other differences. Being explicit has a clear theoretical basis; Sullivan (2006) refers to the current privileging of whiteness as an 'unconscious habit' and describes how people and institutions resist naming it, but, as she explains,

> White domination is located . . . in both the individual person and the world in which she lives. Since habits are formed through transaction with the world and since habits compose the self . . . in a world filled with white privilege, habits that privilege whiteness will result and these habits in turn will tend to reinforce the social, political, economic and other privileges that white people have.
>
> (4)

Saying nothing would collude with, rather than challenge, this default position.

Being upfront has also been our way of managing these dynamics between us as co-trainers, in that while conducting the groups we work hard to process issues and reach shared understandings. When we are teaching in Bangalore there is no fudging the issues of difference. JE connects to the city, its landmarks, culture and language, from her childhood days, whereas HB had never set foot in India prior to teaching the course and speaks no Indian languages. She is not competent in day-to-day exchanges and is very visibly different. Processing the impact of this on our relationship as co-trainers and on our teaching has sometimes been difficult, but it has always proved to be a spur to clarity and a powerful safety net. We would suggest that other supervisors working in cross-cultural settings build in this kind of feedback as a precaution against the temptation to gloss over things.

At the outset we had to find the zone of proximal development (ZPD) of a large and disparate group, drawn from different language groups and regions of India, Tibet, and Middle Eastern and North African countries, and to tune into the theoretical frameworks they were using, so that we could scaffold a more socially conscious and CAT-like approach. We found a group espousing communal structures of family and caste but using individual and predominantly medicalised models of mental ill-health. The local services in which our students were interning did not have protocols to assist them with risk management, protection issues or escalation of concerns. For example, young women were often sexualised in their counselling encounters but had not been offered ways of thinking about how to manage this or when to seek assistance. Suicide risks and self-harm had to be contained by the counsellors and their immediate supervisors, and there were no formal frameworks for child protection nor for addressing sexual abuse. The trainees were also working across regional cultures and this was especially difficult where they did not share their clients' primary language.

In supervision groups trainees brought stories that can only be described as shocking, and we were shocked. They often described situations in which people had suffered significant breaches of their human rights and violations of their bodily integrity. But these accounts also had a subtext. They were presented from, and to, different reciprocal roles and triggered specific self-states in us as teachers and supervisors. Some trainees spoke from a panicked, unsupported, *'helpless in the face of seemingly unfathomable need, out-of-my depth'* state, that triggered in us a *'somewhat grandiose, parental and knowing'* position. Others reported these difficult and traumatic stories more as a kind of test – 'you don't know our culture', 'you couldn't deal with clients with problems as complex as ours' – a challenge that triggered a sense of incompetence. So we would be batted between these two poles, either occupying a *know-all* or a *know-nothing* position. This split seemed to be one way that cultural difference could be obliquely managed, and we came to understand how the presence of 'others' questions everything that is taken for granted about oneself, so that any 'outsider' comes to occupy a *mystic and powerful imagined* place or a *rubbished and useless* one. This is exacerbated when one culture has historically and economically taken advantage of the other.

So during the early sessions we heard about people whose childhoods had been marked by cruelty or indifference but whose experiences elicited no surprise or outrage. Children had often been beaten or cruelly treated behind closed doors. We heard about the gulf in understanding between generations and the pressure to hide aspects of urban life from rural relatives. We heard how a village might invest in sending an older son into the city to take up a high paid IT job when the reality was that they ended up working gruelling and poorly paid call centre shifts. Younger sons came to embody a competitiveness and rebellion about this state of affairs while older sons seemed to carry a kind of communal disappointment. We heard about a gulf between young men and women as each tried to find a compromise between the old constraints and the newly sexualised culture of the internet. We heard about two women whose mothers had been murdered by relatives, seemingly with no consequences for the perpetrators, who had continued to be involved in bringing them up.

In these case discussions there was often a subtext of not believing the patient's account of the harsh realities of their lives, and we also found it hard to believe some of these difficult stories. We spent time processing our responses. Would we hear about these matters in our own community and, if not, was that because these things don't happen or because they are contained in different ways and by different agencies? It seemed as if the students doubted their patients' veracity as a defence against encountering such extreme helplessness, terror or cruelty. We also came to realise that some were struggling to acknowledge the way that they had themselves been hurt or disciplined – self-knowledge that they habitually suppressed on the grounds that this was a fixed and necessary part of their culture.

But domestic violence, child abuse and sexual violence are not the province of any one culture: they are pushed under the carpet in western countries just as they are in India. CAT offers a way of getting behind the 'defence' that a person deserves to be punished because they have broken rules or taboos. Even long-standing cultural notions can be questioned, especially where painful ways of treating each other – and especially children – are the norm. We refer explicitly to the evidence that these ways of relating result in unmanageable feelings, which the child, and later the adult, has to contain or manage through procedures that outlive their usefulness. So we came to see CAT as a radical way of challenging the prevailing view that oppressive practices in any culture should be defended.

To address these painful issues we adopted five strategies in our teaching and supervision:

1. explicitly positioning ourselves and our respective cultures in relation to each other
2. taking a flexible view of what is inside and what is outside, recognising that dilemmas, traps and snags are sometimes held within the culture rather than within the individual
3. defining cultures as living moving entities, and change as a process achieved through dialogue – sometimes slowly and at other times too fast for comfort, causing instability and societal convulsions
4. using CAT's core philosophy to challenge victim blaming by recognising that procedures that come to be seen negatively would have started as one, and possibly the only, way a person could manage, and
5. drawing lines in the sand around serious human rights issues.

Positioning ourselves

Using our differentness in this very explicit way meant that we adopted a curious stance even when this went against the grain of reserve or politeness. We would argue that naming difference is a first step in *any* cross-cultural setting, especially where there is the potential for white privilege to be in play, or for western values to be idealised (see Msebele and Brown 2011, Ryde 2009). We try to acknowledge, albeit with some levity, the exploitation at the heart of our shared history. In any colonial struggle there will be some who symbolically idealise the colonisers and others who wish to expel them. We noted that those who had reason to feel devalued in their own culture, looked to us 'outsiders' to release them from the feeling of being looked down on, while those who held more confident role positions within their own communities did not seem to need this external validation.

In contrast, not naming difference would unhelpfully have allowed unspoken assumptions to operate beneath the surface, setting the direction for comparison, you differ from me, rather than vice versa. It may not be polite, comfortable or usual to make whiteness/racism explicit, but not to do so colludes with this notion that whiteness, and, to a lesser extent, western-ness, is the *ipso facto* default position. Expressed as a reciprocal role, it is as if there is an *unmarked/ unnamed dominant, superior* position that creates the 'other' as *marked/named, singled out, subordinate and inferior* (see Frankenberg 1997). Sullivan (2006: 173) terms this 'hierarchical' or 'asymmetrical' reciprocity, and it is an issue that has been marginalised in CAT theory and lost in the decontextualised way in which we describe reciprocal relationships.

When we factor in power and status to our discussions of reciprocal roles we can see that the deferring/subordinate person may not be allowed to operate from the dominating pole or perform in active or authoritative ways, so the two poles are not equally available and cannot be incorporated into the less powerful person's repertoire. Naming these dynamics allows us to think about the reciprocal roles that are played out in the room because they too have been crafted out of inequality within the wider society. We therefore work explicitly with the reciprocal roles of *superior* to *inferior*, which operate so powerfully in western cultures through the class system and which are present as 'caste' in the Indian context. We also recognise the extent to which these unequal positions continue to underpin unequal gender roles, the status of sexual minorities and religious divisions. Although they are usually unstated, on whatever axes the dynamics of superiority and inferiority are encoded, we find their operation understood by all.

But, however much we all know these hidden rules, we are rarely invited to think about the impact of inequalities on our inner worlds. Even in subjects like psychology and sociology, where these issues are the specific focus of study, they are usually viewed from a distance, in statistics rather than stories, and not named as an active form of positioning that is done to, performed by, and internalised by us all. Moreover, many therapists in training do not adequately consider how their patients position them and how this affects the therapeutic alliance. That is why we work with these issues between us and our supervisees and between them and their patients *on an ongoing basis.*

Seeing the boundary between inside and outside as more permeable

Over the several iterations of the course we evolved a structure that focused first on CAT as a 'model' for treating individuals as opposed to a radical set of theories about society and its values. Only when we had explored its use in one-to-one therapy did we return to it as a lens, through which we could examine culture and identity, and the reciprocal roles that operate between, as well as within, groups. This progression worked well – we started by saying that what is outside gets inside and that individuals have to find ways of managing it, but then we turned the spotlight back onto exactly *what it is that is getting in* that creates these painful internal rifts.

Our way of understanding the internal world as a reflection of the lived experience of our patients is a powerful mirror that can be turned back on society. Using Freud's analogy of psychotherapy as being akin to archaeology, it is as if we become near-sighted when 'reading' our finds. Just as Mikael Leiman (1998) can infer dialogical positions from short pieces of transcript, so we can use our sense of internal worlds to infer where the fracture lines lie in the wider social system. We can understand cultural identities as a set of familiar and/or shared reciprocal roles that shape feelings, relationships and confidence. People who share a 'culture' can read these contours, and respond, whether by accepting or resisting predominant ways of 'being' in the culture. So it is as if everything a therapist understands about their patient provides a cue to thinking about their culture and, if this thinking takes place within a shared dialogue, the default position with its dominant ideas can be challenged rather than colluded with. This accords with Ryle's preference for theories that explain 'psychology in terms of culture' rather than the other way around (Ryle 1995: 12).

So through our case discussions, we came to think about dilemmas, traps and snags as being held in the culture rather than exclusively in the individual. A snag might actually be a prohibition, a dilemma a threat of exile as the punishment for non-conformity and a trap a vicious cycle created by poverty and disadvantage. These do not need to be lodged internally insofar as they continue to be voiced in the culture and enforced externally. We came to the view that one way of thinking about 'cultural' difference is to become conscious of where we draw this line between what is inside and what is outside. We adopted as our mantra that what is unconscious in the society will be unconscious in the individual and referred often to the following quote,

> Individuals do not realise that the source of their motivation to act . . . is social, that the acts they feel impelled to engage in do not well up from inside themselves, but only find their sense, meaning and motive within the overall structure of social activity and relations . . . many of the motives created in social activity will be unconscious to individuals *because the wider system of social activity itself remains opaque.*
>
> (Burkitt 1991: 159)

In response to these issues we work by moving constantly between the inside and outside. Questions that get beneath the surface, 'What did it mean for this person at this stage of their life?' 'How else could he have coped at that time?' 'What resources could she draw on?' 'Was there anyone who took her side?' 'Did it help her to know that this was what happens to other women?' 'Was he able to self-soothe in other ways?' 'How did that help him to manage his feelings in that situation?' 'How did her poverty impact on the choices that were available?' 'How did family members deal with his addiction?' This non-aligned curiosity takes nothing for granted but allows us to respond without adopting a position of cultural-, race- or class-based superiority.

This also helped us to reach a new place in our own understanding of CAT theory and to challenge the primacy it gives to the individual over the social, in its predominant ways of working. The metaphor of the 'dance' in which each individual seeks reciprocation from others, fails to acknowledge the power dynamics at work in a society. The dance does not happen in a vacuum but is structured on the basis of positioned roles, selectively occupied on the basis of class, race, age or gender. Panning out from the dancers' dyad and the interactions between them, we see the unacknowledged rules at play – exiled at the side of the room are the ones who are not 'asked' to join in who stand alongside the servers and waiters. Powerful gendered expectations determine who leads and who is led. Before the anarchic eruption of rock-and-roll in wealthy countries, dancing involved following rules, using pre-ordained and pre-learned steps, not 'stepping out of line', not being too close, too sexual or not sexual enough. Moreover these positionings have always been policed, implicitly by peer pressure but more formally by 'authorities' who impose dress codes or draw boundaries around legitimate moves. In Baz Luhrmann's wonderful film, *Strictly Ballroom*, (1992) the young lovers are disqualified from the Pan-Pacific championships for dancing their own steps; as the old adage says 'He who pays the piper picks the tune'. Indian society tends to be more explicit about these dynamics, there is no pretence that a person can step out of line without alienating those around them, and we found it important to acknowledge these constraints as well as to challenge them.

Refuting the idea that culture is fixed and unchanging

So we could see that this generation of young Indians have found themselves at a crossroads. After not enough change it is as if there is too much happening and too quickly. Capitalism, with its material freedoms but economic pressures, is changing the face of their lives and cities, but the old ways still rule in people's minds. We would be presented with 'givens' which we had to decode and manage collaboratively with the supervisees: the idea that challenging someone who is older is wrong even when that person does not understand the realities a young person is facing. We challenged the extent to which exaggerated striving roles are seen as healthy and normal, compounding the exploitative demands of modern workplaces. We saw that young women in particular end up in the 'trying to please' trap that is framed as a fixed cultural expectation, because expressing needs is characterised as being disrespectful. Explicit prohibitions would be voiced about querying one's sexuality or religious traditions, particularly in the light of legislative changes that had rescinded rights for gay people. Whereas in our first cohorts we worked with openly gay and lesbian trainees, this retrenchment signalled an end to openness and a return to the old reciprocal role of '*hiding*' to '*persecuting*' or '*pathologising*' in relation to sexual orientation. The work of trainee counsellors in what is a fledgling profession, often meant approaching these T-junctions confidently but then feeling too insecure and backtracking.

As we continued our supervision through Skype for those supervisees who decided to complete CAT cases, the phrase '*in our culture*' became our pet hate. Every time the supervisees were confronted with difficult issues this phrase would be like a roadblock stopping us from thinking further. Absent fathers, physical abuse, forced marriages, ill treatment, strong beliefs, not sticking to contractual arrangements, breaching boundaries around confidentiality or time frames were all described by our supervisees, and by their patients, as normal and accepted within the culture. So unpacking culture is a necessary prerequisite for conducting both therapy and supervision.

We also work with the idea that culture is carried within the language and, even (perhaps especially) where the supervisor is monolingual (HB), we try to connect with potent words and phrases that carry the emotional timbre of particular issues.

> One example of this occurred when a Tamil therapist was working with a man from an impoverished rural community, who had become disabled and felt increasingly dismissed within his own family. The younger members of the family took advantage of him, and his wife had taken over 'his' roles. Although both therapist and patient were fluent in English, his therapy came alive when the therapist moved into their shared primary language using the Tamil word for manliness, Āṇmaiyai, that carried the feelings that he was struggling to articulate. Tuning into the emotional weight and complexity of words in a person's mother tongue is an important aspect of cross-cultural therapy in the UK as well as in India with its array of languages.
>
> Another powerful example of this occurred when JE was working with a Turkish woman in her late 30's in the UK (see Emilion 2011 and 2016). The woman had been referred for depression having been divorced after 15 years of marriage. Her husband had been having an extramarital relationship throughout the previous 5 years and told the patient he was leaving the marriage because there was no child and also because she was no longer slim and attractive. She had been living in the UK for over 10 years by this time, but had not learnt to speak much English, and this kept her tightly within the Turkish community where she had very little contact with English culture and values. She signalled this partly by dressing traditionally as a Turkish woman.
>
> At the first session the interpreter, though booked, did not turn up. The client agreed to meet and managed to tell JE her story. Though she looked distressed she told the story in a contained manner. JE was struck by the emotional cruelty she had experienced in her marriage and early life but also by her lack of affect as she described this history.
>
> At the second session the Turkish interpreter was present. The patient told the same story but this time with tears, wailing and beating of her breast. It felt as if this was a different person in the room. She went on to talk about what it meant in her community to be divorced and to be told that she was unattractive and barren. The session was heated, painful and alive. The interpreter also explained the shame in not being able to have a child and in being labelled as a 'divorcee' within the culture and the community. The Turkish word for divorcee (Ayrilmis) carries a derogatory meaning and positions women in a shameful and powerless role position.

Bakhtin (1984: 293) describes open-ended dialogue as the essential and most valued basis of human consciousness: 'to live means to participate in dialogue: to ask questions, to heed, to respond, to agree and so forth. In this dialogue a person participates wholly and throughout his whole life: with eyes, lips, soul, spirit, with his whole body and deeds'.

The patient was only able to participate wholly in the dialogue when the Turkish interpreter was present. Bakhtin (1986: 95) added the highly significant idea that this third voice, or *super-addressee,* represents or carries the wider culture or some part of it. Hence the word divorcee ('Ayrilmis') in Turkish was value-laden when the interpreter was in the room. The English word, 'divorcee', when used by the Turkish client did not bring out the same response, as the word carried no emotional baggage. In 'broken' English the patient was able to describe her experience from an observing role position which did not trigger the same shameful feelings. The dialogue emerging from the observing position was not unhelpful but had different values and meaning.

In our Indian work we try to move between these voices, we try to stay aware of our own positioning but give permission to our students to move out of the confines of their own languages and culture. We try to stand with them when they are challenging the rights of elders to interpret the modern world, but also to acknowledge the helpful containment of tradition and the pain of having to go against it.

Challenging victim blaming

Counselling is a relatively new profession in India and students had interned in organisations where there was no professional or organisational infrastructure to support the provision of talking therapies. What stuck out for us was the tide that these young people were already pushing against in their brave decision to become counsellors. Mental ill health remains stigmatised and marginalised in Indian society and, without a state-sponsored health service or welfare system, it tends to be seen in exclusively medical terms and/or as a responsibility of the individual and his or her family. It is not seen as a consequence of inequality or marginalisation in society at large or within the family system.

Supervisees often expressed disquiet, but could do nothing, about patients whose rights were being violated, for example, where family members had brought their troublesome relatives to be locked up indefinitely in rehabilitation or detention centres as a response to addictions. In some of these services 'beating someone senseless' was considered a valid method of detoxing and they were drawn into witnessing these brutal encounters. In other situations, they had to hold the awareness of their patients' vulnerability and to maintain confidentiality when faced with high levels of risk, thereby carrying a heavy burden on their own shoulders. This happened when young people shared histories of self-harming or suicidality but would have been persecuted rather than helped, had these matters been discussed with 'authorities'.

Framing self-harm as a procedure, rather than a manipulative ploy, started to help the supervisees to get behind 'symptoms' to see their original functionality, but also to dismantle the defences that these things were inevitable and that, because they conformed to cultural norms, they would have no consequences. This became a regular theme in the supervision groups – that even if something is normal it leaves its mark. We framed our work as equipping the supervisees to reflect on what might be going on for the patients, to normalise the rage and the distress patients were displaying, but also to recognise that raging, self-harming or not achieving well in academic work were understandable responses and valid ways of communicating emotional pain, that is to understand that symptoms are not always 'pathological' and that organisations may sometimes exacerbate, rather than support alternatives to, painful procedures.

> *Some students had interned in HIV centres for children and young people, but we heard that when children got ill, other children had to do their share of the chores, so that their suffering was met with resentment rather than care. It seemed as if, when the illness took its toll, the adults took a step back and left ill children to fend for themselves. The workers in turn were deprived of support, they owned the fact that they were afraid of the illness, did not have accurate information about its transmission, and, even if they knew it was illogical, 'blamed' the children for their illness and located the stigma and fear associated with the disease in them.*

In some of the detention centres, women with mental health problems were pathologised and blamed, especially if they had broken taboos by working as prostitutes to support their children or to survive.

> *In one case presentation, we drew a map for a woman who had 'placed herself' beyond the pale in every sense. She was a sex-worker, a drug addict and someone who regularly took risks in relation to HIV, by not insisting her clients use condoms. But as we reformulated her life story we found that she had been betrayed into becoming a sex-worker as a trafficked woman and was being forced into, rather than choosing, what she did. Her use of drugs helped her to blank off from what she had to endure. The risks she took enabled her to charge more for her services and the small percentage of this money that she was allowed to keep, she sent home to her daughter keeping a hope alive for the next generation that had died in the context of her own life. When the map was drawn we could all see that these strategies were the only ones that she could muster against the backdrop of this unbearable hardship. The process of mapping turned assumptions and blame on their head – these patterns had not even run their course, they remained functional within the constraints and horrors of this woman's life.*

We would meet any victim blaming by restating CAT theory to support the view that people do things for a reason, and that even stigmatising behaviours would once have had a helpful function. We urge our supervisees to respect survival whatever its cost.

But we have also been anxious to take away the burden of responsibility from these young people by acknowledging that, as newly qualified therapists, they would inevitably be speaking from a 'new' and insecure position. We mapped

Intercultural supervision 119

out the dilemma of '*being silent*' or '*speaking up injudiciously*' (see Figure 8.1), so that they could occupy the middle ground when facing these difficult situations. Aligning themselves with their patients risked taking them out of dialogue with their seniors, and we urged them to be careful while they were establishing themselves within their profession, taking a longer view of their life's work. We

Parental/cultural voices:
- Have some respect for elders
- Don't get on your high horse
- Is this what I am paying for for 5 years?
- If this is how you behave how can you help others?

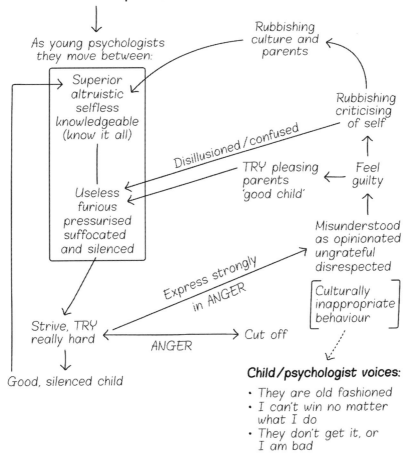

Figure 8.1 Sandwich generation's cultural conflict

expressed a hope that they would continue to embody this empathic understanding of their patients when they reached positions of influence within their organisations and seniority within their profession. In the meantime we consciously urged them to keep dialogue open, rehearsing how to counter victim blaming and modelling how to add one's own, different, voice to these discussions without provoking dismissal.

Upholding human rights

At the heart of the most shocking cases brought to the group were important breaches of human rights, especially to women, that often left us and our supervisees feeling hopeless. But, having lived in India, JE had enough knowledge of the organisations that work with these issues and of the values of human kindness and Dharma to know that, *in extremis,* there are places for women and men to go where they can be safe and protected. We challenge trainees who act as if a person should do *anything* to stay within situations of danger and humiliation when there are safer havens outside. We frame this as a snag whereby conventional values are allowed to sabotage the flourishing, or even sometimes the survival, of a person who wants to make changes. We pull the rug out from under assumptions that abuse is deserved or 'fate' and therefore to be tolerated. Where there are gaps in service provision we urge our students, as and when they reach positions of influence, to become innovators by creating new options that take CAT from a model of individual therapy to a way of thinking about respectful service development and social change. Moreover we remind students that India is a signatory to the United Nations Convention on Human Rights and that this should always be placed above harmful custom and practice.

Concluding remarks

In writing this chapter we have tried to articulate the overarching principles we bring to cross-cultural supervision, that are enshrined in

- CAT's explicit values of respect for patients, collaboration, dialogue and transparency
- Scientific discourse and the bodies of evidence that now exist in relation to early development, punishment of children, the impact of trauma and abuse, neuropsychology, diverse human sexualities, social causes of mental ill health and the association between inequalities at a societal level and distress at an individual level
- International commitments to the welfare of children and adults expressed in human rights declarations and enforcement structures.

Taken together these provided for us, and we hope for our supervisees, a containing ethical and theoretical framework within which the CAT model could be adapted, delivered and supervised. These also provided a safe space within which we could push past the notion that because 'it happens in our culture', it is automatically 'ok' and will never change.

India is a society in a state of flux: change is fast and chaotic. In our supervision we try to validate the personal consequences of this for the self-styled 'sandwich' generation, that present as heightened intergenerational conflict, misunderstandings and stand-offs. We try not to get drawn into colluding from an omnipotent position but to encourage our supervisees to keep dialogues and minds open. We move beyond teaching CAT as a model to thinking more deeply about how culture gets inside people and about the potential for change through dialogue, because it is this generation of young Indians who are going to shape their profession, its infrastructure, discourse and regulation. They are the ones who have the greatest potential to destigmatise mental ill health and to challenge social exclusion.

References

Bakhtin, M.M. (1984) *Problems of Dostoevsky's Poetics*, edited and translated by C. Emerson, Manchester: Manchester University Press.

Bakhtin, M.M. (1986) *Speech Genres and Other Late Essays*, Austin: University of Texas Press.

Burkitt, I. (1991) *Social Selves: Theories of the Social Formation of Personality*, London: Sage.

Emilion, J. (2011) 'Is three a crowd or not? Working with interpreters in CAT', *Reformulation*, 36: 9–12.

Emilion, J. (2016) 'Bilingualism and CAT', *Psychotherapy and Counselling Psychology Reflections Journal*, 1, 1: 47–52.

Frankenberg, R. (1997) *Displacing Whiteness: Essays in Social and Cultural Criticism*, Durham, NC: Duke University Press.

Leiman, M. (1998) 'Words as intersubjective mediators in psychotherapeutic discourse: the presence of hidden voices in patient utterances', in M. Lähteenmäki and H. Dufva (eds) *Dialogues on Bakhtin: Interdisciplinary Readings*, University of Jyväskylä.

Msebele, N. and Brown, H. (2011) 'Racism in the consulting room: Myth or reality?', *Psychoanalytic Review*, 54, 4: 451–492.

Ryde, J. (2009) *On Being White in the Helping Professions*, London: Jessica Kingsley.

Ryle, A. (1995) *Cognitive Analytic Therapy: Developments in Theory and Practice*, Chichester: Wiley.

Sullivan, S. (2006) *Revealing Whiteness: The Unconscious Habits of Racial Privilege*, Indiana: Indiana University Press.

Section 3

Methods and tools of supervision

Chapter 9

CAT group supervision
The social model in action

Jane Blunden and Hilary Beard

CAT was originally developed as an individual therapy and continues to be delivered most often in that format. However, from the earliest days of CAT the preference has been to provide supervision within a group setting. Anthony Ryle explained his preference:

> There are many advantages in the group format, both in terms of learning from the work of others and because the authority of the supervisor is more likely to be challenged. Different previous trainings, cultural perspectives and life experiences among the supervisees enrich discussions and benefit all, including the supervisor.
>
> (Ryle and Kerr 2002: 129)

This chapter will enlarge on that premise, drawing on CAT theory, group analytic theory and practice and the authors' supervisory experience.

Foulkes, the originator of group analysis, characterised group analysis as 'a form of psychotherapy by the group, of the group, including its conductor' (Foulkes 1975: 3). This links well with the Ryle quote above and could be paraphrased, so that we could describe CAT group supervision as 'a form of supervision by the group, of the group, including its supervisor.'

CAT theory and clinical practice are founded on a social and dialogical understanding of human development and distress. The self exists as an amalgam or sum of many parts, which cohere with variable degrees of integration to shape a unique individual. The many parts that contribute derive from lived relationships across the life span with early primary relationships having more impact. These relationships in turn are vessels for the transmission of cultural meanings and forms of expression that derive not only from the explicit culture into which the individual is born, but also from the family and transgenerational cultural patterns that reside in all participants in each significant relationship. Thus in any dialogical exchange the conversation is not just between distinct people but also reflects multiple cultural histories and meanings. These are the 'mosaics or communities of different voices' described by Stiles (1997: 169).

It therefore seems consistent with CAT theory and practice that the usual medium for CAT supervision is that of a group. This places the rich dialogue between multiple voices at the centre of the CAT supervisory process. Supervisees may have diverse professional and cultural backgrounds, be at different life stages with varying experience of life events, and will have their own internalised reciprocal role repertoire derived from their personal history. It is the supervisor's primary task to harness this diversity in the service of the patient and in the service of the supervisee's development as a CAT therapist. A further layer of cultural meaning is supplied by the values inherent in the CAT community and in the organisational context in which the therapeutic work is carried out, for example, NHS or private practice. To harness these multiple cultural and dialogical voices in supervision it is necessary to engender a respect for diversity and to value each person's contribution regardless of seniority or other symbols of status.

CAT supervision is not individual supervision with listening companions. It is co-supervision with each supervisee being able to move in and out of a supervisory role in relation to other members, whilst being steered, contained, facilitated, confronted and sometimes led in this process by the designated supervisor. This process of 'supervisor-led co-supervision' offers a rich potential for experimentation, play, discovery, challenge and general broadening and deepening of each supervisee's reciprocal role repertoire in the service of the therapeutic encounter with their patients. It also offers potential for the presented patient's difficulties to reverberate within and between different group members, therefore offering additional therapeutic insight to facilitate the supervisee's understanding of the patient and the clinical work.

Some helpful concepts from group analysis

Dynamic administration

The CAT supervisor who runs a supervision group is, in group analytic terms, the conductor of that group. As such she is responsible for growing the group, and for maintaining the conditions which encourage all members of the group, including the supervisor, to develop. The creation of a safe enough space in which to work, and maintaining it over time, is called 'dynamic administration' by group analysts (Barnes et al. 1999, Behr and Hearst 2005). The term 'dynamic administration' captures both the practical tasks involved, such as ensuring a regular, reliable room in which to meet and the attention that needs to go on contracting (formally or informally), ethical concerns and boundaries, but also keeping in mind the psychodynamic nuances of the tasks and responsibilities of being the group conductor. It is the latter point that distinguishes 'dynamic administration' from simply 'administration', and to an observer the difference can be subtle. Keeping in mind the various stages supervisees have reached with each of their patients is an element of dynamic administration which quickly becomes second nature to the developing CAT supervisor though is never easy. Other important tasks include time-keeping, managing entries and exits by group members, including deciding who joins the group and when. This is not an exhaustive list but gives some idea of the scope of what is meant by the term 'dynamic administration'.

Group dynamics

The CAT supervisor who conducts a supervision group will find it helpful to be aware of common group dynamics. 'Group dynamics' is a massive and multi-faceted topic, and cannot be covered in detail here. However, there are some ideas that can be simplified from group analysis and other sources which may be helpful to bear in mind while supervising.

It can be useful to think about the group dynamics at play at any particular moment by using two different perspectives and holding them in mind in parallel. One perspective is to consider the developmental stage of the group, and the other is to think about the relative balance between the forces of similarity and difference between group members.

The development of the supervision group

A simple metaphor is to compare the supervision group's development to that of a human individual: to begin with, group members are very dependent on the supervisor and rely on the supervisor to guide them in what to do, to feed them, and they look up to the supervisor as an authority. As they progress further, they often go through an adolescent-like phase of challenging the authority of the supervisor and placing more value on finding their place of belonging amongst their peers while also trying to define their own individuality. Finally, they might end up in an adult to adult relationship with the supervisor and their peers in the group, at which point the relationships are those of mutually nurturing, trusted colleagues. These phases of group development have been famously described as 'forming, storming, norming and performing' (Tuckman 1965) and usefully expanded upon by Proctor (2008).

Foulkes (1984) talked about a multiplicity of dimensions present within a group, including what he called the manifest level and the primary level. The manifest level refers to what actually goes on, 'adult contemporary reality'. The primary level consists of the processes that are predominantly unconscious, referring to primitive, infantile and primordial behaviours. Applying Foulkes' ideas to a supervision group, at the beginning of its development the group projects onto the supervisor the position of a primordial leader – someone who is omniscient and omnipotent and from whom the group expects magical help. The job of the supervisor is to accept this god-like projection, while resisting the temptation to take it personally (that is, to believe it) or exploit it for her own needs, and to use it initially in the service of building up the integrative, constructive and supportive processes within the group. As time goes on, the supervisor's task is to encourage the group to bring the supervisor down from that god-like pedestal and to recognise and use their own authority in the service of the group, rather than relying on the authority they originally projected into the supervisor alone. Thus, as the group develops over time, the supervisor aims for a crescendo on the manifest level of integrating processes accompanying a decrescendo on the primary level of the authority of the supervisor.

Similarity and difference within the group

This perspective relies on keeping in mind the twin concepts of similarity and difference. When people come together in groups, they consciously and unconsciously compare themselves with other group members along these two dimensions, and this is an ongoing process. When people find similarities between themselves and others, this can be comforting especially at the beginning of a group when anxiety about meeting is high. So searching for and finding similarities is often a mechanism that builds group cohesion and feelings of safety. 'Cohesion has been defined as the sum of all forces that keep members of a group together and consists of a feeling of belonging to the group, that single members feel accepted and that they are participating in something important' (Lorentzen 2014: 48). If, however, there is nothing but similarity the group can begin to feel stagnant and even boring and overdependent, eventually cloying, smothering and fused (Ettin 1999). This is not usually a problem though, because differences amongst members inevitably exist and become apparent early on. These might lead to differences of opinion and even arguments, but also offer opportunities to learn from others and discover things as yet unknown or a new perspective on something otherwise taken for granted.

There seem to be inherent assumptions that people bring into groups; that similarities with other members equate to liking and being liked whereas differences equate to disliking and being rejected. The more experience one has in groups however, the more one is aware that difference does not necessarily end up in dislike and rejection but can often lead to the opposite (Nitsun 1996). Battles can be fought and worked through, often with protagonists coming closer together in their views and their respect for each other growing in the process. Thus differences can either be an anti-cohesive force in a group (as often initially feared) or a cohesive force which ultimately builds a stronger, more resilient and more self-confident group. The overall effect is anti-cohesive if there is too much difference and people feel misunderstood, embattled and alienated – they will then either leave the group or may dig themselves into an entrenched position, where it is difficult to reach them and difficult for them to reach out to others.

Most groups come together and have enough of a balance between members' similarities and differences that the overall effect over time is one of cohesion and belonging rather than of alienation and dissolution. Usually, but not always, themes of finding similarities dominate in the earlier stages of a group when members are new to each other and want to find comfort in each other. As group members become more confident in the group setting, they feel more able to reveal their own differences and to engage with those of others. An ebb and flow between seeking similarity and noticing difference continues throughout the lifetime of a group. It can be helpful for the supervisor to ask themselves from time to time what the relative balance is between the seeking and expression of similarity and difference in their group and, if there is an imbalance one way or the other, to nudge the group in a balancing direction.

A balance in the diversity of the membership of a CAT supervision group is helpful. A CAT group consisting of one professional group or derived from one stage of CAT training may offer less diversity than a group of mixed professional backgrounds and at different stages of training. A more varied group can also generate more creativity and may stop inadvertent collusive avoidance of particular areas for exploration. For example, a CBT trained supervisee can offer valuable ideas to a dynamically trained supervisee who is working with a patient with symptoms of obsessive compulsive disorder, and this second trainee may in turn offer insights about countertransference experiences, while their third colleague may offer skills in using imagery and metaphor to help access disallowed feelings. Supervisees can offer rich insights and increase awareness of issues of difference and cultural diversity through sharing their own experience and knowledge of these crucial issues. Many heads and hearts are better than one!

In this way the CAT value of respectful collaboration is engendered and supported within the CAT supervision group and hopefully is equally maintained in the therapeutic work with patients.

George, a senior clinical psychologist, was supervising a group of two clinical psychologists and one junior psychiatrist during their first year of CAT practitioner training. The supervisees were on their second or third cases each and were all really enjoying the training. For the last few weeks, George had noticed in himself a feeling of 'going through the motions' and beginning to feel a bit bored. This thought came to the front of his mind as the group talked about one of Julie's cases, which seemed to be going along all right but with nothing much changing; the group was warm and encouraging but also seemed a bit stuck with nothing extra to offer Julie. Julie, one of the psychologists, had written a very empathic and insightful reformulation for her patient, a young mother who had just separated herself from a situation of domestic violence. George paid attention to his own feelings and realised that the group, including him, was stuck in a comfortable bubble of too much similarity – everyone admired and agreed with Julie's reformulation and each group member was in a similar relationship to Julie and to her case. And so George thought about where in the group there might be some difference which he could call on to help the group out of this rut. The first difference that came to mind was that Ella was a psychiatrist and so he said to Ella, 'If you saw this patient in a clinic as a psychiatrist, would you think about her any differently?' Ella looked a bit surprised, but then stopped to think and said that she would ask more about the patient's drinking. This led to an animated discussion in the group, in which alcohol was identified as a possible substitute for the abusing partner in the same procedural loop – initially comforting but then increasingly damaging and difficult to get away from. Julie pursued this tack in her next session, and it turned out to be a fruitful line of enquiry which unstuck the case.

Groups are complex entities, especially if observed in detail, because so many different things are happening simultaneously in each moment and can be thought about from different perspectives and on different levels. The two frameworks offered above, can help a supervisor to think about the developmental stage of a group, or about the individual members within a group, and to begin to find some meaning amongst the apparent chaos.

The Clinical Hexagon

Many models of supervision focus mainly or exclusively on individual supervision. The *Clinical Hexagon,* developed by the group analysts Margaret Smith and Robert Plant (Smith and Plant 2012), differs from other models as it regards the supervision group as a core feature of supervision. It can be used by anyone who is supervising in a group context. The Clinical Hexagon has six sources of supervisory reflection or exploration:

1   The patient or group being presented
2   The therapist who is presenting
3   The supervision group process, which may parallel the therapy
4   The organisational context
5   Dynamic administration
6   The supervisor's self and countertransference

A mature group will move between the six vantage points and over time will internalise the process of doing so. A supervisor can use them to reflect on the group's work as it is happening and to look out for what might be missing or unexpressed. Figure 9.1 is a pictorial representation of the Clinical Hexagon which can be used as an aide memoire.

CAT group supervision 131

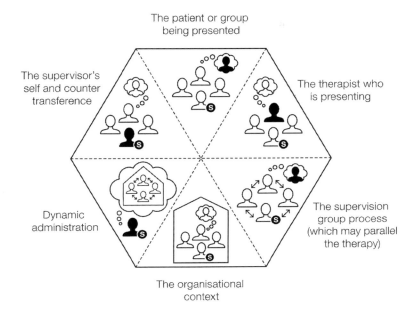

Figure 9.1 The Clinical Hexagon

Key issues in supervisor-led co-supervision

Beginnings, endings and limitation in the supervisory process

Beginnings and endings are of paramount importance in CAT, as a time-limited therapy. Any departure or arrival within the supervision group influences the group dynamics and supervisory process. It is important to give notice of such changes of group membership so that their relational impact in the group can be acknowledged. This includes the supervisor's scheduled absences and any changes of supervisor due to holidays, illness or departure from the supervisory role. It is worth remembering that each supervision session has a beginning. It can be helpful to start each supervision group with a brief personal 'check in' concerning supervisees' current preoccupations and mood, in this way inviting members' individuality to be present as well as their professional selves. This also alerts the group to any prevailing preoccupations among its members which may influence the supervisory group process. This includes the supervisor sharing major concerns which are directly relevant and helpful to the ongoing group process.

Lateness, early arrivals and absences in the supervision group can all become means through which supervisees express their relationship with the group, with change, and with loss. Such issues have added impact when witnessed by several others in a supervision group and can profoundly affect and change the supervisory dynamics. Attention to this impact in the supervision process equips the supervisee to become equally alert to these issues in the therapeutic work.

Ending is a crucial time in supervision as in therapy. Much is written about establishing the supervisory alliance whilst less attention is paid to the importance of ending the supervisory relationship. Endings may involve experiences of sadness and loss of the companionship and support gained in the group, or separation anxiety derived from 'going it alone' or regret and anger about unfinished or disappointed expectations, or relief, joy and other celebratory feelings derived from a sense of achievement and completion of a supervisory process. Suitable sensitivity and humility are required to puncture therapeutic omnipotence and enable acceptance of what is possible from the perspective of both supervisee and supervisor.

Just as goodbye letters are exchanged to mark the ending of CAT therapy, suitable rituals can be put in place within the supervision group to mark departures from the group. These may include experiential exercises which safely offer a chance to give feedback and say goodbye. For example, each member can be invited to comment on one attribute they appreciate in the group/individual members and convey one wish for their ongoing development as clinicians. Alternatively there are the ordinary rituals such as tea and cake!

Holding the tension between knowing and not knowing

The supervisor needs to carefully balance when to intervene and when to wait (Dalal 1995) and to be alert to opportunities to invite one supervisee to contribute to another, e.g. someone who has completed a prose reformulation sharing their experience with someone approaching this task for the first time.

If CAT clinical knowledge is voiced mostly by the supervisor then this will encourage a more didactic, dependent, '*knowing*' to '*not knowing*' reciprocal role in the supervisees. If knowledge is elicited from all, there is more potential for the supervisee's self-confidence and security to grow and for a '*partially knowing*' to '*more bearably uncertain*' reciprocal role to be experienced. This means the supervisor only intervenes when necessary and facilitates the supervisee's own discoveries. This mirrors the hoped-for transition in therapy as the patient moves from dependency and investment in their therapist towards a steady withdrawal and increased recognition of the relational patterns behind their distress.

It is useful to discern when it is necessary to assume a more directive role as a CAT supervisor. Times when this might be more appropriate include the following: at times of change in group membership, when there is conflict in the group that is causing unhelpful group dynamics, when a crisis occurs in the clinical work or in the supervisee's professional or personal life that impacts on their clinical work, when a supervisee is unable to assume appropriate clinical, ethical or professional responsibilities, or when an anxious or less stable supervision group needs containment. This attention to both process and structure within the supervisory group reflects the need to balance both these dynamics within the CAT therapeutic work with patients.

Institutional practices

The impingement of institutional-based policies concerning such things as risk recording and evaluative questionnaires can potentially foreclose detailed clinical exploration of the patient's lived experiences in supervision and stifle the reflective, playful space in the supervisory encounter. The opposite dynamic may be to create an illusion that such institutional demands can be avoided. This creates a false dilemma between obedient over-conformity and covert rebellion, or avoidance. These tensions are exacerbated in group supervision and can manifest strongly in several different ways. One pole of the dilemma/conflict can 'infect' the whole group, with the opposite pole being relegated to the 'others' outside the group, or alternatively the group members play out the conflict in the group between different group members. Both these examples can be seen as an avoidance of personally holding the tensions as an individual. It is important to explore how these tensions affect and pull supervisees into particular reciprocal roles.

Releasing stuckness in the supervisory dynamic

The concept of reciprocal roles in CAT theory offers a powerful instrument through which CAT supervisors can reflect upon the prevailing role positions that each supervisee inhabits and how these role positions are evoked inwardly in the supervisee's own internal dialogue and interpersonally between all members of the group including the supervisor. An important theme to identify through personal reflection is whether a particular reciprocal role in the supervision group is becoming stuck with one person. For example, one member may be struggling to learn the model and may feel isolated in the group in this respect. This can foster a misplaced belief that only this person struggles with theory, while other members inadvertently feel complacent, locating their own inexperience and struggle in one person rather than expressing this directly. The supervisor needs to identify and carefully name this stuckness as being within all members and invite each to take their own share and release it from dwelling in one person. These dynamics are present in any group encounter with varying intensity, and need not become focused within one supervisee who struggles seemingly alone.

During the life of the group each member will feel varying degrees of being central and respected in the group or marginalised and disregarded. This may be a countertransference reaction to a particular patient being discussed in the group. It may represent a particular current issue in a supervisee's personal and professional life. It also reflects a normal, if uncomfortable, existential conflict between the wish to belong and feel part of a kinship group whilst also wishing to differentiate and express individuality.

Where difficult group relationships are significantly impeding the supervisory process the supervisor can sometimes use a CAT contextual diagram to summarise the impasse, drawing the supervisees into the process of generating this diagram. In this way a reflective space is jointly created, just as it is in therapy. Once the map is established then the group can think about how to address this impasse and what other reciprocal roles need to be fostered to move onwards. It is important that the focus is on freeing up the reflective supervisory process and not on a particular individual. Supervision is not a substitute for personal psychotherapy although inevitably personal issues will be present.

For example: one member of the supervisory group was in a stable work setting which had remained unaffected by institutional reorganisation. The other members had had to apply for their own jobs in the context of significant cuts to services. The supervisor noticed a marked increase in criticism and impatience about the clinical material brought by the supervisee who was not facing reorganisation, and this supervisee's attendance and punctuality became less consistent. Concurrently there seemed to be a preoccupation with issues of power, powerlessness and injustice within the material discussed in supervision. With the group members' agreement to explore this development, it became possible to acknowledge the discomfort of both parties and link this to similar issues in their patients' experiences. Attendance improved and the supportive atmosphere of the group felt more robust.

Size and frequency of supervision

The size and frequency of CAT supervision groups vary according to need and circumstance. However, the most common format is that used for CAT training, which is a group of three supervisees and one supervisor meeting for 90 minutes every week to discuss two patients per supervisee. Size and frequency is also guided by ACAT codes of ethics and practice and UKCP guidelines for training.

CAT supervision groups need to meet regularly and have consistent membership over time. Weekly meetings work best for inexperienced therapists, while fortnightly meetings work well in later professional practice. Longer intervals make the group less effective as the group process is diluted. It becomes harder for group members to trust or engage, the memory of supervisees' patients fades and the clinical material becomes less 'alive'. Additionally supervisees can store up too much and expect too much from infrequent supervisory meetings and can feel frustrated and deprived of reflective space. Similarly inconsistent membership results in the group becoming an insecure container for the intimate clinical discussions that are an essential part of the supervision process.

Time distribution in supervision groups

The way time is distributed in the supervision group is crucial. This can feel like a pressure, particularly for new supervisors, as time in supervision, as in therapy, is limited. Attention needs to be given to each member. Too much attention, too little, peer rivalry, perceptions of favouritism and competitiveness for space or avoiding taking space are all relational processes which need awareness and self-reflection by the supervisor before being discussed within the supervision group. Supervisors vary in how they manage these tensions. Some supervisors divide time up into equal parts for each supervisee. Others invite supervisees to check in with their priorities at the beginning of each group and arrange time accordingly. Generally supervisees need more time when beginning and ending with patients, when sharing drafts of prose reformulations, diagrams and goodbye letters and at times of clinical crisis. A mature established CAT supervision group will usually be open to jointly managing these issues, whilst a less experienced supervision group may seek authority and clear boundaries from the supervisor. The supervisor can accept this role, or step away from it and work with the issues as a group responsibility.

Managing clinical appraisals

The supervisor often carries a responsibility to a training course and this may well involve an evaluation of the supervisee's clinical skills, for example, completing a clinical appraisal for a CAT Practitioner Training. Some CAT supervisors perform these evaluations within the supervision group sessions. This can facilitate group cohesion and offer diverse views in a joint peer- and supervisor-led evaluation process. Some CAT supervisors meet individual supervisees outside the group and complete these evaluations in a one to one setting. This can be helpful if a supervisee is less experienced, or if complex personal or training issues need to be discussed. It may be less helpful for a supervisee who resists the supervisory process; here a group evaluation may be more appropriate. If individual evaluation is used it can still be helpful to share some aspects of the evaluation, with both parties' consent, with group members. The choice is ultimately one of preference for the supervisor, and probably transgenerational transmission plays a part – so that supervisors tend to do what their own training supervisor did. However, there may be circumstances that indicate one choice may be preferable. Before instituting a culture, it is helpful to think through some problematic scenarios. For example, how would an appraisal be undertaken with a supervisee who is making much slower progress than their peers; or a trainee who appears to engender negative reactions; or who disregards advice or clear direction from the supervisor and the group? Consideration of which method to use will need to take into account the supervisee's and supervisor's personal resilience and vulnerability and the level of trust and support within the group. This will vary across the life of the supervision group.

CAT culture and values

CAT supervision groups also fulfil an important task as the 'culture carriers' of the CAT community, carrying the model's values and history. Whilst other aspects of the CAT community such as the formal training courses, conferences and professional development events also fulfil this task, perhaps supervision is one of the most consistent culture carriers across a professional career. The distinct relational/dialogical focus which CAT emphasises is possibly counter to the prevailing culture in psychological services, mental health services and in talking treatments, which at the time of writing seems to emphasise symptom resolution, model adherence, manualisation, targets etc. If CAT is to sustain its respect for diversity, collaborative endeavour, relational complexity and social history then its values and attitudes need fostering, transmitting and replenishing across the generations of CAT supervisees. The supervision group can offer this possibility as different generations meet to explore and support each other in their clinical work.

References

Barnes, B., Ernst, S. and Hyde, K. (1999) *An Introduction to Groupwork: A Group-analytic Perspective*, Basingstoke: Palgrave Macmillan.
Behr, H. and Hearst, L. (2005) *Group-analytic Psychotherapy: A Meeting of Minds*, London: Wiley.
Dalal, F. (1995) 'Conductor interventions: To "Do" or to "Be"?', *Group Analysis*, 28: 379–393.
Ettin, M.F. (1999) *Foundations and Applications of Group Psychotherapy*, London: Jessica Kingsley.
Foulkes, S.H. (1975) *Group Analytic Psychotherapy: Method and Principles*, London: Gordon and Breach (reprinted 1986 London: Karnac).
Foulkes, S.H. (1984) *Therapeutic Group Analysis*, London: Maresfield Reprints.
Lorentzen, S. (2014) *Group Analytic Psychotherapy: Working with Affective, Anxiety and Personality Disorders*, Hove: Routledge.
Nitsun, M. (1996) *The Anti-Group: Destructive Forces in the Group and Their Creative Potential*, London: Routledge.
Proctor, B. (2008) *Group Supervision: A Guide to Creative Practice*, London: Sage.
Ryle, A. and Kerr, I.B. (2002) *Introducing Cognitive Analytic Therapy: Principles and Practice*, Chichester: John Wiley.
Smith, M. and Plant, R. (2012) 'Group supervision: Moving in a new range of experience', *The Psychotherapist*, 50: 14–15.
Stiles, W.B. (1997) 'Signs and voices: Joining a conversation in progress', *British Journal of Medical Psychology*, 70: 169–176.
Tuckman, B.W. (1965) 'Developmental sequences in small groups', *Psychological Bulletin*, 63, 6: 384–399.

Chapter 10

Using CAT mapping in relational supervision

Steve Potter

Mapping is a specific CAT method but can also be a general aid to the relational aspects of any therapy. This chapter describes mapping in therapy before looking at mapping in supervision. It covers the supervision of diagrammatic reformulation, mapping therapeutic moments and enactments. The chapter emphasises making maps as a shared therapeutic process as well as maps as a product. What the map is about and how it is made are two sides of the same therapeutic coin. The dynamics of therapy, and their parallels in supervision, can be more accurately described and negotiated with a map. What happens relationally in this way in supervision, can then happen more easily in therapy.

What is mapping?

Mapping at the beginning of therapy may involve simple sketches of several key patterns of interaction between self and others. Over the first four or five sessions, the process of reformulation results in a carefully reworked therapy map which lays out an understanding of the client's problematic patterns. Such diagrams serve as therapeutic maps that can shape, contain and guide a therapeutic journey. They can become a focal tool and reference point for the client and therapist during therapy – and, for the client, beyond the end of therapy. The making and shared ownership of such a map by client and therapist is one of the central concerns of supervision. With a map the therapist, client and supervisor can hold in mind several parts to a conversation and make links across several stories, between past and present and inner and outer realities. A map can link the bigger picture and small details of life experience and also link symbolic thought processes with actions and behaviours.

Mapping as a process, whether in therapy or supervision, is like working together with a sand-tray. It is a shared activity in a creative and uncharted space. Words are mulled over. 'Thinking' words might be replaced by 'feeling' words. Language which is too intense, might be softened, or vice versa. Words that are too particular to one story might be replaced by a more general phrase that resonates with several stories.

Mapping is a vehicle for establishing and experiencing little by little, a stable, transparent but also creative working alliance. As the map develops through recapping and working across several stories, more high-level reciprocal role procedures of self-criticism, doubt, shame, flight or idealisation become visible.

Mapping aids open enquiry: tolerating and modelling vulnerability and thinking out-loud. It offers tangible evidence that two heads are better than one. It signposts the way to help the client develop for the first time, or recover from earlier healthy times, the capacity to be their own therapist. In the process, client and therapist are fostering the *compassionately noticing* to *kindly understood* reciprocal role as they negotiate the emotional and historical meanings being written on to the map between them. This is sometimes put on the map as an observing eye though this may obscure the reciprocal role at the heart of the observing process.

Mapping involves seeing and touching the spaces between (and the arrows linking) the words for different states and different procedures. This tactile, hands, eyes and ears, process of mapping is as important as the product it produces. The capacity to simultaneously hold in mind several feelings and responses draws upon the dialogic idea (Holquist 1990) that in any moment of therapy there are several processes in play – as in the interactions between plot and characters in a good novel. This poses the question of where to focus whilst also keeping in mind alternative calls on attention. As Bromberg (1998) evocatively argues with his notion of 'standing in the spaces,' the therapist needs to close in on one line of enquiry and stay open at the same time. This challenging therapeutic skill is more easily achieved with a map than without one.

However the extent to which mapping is used will vary with the therapist, the client and the context. The activity of mapping should always be secondary to, or in support of, the interpersonal experience of engaging with feelings, developing a shared reformulation and building an alliance. Mapping and maps, like any element of therapy, can be used inappropriately: to control the direction of therapy, mystify its processes or defend against feelings. Or there are times when the map is no longer an accurate or necessary guide for the therapy. The map occupies one point in a triangle; the other two points of which are the client and therapist. The client and therapist work side by side with the map, but at important times of emotional engagement or of working through loss or conflict, the map may fall into the background as client and therapist meet more face to face. Mapping is always a means to an end and not an end in itself.

Mapping can also be a process where the blank spaces of the paper invite reflection on what is not on the map – because it is outside of awareness, or defended against because it is shameful, dissociated or forbidden. One supervisee described how her client put her hand on the blank space at the bottom of the map and, as if covering it up, said 'I am not ready to go there yet. It is too deep water'. They drew a 'beware deep water' sign over the blank space and in so doing were negotiating the terms of the therapeutic journey. In a time-limited therapy, the path we choose not to take is as important to name as the one we choose to take. A shared map can help negotiate these choices of direction.

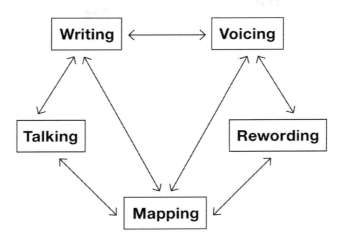

Figure 10.1 Multiple modes of communicating

Mapping can help contain, reveal and explore how we routinely interact simultaneously with all our senses and faculties. Mapping on paper together is an extension of the mental mapping that our brains/minds are evolved to do all the time. We are mental map-makers through our affective neural networks (Panksepp and Biven 2012), through language and memory, through our long evolution (Donald 2001) and through our co-embodied, multi-sensory experience of each other (Malloch and Trevarthen 2010). Therapy offers a space to negotiate the tightness or looseness, the integration or splitting of this multi-layered experience. To get alongside such complexity, we need heuristic tools such as reciprocal roles and maps to help us. As indicated in Figure 10.1 we can be simultaneously talking, writing, voicing and re-wording when we work therapeutically. The map can signpost and facilitate movement between, and therapeutic integration of, these distinctive forms of communication. It can be easier to let the client talk at length, or sit with silence, or share difficult feelings if a map is in the background.

Mapping may start as a literal process of putting pen to paper but it becomes a metaphorical process in which the map of one story, person or stage in life begins to hold and track other stories and more general patterns of life experience. Maps can reveal and track moments of transference between client and therapist, supervisee and supervisor. These can be explored by the often used question in CAT practice 'Where are we on the map?' It enables thinking about patterns of transference which otherwise could be too intensely felt between client and therapist or too automatic a part of the therapist's professional and personal style of working to notice, name and negotiate. In sum, mapping is a very practical and flexible activity that has also played a central part in the development of CAT theory (Ryle and Kerr 2002). While there is no published research on the value of mapping specifically, it has strong face validity among CAT practitioners (and many therapists use mapping in their CAT informed practice). Unpublished data (Potter 2015) shows that mapping as a process is perceived very positively as an aid to holding, guiding, tracking and sharing a therapeutic or reflective conversation.

Tools for mapping

The most obvious tools for mapping are practical common sense: paper and pens, clipboard (A3 size). All maps need dating and initialling with an indication of where made and for what purpose. Mapping offers a containing structure to the therapeutic space and there are advantages to client and therapist sitting at a suitable table in such a way that allows free movement between face-to-face engagement and side by side work with pen and paper.

The key conceptual tool for mapping is the reciprocal role procedure. It depicts a key pattern of interaction in a person's life story that has shaped their personality and identity. It can describe what established and what maintains current problems. In CAT this is called a *target problem procedure*. On a map, the reciprocal role is put in a small box with the words (usually verbs with adverbs e.g. coldly dismissing, lovingly admiring) at the top end of the box describing the initiating action from without or within (often the more powerful, parentally derived one). A downward line links the role to the subjectively felt impact of the action (in terms of feelings or gut reactions) which is written in at the bottom end of the box (e.g. dismissed and unloved, loved and respected).

The procedural part of the reciprocal role procedure is a short sequence of words linked by arrows which depicts the understanding or appraisal in response to the reciprocal role. From this understanding emerge the aims, beliefs or secondary feelings, actions and consequences like a chain reaction. This 'understanding' shapes habitual helpful or harmful behaviours, and interactions with self and others. It is usually outside of conscious attention and the most important reciprocal role procedures may have been internalised before language. These procedures are sequential and weave back into one end or another of the original reciprocal role or to another reciprocal role. They orchestrate the mix of several complementary or contrasting reciprocal roles which mapping can explore therapeutically as shaping a story, a system or the structure of personality and identity. This often complex orchestration is more easily seen on a map, though some of the sequences of feelings produced can be more richly explored through the compassionate voicing of prose description.

The shared process of mapping out the reciprocal role procedures is done tentatively and openly with the client. The addition or revision of words on the map can be rich therapeutic moments of increased awareness, connection with hidden feelings and memories of past ways of relating and responding. The aim of mapping is to achieve a shared, accurate description of the client's changing orchestration of their reciprocal role procedures with self and others in the world, whilst simultaneously nurturing a more kindly, self-conscious reflective capacity.

Mapping in supervision

There are many uses of mapping in supervision. For the beginner in CAT, the supervisor may show how to map a moment or recast the supervisee's narrative description of a client in diagrammatic form. In the earliest stages of a therapy initial sketches of patterns can be brought to supervision as a prompt to case discussion. Subsequently, the skills and concepts involved in developing a complete reformulation diagram (known as an SDR) can be supervised step by step. The process of making maps in therapy has a parallel process of reviewing them in supervision.

The most common mapping activity in supervision is for the supervisee to bring a draft map from working with their client and use it to explain and explore their understanding. Supervisees may bring a single reciprocal role, and want help to connect with it. The slow and open-minded remapping in supervision of one reciprocal role can allow access to the emotions that until then have only been understood cognitively. Solo mapping for self-reflection after a session and before supervision can also be helpful for this.

The supervisor needs to see any mapping work currently being done by the supervisee with a client. The purpose and context of the mapping needs to be known. Has it been done with the client? Or is it for self-reflection afterwards? Has it been done as last minute preparation for supervision or laboured over? It is helpful for supervisees to bring photocopies of the map which they have done with the client, so that it can be modified in supervision without interfering with the original. All parties to the supervision group need to sit so that they can see, interact with and touch the map. It is tempting for supervisees to restrict their discussion to the story told by the map, but it is an equally important task of supervision to enquire how the map was made and whether any enactments arose in the process. Throughout, the supervisor can guide the supervisee in thinking about the accuracy of the map and also its utility, legibility, simplicity and appropriateness for the client.

Mapping out reciprocal role procedures in supervision can help supervisees to notice blind spots and access transference and countertransference.

(See Figure 10.2) John brought an example to supervision of his client Bill who, when seeing his word bullying (of his father to him) out on paper, wanted the reciprocal to be soldiering on. In supervision John thought this bypassed Bill's core pain of hurt. As the map developed, the single-worded reciprocal role of bullying to bullied opened up into one of criticising and bullying to bullied and bad. Bill lived a life of simultaneously switching role positions of being bullied, bullying himself and soldiering on under the weight of seeing himself as criticised and bad. He called the map his yo-yo map. John when sitting with Bill in the therapy felt strong feelings of hurt, but for Bill the hurt only meant more bullying and he had no conscious dialogue with it. In supervision John said he felt reluctant to push Bill to name and touch these painful feelings of

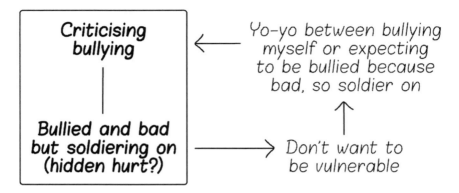

Figure 10.2 Opening up the 'yo-yo' map

hurt for fear of being in the bullying and criticising role, even though, or especially because, Bill seemed to be inviting him to have a go and bully him into feeling something. Working through the push and pull of these feelings with the map in supervision gave John confidence to use the map in therapy to name his bullying dilemma. It was something he and Bill needed to name and negotiate between them in order for Bill to explore his disavowed feelings of hurt. As they worked with these feelings, the reciprocal role of hurting to hurt got added to the map as a fully voiced position and they separated out the bullying to bullied reciprocal roles from the criticising to criticised reciprocal roles, thus ending up with three distinctive but interacting reciprocal roles. This created enough emotional space on the map and in the room to get beyond the 'yo-yo,' enabling them to integrate past hurt and fear of hurting into the therapy.

Supervision of diagrammatic reformulation

There is no fixed sequence in how supervision of the development of the therapy map (SDR) (see page 40 and page 90 for examples of full diagrams) will progress but typically it involves the following elements:

- The supervisee will bring some initial sketches done with the client: a procedural sequence that details a problematic pattern of living, a dilemma of switching between two contrasting reciprocal roles, or a single reciprocal role procedure which holds both an earlier and current interpersonal story and its internal enactment.
- The supervisor, with the aid of the supervision group, will be responding to the emerging map's clarity and coherence and its capacity to bring the therapy alive.

Using CAT mapping 143

- The supervisor needs to keep in mind that the map is partly for the client but partly to hold and guide therapy. It should help the therapist as much as the client.
- The reformulation diagram goes hand-in-hand with a written description of problems and patterns, and supervision will discuss what works best in writing, or on a map or by being voiced.
- No therapy map is ever complete but by session four, five or six it should be complete enough to become a key therapy tool that can survive the 'fridge door or back pocket' test of being kept by the client somewhere for easy access and for regular use in monitoring change.
- A typical reformulation diagram, once fully developed will have three or four reciprocal roles and key word summaries of the patterns that bind them or segregate them.

When supervisees are daunted by the prospect of drawing a full reformulation diagram it can be helpful to build up to it week-by-week in supervision, with one or more reciprocal role procedures being joined together through a cycle of discussion in the supervision group, testing in the therapy room and then further revision in supervision. Learning to map in this way seems to take a year or so of small group or individual supervision alongside formal training.

Mapping the dance not the dancer

It is a useful catchphrase to speak of *'mapping the dance and not the dancer'*. This means talking of a pattern of reciprocation as something that could belong to, or be joined by, any or all of the parties to the therapeutic enterprise: the client, therapist or supervising group, or the supporting cast of family, friends and, not least, health service staff.

> (See Figure 10.3) *Sally tells the supervision group that her client, Bob, was insistent on seeing his words 'cutting up' at the centre of the therapy map. The words 'cutting up' evoked the client's feelings of muted rage about two painful losses: when his father died suddenly when he was a child and when his wife left him some years into their marriage. 'Cutting up' had a reciprocal role named by the client and therapist as being and feeling 'in pieces'. The supervision group looked at these words on the paper of the map and one co-supervisee spontaneously said they felt harsh. The supervision group felt they also described an attitude to himself, as in: 'I cut myself up and put myself now in pieces'. But it was a pattern to which he felt desensitised. 'It is the way it is,' Bob said to Sally. From supervision, Sally took the idea of helping Bob to stand apart from this painful relationship which was so much part of him. In therapy a new reciprocal role of 'noticing' in relation to 'noticed' (softly, more kindly and without blame) was added alongside the cutting up. As these words went on the map, Bob winced, noticing for the first time the harshness of the words towards himself and feeling touched by the presence of the soft words on the*

144   Steve Potter

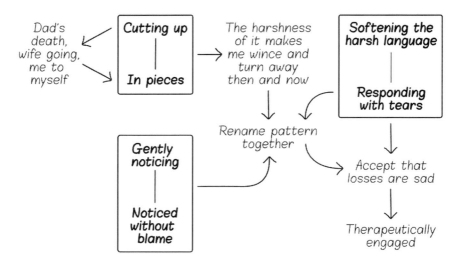

Figure 10.3 Softer words in supervision reach the therapy

> map and, by implication, the soft or caring intent of the therapist. Sally and
> Bob wondered whether to add 'wincing' to the map. The very act of wondering
> whether to add 'wincing' to the map brought the painful emotion a little more
> into the room. Sally said, pointing to the cutting up words on the map, 'We don't
> have to do this dance'. Bob hesitated and responded in a surprising way with
> a direct question, 'You mean we are doing this dance?' Sally had the voices of
> her supervision group at the back of her mind. 'Take the dance away from the
> dancer.' 'Name the dance without blaming the dancer.' This gentle work with
> the map was the means to safe expression of long-forbidden hurt and tears,
> during which Bob said: 'It is I who does this dance.' This emotional expression
> and agency were discouraged at the time of his childhood bereavement and
> denied and self-restricted during his divorce. Bob now had an exit procedure
> and could cast an 'accepting' eye on himself, seeing the losses and allowing
> the sadness as well as making a step towards connecting with forbidden anger.

This process of reworking a map in supervision offers a way of both engaging without being too immersed and standing back without being too detached (Bromberg 1998, Safran 2000). It is a gentle art of finding more open spaces where mixed feelings can be tolerated and reflective capacity can develop.

Mapping enactments

A common focus of mapping live in supervision is the dynamic of a particular enactment. This may occur at any stage of the therapy. It may be an early enactment affecting the development of the therapy alliance, an enactment in the middle of therapy to do with the struggle to help or resist change or an enactment at the end of therapy associated with attachment to the therapist and earlier losses. Enactments that threaten the therapeutic alliance are often missed by therapists (Safran 2000) and mapping them in supervision not only helps regain the flow of therapy in any model but can also teach more general relational competencies. The more or less 'one-third' rule is helpful here (Potter 2014). This encourages shared responsibility for transference and countertransference, and sees enactments as coming in part from the client, in part from the system or context and in part from the therapist. The proportions will always vary – the one third phrase is just a peg to hang discussions on. Maps can help the therapist and client to 'wonder how we are creating this' and offer a better starting point for a therapeutic discussion than the potentially accusatory 'I wonder what you are doing'.

Enactments explored through the map are likely to be more visible, more negotiable and less intensely enacted interpersonally. A primary task of any relational supervision is to help the therapist narrow the gap between noticing an enactment in the therapy room and negotiating some form of resolution of it. Mapping in supervision, whether reworking an existing map or creating a new one, allows a space for hovering over the push and pull of transference and countertransference feelings.

Maps in therapy and maps in supervision are themselves magnets for enactments. There is the uncanny experience of finding the role being mapped is also being enacted in the moment of mapping it. This can be helpful.

Mapping the moment in supervision

It may be useful to map the immediate interactions of supervision along the lines of wondering 'How are we doing just now?' Such mapping needs to start as the micro-mapping of a moment, for example, the classic problem of an apologetic and self-denigrating therapist who is critical of her own emerging competencies, and uses phrases such as 'I know this is a terrible map', as she begins to share it. The supervisor can suggest, 'Could we just map that moment between us?' The triangular relationship in that moment between therapist, supervisor and the map makes support and challenge easier to negotiate. There is a world of difference between a supervisor saying to the supervisee: 'I think you have got this wrong' and saying of the map: 'This sequence from here to there doesn't seem helpful.' Again the map gives scope to naming the dance more than the dancer. This reflective process can be enriched by co-supervisees simultaneously mapping the same moment (see below). For example, one co-supervisee may pick up on the longing of the supervisee to fix things, the other on the supervisee's self-critical voice about feeling helpless. With both positions on paper between them as fleeting sketches of the supervisory moment they can help hold these differences delicately in mind.

Cheryl Delisser, CAT psychotherapist and supervisor, describes mapping two moments simultaneously in supervision – a moment in the therapy session being presented by a supervisee and a moment in the supervisory relationship:

> Mapping plays a key part in my work as a supervisor. It helps supervisees become more fully immersed in the model and become more open, honest and self-reflective. It increases the relational focus of the therapy. A key use of maps in supervision is 'mapping the moment' (Potter 2010).
>
> Time and time again my supervisees and I are taken aback by how much we can learn about a client, their methods of coping and their relationship with the therapist/supervisee, through spontaneously mapping one very specific moment in a therapy session. Encouraging the other supervisees in a group to simultaneously map the moment occurring between supervisor and supervisee can pick up parallel processes offering further insight into the therapeutic relationship. Supervisees say how mapping a moment has enabled them to think and work more relationally. It has brought the concept of using transference and countertransference, and therefore reciprocal roles, to life. It also increases the likelihood that the supervisee and client will mark their therapy relationship on the client's map, enabling them to think about it in a safe and open way.

Mapping the supervisor's style

One part of CAT supervisor training involves a paired exercise of mapping each other's style of supervision. The same exercise can also be used in supervision to build supervisees' reflectiveness and confidence in mapping and to foster an open, playful, respectful, trusting supervisory alliance. Cheryl Delisser describes doing this with new supervisees:

> I use a reflective exercise called 'Mapping my CAT style' as an introduction to mapping in supervision. I encourage new supervisees to put words spread out on paper in response to my description of my style of supervising. We then look together at what the supervisees have mapped out. I encourage each of them to ask me questions which might help develop the map. Whilst they are mapping my supervisor style with me, they are feeling, at the same time, a lively involvement in the process of meeting me and each other. A key element of this exercise is to demonstrate touching the paper and asking questions such as 'How do you think you get from here (touch) to here (touch)?' This curious and non-judgemental enquiry demonstrates the fluidity of the mapping process. Supervisees are then usually able to establish at least one of their own patterns of relating in supervision and to begin thinking about their response to that pattern. We discuss how this may affect them as supervisees and look at any potential exits to hold in mind during supervision. I usually share how this pattern can play out for me in my therapy sessions.

We repeat the mapping of the style of being in supervision in turn for each supervisee. We take care to go at an appropriate pace which is not too exposing.

The benefits of mapping supervision style are:

- *Modelling that the supervisor has 'flaws' allows supervisees to feel safe enough to share openly and honestly without fear of judgement or criticism*
- *Showing how an initial 'messy map' can be good enough in making sense of things*
- *Demonstrating the value of putting words on paper from the initial contact*
- *Reducing anxiety and increasing confidence in the ability to map.*

It highlights how our relational styles go with us. As supervisees note their 'style' of relating in supervision, therapy, professional and personal life they are able to share this, as appropriate, during the course of supervision. It increases our combined capacity for self-reflection (helping supervisees to consider: 'What am I bringing to this therapy relationship?' and 'How are my procedures being enacted in the therapy relationship?').

Conclusion

Mapping is a rich aspect of CAT and potentially has uses across models and modalities. Relational supervision can be enhanced by mapping, whether the focus of therapy is psychoanalytic, dialogic, interpersonal, cognitive or eclectic. Mapping might be compared to mindfulness as an addition to therapeutic practice. Like mindfulness, mapping cannot just be an approach that is added on to therapy, but must be a sustained practice that the therapist takes to heart at the core of his or her relational work.

This chapter has highlighted how supervision can be the containing space and training ground for the technical and conceptual skills of map making and the therapeutic process of mapping. Ryle (1997), in reference to Vygotsky's view that what children do with the care and guidance of an adult today they will do on their own tomorrow, adds that, what the parent or carer does not do today, the child will not do tomorrow. Similarly, what is not done in supervision today will not be done in the therapy room tomorrow.

References

Bromberg, P. (1998) *Standing in the Spaces*, New York: Psychology Press.
Donald, M. (2001) *A Mind So Rare*, New York: Norton.
Holquist, M. (1990) *Dialogism*, London: Routledge.
Malloch, S. and Trevarthen, C. (2010) *Communicative Musicality*, Oxford: Oxford University Press.

Panksepp, J. and Biven, L. (2012) *The Archaeology of Mind, Neuroevolutionary Origins of Human Emotions*, New York: WW Norton and Company.

Potter, S. (2010) 'Words with arrows – The benefits of mapping whilst talking', *Reformulation*, Summer, 34: 37–45.

Potter, S. (2014) 'The helper's dance list', in J. Lloyd and P. Clayton (eds) *Cognitive Analytic Therapy for People with Intellectual Disabilities and Their Carers*, London: Jessica Kingsley.

Potter, S. (2015) *Talkability Test*, Unpublished research report.

Ryle, A. (1997) *Cognitive Analytic Therapy and Borderline Personality Disorder*, Chichester: Wiley.

Ryle, A. and Kerr, I. (2002) *Introduction to Cognitive Analytic Therapy*, Chichester: Wiley.

Safran, J. (2000) *Negotiating the Therapeutic Alliance*, New York: Guilford Press.

Chapter 11

Integration of competency assessment into CAT supervision
A practical guide

Stephen Kellett and Dawn Bennett

Introduction

The aim of this chapter is to provide a guide to both supervisors and supervisees on how to effectively integrate competency assessment into supervision in a way that maintains relational awareness and, crucially, improves the skilfulness of the therapy delivered. As CAT was designed for the public sector, patients, carers and commissioners deserve to know that the time/money invested enables the delivery of a safe, trusted and skilful psychotherapy. The tool with which supervisees and supervisors can achieve this is the Competence in Cognitive Analytic Therapy measure (CCAT) (Bennett and Parry 2004b). The aims of the chapter are (a) to understand the importance of competency assessment, (b) to explain what competency measures actually measure, (c) to describe the CAT competency tool, (d) to detail how competency assessment can be used effectively in supervision (and identify the rupture markers for ineffective usage), and finally (e) to provide an account of the supervisee experience of competency assessment.

During competency assessment, the supervisor needs to retain relational curiosity and awareness at all times. The supervisor therefore adopts a position of an 'observing eye' on the process of the supervision and is constantly inquisitive about how competency assessment is experienced by the supervisee (and so seeks regular feedback from the supervisee). CAT theory is useful here in terms of anticipating or describing the reciprocal roles and procedural sequences that may occur. This helps to ensure that competency assessment enhances (rather than inhibits) the supervision experience. Supervisors need to be willing to work collaboratively and diagrammatically with supervisees, whilst also courageously naming and exploring supervisory reciprocal role enactments. The supervisor needs to adopt a straddling position during supervision of having one foot in the supervisory alliance and one foot in CAT theory. Supervisors' beliefs about competency assessment are important – if supervisors assume that it is too exposing an activity, they can potentially collude with never hearing actual examples of supervisees' work, or if they believe it is too difficult to integrate usefully into supervision, the CCAT remains a remote tool used for research purposes only.

Tyrer (2013) described CAT as a 'humanised and skilled' psychotherapy and therefore formal assessment of the degree of skilfulness displayed is appropriate.

It is reasonable to assume that a certain level of competency in the delivery of CAT in routine practice is necessary to achieve results consistent with CAT trial evidence. This argument is similar to the 'threshold theory of IQ' (Karwowski and Gralewski 2013), in that an individual only needs to be intelligent enough in order to pursue a chosen career, and then their ultimate success is dictated by their ability to work effectively with people and systems. In terms of a threshold theory of CAT competency, the therapist needs to be competent enough, before being creative in their use of the model. The cart cannot be put before the horse. In terms of each of the items of the CCAT, the supervisee will have a zone of proximal development (ZPD). What is useful about the CCAT is that the zone of competence can be quantitatively and qualitatively named – and then subsequently scaffolded.

Competency versus effectiveness

CCAT assessment is explicitly concerned with *delivery* of CAT and so is distinct from the assessment of the *outcome* or *effectiveness* of the therapy. Such is some patients' resilience and/or desire to change, that they can use therapy, although the therapist may be delivering it incompetently. At other times, a therapist may be delivering competent CAT, but the patient cannot make use of it and so outcomes atrophy. Use of the CCAT particularly helps to decide whether adverse events (or poor outcomes) during CAT are the result of inadequate delivery, rather than poor model selection or inappropriate treatment.

Adherence versus competency

Controlled trials of psychotherapies demonstrate treatment *adherence* in order to verify that an intervention has been delivered. Competency alternatively refers to the *quality* of the therapist's interactions and interventions with the patient (Shaw and Dobson 1988). Competency demands practical wisdom in exercising consistent CAT judgement, reliant on the peculiarity of the session and the individuality of the patient. Adherence neglects this notion of skilfulness, as it concerns whether an intervention was delivered, not how well it was done. Over-adherence can be associated with negative outcome, regardless of model of therapy (Castonguay et al. 1996). The CAT evidence base provides examples of competency assessment of CAT therapists delivering the model consistently during the treatment of patients with borderline personality disorder in both routine practice settings and randomised controlled trials (Chanen et al. 2008, Clarke et al. 2013, Kellett et al. 2013).

Why competency?

1 The notion of auditing the *intervention competence* of therapists represents a key ethical practice issue.

2   During training it enables courses to evidence that CAT trainees are learning and mastering the skills being taught.
3   As a CPD activity, competency assessment can be a method of enabling and structuring self-reflection.
4   Like practitioners of any craft, CAT therapists want to maintain high standards for both themselves and their patients.

Competence in Cognitive Analytic Therapy (CCAT): Measure description and implications for the supervisory relationship

The CCAT was developed and validated by Bennett and Parry (2004a). It contains 10 domains of competency; each rated from 0 (incompetent), 1 (unsatisfactory), 2 (satisfactory), 3 (good) to 4 (very competent). This produces a score range of 0–40 with a score of 20 used as a cut-off as 'satisfactory' (i.e. competent) CAT. The CCAT has adequate inter-rater reliability, high internal consistency and concurrent validity (Bennett and Parry 2004a). Table 11.1 describes the CAT competency ratings with associated supervisee descriptors.

Competency is likely to be in a constant state of flux and renewal regardless of the experience of the therapist. When gaps in competencies are identified using the CCAT, supervisors support supervisees in their development, choosing the most suitable method out of a possible range, including teaching, modelling, directing

Table 11.1 Competency and supervision markers

CCAT competence descriptor	Session and supervision markers
Incompetent (novice)	Rule-governed during the session, poor understanding of the model overall and gives little coherent sense of the patient during supervision. Heavily dependent on supervisor to provide direction. Low relationality.
Unsatisfactory	Therapy remains deliberative, but some grasp of the model. Some actions can be taken independently of supervision. More able to discriminate appropriate relational actions at a higher level.
Satisfactory	The organisation of sessions and associated relational actions are taken appropriately to ensure responsivity. Presents patients during supervision in a distilled manner and treats patients according to their needs. Model internalised.
Good	Actions in sessions driven by intuition rather than rule, and modified in an on-going manner. Increased responsivity. Use of supervision to reflect. Model flexibly applied.
Very competent (expert)	Model is fluidly present in all interactions, without conscious choice of action. True relationality evident. Able to critically evaluate intuition. Able to play in supervision.

supervisees to relevant literature, encouraging self-assessment by the supervisee and role play of specific CAT approaches (e.g. rupture repair sequences).

CCAT domains with associated implications for supervisory practice

1. *Phase-specific therapeutic tasks:* (1a) concerns competencies related to early sessions and includes the therapist engaging the client in identifying areas for work, raising hope, establishing the client's motivation and commitment and establishing therapeutic roles. (1b) concerns competencies relating to middle or late sessions and includes reviewing progress, engagement and the value of the work.

    Supervision implications: Is the supervisee's work being sampled across the CAT phases of early, middle and late stages? Does the supervisory work tend to over-focus on certain phases and/or collude with avoiding assessment of other phases? Is the supervisee aware of the necessary CAT phase-specific tasks and able to reflect on these? And if not, why that might be?

2. *Theory-practice links:* Concerns the therapist's application of theory to practice, including the use of the CAT model to plan/structure the work and to make sense of the client's material.

    Supervision implications: To what extent is the supervisee noticing and taking opportunities to use the CAT model to plan/structure sessions and conceptualise the patient's experience of the therapy? Simply, is CAT theory guiding this work? Can the supervisor use the CAT model to plan/structure supervision sessions and use theory to conceptualise the dynamics in the supervisory relationship?

3. *CAT-specific tools and techniques*: 3a is specific to the early reformulatory sessions, and includes the therapist's skill in identifying target problems, procedures and reciprocal roles, developing and sharing CAT tools. Section 3b is specific to sessions after reformulation, and includes the therapist's use of CAT tools to recognise and revise procedures within and outside sessions.

    Supervision implications: How can the supervisor facilitate the supervisee's understanding and application of reformulation, recognition and revision skills?

4. *External framework:* Competencies in establishing and maintaining the boundaries of the therapy and therapeutic relationship.

    Supervision implications: How effectively does the supervisee establish and maintain a containing frame for the therapy and observe boundaries in the therapeutic relationship? Does the supervisor establish the containing frame for the supervision and observe the boundaries and roles of the supervisor-supervisee relationship? Are there parallel processes in the supervisory relationship that mirror the therapeutic relationship in terms of boundary violations or enmeshment?

5 *Common factors:* Concerns basic common factors and includes support and attentiveness to the client's readiness for the work.

   Supervision implications: Are the common factors present in the therapy? Does the supervisor establish and maintain a relationship with the supervisee that includes warmth, supportiveness and attentiveness to the challenges of completing the work and continued personal development?

6 *Respect, collaboration and mutuality:* Concerns establishing a mutual, collaborative, respectful and authentic therapeutic relationship.

   Supervision implications: Is mutuality evident in the therapeutic relationship and in how the CAT tools are developed and shared? Is it a co-production? Does reflecting together in supervision feel an authentic, joint learning encounter and reflect a genuine shared purpose and sense of teamwork?

7 *Assimilation of warded off emotions and problematic states:* Competencies including the therapist's capacity to experience, stay with and tolerate painful affect and to facilitate assimilation and integration of these experiences.

   Supervision implications: Does the supervisor encourage, contain, conceptualise and assimilate the supervisee's experience both of the clinical work and also the supervisory process?

8 *Making links and hypotheses:* Concerns the therapist's ability to offer links and hypotheses about the client's past and other relationships including the therapy relationship, in an appropriate and timely way.

   Supervision implications: Can the supervisor enable the supervisee to see their relational ZPD both within and across their therapeutic relationships, so that they can become more aware of unhelpful procedures with clients (such as steering away from painful affect, not naming what is occurring in the therapeutic relationship, not introducing ending work early enough etc.)? Can the supervisor help the supervisee to see any parallel processes between the position they find themselves in with the patient and the position they find themselves in during supervision (e.g. fear of criticism)?

9 *Identifying and managing threats to the therapeutic alliance:* Competencies in identifying and managing in-session reciprocal role enactments that represent obstacles and/or threats to the alliance but also opportunities.

> *Supervision implications*: Can the supervisee use the model so that they are alive to identifying, and then exploring reciprocal role enactments within supervision, that represent threats to the supervisee's learning/development, pose a threat to the supervisory alliance or are an important opportunity for gaining awareness?

10 *Awareness and management of own reactions/emotions:* Concerns the therapist's ability to appropriately reflect, express and manage their own feelings and reactions.

> *Supervision implications:* Can the supervisor and supervisee reflect on and manage their emotional state during supervision and in reaction to the supervisory relationship and then use this information to inform the process of the supervision?

Getting started

The use of the CCAT in supervision can be discussed when agreeing the supervision contract (in which the expectations and responsibilities of supervisor and supervisee are clearly named). Before using the CCAT, it may be helpful to use recordings of sessions in supervision in a more unstructured manner, to help the supervisee become acquainted with their own relational approach and, crucially, with receiving feedback on live material. It is important to move on quickly to using CCAT, so that the measure does not become a looming spectre.

It is useful for supervisors to acknowledge and normalise that competency assessment can raise anxieties but, in keeping with effective exposure, this anxiety can reduce over time. The supervisor should make sessions of their own available for rating initially, in order to model both delivery of 'good enough' CAT and general openness. Supervisors can initially practise using the CCAT on their own sessions. The supervisor should state their explicit intent of helping a supervisee to improve the skilfulness of their CAT work and to shift from a potentially unhelpful criticised/humiliated/crushed position in supervision, to one in which they can tolerate, and become interested in, their struggles both during sessions and with the model. The CCAT should not be introduced reverentially as a 'special' tool in the supervision, but rather just another method that will be used and integrated alongside case discussion and other experiential methods. There should be an understanding that not all sessions will reach 20 on the CCAT and that such a level of competency consistency would be highly unusual.

As CAT supervision is normally conducted in a 1:3 supervisor: supervisee ratio in a 90 minute per week group, it is useful to have a rota for presenting live material. The supervisee presenting the live material can have 60 of the 90 minutes and this occurs every three weeks. This person can usefully prepare the recording by listening to it beforehand and bringing a focused excerpt, with an attendant question or reflection. This ensures that the supervisee is not passively presenting the material, but is interested in a specific aspect of their ongoing development that has been previously identified via the CCAT. The supervisee can ask for an excerpt to be listened to and scored on a specific CCAT item.

It is important in supervision groups that all supervisees rate each other and that rating is not the sole role of the supervisor. The importance of peer feedback and the manner in which this is done is a matter for the supervision contract. Supervisees can therefore actively participate, contribute and scaffold each others' development through the CCAT. Using the measure allows increased awareness of the competencies as a frame for skill development. The CCAT can be used creatively in supervision, for example, a supervisee, aware of a performance issue, stops the recording at the relevant point and the supervisor listens to it, then models how they would do it differently or asks the supervisee to role play doing it differently.

CCAT rating guide

The purpose of this section is to enable the CCAT be used consistently and fairly:

1 *Identifying presence or absence of competency*

Raters (whether supervisors or supervisees) need to decide, on reviewing the session, whether each element of CAT competence was present or absent in the session. If the competency was present, raters needs to decide how skilfully it was demonstrated. If the competency was not present, then the rater needs to consider whether this was a crucial omission. The CCAT acknowledges that it is sometimes inappropriate for a particular competence to be apparent, due to the phase of therapy the session is sampled from (i.e. the context of the session in the timeline of the therapy). For example, if the therapist is engaging the patient in mapping a procedural sequence during the reformulation phase, it is too early to rate ability to create change (CCAT 3.12). The way the patient presents in the session is also considered; it may be difficult for the supervisee to demonstrate the competence (e.g. a recent negative life event overshadowing the session). There may be occasions when supervisee should have demonstrated a competency and did not; this creates a key supervision opportunity.

2 *Rate each therapist interaction on all applicable CCAT items*

If rating a whole session, raters work through the measure, reading each item in a domain, and then ask themselves, 'Did I hear an example of that competency? Was it appropriately done?' etc. Raters need to recognise when competencies are demonstrated; yes or no and, if yes, how well was it practised across the examples heard? If there was no example of a particular competency in a session, why was this?

Any single statement by a therapist may also be pertinent to several CCAT items. Raters should therefore carefully consider what they have heard in the session and code their observations on all CCAT items that apply.

3   *Use the CCAT during rating*

All supervisees need to read the measure, so that they are aware of what is being asked of them. The CCAT provides item definitions, scoring guidelines and specific examples to promote accurate rating. Because of the complexity of the CCAT items, it is essential that raters are well acquainted with specific item definitions before rating them and regularly refer to the CCAT when rating a session. If raters feel unsure about how to rate what the therapist has said, raters should stop the recording and refer to the measure in order to identify the best-matched item descriptors. Throughout this process, raters are exercising clinical judgment about often very subtle differences between items.

4   *Reviewing the session*

Raters should listen to the entire session before making final ratings. When listening, it can be useful to tally when an item has occurred and write associated notes. Tallying and note-taking can improve rating accuracy, by keeping raters focused on what actually occurred in the session and providing them with information critical for making final ratings on all the items.

5   *Rating items by circling whole numbers*

Although raters may feel drawn to give a score between whole numbers (e.g. 4.5), only whole numbers are acceptable CCAT scores.

6   *Protecting confidentiality*

All recordings and rating scores are confidential material. Raters need to listen or watch recordings and rate sessions in a place where no other person can hear the sessions. They should treat recordings like private medical records and not leave materials unattended nor discuss the content of sessions in any other context than supervision and supervision of supervision.

CCAT selection and methodological issues

There are many varied methodological issues relating to competency measurement during CAT.

First is the source of the clinical material used for ratings, which could range from audiotapes and video footage to transcripts of therapy conversations. Supervisors should encourage use of video footage during supervision as this makes it easier to consider the dynamics between supervisee and patient (e.g. are the therapist and client sitting shoulder to shoulder, with both parties having and using a pen, or is the therapist mapping in relational isolation in the room?).

Second, whether to rate parts of sessions or whole sessions? The CCAT is designed for use with whole sessions and, if scoring a therapist's performance on the measure, the rater needs to hear a whole session, in order to judge the therapist's use of 'timing' in therapy, e.g. therapists may hold back on interventions but use them later in the session. It is useful to rate one full session from each therapy a trainee therapist completes. However, part sessions, either selected or randomly chosen, can be used for training or self-reflection. In using the measure in supervision, supervisees should be encouraged to prepare part sessions for supervision, by bringing a question related to the CAT competency measure for that section of the session (e.g. ability to identify target problem procedures), and by self-rating prior to supervision on specific items.

Third, the stage of therapy? Supervisors need to be mindful of the need to sample the work of their supervisees across treatment contracts and not collude with supervisees in over-assessing single phases. Assessing competency across the duration of any single therapy will highlight relative strengths and weaknesses, e.g. regarding skilfulness of reformulating (narrative and diagrammatic), helping patients to notice their key roles and procedures that maintain their distress (recognition phase) and also the effective application of change methods in the revision stage. Competency assessment of the later stages of CAT is particularly useful, as there may be a tendency to reformulate endlessly (e.g. adding to or tinkering with the SDR) or to approach change in a piecemeal manner (e.g. simply writing an exit that the therapist suggests on the SDR).

Fourth, general versus model specific items? If the supervisee is choosing items for rating in supervision, is there a spread over the supervision sessions of common/general psychotherapeutic competencies (e.g. engagement and empathic abilities) and technical CAT specific competencies (e.g. ability to analyse reciprocal role enactments within the therapeutic relationship)?

Fifth, supervisors need to be aware of a 'halo or horns' effect in which they rate all items in a similarly positive or negative manner for an individual supervisee (Blackburn et al. 2001). The accurate assessment of competency in CAT does arrive at a composite score, but effective supervision will be based more on a 'graphic equaliser' metaphor, i.e. on what the supervisee is doing well (or possibly overdoing) on specific items and what is being neglected and needs attention on others.

Sixth, supervisors need to be aware of their own CCAT bias. If they are particularly (perhaps overly) concerned with CCAT items tapping common factors (CCAT items 5 and 6) and the supervisee struggles or excels on these items, this may cast a shadow regarding the impartial assessment of other CCAT items.

Seventh, supervisors need to match quantitative and qualitative CCAT feedback. This means that supervisors do not give a low mark on one item and then describe all the useful ways in which the supervisee has skilfully worked with that item in the session (or indeed, vice versa).

Eighth, supervisors need to use the whole of the scale for each item to facilitate accurate competency feedback. A supervisor may want to protect or rescue the supervisee (or avoid a difficult enactment in the supervisory alliance) by always giving the middle (i.e. 'satisfactory') rating on each CCAT item. Use of the whole of each item scale enables supervisees to unambiguously understand where they stand. A rating of 0 or 1 (with attendant qualitative comments) enables a supervisee to know this is an issue, and supervision time is given to problem-solving ways to improve competency. Similarly, if a supervisor is impressed with the degree of skilfulness on a specific item, this should be reflected in associated high scores (and matched associated qualitative comments).

Finally, supervisees do not learn and master one aspect of CAT at a time in a sequential process, but tend to develop competency in a more global fashion. Improvement in one aspect of CAT practice and competency (e.g. theory-practice links) tends to fertilise, and lead to change in, another aspect (e.g. assimilation of warded off states). Through getting a 'baseline assessment' of supervisee competency, the supervisor is then aware of where to target supervisory attention.

Competency assessment: The supervisees' perspective (Fiona Purdie, Ben Hague and Nick Firth, trainee clinical psychologists)

Building an effective relationship with the CCAT relied upon the principles of curiosity, trust and patience. The role of the supervisor was crucial in facilitating a constructive relationship with the CCAT, as was shared commitment to the formation of a robust, open and supportive supervision group. Using these principles, we became able to shift from less helpful performance-driven procedures towards a more constructive development-oriented process. However, some recurring challenges remained as described below.

CCAT as judge and punisher?

Almost anyone who has been in group supervision will be familiar with feelings of performance anxiety, associated with covert or overt comparison and potentially unhelpful competition between group members. Initially we felt uncertain and exposed as we faced the prospect of evaluation, and at times we each privately wondered whether we could 'measure up'. As the group formed, the CCAT and supervisor had the unspoken potential to align in enacting the role of judge and enforcer, as we (supervisees) fell into anxiously striving, competitive or pleasing roles. Feelings of insecurity and lack of safety risked stifling group reflection and honest feedback. At times this led to avoidance of the CCAT and growing uncertainty. The reciprocal roles and procedures associated with the CCAT as a potentially unhelpful tool during supervision are summarised in Figure 11.1.

The contracted time at the end of each group supervision session to reflect on group processes gave us the opportunity to connect with, and be open about, our reciprocal roles and procedures and how the evaluative process elicited them. As anxieties were explicit and shared, greater cohesion

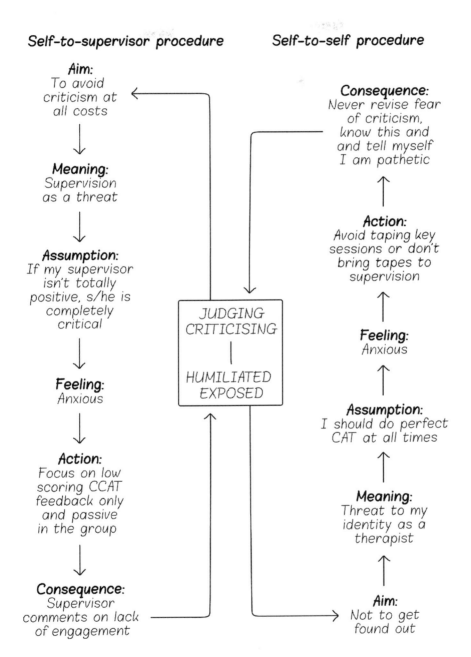

Figure 11.1 SDR of rupture-inducing competency assessment

developed. The supervisor helped us to exit unhelpful roles and procedures through modelling 'good enough' supervision, and paying consistent, balanced attention to individual strengths, weaknesses and associated learning needs. These processes fostered a secure but challenging environment.

The 'shackling' to 'fettered' CCAT

A related challenge was how to use the CCAT to support development without feeling that it was invasive or constraining. Frequent anxieties regarding best use of our time made the CCAT feel critical and constraining, with supervisees falling into a shackled role. This role often resulted in a dilemma, where we perceived that the CCAT could either be used each meeting, in full, to dogmatically assess competency OR we must avoid it, to allow time for other pressing clinical issues. The supervisor helped facilitate the group's awareness of the dilemma, and encouraged us to neither avoid nor feel constrained by the CCAT, but to use it flexibly.

We found it particularly beneficial to bring specific domains of the CCAT to a supervision session for attention, based on identified development goals. This made sense in the context of group supervision, in which it was not usually feasible to listen to a whole taped session (a segment of 5 to 10 minutes per supervisee was common). Full session recordings were submitted for full CCAT ratings outside supervision. It was important to ensure that we did not collude in avoiding certain areas of competency development. The supervisor's balance between focusing on specific domains requested by the supervisee and responding flexibly to additional competency development needs arising within the material aided this.

The 'scaffolding' to 'nurtured' CCAT

As the group became a more established, safe, containing space, we were more able to tolerate and engage with the CCAT. Through understanding our individual CCAT strengths and areas for development, our learning (within our personal zones of proximal development) became more effective. Subsequently, we used the CCAT similarly in some ways to the use of a diagram (SDR) in therapy. Domains of the CCAT were attended to like procedures were with clients. We recognised recurring domains in recordings as areas for development. We formulated, tested and role-played exits in supervision, put them into clinical practice, and reviewed them in later sessions. The supervisor played a role in encouraging a focus on a limited number of important domains, and prompting supervisees to revisit and practise a given domain on multiple occasions. This avoided the danger of shallow and vague learning across all domains without consolidation, helped to scaffold success with exits and provided a model for future independent development after the supervision group ended. The potential positive reciprocal roles and associated procedural sequences are summarised in Figure 11.2.

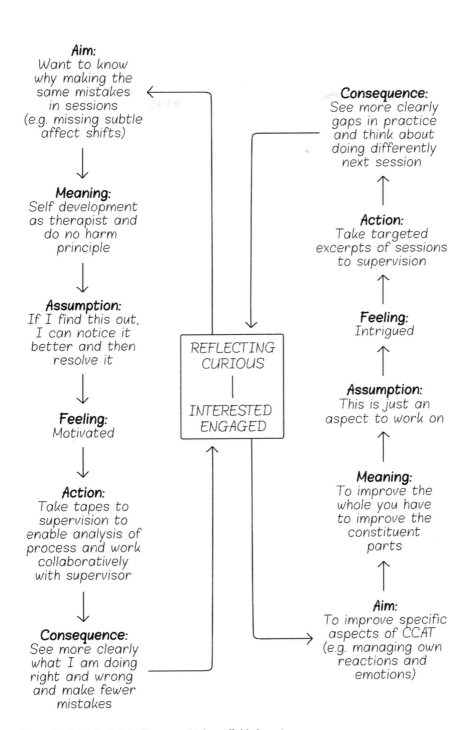

Figure 11.2 SDR of CCAT usage which scaffolds learning

> In therapy, we become familiar with the stories of the people we work with and see their roles, strengths and struggles. So too, within the supervision group, we learnt each others' stories, noticed strengths and also developmental targets using the CCAT. We recognised that rather than using the CCAT as a stick to beat ourselves with, it was best used as a tool to facilitate relational awareness and associated competency development.

Conclusions

Although competency ratings can be difficult to make, they appear useful in the supervision, training and continued (post-training) learning of the CAT model. For the CCAT to grow in widespread acceptance in the CAT community as a useful supervision tool (equal and complementary to other supervision methods), supervisors need to accept its value in documenting replicable observations of supervisees' theoretical grasp and associated relationality within and across sessions and cases. This chapter has hopefully illustrated that it is possible to do this in a manner which is both relationally informed during supervision and supportive of supervisees' personal and professional development.

References

Bennett, D. and Parry, G. (2004a) 'A measure of psychotherapeutic competence derived from cognitive analytic therapy', *Psychotherapy Research*, 14: 176–192.

Bennett, D. and Parry, G. (2004b) *A Measure of Cognitive Analytic Therapy Competence – CCAT*. Online. Available HTTP: <http://www.acat.me.uk/document_download.php/30> (accessed 2 November 2015).

Blackburn, I.M., James, I.M., Milne, D.L., Baker, C., Standart, S., Garland, A. and Reichelt, F.K. (2001) 'The revised cognitive therapy scale (CTS-R): Psychometric qualities', *Behavioural and Cognitive Psychotherapy*, 29: 431–446.

Castonguay, L.G., Goldfried, M.R., Wiser, S., Raue, P.J. and Hayes, A.M. (1996) 'Predicting the effect of cognitive therapy for depression: A study of unique and common factors', *Journal of Consulting and Clinical Psychology*, 64: 497–504.

Chanen, A.M., Jackson, H.J., McCutcheon, L.K., Jovev, M., Dudgeon, P., Yuen, H.P., Germano, D., Nistico, H., McDougall, E., Weinstein, C., Clarkson, V. and McGorry, P.D. (2008) 'Early intervention for adolescents with borderline personality disorder using cognitive analytic therapy: Randomised controlled trial', *British Journal of Psychiatry*, 193: 477–484.

Clarke, S., Thomas, P. and James, K. (2013) 'Cognitive analytic therapy for personality disorder: Randomised controlled trial', *British Journal of Psychiatry*, 202: 129–134.

Karwowski, M. and Gralewski, J. (2013) 'Threshold hypothesis: Fact or artifact?', *Thinking Skills and Creativity*, 8: 25–33.

Kellett, S., Bennett, D., Ryle, T. and Thake, A. (2013) 'Cognitive analytic therapy for borderline personality disorder: Therapist competence and therapeutic effectiveness in routine practice', *Clinical Psychology and Psychotherapy*, 20: 216–225.

Shaw, B.F. and Dobson, K.S. (1988) 'Competence judgements in the training and evaluation of psychotherapists', *Journal of Consulting and Clinical Psychology*, 58: 668–672.

Tyrer, P. (2013) 'From the editor's desk', *British Journal of Psychiatry*, 202: 162.

Chapter 12

The value of mindfulness in CAT supervision

Elizabeth Wilde McCormick

> A contemplative approach to therapy differs from conventional psychological work in that it is more concerned with presence of being – revealed through opening directly to experience – than with problem-resolution.
>
> John Welwood (1996: 122)

What is mindfulness?

Mindfulness is a learned process of paying particular attention, moment by moment, to our immediate experience, just as it is, and kindly, without judgement. Bringing the practice of mindfulness into supervision supports supervisees' practice of mindfulness psychotherapy, and also helps deepen therapists' understanding of their patients. This chapter includes examples from my own practice of mindfulness supervision and also pieces written by supervisees about their experience of mindfulness in supervision.

Mindfulness has its roots in Eastern contemplative and spiritual traditions and was first practised over two thousand years ago. It is the heart of Buddhist meditation. The Buddha was a real person trying things out for himself before passing them on. These early experiential roots establish a well-tested way of being with suffering, showing that it is possible to be alongside, rather than dominated and limited by, suffering. Suffering is the business of psychotherapy and its supervision, and refers to being caught up in struggles with life and oneself, and to a mind dominated by emotional reactions and patterns rooted often in the past. Renowned Buddhist nun and teacher Pema Chödrön describes how the investigative aspect of mindfulness helps to begin to melt the frozen ice in oneself in order to discover potential for a more fluid nature; that the fruits of regular mindfulness meditation are a more settled mind where we are more likely to wake up to our natural human warmth and wisdom (talk at Omega retreat, 'The Present Moment', Rheinbeck, New York, USA, May 2015). As we warm up to ourselves, we warm up to others, we develop compassion. With wisdom we are able to see clearly. The energy generated by two or more people sitting together in mindfulness can be enough for insight, even into what have seemed to be intractable problems or symptoms.

Consultant clinical psychologist and CAT therapist and trainer, Rene Bosman writes:

> *For me the ancient and well-developed practice of mindfulness brings with it the potential for a transpersonal connection with others. These real connections carry the universal values of peace, kindness, integrity, equality and shared vulnerability and are therefore value-based rather than evidence-based.*

Christopher Germer, in *Mindfulness and Psychotherapy* (Germer et al. 2005: 9), states: 'Moments of mindfulness have certain common aspects regardless of where they lie on the practice continuum' and he describes these moments as being:

> *Nonconceptual* – mindfulness is awareness without absorption in our thought processes.
> *Present centred* – Mindfulness is always in the present moment. Thoughts about our experience are one step removed from the present moment.
> *Nonjudgmental* – awareness cannot occur freely if we would like our experience to be other than it is.
> *Intentional* – mindfulness always includes an intention to direct attention somewhere.
> *Participant observation* – mindfulness is not detached witnessing, it is experiencing the body and mind more intimately.
> *Nonverbal* – the experience of mindfulness cannot be captured in words, because awareness occurs before words arise in the mind.
> *Exploratory* – mindful awareness is always investigating subtler levels of perception.
> *Liberating* – every moment of mindful awareness provides freedom from conditioned suffering. (Germer in Germer et al. 2005: 9)
>
> (Reprinted with permission from Guilford Press)

My own practice

I have been practising as a supervisor with therapists and psychologists from different backgrounds and trainings, individually and in groups, in hospital, day centre and private practice settings, for over 30 years. For the last 15 years my interest in, and experience of, the practice of mindfulness have grown, and I now describe my work as being that of a mindfulness based cognitive analytic therapist and supervisor. The interface between clinical understanding and contemplative practice is particularly alive in therapeutic work and especially in supervision. In the shared space of supervision clinicians are in deep contemplation on the drama of the emerging journey of the patient with all its attendant complexities, frustrations and joys. I see the tasks of a supervisor as helping therapists find their own style and expression and supporting them during each therapy they undertake. I see the work of supervision as being guided by the supervisee's personal and professional needs and within the stages of their zone of proximal development.

A CAT supervisor uses left and right brain at the same time. This involves setting an example of focussed thinking by helping the supervisee to condense the presented material into reciprocal roles, traps, dilemmas, snags and unstable states, and also helping supervisees to pause mindfully in order to feel into and find words for both core pain and reciprocal role procedures. In this way mindful approaches to supervision help supervisees to get under their patients' presenting problems and embedded story lines and begin the journey of recovery of being, which I see as the primary work of psychotherapy.

Research into mindfulness

There are many research studies into the effects of mindfulness (Baer 2003, Kabat-Zinn 2003, Shapiro et al. 2006). Whilst most researchers emphasise the need for continuing research, there are indications that regular practice has a positive effect on self-regulation and that mindfulness fosters a decentred relationship with experience, 'a stepping away'. Segal et al. (2002: 58), in *Mindfulness-based Cognitive Therapy for Depression*, illustrate that the mode of mind we bring to decentring is crucial – it is not ignoring or dissociating from experience but approaching and welcoming it; it encourages 'opening up' to what is difficult and adopting an attitude of gentleness to all experience. This process helps to develop spaciousness around ways of being and in the space kindness and compassion can emerge and be fostered. This can develop into a process which interrupts learned maladaptive habits, which Shapiro et al. (2006: 377) refer to as 're-perceiving'. We become less controlled by particular emotions and thoughts and more able to develop reflective responses to our emotional experience and to life's stimuli rather than being repetitively reactive.

The research of Wendy Hasenkamp (2014), senior scientific officer at the Mind and Life Institute, examines the neural correlates of attention and mind wandering during meditation. She writes (2014: 4), 'neuroscience – in part because of its engagement with Buddhism – has discovered a previously unknown potential for brain plasticity throughout one's lifespan. Indeed, because neural plasticity is always operative, the brain is continuously being "rewired" based on our experiences. The key is to put some conscious intention into what those experiences are'.

Neuroscientists have also conducted research into mindfulness practice and one of the results (Farb et al. 2012) shows that the insula – the part of our brain that helps to mediate empathy in a real and visceral way – becomes more energised. The longer a person has meditated, the more highly developed is the insula.

The value of regular mindfulness practice

As mindfulness becomes better known and popular in Western imagination and is introduced into different aspects of management and health care approaches, it is at risk of being seen as a sort of 'cure all' or panacea, at worst an 'add on' to therapeutic work, that can be learned in a weekend. But mindfulness is not, strictly speaking, a technique or method, although there are many different techniques and methods for its cultivation (Kabat-Zinn 1990). For mindfulness to become a genuine practice, and thus have its effect, we need to be in true relationship with it, and this relational aspect is at the very heart of CAT theory and practice. A dialogic relationship with mindfulness means that we stop, drop the content of consciousness, and place our attention on whatever we have chosen as our 'object' of mindfulness. This may be the breath, our steps, eating, washing up or a particular word or sound. It may be our engagement with another person, with a difficult body sensation, or a feeling. On Plum Village Retreat at Arnhem, Holland in 2003, Vietnamese Zen master and teacher Thich Nhat Hanh said: 'Mindfulness carries with it the energy of concentration and only when mindfulness is established can we develop the capacity to see things deeply in their own nature because we are so concentrated'.

Segal et al. (2002) write of their experience of initially approaching their research without developing their own mindfulness meditation practice themselves. They soon realised they could not conduct their studies, nor train others, properly without experiencing the practice 'from inside' individually. In order to integrate mindfulness from the Mindfulness Based Stress Reduction (MBSR) training of Jon Kabat-Zinn into their cognitive programme they had to take part in it, to get up every morning and practise for 45 minutes, and it was not easy! But it was out of their individual practice and sharing the fruits of their practice that the coherent integration of mindfulness within the cognitive therapy occurred.

Training in Mindfulness Based Stress Reduction (MBSR) developed by Jon Kabat-Zinn at UMass Medical Centre in the USA was taken up in the UK at the North Wales Centre for Mindfulness at Bangor where I trained as a MBSR teacher. The training guidelines list the attitudinal qualities associated with mindfulness practice. They include: nonjudging; patience; a beginner's mind; trust; nonstriving; acceptance; and letting go.

My personal experience is that I could not practise as a mindfulness based therapist without the nourishment of my own daily practice and also the support of the group with whom I practise weekly. I believe that this is because mindfulness interventions need to arise naturally from the ground in which the energy of mindfulness has been nourished within the individual. There is a vast difference between experiencing something with full mindful attention, and an idea about what this might be. And it is not for everyone! I always check out whether a patient or supervisee is interested in the experience of mindfulness.

Sydney Bayley, a core process psychotherapist writes:

> My training in mindfulness has helped me to deepen into a state of presence, and to bring this awareness into my work. For me, it is a process of embodiment in relationship, of feeling into what is happening in my body from moment to moment so that my attention is both in and out at the same time. Psychotherapy becomes a joint practice, in which I encourage my client to also develop awareness of the body process and how it relates to the content and states of mind that arise, in order to understand the nature of suffering.

Mindfulness and Cognitive Analytic Therapy

The practice of Cognitive Analytic Therapy (CAT) lends itself well to the key components of mindfulness – stopping, and then noticing – over and over again. In noticing what happens, holding thoughts and feelings in awareness without trying to change them at this point, we become close observers of our reactions, and out of our observation arises reflection. CAT's focus on the accurate description of procedural sequences arises from the encouragement to notice, self-monitor and write down what is noticed. Learned patterns become clear, and the resulting spaciousness is a first step to getting nearer to the emotional suffering that maintains these patterns, and eventually to trying something else. Not only does the energy of mindfulness help to connect both therapist and patient to the reality and feeling of reciprocal role procedures, and find the appropriate words to describe them, it may also be applied to the experience of core pain, and can help in forming exits.

Once the reformulation stage has mapped out the chronically endured emotional pain and the procedures that have been developed to cope with this pain, we have the words to describe it and the opening for manageable exits has begun. With mindful attention this pain can be tolerated and new procedures developed. The actual practice of mindfulness itself needs to be developed within the therapeutic relationship and arise within it, using words that evolve from the joint collaboration. What emerges from these mindful experiences can be checked out within supervision, so that supervisor and supervisee experience what it feels like and can design words or exercises that are closely tailored to what the patient may need. The practice can also take the form of an 'exit' such as 'being alongside my feelings of anger with mindfulness', 'breathing into my anxious feelings and breathing out from them', or, 'I place my past suffering within the balm of mindfulness'.

Rene Bosman writes:

> Mindfulness helps me to be more aware and to clarify my own emotions and procedures in relation to the therapy and what the client brings. The ability to distinguish between what may be personal countertransference, and what may be elicited countertransference facilitates a balance. So that there is a constant movement between fully attending to the client and the moment, and reflecting and making sense of relational and emotional concerns underlying

their predicament. For me, mindfulness enhances both intuitive and reflective ability.

In my clinical work with people with a history of trauma I have found it essential to introduce the concept of mindfulness in order to enhance reflective ability and manage emotions, memories and relationships more constructively. Modelling how to do this in a session can be very helpful to the client. For me mindfulness enhances both intuitive and reflective ability. This helps create a meta-perspective which ultimately leads to more freedom to think, choose, act, relate and be.

CAT has an excellent way of naming and understanding how human behaviour can be described in terms of traps, dilemmas, snags, and unstable states of mind. CAT theory allows therapists to offer patients an understanding that, whilst the development of these patterns has helped survival, real freedom comes from the revision of learned patterns that are restricting and unhelpful; that there is the possibility of establishing a wider repertoire of being in the world as well as in relation to ourselves. In CAT practice patients observe the patterns they have developed, monitor them and then experiment with stopping. This means entering the unknown, eventually trying something differently.

We often use the concept of the 'I' that sees me, and many practitioners draw a seeing 'Eye' on the diagram. This action is where the intentional aspect of the practice of mindfulness (Germer 2005, Shapiro 2006) is valuable, for it helps patients to focus on what could be developed within them rather than what has gone before.

Mindfulness can bring kindness and acceptance – qualities often alien to Western minds – to self-observation. Kindness and acceptance can develop into compassion, and add another dimension to the CAT invitation to become observers, which is to become compassionate observers. Changing hard-learned patterns of thinking and reacting is not easy and many patients we see, and we ourselves, can be overly harsh and self-critical. The combination of becoming a compassionate observer and developing clarity of seeing assists with the development of choice about how to respond, creating an exit from the habit of reactivity. Mindfulness helps to develop concentration and focus and the practice helps to discriminate feeling from thought and sensations. The by-product is often a greater sense of calm. The reality of most mindfulness practitioners is that they are always in the process of forgetting and remembering in order to re-establish a stable ground of being.

The practice and value of mindfulness within supervision

Mindful interventions arise within the shared space and joint enterprise and shared language jointly understood. The habit of standing back, noticing, inviting supervisees to feel into their bodies, to notice where a certain word or phrase has touched them and step beneath the word, is a first step.

Embodying mindfulness and modelling it in supervision can filter down into the supervisee's own practice, where a supervisee is helping a client to use mindfulness as a tool for self-awareness and acceptance during the complex process of change. Supervisees may or may not integrate the practice of mindfulness into their work. Sometimes supervisees are able to use just moments of mindful attention that have arisen in their supervision to help support their work with clients. My experience is that when invited, many supervisees find mindfulness a very helpful discipline for both themselves, and for their work.

Kosko (in Sturm et al. 2012: 223) quotes the Zen philosopher Suzuki, who said 'in the beginner's mind there are many possibilities; in the expert's mind there are few'. This describes one of the foundations for mindfulness and is also a useful reminder for supervisors; we are not experts! Sturm et al. conclude their paper with: 'in a truly mindful, respectful, and intentional supervisory relationship, we too are using relationship to nurture the never-ending beginner's mind of wonder, curiosity and openness' (Sturm et al. 2012: 231). They emphasise the way in which the ideas from Buddhist concepts have been passed down orally through generations of teachers in relationship with their students.

Both Sturm et al. (2012) and Safran et al. (2007) comment that mindfulness, as a metacognitive skill, is an important component in psychotherapy training and for supervisees in the early days of their work, when there is more anxiety, and also when there are ruptures in the therapeutic alliance. Safran et al. (2007) write that one of the valuable by-products of mindfulness is the gradual development of a more accepting attitude to internal experience as it arises and is reflected and shared within the supervisory relationship.

The invitation to a short (2–3 minutes) mindfulness practice can be offered as a shared joint activity at the beginning and end of a supervision session, for both group and individual supervision. The invitation comes from the supervisor's own practice. The practice may take the form of just sitting with eyes open or closed, taking three breaths, or focusing on the body in the chair, or the feet on the ground. Different approaches to practice may be developed within the joint activity. Mindfulness practice is usually something that develops over time and with familiarity and regularity of practice. I introduce it as a suggestion – shall we try sitting together for a few moments, with the instruction to concentrate on the breath or the feet on the ground and let the busy mind settle. With new supervisees it may also take the form of 'experiment' or 'shall we try this' and can be maintained, or not, according to its value to the supervisee.

Liz Hall, clinical psychologist and advanced practitioner in sensorimotor psychotherapy, writes:

> *Doing a shared piece of mindfulness at the beginning of a supervision session is really useful for several reasons. It quietens a busy body that has had to make its way to supervision. The invitation 'shall we sit together' invites the supervisee into the relational space. For me this reminds me that I am*

sharing a space with my supervisor rather than having to battle through things on my own.

Rene Bosman also writes about the centring experience of practising mindful attention at the beginning of supervision:

I have found this very helpful in centering myself. It allows me to make the transition between the busy feelings and thoughts of every day and the creation of a calm and reflective space for learning. The fact that both my supervisor and I are engaged in mindfulness enhances rapport and sets the scene well for collaborative focus.

In mindfulness-based supervision our object of mindfulness is the exchange within the relationship between supervisor and supervisee, at the same time as holding in awareness the third person in the room, the patient. The 'clearing a space' for the reflective aspect of mindfulness facilitates several processes. The slowing down and rest generated help clarity of thinking and observing; it also allows both participants to drop down away from thinking and analysing and to connect with what has not been said or expressed, allowing space for the unheard or neglected voices.

Very often, after a period of mindfulness contemplation on a particular aspect of core pain or procedural repetition, clarity about description occurs. Liz Hall writes:

I have found that using mindfulness when a little uncertain what to bring into supervision is really helpful. The invitation is to see what rises to the surface – this might be a client I had not thought of discussing or an issue that has been avoided or buried. Using mindfulness to increase my awareness of my own reactions has helped me look at the various ways I can inhibit or facilitate the therapeutic process. Alongside this is the willingness of the supervisor to share mindfully the feelings evoked in her by the issues brought by me. Again this has revealed what I might have been avoiding! This has included anger, frustration, boredom and at times over-fascination! Doing this in mindfulness with curiosity and without judgement increases the honesty of transaction and prevents it becoming overwhelming.

The benefit of practising mindfulness together in supervision is that it nourishes the quality of the shared space for both supervisee and supervisor. CAT is a very active therapy and CAT supervision can be very busy, especially in groups. Many professionals' minds can be dominated with theory, ideas, concerns, risk assessment procedures and patients' emotional milieu. The shared intention and action of focusing on the breath or the body allows the more pressing thoughts and preoccupations to settle and for other aspects of the work to come forward. It can allow for a sifting process, re-prioritising those things that might have been beneath the surface to arise.

An example of this is, some years ago, working with a supervisee who tensed her left shoulder whilst speaking of one of her clients. I had noticed this in a previous supervision and when it happened two more times decided to ask her about it, and whether she felt OK about being curious about it. She agreed to place her mindful awareness on the feeling in the shoulder in the spirit of curiosity. I invited her to stay with it, just noticing what happened and she reported some movement and tension in her shoulder.

'I feel tearful now', she said after about two minutes of staying with her experience of the shoulder. I asked her to stay with this feeling of tearfulness and notice where she experienced it in her body.

'In my chest here', she said placing her hand on her heart area.

I invited her to stay a bit longer with the feeling and just notice.

'It's as if my heart is very very heavy'.

Then: 'as I just said that I sensed that the heaviness was due to unshed tears, like a dam ready to burst'. We sat with this image and feeling for perhaps one minute. Then she opened her eyes and said: 'I know that some of these tears are mine, I own that and that's good, for I can look at this in my therapy. But with my patient it's really interesting. We've been working away at her procedures of placation and the running away and avoiding contact, and when I've asked her to find what's under this, the core pain from the reciprocal role of dismissing in relation to dismissed, she just laughs and shrugs her shoulders – both of them!! And now this heavy heart has been inviting me to connect'.

I asked her if she could connect now with the heavy heart of her client. What it might be like. She became very quiet 'I've just realised that her father died when she was only seven and I have asked her about what happened at the time her father died but she's always said she doesn't remember. I've been afraid to make too much of it, especially because my own experience is similar and I didn't want to confuse the two. But now I can see that within our relationship it's as if I've been invited to carry some of that unlived grief. Now this is very clear'.

We looked together at how she might continue in mindfulness with the feeling in her chest and shoulder in order to digest it fully and to know clearly which was hers and which she was invited into by her patient and also how she might work with this in the next session.

Mindfulness in supervision offers an opportunity of opening to the relational capacity of the self. Sydney Bayley writes:

Mindfulness-based supervision differs from other supervision practice in so far as the encouragement to be mindful develops and heightens my capacity for being present with the relationships involved, thereby allowing greater and quicker access to subtle, subliminal and unconscious material in the supervision session. What facilitates this for me is the invitation, in the supervision session, to slow down, to feel into the way in which I have experienced

> *the client in my body and to be aware of what comes up as a result of doing this, whether it is a feeling, a thought, an image or a felt sense. Or, my supervisor, being mindful of what is going on in her body, through mindfulness, and letting me know about this, so that we can explore where it resonates with my experience of the client and how it might be useful in understanding their process.'*

Mindful attention can be offered at times when supervisees feel stuck, or feel they are doing a continual dance of reciprocal roles, or feel caught in the 'if I must then I won't' dilemma with clients. Mindfulness as a practice can help both supervisor and supervisee study the energy of the pull of each end of a reciprocal role and the power of transference invitations.

> *Recently during the second half of a supervision session I noticed my body feeling very tense and I remained curious about this whilst we continued our conversation which, was largely my asking questions and my supervisee answering them with more literal interpretations than usual. I also noticed that I had to work very hard not to let my mind run away with distractions. I kept thinking of all the things I had to do in my lunch hour and all that I had not completed before I started work. I could see that my supervisee was sitting hunched forward, leaning toward me earnestly whilst we were discussing the fact that the therapy felt very stuck. We were both trying so hard to understand, to grasp what was underneath the 'if I must, then I won't dilemma' and the continual sabotage in this person's life! After noticing the intensity of my body sensation and distracted thinking, I said, 'it feels as if we are both caught up in the energy of this dilemma, and each time I say "Have you asked about x?" or "What about y?" you say, "I've tried that" somewhat triumphantly before we descend into the reality of frustration and despair. Let's just stop and feel into what is happening, let's just concentrate on the in breath and out breath and clear the space'.*
>
> *We sat with this shared instruction for a few moments. Then she said, 'It's something unbearable'. We sat together with this. Then: 'It's something so tense and restricted that we are skirting around it so as not to actually feel it'.*
>
> *Then she and I touched into the feelings of despair together and the energy softened, we sat back in our chairs. We reflected on this man's life and how it might have been, how he might have felt, trying to put ourselves there through the felt sense of our shared mindfulness, so that my supervisee could take this insight back into her session. In doing so she carried inside her a felt understanding of his suffering and this, although not yet named, helped him to lessen the defensive control around his feeling. He was able to lean back also, and not have the encounter with the therapist so tightly controlled, not have to outwit her at every opportunity, because now there was something they shared, non-verbally, non-threatening, and this was the turning point of their work.*

The contemplative and investigative aspects of mindfulness have a great deal to offer psychotherapy supervision. Within this practice both participants in the supervisory relationship enjoy their 'beginner's mind' together, and thus enable a fresh, open, curious and deeply relational space, in which an insightful and compassionate understanding of both themselves and the patient becomes possible.

References

Baer, R.A. (2003) 'Mindfulness training as a clinical intervention: A conceptual and empirical review', *Clinical Psychology: Science and Practice*, 10, 2: 125–143.

Farb, N.A.S., Segal, Z.V. and Anderson, A.K. (2012) 'Mindfulness meditation training alters cortical representations of interoceptive attention', *Social Cognitive and Affective Neuroscience*, 8, 1: 15–26. Online. Available HTTP: <http://scan.oxfordjournals.org/content/8/1/15.full.pdf+html> (accessed 15 September 2015).

Germer, C.K. (2005) 'Mindfulness: what is it? what does it matter?' in C.K. Germer, R.D. Siegel and P.R. Fulton (eds) *Mindfulness and Psychotherapy*, New York: Guilford.

Germer, C.K. (2009) *The Mindful Path to Self-compassion*, New York: Guilford.

Hasenkamp, W. (2014) 'Brain Karma, is delusion hardwired?', *Tricycle Magazine*, Fall 2014.

Kabat-Zinn, J. (1990) *Full Catastrophe Living*, New York: Delta.

Kabat-Zinn, J. (2003) 'Mindfulness based interventions in context: Past, present and future', *Clinical Psychology: Science and Practice*, 10: 144–156.

Safran, J.D., Muran, J.C., Stevens, C. and Rothman, M. (2007) 'A relational approach to supervision: addressing ruptures in the alliance', in C.A. Falender and E.P. Shafranske (eds) *Casebook for Clinical Supervision: A Competency-based Approach*, Washington, DC: American Psychological Association.

Segal, Z.V., Williams, J.M.G. and Teasdale, J.D. (2002) *Mindfulness-based Cognitive Therapy for Depression*, New York: Guilford.

Shapiro, S., Carlson, L., Astin, J. and Freedman, B. (2006) 'Mechanisms of mindfulness', *Journal of Clinical Psychology*, 62, 3: 337–386.

Sturm, D.E.R., Presbury, J. and Echterling, L. (2012) 'The elements: A model of mindful supervision', *Journal of Creativity in Mental Health*, 7, 3: 222–232.

Welwood, J. (1996) 'Reflection and presence: The dialectic of self-knowledge', *Journal of Transpersonal Psychology*, 28, 2: 107–128.

Chapter 13

The microcosm in CAT supervision

Jason Hepple

Introduction

I realised that when I got down to writing this chapter, I had taken on an idea that is very difficult to define or explain simply. The idea of microcosm has connections to many of the other concepts discussed in this book under the general heading of relational supervision. Particularly, it has affinity to the idea of parallel process discussed in Chapter 1. I do not want to repeat the same discussion here but I do want to offer something different and original by describing the idea of the microcosm; an idea that will add to the experience of supervisor and supervisee.

In a nutshell, the idea of microcosm, in my way of thinking, has within it two components. The first is the idea that a lot of meaning can be condensed into a small occurrence. The second is that these occurrences are replicated dialogically across time (generationally) and through space (systems or contexts). I will cover some of the theoretical sources of this idea, which include Neoplatonic thought, Mikhael Bakhtin's dialogics and the literature around trauma and its effects being communicated trans-generationally. I will then consider how we, as humans, are naturally incredibly intuitive in our dealings with each other and that by finding ways to increase our awareness of all the information available to us in our clinical contexts (words, thoughts, feelings, behaviours, day dreams, non-verbal and somatic experience) we may be able to unpack the microcosm and trace back some of its roots in the client's story. The point of this is to find a creative way to make progress, often when the therapy is 'stuck' or going nowhere useful, which often means uncovering material from the client's story that has been disavowed, neglected or forbidden. It attempts to answer the question: 'What is really going on here?' To help with this process I will offer an exercise or technique that may be useful and also some fictional examples of how the microcosm can be used in supervision: in direct relation to the client's material, in the supervisor's experience of the therapist, in the supervisor's experience of the client through the therapist and finally in the context of a supervision group.

Theoretical considerations

Dialogic complexity

CAT offers a fundamentally dialogic therapy and theory of relational development and psychopathology. In CAT the 'self' is not fixed but defined in relation to others; past, present and future. It is firmly embedded in a social and cultural context. It can never be fully pinned down and is always in the process of dialogic progression; posing a question or providing a response. In dialogic terms the self is 'unfinalisable', meaning that it can never be completely 'consummated' or described as a finished work, but always remains a work in progress. Even when someone is physically dead, for example, it is quite legitimate for an historian to ask: 'Who was Alexander the Great?' A person's self extends before and after the embodied life of the individual and beyond the body and mind of the individual. Consider 'my family', 'my legacy'. This dialogic self draws heavily on the work of Mikhail Bakhtin incorporated into CAT by Mikael Leiman (Leiman 1997). For an introduction to dialogism I would recommend Michael Holquist's book of the same name (Holquist 2002).

This is seemingly complex. To put it simply, the dialogic self has roots deep into the past and is manifest at a point in time in terms of the unique social and cultural context it finds itself in. This idea is incredibly rich but also impossible to reduce or categorise in a fully meaningful way. I was struck, when reading about parallel process, that authors were considering some of the complexity when asking questions like: 'Is this client's material seeking expression by unconscious transmission through the therapist or is this the supervisor's countertransference to the therapist?' It is tempting to try to define a number of sub-types of parallel process etc. but I am unsure if this is very useful as quite quickly the attempt at reduction becomes too simplistic or evolves overlaps and incompatibilities. It is important to realise when dealing with dialogical complexity that the best language for communicating the ideas is that of metaphor, and that an idea may require the use of more than one metaphor. Metaphors do not take themselves too seriously and can sit alongside each other without contradicting each other.

In CAT the core concept of reciprocal roles is a metaphor as are the CAT tools; the reformulation, maps and goodbye letters. They are allowed to co-exist with differences and inconsistencies. I might represent something that is going on in supervision by writing down a reciprocal role. If it is jointly owned by supervisor and therapist in that moment, it is both a metaphor and a sign. It has done its dialogic work and has started something in motion.

To define the idea of the microcosm I will therefore use three metaphors:

> *The Tree* ~ the tree has roots and a direction of growth, it branches and each branch becomes the start of another replication; another miniature tree if you like. The tree represents history, family history and cultural history (time).

The Ripple ~ a stone dropping in the water causes a ripple that extends out in all directions. The ripple represents the effect of an occurrence in a particular time and context (space).

The Onion ~ the onion has many layers. The onion represents the layers of meaning of an occurrence. It is always possible to understand something at a deeper level (depth).

As Mikhail Bakhtin, speaking in 1971, describes:

> The history of each human individual begins a long time before the awakening of his consciousness. . . . In this great experience everything is alive, everything speaks, this experience is essentially and profoundly dialogic.
>
> Mikhail Bakhtin, cited in Pollard (2012: 34)

Microcosm and macrocosm

The idea of microcosm dates back to Neo-Platonic thought. It is the idea that problems are replicated at the scale of the whole universe (the macrocosm) down to the smallest level (the microcosm). Human beings are seen to be right in the middle. It is interesting that black holes are thought to be able to swallow up whole galaxies but also to exist, in miniature, at the quantum level. This idea of replicating patterns can be summed up by the Hermetic expression: 'As above, so below'; the words that were supposedly found in the tomb of the mythical sage-philosopher Hermes Trismegistus (hence 'Hermeticism' and also the expression 'hermetically sealed'). Many writers and poets of the 19th and early 20th century were interested in Hermetic ideas; people like William Blake and T.S. Eliot, for example.

Another figure from the end of the nineteenth century was Madame Blavatsky who is a central figure in the modern day Theosophical Society. In her book *The Secret Doctrine* she writes:

> The Universe is worked and guided from within outwards. As above so it is below, as in heaven so on earth. . . . We see that every external motion, act, gesture, whether voluntary or mechanical, organic or mental, is produced and preceded by internal feeling or emotion, will or volition, and thought or mind.
>
> Madame Blavatsky (1888, Vol.1: 276)

> More than this; that no such form or shape can possibly enter man's consciousness, or evolve in his imagination, which does not exist in prototype, at least as an approximation.
>
> Madame Blavatsky (1888, Vol.1: 282)

Applied to psychology – this could be seen as an early description of a theory of mind and behaviour that relies on the existence of underlying traces, schema or perhaps reciprocal roles; internalised patterns of relating that are enacted and re-enacted in future relationships. It is perhaps saying that, 'there is nothing new under the sun', or in CAT terms that a reciprocal role enactment is always a re-enactment of something that has gone before. The word 'prototype' I think is important as it infers that the current enactment, that is perhaps being experienced in the therapy context, is based on, but not identical to, a previous enactment or prototype.

Transgenerational communication of trauma

CAT is often used to help people who have experienced abuse, trauma or neglect earlier in their lives. It is a central tenet of CAT's theory of psychopathology and human development that people learn to expect their world of relationships to go on repeating the patterns they have experienced, without being aware that other ways of relating are available. In order to survive harsh, neglecting or abusive experiences, people develop strategies or procedures based on moving around the world or map of relational patterns they have experienced. For example, it is a common theme in the story of boys who have been physically abused and brutalised in childhood that one day, often when they are in their teens, they decide they have had enough and 'turn the tables' on the abuser by hitting them back. There may seem to be only one reciprocal role available in this relationship: *powerful/intimidating/abusing* to *weak/intimidated/abused*. As a CAT dilemma this represents a choice between attacking or attacked. Even for clients who have experienced severe abuse and neglect, there is often an awareness during therapy that the parents who did this to them were treated badly in their own childhoods in the social and cultural context of their own generation. This realisation may allow a degree of acceptance and understanding and is a way of using the tree metaphor to track back a line of causation.

To take this to the next level of the tree, there has been much written about trauma somehow missing a generation or being replicated in some way across time without the obvious chain of events and experience that links grandfather, father and son engaging in very similar reciprocal role procedures. This idea is particularly relevant when trauma has been annihilating or deeply shameful. A more palatable layer has been added to the onion but inside the trauma is contained with all its power and nuances. In some ways it may be negatively transmitted; inferred by what is not said, not allowed, not done. It is thought that the means of transmission of this trauma could be both psychological / dialogic and physiological / epigenetic (Kellerman 2013). For example, a child will be influenced by the psychological effect of what is not spoken about by a parent but also may have been exposed, in the womb, to stress hormones that then have a physiological effect on the developing body and mind. There is also growing evidence that abuse, trauma and neglect in childhood can influence the way genes are expressed as the child develops (Mehta et al. 2013).

Human intuitive ability

To be able to use the idea of the microcosm in psychotherapy supervision relies on developing the use of the human intuitive abilities that are present in all of us. It is my conjecture that we are much more intuitive than we realise and that we are constantly experiencing the world using all our senses and pattern-identifying abilities without this necessarily manifesting in consciousness as thought. We regularly talk about thoughts, feelings and behaviours. We are able to discern the subtlest of nuance in the choice of words someone uses (for example, the restrained contempt in: 'I was somewhat surprised that you . . .'). We notice an enormous range of emotional states in others by watching and unconsciously replicating their facial expressions and bodily movements (Adolphs 2002).

Jung described four sub-divisions of the personality (Storr 1986) and these have been linked to the four elemental signs of astrology, which I think adds something to the exploration. They are: thinking (air), feeling (water), sensing (earth) and intuition (fire). It is the fourth of these functions, the intuitive, that is the hardest to pin down and describe. The verb that goes with intuition is 'I know'. Intuition considers a time dimension and makes judgements based on context and the 'big picture'. Having done some psychometric tests myself in the past I have realised that this is my dominant way of weighing up the world (which is probably why I am writing a chapter like this and not one on statistics!). I am aware that I often make decisions that are warned against by any rational, thinking analysis and may feel emotionally difficult, but somehow I know what, for me, is the right thing to do. Our experience of our dreams, for example, often leaves us with some intuitive knowledge that is difficult to put into words. In the daytime this dream world is still going on underneath the stream of consciousness that seems to give our selves a sense of continuity and agency. The language of this world is based on sensation, feeling and imagery rather than cognition or thought.

In order to develop any capacity to explore more fully what is happening in therapy we need to use all the capabilities of our personality. In many cases the exact word used, on further thought, holds rich meaning. Words may be coming out of your mouth that have been used in your family for generations; used by people you have never met or even heard of. Mikael Leiman makes excellent use of this richness in his Dialogical Sequence Analysis (Leiman 1997). We can learn to be more observant of clients' feelings, emotional states and non-verbal language. We can be aware of how our own experience of our body and bodily sensations change in response to a client. Finally, we can hone our capacity to bring into awareness the intuitive dream world that is constantly feeding us with imagery.

Psychoanalysts have been aware of this, of course, since Freud started using free association and dreams. There is an assumption here that the content of an uninhibited stream of thought or remembered dream is not random but may contain meaning in the form of metaphors, multi-layered images and, I think importantly, the connection of emotional states to dream imagery, sometimes in a surprising way, for example, a dream about a dog laughing that fills you with terror. It is thought important in many types of psychotherapy for the therapist to be able to attend to the client as well as being able to take a 'meta-position' with regard to other things that are going on in the room. Wilfred Bion (in Casement 1990: 10) writes about starting a psychoanalytic session 'without memory, desire or understanding,' and I think this is a good description of a way to temporarily suspend the dominance of the stream of conscious thought or spoken conversation in order to allow awareness of other information available to us. In CAT we use the metaphor of the 'observing eye' to describe, particularly, a reflective capacity that can take an overview of a range of dissociated self-states. This is quite a thinking eye that sees and describes. Perhaps to be aware of more of 'what is going on', we need to develop a 'dreaming eye' as well?

A supervision exercise

I would use something like this in supervision when I start to feel unhappy that we are missing the point in some way or that I am failing to connect with the therapist I am supervising with regard to a particular client. It could also be used if the therapist acknowledges feeling stuck or lost.

If there are others in a supervision group then they can take an observer position; closing their eyes and suspending their cognitive selves as much as possible.

> *Press Pause.*
> *Stop the normal supervisor's dialogue and explain that you would like to try to explore the question: 'What is really going on here?'*
> *Find a point of departure.*
> *As supervisor you may have already chanced on something that seems meaningful! Examples could be:*
>
> - *The exact words used by the therapist*
> - *A strong emotional or bodily response (particularly a surprising or paradoxical response) to part of the story*
> - *A dream-like image or association*
>
> *To elicit a point of departure from the therapist you could ask questions like:*
>
> - *What is the one thing you need to tell me about this client?*
> - *What do you need to say to the client?*
>
> *Name the point of departure.*
> *Explore the places accessible from the point of departure, with the therapist, using the metaphors of the onion (depth or layers), the tree (history) and the ripple (the current context).*
> *Questions that may help this exploration include:*

- *'Who do you think said that to the client in the past?'*
- *'How would you feel if that happened to you?'*
- *'Have we overlooked something deeper in the client's story?'*

Do not stray too far from the point of departure. Have confidence that what you need to know today is contained within it. Use your imagination.

Ask the observers to contribute.

Together try to link your discoveries to what is known or not known about the client's story.

Make a plan as to how to bring this discovery into dialogue with the client. This may take the form of naming a reciprocal role, mapping a procedure or working out an enactment that has been occurring in the therapy relationship. What can the therapist now do that is not colluding with the enactment? How can the enactment be explained to the client? What words could be used? Sometimes it will be necessary to ask the client for more information and to explore an area of their past that has been overlooked. It is always possible to go back into a session and say: *'I have been thinking about what you said last week . . .'*

At the end of the exercise check out how the therapist(s) are feeling. Have they debriefed sufficiently? Do they feel that they have had their say?

Illustrations

I am now going to illustrate the idea of the microcosm with reference to some fictional examples. All demonstrate the metaphor of the onion. The first also demonstrates the tree. The other three show how the ripple works.

The microcosm in relation to the client's material brought to supervision

'Psychopath'

The therapist had developed a good therapeutic alliance with a female client who had a diagnosis of schizophrenia and had experienced paranoid and accusatory hallucinations over a number of years. The client had also experienced sexual abuse as a young child.

The CAT map contained a description of the client's unmanageable feelings; fear, shame and a powerful feeling of being ruined, irretrievably damaged and beyond repair. There were marked similarities between the unmanageable feelings and the things that the voices said to the client about herself. They often accused her of being a sex offender and also a 'psychopath'.

The supervisor became interested in the meaning of the word 'psychopath'. It is a term that is not clearly defined in common usage and can refer to a selfish person, a psychotic person, a remorseless serial killer or even to someone

The microcosm in CAT supervision   181

who is just reckless and hedonistic. Following supervision the therapist was tasked with exploring the history of this word in the client's story.

It turned out that the client's mother had been labelled as a 'psychopath' at the age of seven by a family doctor where she had grown up in Ireland. This was because she was difficult and rebellious in some way. Culturally this proved very interesting as at that time in Ireland girls could often be written off as 'fallen', especially if they became pregnant, and were sent to Magdalene Laundries. (These were harsh and abusive 'asylums' for women and girls in Ireland that existed up to near the end of the twentieth century. They were often run by nuns and there are many accounts of physical, sexual and psychological abuse. Some 30.000 women experienced confinement in these institutions).

The word 'psychopath' therefore holds within it the idea of a fault so deep that it can never be recovered from. It is also a blaming word and generates guilt and shame. 'Psychopaths' do not deserve love or care and should be excluded and forgotten. It turned out that the client felt that the therapist secretly believed her to be a 'psychopath' and not a 'schizophrenic', which created an enactment where the therapist was felt to be deceitful / damning / neglecting and confirmed the client's unmanageable feelings about herself.

This was successfully brought into dialogue with the client. The therapist was able to explain that he did not hold this view and was hopeful for the client. It also helped the client understand her mother's guilt for having passed on her 'psychopathy' to her.

This illustration demonstrates the metaphor of the tree and the presence of the generational past in the meaning of the client's experience and also the metaphor of the ripple in the way the term 'psychopath' retained its resonance in the present enactment in the therapy relationship.

The microcosm in relation to the supervisor's experience of the therapist

'I don't know'

The therapist had a number of clients that he was currently seeing but the supervisor became curious about a reaction he was experiencing in regard to the therapist and attempts to discuss the final client for the day. In contrast to the supervision of the preceding clients, the supervisor was finding the therapist disconnected and vague with regard to a female client in her thirties who was known to have been sexually abused as a child. When asked questions about the nature of the abuse the therapist repeatedly said: 'I don't know'. The supervisor wanted to push for more detail but quickly felt uncomfortable and intrusive. Often a lack of knowledge about the client is due to the re-enactment of a neglecting to neglected role. In this case, however, it felt different.

The supervisor allowed his imagination to understand the experience of: 'I don't know' in relation to the client. He soon 'saw' a little girl being groomed and abused by an adult. Frightened to say 'no' she simply replied: 'I don't know'. The words took on horrible meaning in the imaginary exchange: 'Did you enjoy that? Shall I do that again?' 'I don't know'. It was not a churlish, rebellious 'I don't know', but a terrified, frozen, survival strategy that alluded to the violence and coercion that could be used if the child were to resist.

The reciprocal role: abusing / threatening (as if friendly) to abused / terrified (passively compliant) was named in relation to the supervisor / therapist and in the context of the therapist / client relationship. On later exploration the details of the abuse were disclosed and they revealed this pattern. The therapist was able to understand that attempts at friendly 'probing' were likely to be experienced as threatening and intrusive, unless the client could think with the therapist about the enactment and give genuine consent to proceed.

This illustration demonstrates the metaphor of the ripple in the way the meaning of: 'I don't know' is replicated in the enactments in the therapy and supervisory relationships.

The microcosm in relation to the supervisor's experience of the client's story via the therapist

'Alien abduction'

A female therapist was seeing a highly dissociated female client, who was known to have been one of a number of children who had been sexually abused at a young age by a group of adults on a regular basis (who were later convicted). The client reported no memory of the events at all and presented in sessions as regressed and childlike; cuddling toys and unable to engage in an exploratory dialogue with the therapist. In supervision the therapist owned feeling lost and out of her depth and very disturbed by what she did not know about the client's experiences.

After several weeks of this the supervisor had a terrifying dream. He felt that he was awake in his own bed and was being somehow pulled by the feet towards a very bright light outside the window. The supervisor brought this to supervision, wondering whether it might shed light on this faltering therapy. The discussion turned to the topic of 'alien abduction', something both therapist and supervisor had seen documentaries about. Abduction took the form of the supervisor's dream but the abductees would typically have no clear memory of what happened to them on board the alien space-craft except for the idea that they had had things inserted into them (alien medical probes).

The key elements of this explanation proved over time to connect to the core experience of the client's abuse. With careful questioning, the client revealed that children were selected out of a group of children and taken to a room where they were put on a table and anaesthetised. When they woke up later they only knew that something had been done to them because of internal pain and bleeding. Although this material was deeply disturbing, it was important for the therapist to be able to witness and empathise with the true horror of the experience in order to help the client move forward.

This illustration demonstrates the metaphor of the ripple in that the disavowed experience of the client spreads out to encompass both the therapist and supervisor.

The microcosm in relation to enactments in a supervision group

'Not one of us'

A female therapist was in a supervision group with a male supervisor and two other male therapists. The female therapist had been conducting a group for female abuse survivors. The supervisor noticed that the two male therapists seemed disinterested in the supervision of the group, perhaps wary of such a rich source of material taking up a lot of the supervision time to the detriment of their individual clients. Perhaps there were gender issues along the lines that the female survivors' group was 'women's business' and that they had nothing to offer or felt excluded?

Tensions came to a head when the female therapist owned that she felt that she was: 'not one of us' – that she and her group did not fit in with the unspoken 'rules' of the supervision group. She felt excluded, inexperienced and lost as to how to explain her feelings in both the supervision group and the therapy group itself. The supervision group recognised this as an important revelation and made extra time and affirmed their confidence and respect for the therapist. The supervisor had the feeling that this apparent gender issue in the supervision group may mirror another, but different, split in the therapy group.

On further exploration it turned out that a few weeks earlier the therapist had had to briefly leave the therapy group to use the bathroom. She had felt guilty about doing this and had not mentioned it in supervision. Focussing on the expression: 'Not one of us', she then made a link with what a client said when the therapist returned to the room. The clients had been whispering together and as she sat down one said: 'We were discussing whether you are one of us or not and we think you are'. The therapist had felt deeply exposed by the comment and unable to stay with it in the group. It clearly brought up many issues around self-disclosure and feelings of inadequacy. As the therapist had not been sexually abused herself, she could never be in the group as 'one of us'.

The therapist was able to go back to this comment in the next group and explore the extent to which a therapist could empathically connect with and help clients who had experienced things that were outside the therapist's own experience, and the boundaries around self-disclosure.

This illustration again demonstrates the metaphor of the ripple spreading wider to encompass the whole supervision group.

Conclusion

I hope that this exploration of the ideas of the microcosm in CAT supervision has been illuminating and helpful. Particularly, I hope that the metaphors of the onion, the tree and the ripple can become tools in relation to the complexity of the material we hear in supervision and perhaps help in the development of both an observing and dreaming eye in supervisors and therapists practising CAT and other therapies.

References

Adolphs, R. (2002) 'Recognizing emotion from facial expressions: Psychological and neurological mechanisms', *Behavioral and Cognitive Neuroscience Reviews*, 1, 1: 21–62.
Blavatsky, H.P. (1888) *The Secret Doctrine*, Pasadena: Theosophical University Press.
Casement, P. (1990) *Further Learning from the Patient*, London: Routledge.
Holquist, M. (2002) *Dialogism: Bakhtin and His World*, London: Routledge.
Kellerman, N.P. (2013) 'Epigenetic transmission of holocaust trauma: Can nightmares be inherited?', *Israel Journal of Psychiatry and Related Sciences*, 50, 1: 33–39.
Leiman, M. (1997) 'Procedures as dialogical sequences: A revised version of the fundamental concept in cognitive analytic therapy', *British Journal of Medical Psychology*, 70, 2: 193–207.
Mehta, D., Klengel, T., Conneely, K.N., Smith, A.K., Altmann, A., Pace, T.W., Rex-Haffner, M., Loeschner, A., Gonik, M., Mercer, K.B., Bradley, B., Müller-Myhsok, B., Ressler, K.J. and Binder, E.B. (2013) 'Childhood maltreatment is associated with distinct genomic and epigenetic profiles in posttraumatic stress disorder', *Proceedings for the National Academy of Sciences*, 110, 20: 8302–8307.
Pollard, R. (2012) 'Great time: From blade runner to Bakhtin', *Reformulation*, 38: 32–34.
Storr, A. (1986) *Jung*, London: Fontana Press.

Section 4

Supervision in different contexts

Chapter 14

The supervision relationship in a training context

Yvonne Stevens

> As a CAT trainee, I recall being infused with feelings of newness, keenness, excitement and anxiety. I didn't know at the time, that I was beginning a journey into uncharted territory, that would take me through my inner relational landscape, unknown and warded off. It's a curious fact that this terrain was both present in some sense, but un-mapped, out of consciousness, obscured from my conscious self-reflective, observing 'I'/eye. It's only through working alongside the guidance of keenly-seeing and containing supervisory relationships that I have come to see the importance of the dialogic stance in supervision.
>
> CAT supervisor

Introduction

Possibly the most rewarding role for a CAT supervisor is taking responsibility for supervising trainee therapists. The demands and challenges of this role require the supervisor to be facilitator, guide, assessor, teacher, mentor, working alongside each trainee as they make their journey towards competence and accreditation in relational and psychotherapeutic skills, with the model of CAT as the therapeutic framework (Ryle and Kerr 2002).

This chapter describes how the dialogue between supervisor and trainee can address anxieties, hopes and fears about the clinical work of therapy (Salzberger-Wittenberg 1970), alongside valuing the skillset that the trainee is bringing from their professional background or training in other modalities of psychotherapy (Hawkins and Shohet 2012, Proctor 1994), and enabling a safe environment in which learning can take place (Casement 1985). Undertaking training in psychotherapy can be an emotionally challenging process for the trainee therapist. The supervisor has a role both in supporting and assessing trainees through appraisal and accreditation, and encouraging awareness of how their emotional well-being, relational roles and procedures interact with their work with patients (Ballatt and Campling 2011). The supervisor-trainee relationship in CAT is intensive, usually involving meeting weekly individually or in a group setting over one or more years. The chapter provides guidance on supervising trainees in the CAT model through the demanding tasks of assessment, reformulation and mapping, and ending. Alongside the CAT tools, this chapter reflects on the dialogical modelling of 'use of self' and joint activity 'in the room.' A capacity for authority and flexibility is required of the supervisor in order to adapt to the needs of the trainee and work within their zone of proximal development (ZPD) (Vygotsky 1978), whilst also holding the clinical governance needs of the patient and the clinical setting (Cooper and Lousada 2005, Denman 2011) and the values of the CAT model (Ryle and Kerr 2002). Included throughout this chapter is feedback from trainees at different levels, from CAT foundation to psychotherapist, and from other trainings such as clinical psychology and psychiatry, concerning their experience of supervision in the CAT model.

What of CAT supervisors and their competence? It seems that the best preparation for becoming a good supervisor is to have had a good experience of supervision as a trainee. 'Without this fundamental step the supervisor lacks a good role model and a solid inner experience of how beneficial supervision can be in one's professional life' (Hawkins and Shohet 2000: 188). I am grateful to both my supervisors during my CAT training at St Thomas' Hospital, who provided me with this experience of good supervision, both challenging and supportive, and whose voices remain a part of my relational interaction with every supervisee.

The CAT training supervisor in dialogue

When meeting a new trainee therapist or group of trainees, supervisors bring to the role their knowledge and experience as CAT therapists and supervisors, but also other influences, the multitude of voices (Stiles 1997) with whom they are in dialogue when with patients and supervisees. These are the internal resources from our lives and experiences on which we draw, the Greek chorus of internal consultants. There is a hierarchy of 'addressees' – these may include Freud, Jung, Winnicott, Bion, Kelly, Laing, Ryle and others whose wisdom is revisited and reworked in an ongoing dialogue; our own experiences as CAT trainees, the failures, struggles and triumphs; learning from past patients, supervisors and trainers, colleagues and supervisees; our own personal therapy which reverberates to provide new insights and markers long after ending; these are alive, dynamic and '*inspiring*' to *inspired* reciprocal and relational conversations that are never complete (Hepple 2010). I seek to encourage trainees' awareness of the richness of their own internal dialogues, which may be inspiring but also restricting or undermining of their development as a CAT therapist. Casement (1985: 31) describes 'the island of intellectual contemplation', the capacity for self-reflection we achieve using the observing eye in CAT.

We can also talk about the relationships of accountability (Hawkins and Shohet 2012); here and now my responsibility is to the trainees and their patients, and within the clinical setting with its particular clinical governance expectations and service restraints, but also to training course directors, ACAT, UKCP; the patients' families, friends, employers, state agencies, and the wider society – any of whom may call me and the trainees to account for our therapeutic work and clinical judgement, and may judge accordingly. This is the alive, challenging and dynamic world of psychotherapy that trainees are entering and progressing through.

Orientating trainees to the CAT model

Initially I was looking for help understanding the main conceptual and structural elements of CAT. I wanted help identifying reciprocal roles and procedures (traps, snags and dilemmas). With time, and some of the core concepts more or less in place, I started to look to supervision to help me think more reciprocally, to think about not just what I was being invited into but what I may bring to the party: help with my 'blind spots', with working with the model, in the context of a therapeutic relationship, that was as non-collusive as possible.

CAT trainee

The task of the supervisor when trainees are new to CAT, is to oversee the bringing together of the CAT structure, theoretical understanding, and CAT tools into the clinical practice of the trainee as therapist, as it has been explained and explored on the training course through lectures, role play, seminars and cases studies. Early on, the supervisor provides the scaffolding for trainees who may be highly anxious and expressing this anxiety in different ways. Casement (1985) describes how trainees may revert to their prior role or modality and resist the new model, or strive excessively to fend off fear of failure, or struggle with the balance between *being* and *doing*. Hawkins (in Jansen 1980) identifies that trainees need to overcome the twin pitfalls of over-identification and being overwhelmed by emotion, and excessive distance and rationalisation, and some may fear becoming psychotic or depressed.

The challenges encountered in learning the CAT model differ according to the trainee's professional role and therapy background. A trainee psychiatrist after her first CAT therapy session with her patient described feeling 'naked without her doctor's coat and prescription pad'. Conversely trainees from other professions may struggle with holding the therapeutic frame, the boundaries of setting, time and self-disclosure. Supervisors may need to induct trainees who have little experience of therapy in to the role of therapist. Both person-centred and psychodynamic trainees may struggle with the speed of the early reformulation process in CAT, fearing distressing the patient and damaging the therapeutic alliance. The collaborative CAT process, brings together the patient's knowledge of their history and the therapist's skill in making connections to create a new narrative framework which promotes reflexivity (Ryle 1994). This more active role of therapist may feel uncomfortable. For less experienced cognitive therapists, trainee clinical psychologists and doctors, learning to use countertransference as an assessment tool and 'being in the room' relationally may be challenging. The supervisor's role is to gain an overview of the core competence of each trainee, of their unique mix of skills and experience, personal qualities and potential to develop with respect to their ZPD.

Differences in CAT experience within the group make it challenging to offer us supervision that promotes learning the model and skills.

CAT trainee

If supervisors do not have responsibility for allocating patients to trainees, they will need to gauge whether cases brought by trainees are suitable for their stage of training. Trainees may wish to hone their skills in their specialist field (e.g. eating disorders), but most CAT trainings will expect some diversity of patient presentation, including experience of CAT in adult mental health services. Increasingly the pressure on services means that even inexperienced trainees are expected to see very complex patients. The supervisor will have oversight of risk issues, and can assess whether the trainee is managing the level of risk and complexity that a patient presents, ensuring that other services, such as the crisis team, are in place when needed. The dialogue between the supervisor and the training course and the service which provides the training patients, requires attentive communication around these issues.

CAT supervision, especially for those in training, is usually conducted in groups, so the negotiation of time and boundaries will need to be spelt out explicitly for therapists new to group supervision. The question of how to present a patient bears some attention early on, as other modalities will conduct supervision differently. The early stages of training supervision are a useful time to start reflecting in the supervision group about reciprocal roles and procedures, thinking about referral letters or patient assessments and the patterns that are described and enacted within them, and allowing the development of some spontaneity, playfulness and creativity in the group.

Early on the reciprocal roles of the supervision group itself begin to emerge as each trainee approaches this new experience, described by CAT trainees as follows:

> *For me it was both an exciting opportunity and somewhat of a threat to my . . . professional pride? My anxiety made me a little too eager to want to prove myself.*
>
> *The focus on thinking reciprocally, of asking, 'What am I being invited into here?' Then the discussion and exploration that would lead to the translating and restating of such transference and countertransference phenomena into abstracted cognitive terms which could be written onto a piece of paper as a reciprocal role. Three years on, this seems 'normal' good CAT therapy. At the time it was a wonderfully new way of working to me. The seamless integration of the psychodynamic and cognitive therapies.*
>
> *At the very beginning it was not just a scaffold to support the learning of the new model, but also newer parts of myself I had not been aware of.*
>
> *When I am learning anything new it is important for me to feel safe with the supervisor, able to be honest about my lack of understanding and confident that my supervisor feels confident in adopting the 'powerful' end of the reciprocal role when I need it.*
>
> *I was able to gently challenge colleagues at times as we have built a very therapeutic, honest supervision group which has been really encouraged and supported by our supervisor. We have also learnt to take risks in supervision – which have then been channelled into sessions with clients.*

Common reciprocal roles in training supervision include:

judged, criticised in relation to *judging, critical*
admiring, special in relation to *admired, special*
anxiously striving in relation to *approving*
exposed, incompetent in relation to *exposing*
rebellious in relation to *controlling, demanding*
engaged, challenged in relation to *engaging, challenging*
supported in relation to *guiding, supporting*

Approaching the first session with a patient may be a new experience for some trainees.

Salzberger-Wittenberg (1970) in her short but seminal manual on the therapeutic relationship describes the hopes and fears the therapist brings to that first meeting: to be tolerant and understanding, not to do harm to the patient, perhaps even to be liked by the patient, a fear of not being good enough, of not helping. The relational position in CAT is that both patient and therapist come together in a position of not knowing, that it is the creative and collaborative process of reformulation that brings understanding, reflection and the possibility of change. My training supervisor used to say 'It's about the relationship – the CAT tools will come in time'. Encouraging the therapeutic use of self from the outset will advance the trainee's ability to practise CAT, and engaging the trainee's capacity to reflect on and report in supervision their countertransference responses will give the best insight into the patient, not only for them but also for the supervisor and the supervision group. Welch (1994) describes how supervision needs to ensure that it is only with the full engagement of the self that the skills of CAT become active enough to effect change in the client. 'Trainee therapists need to use supervision to become aware of their particular tendencies' with respect to personal and elicited countertransference (Ryle and Kerr 2002: 104).

Supervising the development of relational CAT skills

The initial sessions in CAT are demanding for both patient and therapist, and can feel overwhelming for the trainee therapist. The information gathering process (described in Chapter 3) takes place in a relational context, offering the first clues to formulating reciprocal roles and identifying enactments, making connections between 'inside and outside the room' and past and present events, building up to reformulation. As supervisors guide trainees step by step through the process, they stay mindful of the ZPD of both patient and therapist, as they support the trainees in building the therapeutic alliance. I usually recommend trainees read Claire Tanner's article (2002) on the importance of developing good enough target problems and target problem procedures collaboratively, in order to define the focus for therapy and achieve the higher order descriptions that underpin and form the backbone of the reformulation letter.

> Trainees will have to spend a lot of time on writing their first reformulation letters, . . . letters do not have to be exactly right . . . , by stating clearly what their understandings are, therapists offer their patients an opportunity to suggest changes where the account does not fit; in that sense being 'wrong' can serve to clarify the story and can provide the experience of collaboration.
>
> (Ryle and Kerr 2002: 86–87)

Supervisors can offer examples of letters and diagrams as part of the scaffolding process, recommending references to useful articles and passages in books. Ryle and Kerr (2002: 88–91), for example, offer an excellent description of constructing an SDR.

Reading out loud one's first reformulation letter in supervision is a rite of passage for the CAT trainee. I remember what an anxiety-provoking experience that was in those large supervision groups at St Thomas's Hospital, London, in the early 90's. 'Think about what it was like to be that child in that family', my supervisor would say to inspire and encourage our empathic letter-writing. Prior to sharing the reformulation, I encourage trainees to read their letters out loud to themselves, imagining the patient sitting in front of them, and to look out for words that might sting or be placatory, vague or collusive. Supervising a trainee CAT supervisor, who was taking a pen to a trainee's imperfect first reformulation letter, with the view to create a perfect letter, I asked her to think instead about what would be a good enough letter for the patient to receive. I suggested she reflect on the impact on the fragile and nascent skills of the trainee therapist of his supervisor's words replacing his own and also on the intrusion into the relationship between the trainee therapist and patient. How might the supervisor approach the changes needed in the letter in dialogue with the trainee from a point of developing the trainee's understanding of the therapy relationship? We can easily move into a superior magistral voice when we take on the powerful role of supervisor.

> *I guess the theory /model may become more second nature as time goes by, however there will always be room to learn something more about yourself from the client you are working with.*
>
> *CAT trainee*

Supervising the development of the diagrams and mapping in the room requires the supervisor to provide the scaffolding appropriate to each trainee's needs and skill level, actively and collaboratively mapping with the trainees and modelling therapist activity in the room.

The middle stage of therapy, the recognition and revision of roles and procedures, brings about the possibility of change for the patient. For trainees there is scope to use therapeutic techniques from inside and outside CAT, for creativity in their application of techniques. They have the opportunity to bring their own skills and experience into the model or to experiment with new techniques creating their own unique tool kit for enabling integration and change. The supervisor's role is to ensure techniques are embedded in the therapeutic relationship, relevant to the needs of the patient, and in line with CAT understanding of recovery and healing. Trainees may be encouraged to use rating scales to track anxiety management skills, or use creative therapies to uncover hidden emotion or aspiration, or use therapeutic letters to facilitate the expression and healing of core pain. The supervisor has the responsibility to corral this activity within the container of the CAT structure, with reference to the reformulation and diagram.

The structure of CAT – having a beginning, middle and end – may be a new way of working for many trainees, and as ending approaches, and the writing of the goodbye letter, anxiety will run high for patients and trainees.

> *I didn't really appreciate how much CAT would press my own buttons . . . how much my core pain is being impacted on. I strive to excess to avoid failure, and currently my client is sabotaging therapy at session 13 and is anxious about being discharged after therapy is concluded. This is taking me into my core pain of 'not feeling good enough' and I really feel I need to explore this further.*
> CAT trainee

Martin and Schurtman (1985) describe the ways in which therapist anxieties present at the ending of the therapeutic relationship and how this will reflect patient anxieties. The therapist may seek to rescue the patient, or deny the importance of ending, or struggle with the disappointment and loss of an idealised relationship with the patient. Trainees can be encouraged to make use of the reformulation and diagram in supervision and in therapy to understand how termination anxiety is being played out in the relational space between them and the patient, and how to address this in the ending letter. It may be that the ending of therapy will present personal challenges for the trainee with regard to losses in their personal life, and encouraging early arrangement of their CAT training therapy will be advisable. Supporting the trainee to hold the therapeutic boundary at termination will enable the relational learning for both patient and trainee of an enriching experience of at least one relationship that was no less rewarding because it ended.

Relationship with the training course, appraisal and assessment

It is in the clinical work that the trainee's theoretical understanding from the course input and skills development from case discussions, experiential exercises and role plays is demonstrated, appraised and adjusted. Hawkins and Shohet (2000: 52) describe the educational/formative foci of supervision:

> To provide a regular space for supervisees to reflect upon the content and process of their work; to develop understanding and skills within the work; to receive information from another perspective concerning one's work; to receive both content and process feedback.

Proctor (1994) sees that both supervisor and trainee need to take responsibility for clarifying the tasks and the lines of communication and accountability between the course, trainee and supervisor. Supporting a collaborative, relational approach to appraisal and managing issues of power, control and authority, McLeod (2003: 504) argues 'it is important that supervisors work with trainees in ways that are consistent with the aims and philosophy of the course' but also that 'the role of supervisor in relation to a training course represents a challenge to achieve an appropriate balance between involvement with the course and autonomy in the service of the trainee'.

Periodic course appraisals, completed jointly by the trainee and supervisor, are opportunities to discuss progress and plan training goals and also to identify difficulties and raise concerns either may be aware of. Similarly, the supervisor's feedback on case studies and presentations can address the development of relational, clinical and theoretical competences. More specifically these competences include the collaborative development and use of CAT tools; the therapeutic relationship and use of self; and the ability to present the case clearly in writing and in supervision, demonstrating an understanding of the therapeutic process and the ability to communicate this understanding. Divergence from the CAT structure and use of tools needs attention, and, in exploring why the CAT model is not being followed, it can be helpful to discuss its analytic and cognitive strengths with trainees. These can be fruitful discussions in supervision, and, in them, the supervisor can model the relationally curious, thoughtful and emotionally present stance of CAT.

Common problems that can arise for trainees include personal, work-related and mental health issues, conflicts with usual roles and boundaries, feeling deskilled, the challenge of offering therapy in an unfamiliar modality, anxiety about the use of self or too much use of self and the challenge of being versus doing, mentioned earlier. Developing a language of role relationships and encouraging openness within the supervision group can give trainees confidence to voice difficulties and express their feelings. Bruch (1974: 116) asserts that supervision can broaden the therapist's self-awareness of conflicts and issues of confidence and self-esteem, 'supervision encourages the trainee to be explicit about attitudes that usually remain unexpressed . . . to recognize behaviour that is, for example, competitive and striving for what it is'. Bruch (1974: 116) continues that 'trainees need support in accepting . . . that as learners they are entitled not to know something and to overlook certain points that the supervisor recognizes. If a trainee is unable to accept instruction and correction but reacts with undue self-recrimination or sullen anger . . . , the trainee may themselves need therapeutic help'. Yourman (2003) notes that trainees may withhold sessional material from supervisors, and this may be due to shame, which affects a desire to hide oneself. So supervisees who are experiencing shame are less likely to be forthcoming in supervision, especially about material that may be viewed negatively by the supervisor, and this may be to do with the supervisory relationship. A persistent cause of anxiety for trainees is the possibility of patients dropping out of therapy and a fear that they will not complete course requirements in good enough time. This anxiety may lead a trainee to become over-accommodating (e.g. by re-arranging appointments), too active in the room or to avoid challenging the patient. The supervisor's role is to anticipate and address these procedures, which may undermine therapeutic progress, and to work with the trainee to reflect on and contain their anxiety.

If trainee performance is poor or potentially harmful to the patient or if events in the trainee's life are having an adverse effect on their clinical work, these issues need to be addressed in the supervisory relationship, with reference to course and accrediting body guidelines. This may be the hardest part of a supervisor's role, and it may be tempting to overlook or minimise difficulties, or hope that problems will resolve themselves. Careful, attentive use of the appraisal process promotes a collaborative rather than judgemental approach to difficulties. Engaging in a collaborative dialogue with the course directors, while observing boundaries of the supervisory relationship around this, is essential for resolving such issues and for meeting the challenges which often arise in the training context. Supervisors, who see trainees more often than course staff, can have an important role in helping trainees find resolution, which may be an acceptance that to leave the course or take a break from the training would be the most favourable course of action.

On becoming a CAT therapist

Hawkins and Shohet (2012) describe a developmental approach to supervision, as the supervisee develops so must the nature of the supervision, and this requires flexibility and attunement on the part of the supervisor. By encouraging exploration of different perspectives on clinical and theoretical issues, welcoming challenge of standard practices, and promoting personal style, innovation and wider reading, the supervisor is handing over the baton to the therapist. We see learning develop rapidly within groups: for example, in a training session on mapping skills with a group of four junior doctors over the course of an hour, the first person needed me to draw the map as we discussed their case, the second suggested roles and procedures for me to draw, the third took the pen but needed prompting, the fourth drew the map completely herself. Vygotsky's (1978) understanding of the internalisation of higher psychological processes follows the idea: *what I do with another today, I can do by myself tomorrow.* Casement (1985: 32) states that 'as the trainee progresses towards accreditation, supervision becomes a dialogue between the external and internal supervisor'. For the experienced trainee the internal dialogue and capacity for self-reflection enable identification of self to self and self to other procedures and enactments as they occur.

Sue Yabsley, CAT psychotherapist, reflects on her experience of supervision during the advanced CAT training, which prepares CAT therapists for professional accreditation and registration as CAT psychotherapists:

> There was more expectation of therapist competency; by this I mean an understanding and ease around reciprocal role procedures and the place of

> the therapist in this, and a depth of knowledge of the A in CAT and its place in the relationship between therapist and patient, rather than the more 'tool led' interventions at practitioner level.
>
> I brought to the supervisory relationship a broader understanding of the development of different states active within patients' presentations; their roots and development in pre-verbal but known experience; a renewed observing eye on my own pathology and reciprocal role procedures and subsequent more subtle enactments. I was looking for greater challenge both clinically and personally – to be enabled to think and work more widely and less rigidly and to use CAT tools to facilitate more psychodynamic understanding.
>
> Most important in the supervision relationship are openness, challenge and an ability to tussle with ideas and wonderings which may identify what the therapist is eliciting in the transference as well as the patient. A supervisor's willingness not to avoid difficult thoughts or conversations and the trainee's willingness to hear them! For the pair to have mature but different views on a clinical situation or enactment which may not be resolved but which can be worked with. Playfulness both within the supervisor/supervisee relationship and also with the client material – to be able to 'think outside the box'.

Some senior clinicians returning to training may feel unnurtured in their professional roles, where responsibility outweighs support and they may be more used to giving supervision than receiving it. An experienced CAT therapist, feeling a bit stale and under-supervised in their CAT practice, expressed looking forward to supervision where someone would care about him and his patients. Frank (1974) reports that experienced therapists from any modality generally achieve better therapeutic outcomes than trainees and highlights the importance of the healing qualities of the therapeutic relationship over technique and the need to enhance trainees' capacity for empathy, genuineness and warmth.

Conclusion

> CAT training, of which supervision is arguably the most important part, reveals CAT like an onion – ideas and concepts come into focus over time, which can be anxiety provoking for the trainee. My supervisor was able to weather the push and pull of his trainees' anxiety and steer a steady course, trusting (I assume) that it would come into focus in the end, which for me it has!
>
> CAT trainee

Rather like being a parent or even a grandparent, the supervisor's task is to set an example, to teach and learn, to set boundaries and allow them to be challenged, to enjoy successes and laughter, to share tears and disappointments, but above all to care without judgement. In Bakhtinian terms the supervisor is aiming to manage the dialogical relationship between permissiveness and authority; to have faith in the therapeutic process and in the trainee, to allow them the space to grow as individual therapists without shame – so that they can make mistakes and learn from them. The reward is to watch as trainees grow, with increasing competence and take on the mantle as the next generation of CAT therapists.

References

Ballatt, J. and Campling, P. (2011) *Intelligent Kindness: Reforming the Culture of Healthcare*, London: RCPsych Publications.
Bruch, H. (1974) *Learning Psychotherapy*, Cambridge: Harvard University Press.
Casement, P. (1985) *On Learning from the Patient*, London: Routledge.
Cooper, A. and Lousada, J. (2005) *Borderline Welfare: Feeling and Fear of Feeling in Modern Welfare*, London: Karnac.
Denman, C. (2011) 'The place of psychotherapy in modern psychiatric practice', *Advances in Psychiatric Treatment*, 17: 243–249.
Frank, J.D. (1974) *Persuasion and Healing*, New York: Schocken Books.
Hawkins, P. (1980) 'Between Scylla and Charybdis', in E. Jansen (ed) *The Therapeutic Community*, London: Croom Helm.
Hawkins, P. and Shohet, R. (2012) *Supervision in the Helping Professions, (fourth edition)*, Maidenhead: Open University Press.
Hepple, J. (2010) 'A little bit of Bakhtin – From inside to outside and back again', *Reformulation*, 35: 17–18.
Martin, E.S. and Schurtman, R. (1985) 'Termination anxiety as it affects the therapist', *Psychotherapy: Theory, Research, Practice, Training*, 22, 1: 92–96.
McLeod, I. (2003) *Introduction to Counselling*, Buckingham: Open University.
Proctor, B. (1994) 'Supervision – Competence, confidence, accountability', *British Journal of Guidance and Counselling*, 22, 3: 309–318.
Ryle, A. (1994) 'Consciousness and psychotherapy', *British Journal of Medical Psychology*, 67: 115–123.
Ryle, A. (1997) *Cognitive Analytic Therapy and Borderline Personality Disorder*, Chichester: Wiley.
Ryle, A. and Kerr, I. (2002) *Introducing Cognitive Analytic Therapy*, Chichester: Wiley.
Salzberger-Wittenberg, I. (1970) *Psycho-analytic Insights and Relationships*, London: Routledge.
Stiles, W.B. (1997) 'Signs and voices: Joining a conversation in progress', *British Journal of Medical Psychology*, 70: 169–176.
Tanner, C. (2002) 'Target Problems', *Reformulation*, 16: 10–13.
Vygotsky, L.S. (1978) *Mind in Society*, Cambridge, MA: Harvard University Press.
Welch, L. (1994) 'Supervision: Integrating self and skill', *ACAT News*, Spring, 3: 14–17.
Yourman, D.B. (2003) 'Trainee disclosure in psychotherapy supervision: The impact of shame', *Journal of Clinical Psychology*, 59: 601–609.

Chapter 15

Supervising non-CAT therapists

Mark Westacott

Introduction

The cognitive analytic approach offers a remarkably powerful and versatile set of relational concepts and tools for providing supervision and consultancy to individuals and groups. As well as an effective approach to therapy and clinical supervision, CAT is now also used to provide consultancy to teams and services (see Chapter 16, also Carradice 2012, Elford and Ball 2014) and has also moved beyond the health and forensic fields to include applications to business management and executive coaching. CAT offers a fundamentally relational and dynamic view of how people and social systems work and this, along with its tools for mapping and sharing formulations, makes the approach particularly well suited for supervision and consultation across a broad range of services. CAT's emphasis on collaborative working, transparency, and flexibility in the way that the tools can be applied, also makes it a useful approach when supervising professionals who have not received specific training in the model.

Good quality supervision and ongoing professional development for psychotherapists is increasingly recognised as important for clinical practice and for supporting therapist development and preventing burnout and emotional depletion (Orlinsky and Ronnestad 2009). Regular supervision is now also a requirement for ongoing registration with most professional bodies and many of these organisations have developed their own programmes for training and accrediting supervisors. Within-modality supervision is probably the most common type of clinical supervision within the field of psychotherapy. There are occasions, however, when supervision based on the CAT model is provided to therapists and other professionals who may not be trained in this approach themselves and may even be working in an entirely different therapeutic modality.

A CAT approach to supervision is sometimes requested by professionals who have no training in the CAT model and perhaps a limited experience of specifically relational ways of working. This might in fact be precisely the reason they are seeking a CAT approach to their work – to provide a fresh perspective and new ideas about how to progress their clinical cases. This type of supervision, with professionals working in alternative modalities, can provide some stimulating opportunities to demonstrate the adaptability of the CAT framework and also offers the opportunity to enter into a creative dialogue with therapists working with a different model. However, this type of supervision also comes with a number of challenges and there are some important limitations and potential difficulties with this kind of cross-modality supervision.

Particular strengths of the CAT approach to supervision

There are many reasons why someone might seek supervision with a therapist trained in the CAT model and there are also a number of aspects of the CAT approach that make it particularly suited to supervising colleagues from a range of different backgrounds. CAT works through developing relational understanding and attention to the quality of the relationship is central to both therapy and supervision. This is common to a number of therapy approaches of course, but the reformulation tools of CAT are a particularly useful resource for conceptualising and working with relational processes. Marx (2011) notes how the prose and diagrammatic reformulations can create space for thinking creatively about relational processes in a way that is non-blaming and 'out there'. He also describes how the concept of reciprocal roles can provide a useful way of thinking about the different layers of the supervision process – intra-psychic, interpersonal, organisational and cultural (Marx 2011). These tools can be attractive to therapists who are struggling with the relational dynamics of their work, perhaps because their own model does not provide particularly useful ways of formulating such problems, or because they are working with relationally complex issues.

The CAT approach is flexible and integrative and readily lends itself to working with a range of different clients. Because it integrates ideas from a number of approaches, including the cognitive, dialogic and object relational, the model can appeal to a diverse range of therapists looking for an alternative perspective but one perceived to be not too far removed from their own way of working. Although the CAT technical language can be off-putting, this is usually rendered more palatable when working with non-CAT therapists (for example, 'maps' and 'patterns' instead of sequential diagrammatic reformulations and reciprocal role procedures) and most therapists, once they have grasped the idea of the reciprocal role, can begin to develop from this a more relational way of formulating their work.

The CAT model also allows for parallel processes (see Chapter 1 and Binder and Strupp 1997) to be thought about in a straightforward, helpful way. Parallel processes occur when the same interpersonal dynamics are played out in the therapist-client relationship and in the supervision relationship. From a CAT perspective, these are conceptualised and mapped out as re-enactments of particular reciprocal role procedures across the client, therapist and supervisor pairs. Focusing on these processes in this clear and tractable way can help move the clinical work forward and can also promote relational awareness in supervisees and deepen the experience of the supervision.

The CAT model lends itself to being applied at different levels within systems, from supervising individuals to providing supervision and consultation to groups and teams. This again can make the approach highly attractive not only for therapists looking for supervision around particular clinical cases, but also to professionals looking to develop their roles and effectiveness within teams and services.

CAT has a clearly articulated model of learning, based on Vygotsky's work (Kozulin 2013), which emphasises that development occurs through co-created dialogue. Therefore the supervisor needs to be attuned to the current level of development of the supervisee, carefully supporting or scaffolding their learning, within what is called their zone of proximal development (ZPD). This model of learning makes the CAT approach to supervision particularly useful when supervising therapists from a range of different therapeutic backgrounds as it focuses on the current skill level and knowledge of the supervisee and builds from that point forwards. Of course, it helps if the CAT supervisor has some familiarity with other therapy and systems models and can draw on these when needed to facilitate learning.

Examples of CAT supervision for non-CAT therapists

Here are some examples from my own experience of providing CAT informed supervision to non-CAT therapists and other professionals:

1. *A clinical psychologist trained in Cognitive Behavioural Therapy (CBT) requested regular supervision each month to develop her skills when working with staff teams and the organisational dynamics in her eating disorder service. This was alongside her regular monthly supervision with her manager, who was a consultant clinical psychologist trained in Dialectical Behaviour Therapy (DBT) and CBT. She had some familiarity with the CAT model from working with a colleague in a previous post who was a CAT psychotherapist.*
2. *Two occupational therapists in a regional medium secure unit needed fortnightly supervision over a year when running a set of new Thinking Skills groups for personality disordered offenders. They requested supervision on the content of the programme and on how to manage the relational dynamics of the group. They thought a CAT approach would be particularly useful for this client group and also for understanding and working with their own countertransference reactions. Their main way of working was mostly psychodynamic and integrative and they had both previously attended a one-day introduction to CAT workshop.*
3. *An experienced executive coach requested monthly supervision to discuss her emotional reactions and style of working with highly narcissistic and emotionally avoidant clients. She tended to feel de-skilled and emotionally depleted in these situations. Her usual approach to coaching was based on*

neurolinguistic programming (NLP). She had heard about CAT from a colleague who had received a personal CAT therapy but had no training or experience in the model.

4   *A new head of clinical psychology wanted a regular monthly space to talk about the development of her role in a community complex cases service. She also wanted to bring some of her own treatment cases along for discussion. This was alongside her normal managerial supervision with a clinical services manager who had a background in social work. Her main therapy models were CBT and systemic therapy. She had had some exposure to CAT years ago as part of her clinical psychology training and had also attended a number of more recent training events on CAT.*

Is this supervision or consultancy?

There are many more examples of this type of work, including where supervision is provided to groups and teams, but even this small list illustrates something of the flexibility of the model in providing supervision to therapists with diverse clinical backgrounds. In these examples, all of the supervisees had some awareness of the model, found that the approach personally resonated, and wanted to learn more. This is a good place to start from when providing this type of supervision and can make the development of the supervisory alliance more straightforward. Gilbert and Evans (2000) in their book on integrative relational supervision have used the term 'consultative supervision' to describe the type of supervision that is provided to qualified professionals and that can sometimes be with supervisees working in different therapy modalities. This contrasts with 'training supervision' that is required by trainees during their therapy training and is usually carried out by a supervisor who is experienced in the same treatment modality.

After training, most therapists continue having supervision in the same modality and this is perhaps the most common model of supervision. There are clear advantages in having a supervisor who is working with the same model and this is essential for skills development, preventing therapeutic drift, and for the emotional support and understanding that is provided by a close colleague singing from the same hymn sheet. The kind of cross-modality supervision that I am describing here is not meant to replace this. There are times though, as mentioned above, when qualified therapists seek additional supervision. It can also happen of course that therapists may not be able to access supervision within their own model of therapy and so come to the CAT therapist as the next best thing or perhaps because this supervisor has been allocated by the service.

Looking at the examples above it is clear that this kind of cross-modal supervision can sometimes look very similar to consultancy and in practice the two can sometimes overlap and be difficult to distinguish. As a general rule, in supervision the focus is more explicitly on the welfare of clients and the development and support of the supervisee (Inskipp and Proctor 1993) whereas in consultancy the focus is usually on a more specific task, such as guiding care planning (Carradice 2012), resolving specific problems within a team or supporting the development of a new service. In consultancy the contract is also usually for a shorter period of time whereas supervisory relationships usually extend over many months or even years. Whichever type of support is being offered, it is essential to think carefully about its aims and scope at the contracting stage of the relationship. Giving consideration to whether it is consultancy or supervision that is being offered can help focus this discussion.

Common features and challenges of cross-modal supervision

The supervisees are not trained in CAT and typically are not looking to use specific CAT interventions in their own clinical work

The supervisee may, for example, work with a number of different models or have a main therapy model and it is likely that they will have another supervisor who is providing supervision congruent with this. A common example of this supervision is the one mentioned above of the eating disorders psychologist who was trained mostly in CBT and who wanted supervision on the relational aspects of her work with staff teams. In this kind of supervision the extent to which CAT concepts and tools, such as reciprocal role procedures and mapping, are discussed together and utilised can be highly variable. It will not be helpful to overwhelm someone working with a DBT or CBT framework with a new therapy language and often the supervisor simply holds in mind the CAT framework and draws on it to guide thinking and discussion.

At other times however, CAT ideas and tools are explicitly referred to and utilised collaboratively. This might be the case with supervisees who have some familiarity with the CAT model or who are used to working integratively and can draw on different formulations for particular aspects of the therapy. Introducing the idea of the reciprocal role procedure and then scaffolding the development of relational thinking through discussion and joint mapping of reciprocal role procedures and states is usually a key part of this process. Supervisees can keep maps and bring them to further sessions so that the new understanding is held across supervision sessions. The amount of CAT theory that is introduced is variable and largely dependent on the supervisee. Rather like working with clients, the process of joint description and the development of a meta-level 'observing us' position is usually more important than discussions about theory (see Darongkamas et al. 2014 for discussion of the 'observing us' position in supervision). The fact that portable tools like maps are generated and brought back to sessions is also immensely useful, particularly as supervision sessions in this context can be irregular or infrequent.

Cross-modal supervision is often organised 'externally'

If cross-modal supervision is organised externally the supervisor may not be part of the same professional team or even employed within the same organisation as the supervisee.

Common examples in my experience include the provision of external supervision to professionals in forensic, eating disorders, learning disability and complex cases services. This can take the form of regular group supervision, supervision with individual clinicians, or a more limited intervention to supervise a particular piece of work such as a group therapy. The latter is a good example of when supervision and consultation can feel blurred and this should be clarified at the contracting stage of the relationship. Of course, the CAT supervisor may be working in the same organisation as the supervisee, but this is often not the case.

External supervision can add an extra level of complexity to the ethical and dynamic relationships between the parties involved. An example of this might be how the external supervision fits into the governance structures of the service and what action the supervisor should take if there are concerns about the welfare or competence of the supervisee. Confidentiality will also need careful discussion, particularly if the external supervisor has relationships with a number of people in the organisation. Such issues need to be clarified at the contracting stage. This stage is important and supervisory aims and expectations should either be written in the form of a contract or at least noted and agreed carefully in the supervision notes. See Scaife (2008) for a full discussion of the use of supervision contracts.

The goals and purposes of supervision need to be clarified carefully

Inskipp and Proctor (1993) describe three purposes of supervision: a *formative* purpose where the focus is on the supervisee's learning; a *normative* purpose, where client welfare and ethical and professional concerns are the focus; and a *restorative* purpose, where the focus is on emotional support of the supervisee. In cross-modal supervision the goals that supervisees bring to supervision can often be very specific. For example, the supervisee might just want help in formulating with complex clients alongside their usual modality-specific supervision. However, just because a supervisee comes with specific goals does not mean that the other purposes of supervision can be put aside. For example, the supervisor still has a responsibility to ensure client welfare and also has an ethical responsibility to ensure that supervisees are working within levels of competence appropriate to their stage of professional training. They will also want to provide emotional support and assess the impact of the work on the emotional well-being of the supervisee.

For cross-modal supervision it is the *normative*, managerial and ethical aspects of the supervision that are likely to present the most challenges and need the fullest discussion at the contracting stage of the supervision. For example, the roles of other supervisors and the issue of managerial responsibility must be clarified. If the focus is on an aspect of the clinical work, what other supervision is in place and who is available in an emergency? Another common issue is whether the supervisee is thinking of bringing the same cases to two supervisors, perhaps with the aim of having supervision on different aspects of their work. This can clearly create a number of conflicts and tensions. For example, how would the trainee hold and use two perspectives when working with their client? Also, what would be the lines of professional accountability and governance in this kind of supervision? Occasionally, in my experience, supervisees do bring cases where they are feeling stuck and where there is another supervisor providing regular supervision. Usually the discussion centres on a specific aspect of the work and I encourage the supervisee to take this back to the main supervisor so that any conclusions can be integrated back into their main way of working. These are usually 'one off' discussions and having two supervisory inputs with the same client is probably best avoided.

Tensions may arise in the supervisory alliance

The lack of a shared therapy language and sometimes different backgrounds in training and approach can more easily lead to misunderstandings and also to the mobilisation of unhelpful roles and procedures. Common patterns include feeling that the CAT supervisor is an expert in the field and has all the answers, or thinking that the CAT approach is particularly insightful and so is idealised. These can have the effect of leaving supervisees feeling deskilled and disempowered and this is not conducive to learning or effective supervision. The good news of course is that working with these types of dynamics is grist to the mill for CAT supervisors and the emphasis on working collaboratively alongside one another helps the process of naming and reducing these role pressures.

Another potential dynamic is when the supervisee feels resentful of the supervisor and perhaps experiences the CAT approach as somehow questioning or discrediting their own main way of working. In my experience, this is more likely to happen if the supervision has been set up by a manager rather than directly by the supervisee. It is also more likely when the supervisor has little understanding of the supervisee's main model and so is less effective at scaffolding learning.

A useful way of reducing the likelihood of this is to have clear supervision goals from the outset. It also helps to emphasise that the supervisee is the expert when it comes to their work with their clients and that the supervision session is there to help them address their particular learning aims. The supervisor should also be curious about the supervisee's main model if they are unfamiliar with it and about the supervisee's style of working. Doing all of this sets a collaborative tone of two professionals sharing knowledge and working together for the benefit of both the client and the supervisee. The use of joint mapping together and the development of an 'observing us' position on the map and in the dialogue of supervision can also assist with this.

Sometimes, particularly with external supervision, there can be complex invitations into alliances against other professionals in the service, or perhaps even against other supervisors. There might be an unhelpful idealisation of CAT over other approaches, for example, or a general denigration of management or the wider service. Such splitting processes are common in services, such as forensic, eating disorder and complex cases teams, where the dynamics of the patient also involve processes of partial dissociation and powerful pressures on staff to enact unhelpful reciprocations. What is particularly helpful about the CAT approach, of course, is that we have the tools to anticipate and work with these particular dynamics in a way that is non-blaming and promotes insight and integration.

Finally, some supervisees, particularly those not used to psychodynamic ways of working, will need some orientation to the CAT focus on countertransference and the emotional reactions of the therapist to the client and their history. This focus on the responses of the supervisee can feel more personal and challenging for some therapists, and some education and preparation is needed. Again the CAT model is helpful here as the different forms of countertransference – identifying and reciprocating (Ryle and Kerr 2002) – are easily understood as particular reciprocal role pressures to which the supervisee is responding. There is nothing confusing or mysterious, and even intense emotional reactions, sometimes thought of as projective identifications in other models, are conceptualised in this clear way. Modelling of how to use and talk about countertransference responses by the supervisor can be helpful here to guide the supervisee. Referring supervisees to the literature on related topics such as 'internal supervision' (see Casement 1994) can help scaffold learning. Focussing on countertransference in this way can help identify and draw out illuminating parallel processes that can enhance learning for the supervisee and deepen the experience of supervision and the development of the 'observing us' position.

Two examples of cross-modal supervision

Paul – Contracting and setting up the supervision relationship

Paul worked as a newly qualified clinical psychologist in a NHS Psychiatric Low Secure Unit. He requested additional supervision to help with understanding and managing the dynamics within the staff team, to discuss some of the pressures he was already feeling in his new role and to discuss some of his work with patients with offending histories as he was less experienced in working with offending behaviour and understanding its impact on the clinical team.

The lead clinical psychologist, who was familiar with CAT and its uses in forensic contexts, arranged Paul's external supervision with me. The initial meeting in this case was with her as she had also asked for supervision to be provided to another member of staff, in addition to Paul, and so a more general discussion was needed. A number of issues were discussed in this first meeting. We clarified the location, duration, frequency and funding of the supervision. For Paul, this was to be monthly for one hour at the Unit. The supervision would run for six months before being reviewed and Paul would give the lead psychologist feedback about its usefulness. The issue of confidentiality is an important one in this context and we agreed that the lead psychologist would not obtain feedback from me about the content or the engagement of the supervisee but if there were any serious ethical or fitness to practise concerns then I would discuss them with the supervisee first before raising them with the lead psychologist. Finally we clarified that Paul would continue to have regular managerial and clinical supervision with the lead psychologist every fortnight. We also agreed that he would avoid taking the same cases to both supervisors, unless there were specific reasons for this (such as the unavailability of one supervisor in an emergency or the need for help with a specific issue).

In the first meeting with Paul his aims and expectations for supervision were discussed. He felt that his clinical training had given him good skills for assessing and working with clients on their clinical symptoms, using a cognitive behavioural approach, but he was less experienced in working with patients with personality difficulties, offending behaviours, and understanding and working with team dynamics. He also wanted to have a better understanding of his own emotional reactions to the work and how he might best support the other staff in the secure unit. We agreed the location and timing of the supervision and also the boundaries around confidentiality and communication that had been agreed with the lead psychologist.

We discussed Paul's experience of individual therapy and team working. He had some experience of DBT and we also had a shared understanding of cognitive behavioural approaches. Paul had heard about CAT but had no experience or training in the model. We talked through my experience and limitations, particularly my lack of experience and training in DBT, and Paul discussed his wish to understand more about the CAT approach and to be able to use CAT thinking to develop his clinical skills and understanding of team and organisational processes. We clarified in the contract that the aim of supervision was to help him move forward in his role in the Secure Unit and develop skills in working with complex clients, but that the supervision would not equip him to offer CAT therapy and that he would need training in the model if he wanted to do this.

I talked about my interest in learning more about the DBT approach, said I would read up on this and that I would also be guided by Paul when discussing unfamiliar DBT interventions. This seemed important as Paul had asked for a supervisor who could help him work with complex forensic cases and team processes rather than directly requesting supervision by a CAT therapist, so careful work was needed to develop a collaborative and strong supervisory alliance. Some openness to different approaches and ways of working is most likely a minimum requirement for this kind of supervision to be feasible.

Emma – Working with role pressures and enactments

Emma, a clinical psychologist, had been coming for monthly supervision for about six months. Her main treatment modalities included CBT and Interpersonal Therapy (IPT) and she wanted help with managing personality disordered clients living in the community, many of whom engaged in self-harm and other destructive behaviours. She received regular supervision from her line manager, but the focus here tended to be on service rather than clinical issues and she was beginning to feel overwhelmed and emotionally depleted by the work.

Emma was familiar with CAT concepts from her clinical psychology training but had never used the model herself. Initially we mapped out particular roles and countertransference feelings she described. For Emma, a common reaction to many of her patients was that of feeling emotionally overwhelmed and not good enough as a therapist. She tended to manage this by offering additional time and being more available to these clients, reading up extensively on their problems, and also frequently discussing these patients with colleagues. She thought the source of feeling overwhelmed was 'therapy interfering factors' such as her clients' low levels of engagement and their difficulty in doing any between–session work. Emma expressed a deep level of commitment to her work and to helping her patients move forward.

The supervision did not focus specifically on Emma's therapy interventions with her clients. Starting with her feelings of powerlessness and anxiety, we mapped these emotions together along with her pattern of striving to offer a 'perfect' level of care. She identified that this often led to more anxiety as whatever she did never seemed to be enough and problems often even escalated, leaving her feeling overwhelmed again and even more anxious. These reciprocal roles and loops were mapped out. Emma understood enough about personality disorders to be able to make a new link between the internal roles of her patients and what she was being pulled into in her role with them as their therapist. Making the link between the 'perfectly caring – perfectly cared for' reciprocal role of her borderline clients and her own strivings was an example of this. This insight proved to be far more effective in helping her contain her anxiety and formulate and plan subsequent interventions than did the concept of 'therapy interfering factors'.

In conclusion, CAT provides an adaptable framework for supervising therapists who do not have specific training in the model. CAT has specific strengths in areas such as working with complexity, offending behaviour, team and organisational dynamics and relational processes generally, including parallel process. Because of this, a CAT approach to supervision is often requested by therapists working in these areas. Supervision across modalities is not without its problems though and various tensions and areas of potential conflict have been described. These difficulties are not insurmountable but need careful discussion and clarification at the outset of the supervisory relationship.

References

Binder, J.L. and Strupp, H.H. (1997) 'Supervision of psychodynamic psychotherapy', in C.E. Watkins (ed) *Handbook of Psychotherapy Supervision*, Chichester: Wiley.

Carradice, A. (2012) 'Five-session CAT consultancy: Using CAT to guide care planning with people diagnosed with personality disorder within community mental health teams', *Clinical Psychology and Psychotherapy*, 20, 4: 359–367.

Casement, P. (1994) *On Learning from the Patient*, London: Routledge.

Darongkamas, J., John, C. and Walker, M.J. (2014) 'An eight-eyed version of the Hawkins and Shohet's clinical supervision model: The addition of the cognitive analytic therapy concept of the "observing eye/I" as the "observing us"', *British Journal of Guidance and Counselling*, 42, 3: 261–270.

Elford, H. and Ball, Z. (2014) 'Using cognitive analytic therapy in a systemic context with staff teams', in J. Lloyd and P. Clayton (eds) *Cognitive Analytic Therapy with People with Intellectual Disabilities and Their Carers*, London: Jessica Kingsley.

Gilbert, M.C. and Evans, K. (2000) *Psychotherapy Supervision: An Integrative Relational Approach to Psychotherapy Supervision*, Buckingham: Open University Press.

Inskipp, F. and Proctor, B. (1993) *The Art, Craft and Tasks of Counselling Supervision, Part 1, Making the Most of Supervision*, Twickenham: Cascade Publications.

Kozulin, A. (2013) *Vygotsky's Psychology: A Biography of Ideas*, Cambridge, MA: Harvard University Press.

Marx, R. (2011) 'Relational supervision: Drawing on cognitive-analytic frameworks', *Psychology and Psychotherapy: Theory, Research and Practice*, 84: 406–424.

Orlinsky, D.E. and Ronnestad, M.H. (2009) *How Psychotherapists Develop: A Study of Therapeutic Work and Professional Growth*, Washington, DC: American Psychological Association.

Ryle, A. and Kerr, I.B. (2002) *Introducing Cognitive Analytic Therapy: Principles and Practice*, Chichester: Wiley.

Scaife, J. (2008) *Supervision in Clinical Practice, (second edition)*, London: Routledge.

Chapter 16

Supervising CAT consultancy in mental health teams

Angela Carradice

Introduction

Effective team working is essential for quality mental health services and there is well-researched guidance around the essential components of effective teams (West 2012). However, the reality is this is rarely achieved (Borrill et al. 2001) and there is growing pressure on mental health teams to provide evidence-based approaches which often involve psychologically-informed treatment for large numbers of people with complex clinical presentations (Kerr et al. 2007). Team members may have too little training and supervision to do this work effectively (Kerr et al. 2007). Some clients present to services in ways that mean it is difficult to help them, such as having unstable and chaotic lives (Carradice 2013). Many clients seek help when poor outcomes would be predicted (Ryle and Golynkina 2000), for example, because they are at an early stage of their recovery and are not yet able to benefit from psychotherapy (Kerr 1999), or because they do not have enough helpful coping strategies. Teams can experience the client's presentation as challenging and this sometimes results in unhelpful relational patterns between clients and the services, which then unintentionally reinforce the client's difficulties (Kerr 1999). These patterns can also lead to damaging processes within teams, such as team 'splitting', stress and burnout (Main 1957).

The application of CAT to consultancy work is a growing area, with practitioners using innovative approaches to apply the skills from psychotherapy to consultation in ways which suit the context within which they work (e.g. Kerr 1999). I will use the terms 'consultant' or 'practitioner' to refer to the CAT practitioner, psychologist or psychological therapist who is integrated into a team whilst offering consultation. This chapter focuses on 'internal' consultancy, rather than other kinds of consultancy such as 'external' (where the consultant is based outside the team). CAT consultation can be a resource to a team, helping it to address pressures, clarify roles and avoid unhelpful reinforcement of the client's difficulties through its responses to the client. This approach is thought to improve the care provided, or, at the very least, to support the team to 'do no harm' (Dawson 1988). Staff teams report CAT to be an accessible relational model which aids their psychological thinking and provides a shared language (Thompson et al. 2008). The main benefits include how the CAT formulation provides a containing framework which empowers teams to work effectively with their clients (Carradice and Bennett 2012), by helping them express and make sense of their reactions to the client and build (and maintain) their empathy and understanding for the client in order to maintain a therapeutic approach (Carradice 2004). CAT consultation also offers the potential to provide a secure theoretical base for the team (Carradice and Bennett 2012). This is the concept of '*using CAT*' (applying CAT outside the therapy role) rather than '*doing CAT*' therapy (Potter 1999) and a style of working ('*doing with*') that is a vision for client care (Kerr et al. 2007).

Supervision of consultation

The importance of supervision is well established in psychotherapy and is essential for professional accreditation. Supervision of consultation work is as important as supervision of psychotherapy, but, in contrast, consultation supervision is often overlooked both in the literature and in clinical practice. Consultation work can be personally challenging and anxiety provoking. Supervision has an important restorative function and can help acknowledge the emotional impact of the work (Inskipp and Proctor 1993). Supervision can also help the supervisee develop and maintain resilience and self-care. The supervisor can encourage the supervisee to develop their internal reflective capacity (the idea of the 'internal supervisor' offered by Casement 1985) and to nurture a compassionate 'self to self' internal supervisor.

The context of consultation has specific challenges which supervisors need to recognise. For example, consultation work is often experienced as more exposing by practitioners because they are working with their colleagues and this affects the boundaries of the work. In psychotherapy therapeutic boundaries are protective for both the client and therapist (Hamilton 2010), for example, contact is limited to regular sessions with an agreed purpose. However, a practitioner providing internal consultancy will frequently meet colleagues in different situations. This can present a number of challenges to maintaining the effectiveness of the role, for example, it is more difficult to avoid enacting unhelpful team procedures, when also a member of the team.

While the literature on supervisor competence is growing (e.g. Roth and Pilling 2015), there is an absence of guidance about supervisor competence in relation to consultancy work. Just as we expect a psychotherapy supervisor to be both an experienced therapist and competent supervisor, it seems sensible that when supervising consultation, the supervisor is also competent in consultation. However there are real difficulties for both supervisors and for those seeking supervision, in ensuring they have the necessary knowledge and skills in consultation. For example, although there are rich case examples in the CAT literature (e.g. Kerr 1999), there is limited guidance about approaches to consultation, the skills involved and the steps needed to develop these skills. There is a paucity of research about the effectiveness of different approaches to consultation (Mattan et al. 2009) and no National Institute of Health Care Excellence (NICE) guidance on effective approaches to consultation. In addition, although some professional training (for example, clinical psychology) covers consultation, most training is focused on the development of skills for direct client work. Some of these factors may account for the lack of supervision available for this work.

Although the literature on supervision of consultation is relatively undeveloped, it is important that, despite this lack of guidance, practitioners and supervisors continue to work together to develop consultancy approaches further and then share this learning in the literature and contribute to further research. With this in mind, this chapter describes how psychotherapy concepts can be applied to consultancy work and its supervision, presents a model of CAT consultancy (Carradice and Bennett 2012) and illustrates some of the skills used in consultation.

The alliance with the team

The essential ingredients of consultancy work are similar to those in psychotherapy and benefit from reflection in supervision. For example, research consistently reports the alliance between the therapist and the client as the key predictor of outcome from therapy (e.g. Horvath and Symonds 1991). The same is likely to be true for consultancy work. Bordin (1979) describes three components of an alliance: a bond (or connection), shared goals/aims and a shared task which involves activities to achieve the aims. This also involves noticing and addressing potential alliance ruptures.

Developing positive working alliances with members of the team takes time and can be a useful subject for supervision discussions, especially when starting in a new service. The practitioner needs to get to know the team members (individually and as a team), to develop an understanding of team history and culture and to build empathy for the inherent challenges faced in their work. The alliance is developed through building credibility with team members by contributing reliably to the therapeutic work of the team. This involves focusing on the agreed task. If the team is unclear about this, then the practitioner needs to start by encouraging the team to describe and agree the team task. It is important to have an explicit and transparent role that is agreed with the team and to continually reflect on the process of developing alliances. Everything the practitioner does on a day to day basis has the potential to enhance the alliance with the team. So it is important for the practitioner to try to be perceived as 'useful', 'safe', and 'trusted', whilst at the same time demonstrating professional integrity and effective boundaries.

Parallel process

Supervision of consultation involves working with parallel process (see Chapter 1) just as supervision of therapy does. However, when supervising consultation, the supervisor needs to understand that parallel processes may occur not only between the supervisory relationship and the therapeutic relationship. They may involve the enactment of similar relational patterns between any pair of interlinked relationships: e.g. between the client/team relationship, the team/practitioner relationship, the practitioner/supervisor relationship and the team's relationship with the wider organisation.

For example, a practitioner's loss of empathy towards the team, may become apparent in a supervision session. This may reflect a parallel process with a team's relationship with a client, if the team itself has lost empathy. Their loss of empathy may be due to understandable factors like the nature of the work, high caseloads or because of intense relational pressures specific to their relationship with the client. When empathy is lost professionals may adopt unhelpful negative or pejorative appraisals of their client or their role (for example, 'she is a manipulative client' or 'I am no good at my job') and clinical practice can deteriorate. The supervisor will need to help the practitioner to notice the parallel process in their own response to the team and move back to formulating the context, in order to restore empathy and stay in a helpful stance (or quickly return to this stance) whilst working with the team. This in turn can help the team to think in a psychologically formulated way about the clinical context (rather than making personalised judgements), and they may then renew their empathy and provide therapeutic care within challenging conditions. This example also shows how parallel process works in both directions. A practitioner who experiences a safe reflective relationship with an active supportive supervisor (guided by a clear model and transparent approach) may then incorporate similar elements into their consultative relationships, thereby supporting team members in their work with clients.

The way team members seek and use consultation may also reflect a parallel process. For example, if a team is drawn into 'striving to provide too much care' for a client (which the client may be inviting the team to do), it can unintentionally reinforce the client's difficulties and impede his or her recovery in the longer term. In a parallel process the team may seek too much care from the practitioner, and then the practitioner may feel under pressure to strive to provide help to the team in unboundaried ways, for example, by being available to help team members at any time. This approach is not usually sustainable and, over time, it disempowers the team by communicating lack of faith in their ability, which can be replicated in the care they offer clients. When the practitioner brings this consultation to supervision, the supervisor may also feel a pull to offer more, perhaps becoming more active than usual. Reflection in supervision can help the practitioner focus on using balanced boundaries, such as regular bookable slots for consultation and a limited number of ad hoc conversations, to help set the conditions for offering consultation in a more manageable way. This approach can be more containing and empowering for teams over time, although initially, like the client, the team may prefer the consultation to be instant and 'on tap'.

Focusing on task and process

During consultation the practitioner needs to move seamlessly between focusing on the task in hand and addressing difficulties with the process which, if overlooked, may lead to alliance ruptures (Carradice 2013). The task of the consultation session may, for example, involve helping two members of the team describe their 'stuckness', but it may become apparent that the same 'stuckness' is being enacted in the relationship with the consultant. The practitioner must then respond appropriately to this process, before moving back to the task. This skill is essential for consultation work to be effective (as it is in individual psychotherapy). Supervision can also help the supervisee to anticipate, understand, contain and address relational processes, including reciprocal role enactments they may have missed (and their reactions to them), and to stay closely attuned to the needs of the team members and their client. Supervision can help the practitioner to remain compassionate to the team members during difficult interactions, where the team can (without realising) enact the client's difficulties towards the practitioner.

Levels of consultancy work

The diagram (Figure 16.1) below from Carradice and Bennett (2012) demonstrates three levels of consultancy work. CAT mapping is central to each level:

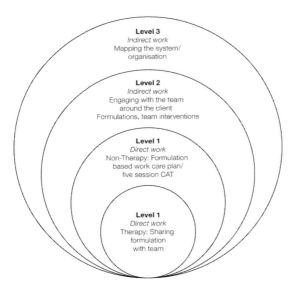

Figure 16.1 Levels of working
(Carradice and Bennett 2012)

Supervision can help the supervisee decide the most appropriate level of intervention for the particular situation and what kind of intervention to offer. The choice will depend on a number of factors, including attitudes in the staff team to the issue concerned (and in relation to the process of change), factors affecting the team's emotional resilience, and other support available to the team (such as reflective practice groups).

At Level one, the practitioner who is undertaking therapy with a client may explicitly share the diagram with the team, to guide team interventions. This can be done with or without the client, but important issues need to be considered such as informed consent, how the client is involved and whether the rationale for sharing is related to the client's needs (rather than an unhelpful enactment of the client's (or team's) procedures. In order to maintain effective therapeutic boundaries, it is important to approach this option with caution and reflect in supervision about whether or not to share information and, if so, how and in what circumstances. Level one does not always involve therapy, but may instead consist of working with the client and a team member to develop a psychologically informed care plan (e.g. Carradice 2013).

At Level two, consultation involves supporting teams to work effectively with the client without the client being directly involved. This can involve informal reflective conversations with individual workers or groups, through to provision of formalised approaches such as whole team interventions (e.g. Carradice 2004). This level emphasises the importance of clinical leadership as a process of 'sense making and direction giving' guided by psychological reformulation.

Level three working involves developing reformulations to support interventions at the team or organisational level. This approach is particularly helpful when there are difficulties around recurring themes, for example, struggling to discharge clients therapeutically (Carradice and Bennett 2012), or when the need relates to team functioning or organisational processes (e.g. Walsh 1996). Even if the consultation work is not focused on Level three working, it can still be useful in supervision to map the organisational context within which the work is done, particularly if there are unhelpful team procedures operating within the team's culture. This map can then inform the supervisee's decision-making about how to target their role most effectively.

Contextual reformulation is usually at the heart of consultation work at levels 2 and 3 and is a process of mapping which takes account of and describes the context, including the responses of staff teams in terms of reciprocal role enactments (Ryle and Kerr 2002). There are many ways of developing contextual maps and they can be comprehensive or summarise simple procedures. Supervision can support the practitioner to develop contextual maps by helping them reflect on the issues faced by the team and practise mapping (e.g. through role play), so that they can begin to develop maps 'live' with groups (in much the same way as during therapy). This involves exploring the patterns within the system in which the client is embedded from a place as observer in the system, whilst also being part of the system (Carradice and Bennett 2012).

An example of a contextual map of team functioning developed in supervision with a psychologist is shown in Figure 16.2.

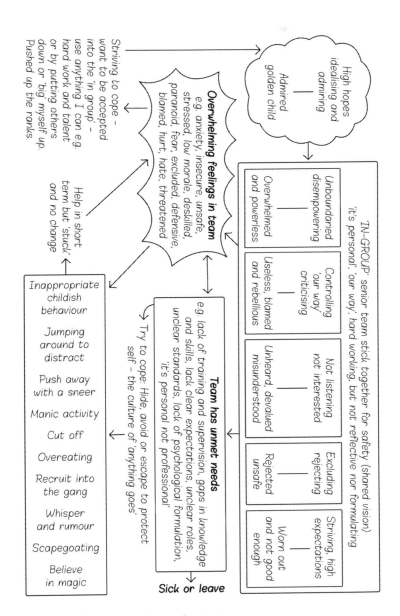

Figure 16.2 Formulation of team functioning

Drawing this diagram in supervision helped the practitioner to express the feelings she experienced about how team members were behaving at work, to describe the repeating patterns in the culture (and begin to resist the invitations to reciprocate) and to build her empathy and understanding for the team, so that she was able to refocus her role. The reformulation helped the supervisee to think more clearly and to focus on how to influence the senior team to incorporate a balanced approach to improving its management style and support, in the form of clear expectations about roles, and professional boundaries, supervision and training, so that the team could function better.

CAT consultancy framework

Carradice and Bennett (2012) offer a framework for CAT consultancy in Table 16.1, to illustrate the steps required at levels 2 and 3, and suggest that success at the later stages comes from spending sufficient time on completing the earlier stages.

Each stage of the framework is necessary, but the length of time needed for each stage varies depending on the nature of the work. The stages can be followed within one meeting or over consecutive meetings. Supervisees may bring various issues relating to the framework to supervision, such as feeling the urge to rush ahead too quickly through the stages. Discussion in supervision can help consider

Table 16.1 Consultancy framework

Steps	Tasks
1 **Letting people talk**	Communicate empathy and understanding whilst hearing their struggle. Validate: listen, support and contain, help to put their experiences into words. Help reduce expressed emotion so that team can begin to gradually reflect.
2 **Reformulation of team 'stuckness'**	Normalise experiences and convey they can be made sense of, help them re-engage with their empathy for the client, e.g. by using narratives of the client's difficulties.
3 **CAT mapping**	Develop a CAT map as collaboratively as possible, identifying main reciprocal roles and key procedures, by asking questions such as: What happens and what next?
4 **Seeking consensus**	Check out where we all agree and get everyone on board. The team may take map away to test and refine.
5 **Further understanding**	Build relational understanding. Ask which parts of map they have observed, e.g. between the client and others and which parts they have experienced themselves.
6 **Planning the intervention**	Support the team to name and understand feelings and to think and develop their own plans, e.g. formulated care plan – *thinking before doing*, whilst trusting their knowledge and skills.

(Adapted from Carradice and Bennett 2012)

whether this reflects a procedure related, for example, to the client's coping style or the team's responses to the client.

CAT consultative tools

The Boundary Seesaw model

Laura Hamilton developed the Boundary Seesaw model (see Figure 16.3) through using CAT contextual reformulation to understand issues relating to therapeutic boundaries within a high secure environment (Hamilton 2010, Hamilton 2014). Adaptations of this model have also been used in other settings with encouraging results (e.g. Hamilton et al. in preparation). The model describes the continuum of therapeutic boundaries and has multiple uses in supporting teams with providing therapeutic care, including CAT-formulated care planning, and in reflecting on clinical work during consultation sessions.

The continuum of the seesaw covers three areas and individual team members (or whole teams) can act from any of the three roles in relation to the boundaries in any given situation (such as, the care offered to a client). The *'controller'* role is when the therapeutic boundaries are too rigid or the team member is under-involved. When a worker (or service) is in this role they may focus on the risks or most challenging aspects of the clinical presentation and their responses can be *critical*, *controlling* and/or *rejecting*, which can reinforce the client's early experiences (such as feeling *not good enough*, *trapped* or *rejected*). The client is likely to respond by either compliance with these roles or rebellion. The *pacifier* stance is the opposite end of the seesaw and is like a *super carer* role, for example, when a worker (or the service) has developed boundaries which have resulted in *being*

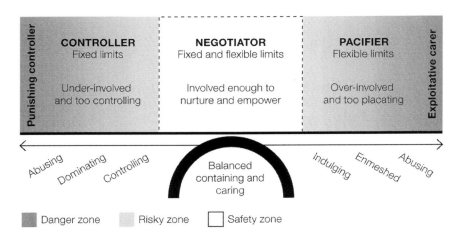

Figure 16.3 Boundary Seesaw model
(Hamilton 2014)

over-involved/doing too much or *too indulging* in their approach. This can be called *offering special care*, and can result in the client *being disempowered* and *becoming more dependent on others*. When workers are in the '*pacifier*' role, they tend to be aware mainly of the client's vulnerabilities which they want to help.

Both ends of the continuum may (or may not) be well-intended roles, but they unintentionally reinforce unhelpful patterns of coping, and so result in clients staying the same or deteriorating. Being at one end can promote flipping to the other end, such as becoming *burnt out* by the *pacifier* role and switching to *controller*. When staff (within one team or across different agencies) are in different roles, there is more potential for splitting, where different people enact different roles, as if they are only aware of part of the client's experience, leading to inconsistencies and/or conflicts in care. The middle area of the Boundary Seesaw is called the '*negotiator*' role that enables teams to provide 'good enough care'. This is when care is provided with explicit limits and there is a flexible, realistic balance of care and control, which is based on awareness of the whole of the client's experiences (and ways of coping) and in tune with recovery.

The Boundary Seesaw model is a useful reflective and/or planning tool both within consultation sessions and in supervision. Megan Black, Clinical Psychologist, provides consultation using CAT ideas and describes an example of using the model in supervision:

> *I took a consultation session I had with Carol, a mental health nurse, to supervision because I didn't feel comfortable after the session. Carol came to see me to discuss her work with Natalie, who has a diagnosis of borderline personality disorder. Carol said that Natalie contacts her every day to express her distressing suicidal thoughts. Carol listens to Natalie, but finds it difficult to get a word in and gets stressed, because, whenever she speaks to Natalie, Natalie won't focus on strategies to help and instead says she wants to be 'looked after' by Carol. Carol told me she visits Natalie at home frequently and thinks Natalie wouldn't cope without the visits and telephone calls.*
>
> *Carol was hopeless and distressed in the session as she described how Natalie's mental health was deteriorating and I felt overwhelmed listening to her. I told my supervisor I struggled to know how to help.*
>
> *My supervisor listened, and asked me what I offered during the session. I explained how, after listening to and validating Carol's experiences, I used the Boundary Seesaw model with Carol, to help facilitate a discussion about her relationship with Natalie. I reflected on how Carol is often drawn into the 'pacifier' role, working hard to meet Natalie's needs, and fearing what would happen if she didn't. This was useful because with this recognition, Carol began to rethink her approach.*
>
> *I explained to my supervisor that although I felt we'd made progress, I left the session feeling that I should do more. I reflected that I had provided lots of reassurance, especially at times when Carol was self-blaming. I asked my*

supervisor to help me plan some joint work with Carol to help her and the client get on track.

My supervisor encouraged me to use the Boundary Seesaw model to think about possible parallel processes. During this discussion, I recognised I was responding to the pull towards the pacifier role, in my wish to rescue Carol. I reflected on how I could empower Carol to take a more balanced approach (associated with the negotiator role), to help her and Natalie develop a more boundaried relationship. I didn't need to see the client with Carol; she would be able to work on this with Natalie herself.

Standard CAT consultation templates

Alongside the Boundary Seesaw model, other diagrams can be useful during consultation work (Carradice 2012). The diagrams in Figure 16.4 can help focus discussion as they show examples of clients' reciprocal roles, the intention to be therapeutic and the potential invitation to provide special care (the *pacifier* role on the Boundary Seesaw model).

These diagrams can be used as 'templates' by practitioners who are developing their CAT consultation skills, and are also useful as an accessible visual guide for team members when discussing their work during reflective sessions or planning for interventions. The words can easily be changed to reflect a particular client's experiences and the team's responses more accurately. Enactments can be discussed together and effective ways of relating with the client can be practised. Within supervision they are just as useful to help the supervisee to predict potential enactments in forthcoming consultation sessions (and to reflect afterwards).

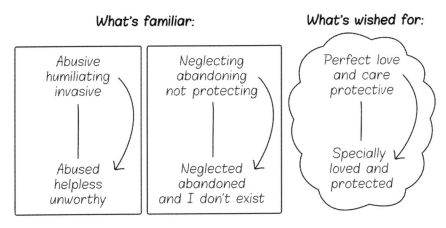

Figure 16.4a Consultancy templates
(Carradice 2012)

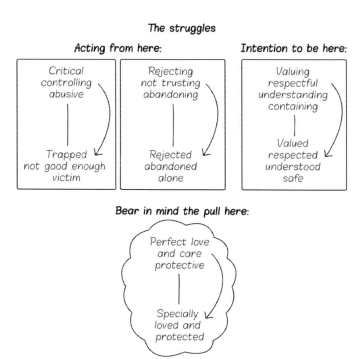

Figure 16.4b

Conclusion

Consultation is a developing field which shows promise in supporting mental health teams to provide effective therapeutic care. CAT consultancy literature is in its infancy and further research is needed. Providing consultation to teams needs as much care as any other kind of work, and supervision is therefore essential. This chapter describes common processes in consultancy supervision and gives an overview of CAT consultancy, with the aim of encouraging practitioners and their supervisors to continue to develop approaches to CAT consultation.

References

Bordin, E.S. (1979) 'The generalizability of the psychoanalytic concept of the working alliance', *Psychotherapy, Theory, Research and Practice*, 16, 3: 252–260.

Borrill, C.S., Carletta, J., Carter, A.J., Dawson, J.F., Garrod, S., Rees, A., Richards, A., Shapiro, D. and West, M.A. (2001) *The Effectiveness of Health Care Teams in the National Health Service*, Final Report to the Department of Health, University of Aston, Aston, Birmingham.

Carradice, A. (2004) 'Applying CAT to guide indirect working', *ACAT News*, 23: 16–23.

Carradice, A. (2012) *CAT Team Training to Support Work with People Who Have Experienced Complex Trauma*, unpublished training manual.

Carradice, A. (2013) 'Five session CAT consultancy: Using CAT to guide care planning with people diagnosed with personality disorder within CMHTs', *Clinical Psychology and Psychotherapy*, 20: 359–367.

Carradice, A. and Bennett, D. (2012) *Beyond the Psychotherapist's Chair: CAT Consultancy*, ACAT conference presentation, Manchester.

Casement, P. (1985) *On Learning from the Patient*, London: Routledge.

Dawson, D.F. (1988) 'Treatment of the borderline patient: Relationship management', *Canadian Journal of Psychiatry*, 33: 370–374.

Hamilton, L. (2010) 'The boundary seesaw model: good fences make for good neighbours', in A. Tennant and K. Howells (eds) *Using Time Not Doing Time: Practitioner Perspectives on Personality Disorder and Risk*, Oxford: John Wiley.

Hamilton, L. (2014) *Boundary Seesaw Workshop – Core Concepts (BSW-CC)*, unpublished training manual.

Hamilton, L. Bancroft, S. and Bloxsom, C. (in preparation) Qualitative study evaluating the impact of the Boundary Seesaw – Core Concepts training in a Low Secure Unit.

Horvath, A.O. and Symonds, B.D. (1991) 'Relation between working alliance and outcome in psychotherapy: A meta-analysis', *Journal of Counseling Psychology*, 38, 2: 139–149.

Inskipp, F. and Proctor, B. (1993) *The Arts, Craft and Tasks of Counselling Supervision Part 1 – Making the Most of Supervision*, Twickenham: Cascade Publications.

Kerr, I.B. (1999) 'Cognitive analytic therapy for borderline personality disorder in the context of a community mental health team: Individual and organizational psychodynamic implications', *British Journal of Psychotherapy*, 15, 4: 425–437.

Kerr, I.B., Dent-Brown, K. and Parry, G.D. (2007) 'Psychotherapy and mental health teams', *International Review of Psychiatry*, 19, 1: 63–80.

Main, T. (1957) 'The ailment', *British Journal of Medical Psychology*, 30: 129–145.

Mattan, R. and Isherwood, T. (2009) 'A grounded theory investigation of consultees' perception and experience of psychological consultation', *Mental Health and Learning Disabilities Research and Practice*, 6, 2: 169–183.

Potter, S. (1999) 'A personal view of ACAT', *ACAT News*, 11: 2–5.

Roth, A.D. and Pilling, S. (2015) *A Competence Framework for Supervision of Psychological Therapies*. Online. Available HTTP: <https://www.ucl.ac.uk/pals/research/cehp/research-groups/core/competence-frameworks/Supervision_of_Psychological_Therapies> (accessed 7 October 2015).

Ryle, A. and Golynkina, K. (2000) 'Effectiveness of time-limited cognitive analytic therapy of borderline personality disorder: Factors associated with outcome', *British Journal of Medical Psychology*, 73: 197–210.

Ryle, A. and Kerr, I.B. (2002) *Introducing Cognitive Analytic Therapy: Principles and Practice*, Chichester: Wiley.

Thompson, A.R., Donnison, J., Warnock-Parkes, E., Turpin, G., Turner, J. and Kerr, I.B. (2008) 'Multidisciplinary community mental health team staff's experience of a "skills level" training course in cognitive analytic therapy', *International Journal of Mental Health Nursing*, 17: 131–137.

Walsh, S. (1996) 'Adapting cognitive analytic therapy to make sense of psychologically harmful work environments', *British Journal of Medical Psychology*, 69: 3–20.

West, M.A. (2012) *Effective Teamwork: Practical Lessons from Organizational Research, (third edition)*, Chichester: Wiley Blackwell.

Chapter 17

Supervising CAT with young people

Louise K. McCutcheon, Lee Crothers and Steve Halperin

Introduction

This chapter focuses on supervision of clinical work and CAT with adolescents and young adults. Although we are particularly interested in the supervision of specific CAT interventions, many of our comments apply to the supervision of clinical work generally, because we believe taking a relational (CAT-informed) approach is helpful. We acknowledge that others might use CAT with younger children, however the majority of our experience is of supervising therapists working with 12–25 year olds, hereafter referred to as 'young people'.

Young people present for mental health treatment for many reasons, ranging from unresolved childhood problems to 'adult' mental health problems (including depression, substance use, anxiety disorders, eating disorders, personality disorders and psychotic disorders) that have their onset and peak period of incidence during these years (Rickwood et al. 2005). The flexibility of CAT makes it a particularly suitable model for younger people. CAT stresses the importance of the therapist attuning to the client's zone of proximal development (ZPD) (Vygotsky 1978) – see Glossary – and working within it. The therapist can be challenging, but it is his responsibility to remain within the client's ZPD, and to adjust the therapy to the person's capacities. It is a respectful, playful model, one that assumes that young people can be encouraged to use their own skills, something that young people want and need to do in a safe way.

The strong emphasis on finding ways to work truly collaboratively provides a new and challenging experience in young people's relationships with adults, confronting the often low expectations that systems have developed of them because of their age, mental health problems and other issues. Supervision can assist clinicians to reflect on these issues, and consider how CAT can be adapted and used creatively.

What is different about supervision of those working with young people?

Although the reasons young people present for treatment are often similar to those of older people, there are some particularly prominent themes and pressures in work with younger clients that are regularly brought to supervision.

We will consider some of these, and how supervision might assist supervisees to address them.

Readiness and the therapy contract

One dilemma supervisees often struggle with is whether or not a particular young person should be offered therapy. As there is little evidence to indicate who will use therapy best, a more pragmatic approach allows time-limited interventions to be offered to as many young people as possible, with review of what each person is able to achieve over time. We supervise those working with young people in both public and private settings, and have found that many young people, even those with moderate to severe problems, including borderline personality disorder, are able to make significant changes in relatively short periods of time (8–16 sessions) (Chanen et al. 2008). Perhaps this is because their maladaptive patterns are more malleable, and dysfunctional relationships are less entrenched.

There are also clearly cases in which there is little change by the end of the therapy. At these times, anxiety from the young person and the system can leave supervisees feeling they should extend the therapy contract. The central issue here is whether changing the contracted number of sessions represents an opportunity for better learning and outcomes, or will collude with unhelpful patterns (the young person's or those of others in the system). We consider the ending of therapy to be different from the termination of care, and some young people might clearly need more support after completing therapy, particularly when risks are high. In general, we encourage young people to try out what they have learned in therapy (e.g. during the follow-up period) before a decision is made to extend the therapy or offer a short contract of booster sessions. Occasionally the therapist, team and young person all agree that a short extension (e.g. four more sessions) will provide the best opportunity to complete work on a particular problem, or allow development of exit patterns. In contrast, some young people request to reduce the number of sessions. This is usually because they are feeling and functioning better or are not willing to work on change at this time. Accepting a reduction in the number of sessions can facilitate a 'good enough' ending, and is seen as a better option than persisting with a contract that the young person is unlikely to complete. A reasonable, if brief, experience of therapy is more likely to facilitate future 'adaptive help-seeking' and result in re-referral when the young person is ready to work again.

The extension or renegotiation of contracts can be delicate subjects and supervision can assist reflection about how much the decisions represent supervisees' avoidant or dependent collusions. Both supervisors' and therapists' expectations can weigh heavily on young clients, and the (perhaps unintended) message that one will need 'long-term' therapy can be unhelpful.

Difficulty engaging

Most young people are referred or brought in for treatment by others (such as primary or acute health care professionals, teachers, family members or friends), and are likely to differ in terms of their readiness to start treatment. A normative desire for greater autonomy can coincide with young people's low levels of mental health literacy and a reluctance to seek care especially from professionals (Rickwood et al. 2005). Although physical attendance at an interview signals at least some level of cooperation or agreement, the young person can concurrently communicate she does not want to be there, and is at best ambivalent about collaborating. Working with a young person who feels coerced to attend or is silent can be particularly frustrating (McCutcheon et al. 2007), and the challenge of how to engage a reluctant young person in treatment is commonly brought to supervision.

A typical exchange might be:

THERAPIST: It's pretty difficult . . . he just plays with his phone and doesn't say anything . . . I have real doubts about whether I can do anything useful for him.
SUPERVISOR: That does sound difficult. What happens if you just sit there a bit? Maybe take the pressure off both of you?
THERAPIST: I guess I did do that a bit more last session. I tried to make it like I wasn't waiting for him to speak all the time and that did feel better. Rather than asking him questions, I might try to suggest some things and see if he can just agree or disagree.

Gender differences in help-seeking are also apparent in young people, such that young men can equate seeking psychological treatment with vulnerability and weakness. Young people's expression of emotional distress can include antisocial behaviour, substance use, self-harm and social withdrawal, all of which can be particularly concerning to others (Rickwood et al. 2005). Assisting supervisees to take these factors into consideration, and where possible explore them with the young person, family and others, can facilitate engagement and collaboration on shared goals.

Common relational themes for young people

Power and control

Young people frequently find themselves in situations in which adults seem to have all the power. Childhood is unavoidably a period in which adults make most of the important decisions, but by adolescence most young people want to 'spread their wings' and assume more responsibility. Therefore, young people are often sensitive to reciprocal roles (RRs) such as *powerful* in relation to *powerless*, and *controlling* in relation to *controlled/trapped* or *out of control*. Adults (including therapists) who are concerned about young people's behaviour and well-being can experience strong pressure to become *controlling*. Therapists are not always aware of these forces, and can find themselves pulled into unhelpful enactments quickly. They can be overtly or covertly invited by the young person, parents or others in the young person's system to step in and become *directive* or *controlling*. Supervision can be a space to explore and understand these pressures and where they come from. It can help supervisees to identify their own reactions to situations, and to separate out which are responses to others' concerns and which are their own patterns.

Young people who feel trapped commonly attempt to gain control over their situation. This might be displayed by talking a lot, strictly limiting what can be discussed, or who can be involved. Sometimes this might take a more avoidant or resistant form, in which the young person is silent, defiant or refuses to cooperate. Enactments outside the therapy room can involve considerably more risk-taking and concerning behaviour. These responses are often the only ways a young person can manage the *powerless* or *trapped* experience, yet they can leave the therapist and others anxious. Supervision can explore ways to address these moments helpfully, in order to avoid collusion and to model an alternative.

THERAPIST: I'm not sure what is going on sometimes. She seems to change the subject at odd moments. Often to something random or unrelated to what we were talking about. I'm not sure if she realises she is doing it, but I just seem to get confused . . .
SUPERVISOR: Have you noticed when it happens? What were you talking about just before that? What do you think is going on, and how might you explore that with her?

Supervisees can be encouraged to notice which presentations or situations are more likely to pull them into enactments. In response to withdrawal and difficulty engaging a young person, therapists' concern frequently drives more directive and intrusive responses. Where young people's risk (towards themselves or others) is increasing, therapists often become more personally concerned, prompting more *rescuing* responses. Therapists who work with highly chaotic and troubled young people are more likely to collude with either *rescuing* or *perfectly caring* type patterns. It is understandable and often quite appropriate for therapists to want to assume responsibility when the young person appears unable to do this himself. Supervision can help therapists explore a bigger picture view ('helicopter up') to see how their immediate response might inadvertently confirm and exacerbate unhelpful procedures and thus risks.

Another common presentation in supervision involves young people who seem stuck, do not get better, and continue to engage in self-defeating or self-damaging behaviour. Those who are seen to be taking support for granted or to be manipulating staff are particularly challenging. Therapists can feel frustrated or angry with these young people, or guilty for not feeling more empathy, or both at once. These presentations can provoke rejecting or placating responses in therapists that are often difficult to acknowledge, as they fit less well with the 'caring' role supervisees believe they should enact. Often the supervisor may need to normalise awkward or challenging feelings in order for the supervisee to name and talk about them openly:

SUPERVISOR: I don't know about you, but this would make most people want to push her away. In fact, I feel a bit like that on your behalf, just hearing about it!

Criticism and blame

Another common theme brought to supervision is young people's sensitivity to feeling unfairly blamed for their problems and the challenges this presents to discussions about agency and responsibility. Developmentally young people are particularly focused on others' approval, and much of the feedback they get (particularly from peers via social media) can be immediate, harsh and destructive, so it is not surprising that young people are finely tuned to possible social rejection. The idea of non-judging self-observation is something young people have rarely considered and can find difficult to contemplate, particularly if they strive to be perfect or have high expectations. Supervisors can model this in their interactions with the supervision group, who in turn can consider how they might take this back into the therapy. Addressing these patterns (and perhaps the associated fear of failure) in therapy, by exploring what reasonable goals might be and by modelling acceptance of making mistakes, can allow the young person to start to reflect on their part in their interactions.

Supervisees can struggle with similar issues. By setting high standards for themselves as therapists, and perhaps inadvertently, high standards for their clients, supervisees can experience supervision as criticising and intrusive rather than exploratory and reflective.

> *A supervisee refused an invitation to discuss a client in CAT supervision, saying the case had been covered adequately in a team clinical review. The rest of the group quickly agreed. The supervisor felt confused and shut down, and noticed that her group had disappeared just like the client did from the therapist, but that the situation seemed too fragile to raise this.*
>
> *The following week, they mapped the client's experience of feeling powerless and scrutinised (see Figure 17.1). The therapist disclosed that her colleagues' suggestions in the clinical review had felt demanding, and she had felt scrutinised, incompetent and inferior – in the 'hot seat'. The supervisor's questions had replicated this. The other supervisees said they had worried about their colleague feeling attacked by the 'scrutinising system' and had jumped in to protect her by shutting down the discussion. The therapist said this felt supportive, but at the same time over-protective.*

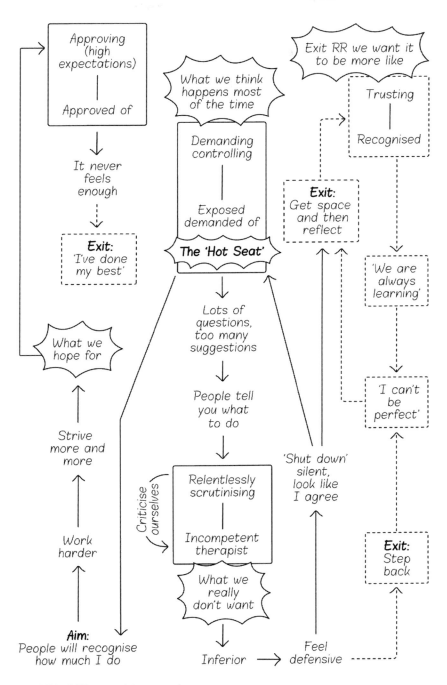

Figure 17.1 CAT supervision group's map

The supervisees reflected on this process:

THERAPIST: [Mapping the situation] helped take the pressure off me. It felt more shared, and I started to feel safer in the group. It was good to see the supervisor not get it right, and talk about how she could have been seen as scrutinising . . . that's what is encouraged in our clients and us as therapists, to notice what part we play. . . . A balance of not feeling too exposed and not avoiding eventually emerged through the mapping . . .
SECOND SUPERVISEE: I liked how I could step back and see that, by protecting my team member, I could have also been avoiding things.
THIRD SUPERVISEE: The diagram allowed reflection and acknowledgement (rather than scrutiny) . . . fires around the hot seat were extinguished.

The concept of the 'good enough' therapist (Ryle and Kerr 2002) can help supervisees, who might tend towards self-criticism or perceiving judgment by others. Supervision is a space in which alternative RRs and responses can be explored (such as *assertively caring for myself* in relation to *feeling empowered and capable*).

Goal-setting

As a goal-directed active therapy, an early task in CAT involves assisting the client to identify what they want to work on. Yet therapists can struggle to identify target problems (TPs) in a collaborative and engaging way, and it can be difficult to estimate how much the young person can tolerate the focus on their problems. Therapists can find themselves expecting too much or alternatively setting low expectations in an effort to engage the young person. Neither is likely to be satisfactory, and supervision can offer the supervisee time and space to step back from this and consider if unhelpful RRs are being enacted.

The fact that TPs can be phrased in relational terms rather than as symptoms can assist the young person to understand and tolerate exploration of them. For example, rather than focusing on self-harm, the TP is redefined as feeling *'evil and out of control'*. The procedure of cutting oneself is linked to the aim to feel more in control and to the consequences of increasing admissions to hospital, which then reinforce the young person's feelings of worthlessness and reduced sense of agency.

Therapists can sometimes struggle with the client who feels overwhelmed by the negativity of a focus on target problems. This young person might feel they have little choice other than to reject the treatment completely, because anything less implies agreement with the interpretation that they are 'the problem'. A range of techniques might be discussed in supervision and tried by the supervisee. Taking more of a strengths-based approach can help, as the therapist acknowledges and elicits positive aspects of the young person as well as the difficulties.

Discussing how the young person might have more say over the pacing of the therapy can also help. Understanding the meaning the young person attributes to attending therapy (e.g. 'the problems must be my fault') can increase the possibility of helpfully reframing this, allowing therapy to be seen as useful and the therapist as being aligned with the young person's goals.

> *A 16-year old girl feels scapegoated for the fighting in her family, and refuses to continue with therapy. The therapist suggests that perhaps the fighting might be a family problem, and that they could consider her anger separately in her individual sessions. They make a plan to talk about the fighting together with the family, and to concentrate in her individual therapy on how she might get her own needs met more effectively. This provides a way for the family to share some responsibility for the fights and a 'face-saving' way for the young person to address her anger.*

Adapting the tools of CAT

CAT tools may need to be modified or adapted for use with young people. CAT tools (primarily letters and diagrams) are designed to reflect the shared conversations and new understanding developing between the therapist and the client. They should aim to be challenging enough to provoke new thinking, but not so much that they are not useful (i.e. within the ZPD). The ZPD is created in the inter-subjective space by the therapist and young person, and is therefore unique to both people, in that moment, on that day. How challenging a therapist can be with this individual, in a specific moment, is something that therapists must learn to tune in to. Supervision can explore supervisees' ideas about how they might assess the young person's capacities and understanding of the work being done together. Discussion about how formal or intellectual letters should be, their emotional content, length, complexity and focus, can help supervisees to predict how their clients might respond to their letters and diagrams. Supervision can also help supervisees to tune in to their own desire to honour the client, to get the letter perfectly 'right', or to include everything that carries importance, and to consider whether these are affecting the process too much. Particularly in shorter CAT contracts, it is important that the letter fits the therapy, and does not include too much. For young people who appear particularly sensitive, the process might need to be even more collaborative, perhaps writing the letter together over more than one session, or giving a second letter later in therapy. Thinking about how to improve the acceptability of the reformulation is vital, as overwhelming experiences early in therapy can be off-putting.

There is also often discussion in supervision about whether to delay the reformulation letter, when the young person is considered fragile or easily overwhelmed. In general, we feel it is better to consider what can be written to young people that will be within their ZPD, and will address the issues of therapy 'well enough', rather than to delay the letter. Our firm view is that a document that is validating, models collaboration and provides evidence of a shared formulation (even if it continues to be added to) is an important starting point for the hard work in therapy, and can assist the engagement process. Supervision can assist supervisees to consider their hesitance and reluctance to write a letter before they think they know 'enough', and how they might involve the young person more in the letter writing.

Therapists often feel they have more space and licence to creatively adapt or 'play around' with diagrams – adding pictures, cartoons, colour and stickers, focusing on simple dilemmas or capturing several interacting patterns at once. We have seen some wonderful examples, such as short graphic novels, some drawn by the therapist, others by the client. It is important that supervisees remember to let themselves make mistakes and explore, so the young person clearly sees it is all right for them to do this too.

It is common to hear that others, such as parents, have read the CAT letters written to young people. Sometimes this is at the invitation of the young person and therapist. At other times it is accidental or perhaps a covert message from the young person. Sharing this validating letter can be a way for both young person and therapist to communicate the non-blaming CAT stance to parents. Nevertheless, it can be daunting for therapists to write to a wide audience who they anticipate might have differing reactions, particularly when there are complex problems in the family. Supervision can play a crucial role in such situations.

Playfulness

Playfulness is often the key to helping both the young person and the therapist talk about anxiety-provoking or challenging issues without them seeming overwhelming. Play is often the bridge between adults and children, it is an equaliser, and is one of the ways we learn and relate to one another (Kravtsov and Kravtsova 2010). As responsible adults we take our work with young people seriously. However, the earnestness of adulthood is often one of the features that young people look forward to least. 'Growing up looks so boring! I don't want to stop having fun' (male client, 17 years). Supervision can be used to 'unstick' the supervisee, and humour and playfulness can free up the supervisee to take a more curious, observing position. Supervisors who are able to be playful and creative in the group, allow supervisees to get richer feedback and feel supported to take calculated risks and make mistakes. Finding a way to bring these qualities into supervision can encourage supervisees to use them in the therapy room.

> Creative and playful supervision pulls for more collaboration in the supervisory relationship, encourages supervisees to become curious about their own potentials, illuminates the possibilities for continued professional development, and emphasises the importance of discovery in the supervision experience.
>
> (Stewart and Echterling 2008: 283)

Focusing on change

While some therapists feel comfortable discussing work between sessions and using rating sheets to monitor progress, many assume that their young clients will be reluctant to complete such tasks, usually because they are concerned about a negative association with school. They may avoid explaining the need to rehearse new patterns and procedures to make them familiar and automatic, and thus limit the effectiveness of the intervention. Exploration in supervision about how to talk about practising new procedural sequences to maintain healthier RRs is beneficial, and most young people have recent examples of learning new skills (e.g. sport, music, driving) to draw from.

Young people have limited life experience and have few examples of being the agent of change in their own lives. They may not have good planning or metacognitive skills, and therefore discussions about change can be completely bewildering. You may as well have asked them to walk on the moon! Changing family relationships and relational patterns can be particularly difficult for them to imagine. For many, it can be a challenging or scary process to question and explore things outside what they already know, and they can seek to manage the ambiguity in the world around them by looking for certainty and the 'right' answer. Sensitive and playful search for the 'colour in the black and white world' can be exciting and fun, and can lead to a broader understanding of themselves and others.

Inclusion of families, parents, partners, friends

In contrast to older clients, young people are often still living with, or interacting frequently with, the people (usually their parents) with whom their early relational patterns were established. Even those who do not live with them have thoughts, hopes or fantasies about how they would like these relationships to be. Supervisees frequently worry about how to talk with family members who might have been at least partly responsible for the establishment of the unhelpful and possibly even punitive patterns with which the young person presents. The vast majority of parents have benign or positive intentions, and are doing the best they can with what they have. This stance towards parents and carers can be helpful and noticing trans-generational relational patterns can also help reduce parents' experience of blame.

The question of whether and how parents or carers are involved in therapy should be addressed both at the commencement and through the course of treatment. This is an issue that can evoke strong feelings in both clients and therapists. Supervision can encourage reflection on how others will be involved. A systemic view would suggest that, as long as the young person and family members are willing to work together towards change, there is potential for greater and more sustainable impact. A number of young people start out refusing to have their parents or carers involved in any way. However the younger the client and the more dependent a young person is on their parents, the more likely there will be pressure to involve parents or carers. Young people's concerns can include: past negative experiences, fear of burdening their parents, or fear that involvement of parents or carers will lead to the therapist aligning with the parents and 'taking their side'. As this is often a sensitive subject for young people, it can be easy for therapists to unwittingly collude with the young person to exclude the parents or carers, especially when engagement feels tentative, or when carers appear judgemental or challenging. It might be useful for the therapist to 'strategically collude' temporarily before revisiting the issue when things settle or change. At times of crisis, therapists might have no choice other than to involve parents, and supervision can assist with the exploration and repair of any rupture. The wider context – families and carers, other institutions such as child services, welfare, or schools – can be heavily involved with younger clients, and potentially consider themselves clients as well.

Involvement of other systems and consultation

Most young people are in contact with a number of agencies or supports, including schools, training providers, employers, other health providers including child health nurses (for young people who are parents), and other informal supports like extended family and friends' parents. A smaller subset of young people with complex needs are in contact with a large number of professional supports. The CAT model can be used effectively to assist relational formulation for consultation with care teams and services, and by intensive outreach teams (Schley et al. 2011). There are sometimes opportunities to do short CAT-informed interventions (e.g. Carradice 2013), contextual reformulations (Ryle and Kerr 2002), or brief personal reformulations with young people when longer therapies might not be possible. These interventions can be surprisingly helpful for the young person, as well as assisting others who work with them to avoid re-enacting punitive and damaging patterns that might contribute to iatrogenic harm.

Endings

Endings, transfers and deadlines of various sorts can provoke concern in the young person, their family and the system, as well as in the therapist. Sometimes these concerns are justified, and at other times they are more anticipatory. Anxiety expressed by the young person or the system about looming discharge dates commonly elicits either *placating* or *perfectly caring* responses from therapists, for example, therapists may try to hold onto their clients or extend their contract for fear of what might happen when they are discharged. Similar enactments might occur because therapists worry they have not done a good enough job with the young person. Supervision can assist supervisees to work out which responses are their own, and which might belong to others. In particular, it can be useful to discuss the need for young people to have opportunities (in relative safety) to try out new skills. Some anxiety can be helpfully addressed by clearly articulating the pathway back to care, or referring to less intensive supports, rather than by delaying discharge.

SUPERVISOR: Do you think you are concerned about ending with her? How much therapy would be enough at this time? What is the message you want her to take away about the ending?

In conclusion

While many young people can utilise standard CAT interventions, there are some for whom the model needs to be modified and adapted. In this chapter, we have attempted to discuss some of the issues that might lead to adaptations. The flexibility of CAT makes it an exciting model to use with young people, but this also raises a challenge for supervision: how much CAT can be adapted without straying too far from the fundamental core of the model – to 'give the experience of being understood, of being reflected upon and of learning to self-reflect' (Ryle and Fonagy 1995: 573).

References

Carradice, A. (2013) 'Five session CAT consultancy: Using CAT to guide care planning with people diagnosed with personality disorder within community mental health teams', *Clinical Psychology and Psychotherapy*, 20: 359–367.

Chanen, A.M., Jackson, H.J., McCutcheon, L.K., Jovev, M., Dudgeon, P., Yuen, H.K., Germano, D., Huggins, H., McDougal, E., Weinstein, C., Clarkson, V. and McGorry, P.D. (2008) 'Early intervention for adolescents with borderline personality disorder using cognitive analytic therapy: Randomised controlled trial', *British Journal of Psychiatry*, 193: 1–8.

Kravtsov, G.G. and Kravtsova, E.E. (2010) 'Play in L.S. Vygotsky's nonclassical psychology', *Journal of Russian and East European Psychology*, 48, 4: 25–41.

McCutcheon, L.K., Chanen, A.M., Fraser, R.J., Drew, L. and Brewer, W. (2007) 'Tips and techniques for engaging and managing the reluctant, resistant or hostile young person', *Medical Journal of Australia*, 187, suppl. 7: 64–67.

Rickwood, D., Deane, F.P., Wilson, C.J. and Ciarrochi, J.V. (2005) 'Young people's help-seeking for mental health problems', *Australian e-Journal for the Advancement of Mental Health*, 4: 1–34.

Ryle, A. and Fonagy, P. (1995) 'BJP annual lecture: Psychoanalysis, cognitive analytic therapy, mind and self', *British Journal of Psychotherapy*, 11: 567–574.

Ryle, A. and Kerr, I.B. (2002) *Introducing Cognitive Analytic Therapy: Principles and Practice*, Chichester: Wiley.

Schley, C., Radovini, A., Halperin, S. and Fletcher, K. (2011) 'Intensive outreach in youth mental health: Description of a service model for young people who are difficult to engage and "high-risk"', *Children and Youth Services Review*, 33: 1506–1514.

Stewart, A. and Echterling, L.G. (2008) 'Playful supervision' in A. Drewes and J.A. Mullen (eds) *Techniques for Child and Play Therapist Supervisors*, Plymouth: Jason Aronson.

Vygotsky, L. (1978) *Mind in Society: The Development of Higher Psychological Processes*, Cambridge, MA: Harvard University Press.

Chapter 18

Dilemmas in relational supervision in intellectual disability services

Julie Lloyd

Historically in the UK, there has been a large divide in the way mental health services have been provided to those diagnosed with intellectual disabilities and the general population. Intellectual disability (or 'learning disability'; I use these terms interchangeably) is often used as a primary 'label' excluding people from receiving specialist mental health services. Workers in intellectual disability teams in the NHS are expected to meet a vast range of health needs in a population whose disability is lifelong, but who are referred not for having a learning disability per se, but for additional problems they encounter. In fact there is substantial evidence that experiences implicated in the development of emotional distress and subsequent mental health difficulties within the general population are more common among people with intellectual disabilities (Emerson and Baines 2010). For example, they tend to suffer multiple separations and abandonments, have a higher than usual incidence of sexual abuse and/or neglect and struggle to know what assistance they need. The traditional trajectories leading to mental health input are often overlooked within intellectual disability services and offering talking therapy is fairly recent. CAT, as a transdiagnostic and relational therapy, is a particularly useful approach for people with intellectual disabilities because relational patterns are rarely built on IQ scores (Lloyd and Clayton 2013).

A dilemma for non-learning disability supervisors

Therapists working in intellectual disability services frequently struggle to find psychotherapy or counselling supervisors, partly because there are not many specialist supervisors available, so they often need to approach supervisors working in other services. Supervisors from other services may worry about supervising therapy for people with intellectual disabilities. From a CAT perspective, we can reformulate this worry in terms of a '*dilemma*'. In CAT, dilemmas are patterns where it seems that there are only two options open to us, leading to 'black and white thinking'. Non-learning disability supervisors can see supervision of learning disability therapy as:

Either so different that I have nothing to offer and wouldn't touch it with a bargepole, or it's all the same and I don't need to adapt what I do, or learn anything new.

This chapter starts by describing how this dilemma can influence supervision and then considers some ways forward. The chapter ends by looking at the reverse situation; the dilemma for specialist intellectual disability supervisors of supervising in fields such as neurotypical adult mental health.

'So different that I have nothing to offer and wouldn't touch it with a bargepole'

Most supervisors who do not supervise therapy for people with learning disabilities have no friends who have learning disabilities. In fact, many say they have never had a sustained conversation with a person with significant intellectual disability. The Intellectual Disability 'profession' has been set up in order to separate out people with intellectual and social impairments, so many mainstream professionals have never worked with anyone with disabilities of this type. Some mainstream supervisors hold similar distancing attitudes towards intellectual disability workers.

Supervisors used to working with people of higher intellectual abilities can be reluctant to see that therapy in learning disability addresses similar relational patterns to the therapy they usually do. Accepting such relational similarities invites collaboration, which may feel uncomfortable for professionals whose respect for themselves is increased by a sense of being clever and by being valued by others for their cognitive prowess.

Supervisors without learning disability experience may feel that the sustained, intimate and deep contact of therapy with someone with learning disabilities would be difficult to tolerate. This position is described within learning disability services as 'the unoffered chair', i.e., the therapy chair that is withheld because of the client's intellectual disability (Bender 1993). In the paper, Bender provided an elucidation and critique of the history of this exclusion from early psychoanalysis through to patient-centred counselling and cognitive-behavioural therapies. He suggested that a psychotherapeutic relationship involves an intense and intimate interaction with another individual over a prolonged time; this intimacy is difficult to tolerate and requires more energy when the individual is perceived as 'unattractive'. Supervisors may feel they would not like to do that work themselves, owing to communication barriers and clients' impaired cognitive skills and so assume they have little to offer supervisees working in such services. They may imagine therapists who do that work are special and must have mysterious extra qualities. Potential supervisors may assume only behavioural skills development would work (Greenhill 2011), and furthermore, dislike behavioural approaches, think the pace of work would be far too slow and anticipate getting bored.

'It's all the same and I don't need to adapt what I do, or learn anything new, in order to supervise learning disability cases'

This may occur when supervisors, perhaps owing to over-confidence, do not know what they do not know and hold rigid views, lack curiosity about difference and disrespect the therapists' skills and experience with this client group. This makes it impossible for supervisees to benefit from supervision, and breakdown becomes likely.

Exits, or finding a middle course

A supervisor can find a middle way out of this dilemma by learning and adapting. When supervisors adhere to the Equality Act 2010 they want to include people with learning disabilities rather than support intellectual apartheid (i.e. models about separate development).

Collaboration

Beinart (2003) identifies collaboration as a crucial component of a constructive supervisory relationship, whilst Hirons and Velleman (1993) argue that 'joint problem solving' and 'soliciting ideas from the supervisee' are fundamental for effective supervision. Supervision is most helpful when supervisors not used to working in intellectual disability services can hold on to their therapeutic relational expertise, whilst acknowledging their lack of experience with this client group and being open to the therapist's knowledge of their working context. This works best when supervisors accept that their supervisee may need to offer them some brief teaching about how the client's intellectual disability impacts on the therapy. In this scenario, the supervisee brings experience and specialist knowledge of the client group, for example, the impact of cognitive deficits, awareness of certain reciprocal roles commonly associated with people with intellectual disabilities (Psaila and Crowley 2006) and behavioural and psychodynamic theory relating to interpersonal experiences of people with intellectual disabilities (Sinason 2010). Complementing this, the supervisor brings specialist knowledge of CAT and the process of relational psychotherapy supervision, focusing both on the therapy relationship and the relationship between supervisor and supervisee and an awareness of how learning occurs interpersonally. The supervisor may be aware of the risk that the therapist is taking on too much responsibility for change, if the therapist is trying to help support workers and professional staff manage their own countertransference. One advantage of supervision by external consultants not working in intellectual disability teams is that they may be freer from assumptions and more objective than internal consultants (Swartz 1974). The collaborative and mutually respectful relationship that CAT tries to build applies as much to supervision as to therapy.

The Association for Cognitive Analytic Therapy's Learning Disability special interest group conducted a survey of its members about their experience of supervising and of being supervised. Thematic analysis produced themes around supervision being supportive, empathic, reassuring, non-judgmental, respectful, compassionate, positive and a safe space. Most of the responses described the type of constructive supervisory relationship that exists in work with any client group, i.e. has little to do with disability. All respondents commented on how flexibility was a key component to successful supervision. Flexibility in this context meant that supervision was structured and boundaries kept to, but not rigidly, so that issues that arose at that moment could be explored. One supervisee described how her supervisor was skilled at moving flexibly between times when the supervisor offered clinical leadership, when the supervisee needed help to manage frustrations, and other times when the supervisor could be very encouraging, giving her the message not to see the supervisor as the expert, but supporting the supervisee to observe and formulate for herself.

Another theme that came through strongly was that supervisees experienced supervision as a supportive learning environment. It was a place where they could develop their skills. Several supervisees commented that they learnt more easily when they experienced supervision as collaborative because a respectful approach made for a good learning environment, helping the supervisor to pitch their comments at the right level. When supervisees were asked about their supervisor's attitude to supervising work with people with learning disabilities, many responses described how interested in and enthusiastic supervisors were about this work. However, responses were mixed. Sometimes supervisees found that because their non-learning disability supervisors felt less competent, they were given less time than other supervisees in more straightforward mental health services and had to be more self-reliant about finding creative ways forward with the work. Comments such as 'it seems like you're doing all the right things' – may in fact be heard as the supervisor feeling stuck about how to provide other ways of working within the learning disability field. Supervisors can find learning disability work challenging, but coming from different clinical backgrounds can also helpfully widen supervisees' knowledge and enable them to develop practice further. This can be two-way as some supervisors have particularly enjoyed the challenge and developed their supervisory skills e.g. by thinking about what the change mechanism is in therapy.

Using our feelings in supervision to develop our relational understanding of intellectual disability

When a supervisor feels disempowered, de-skilled, and downright stupid at the thought of supervising someone in intellectual disability work, we can link these feelings with what it can be like to have an intellectual disability. Disability is something that lies between us and is not the sole property of one party in the client–therapist–supervisor triad. Hinshelwood (1999) describes how it is necessary that the analyst feels the disturbance, and thereby becomes 'disturbed' himself. Maybe in supervising intellectual disability work there need to be three people aware of the limits to their own skills and cognition.

Seeing similarities in relational patterns

When engaging in this supervision, the supervisor will see that therapy involves similar relational patterns to those that occur with people with higher intellectual abilities. They can recognise common histories of trauma and understand how emotional expression can be denied by the client's and service's (and therefore, perhaps the supervisee's) requirement to show a 'happy face' (Sinason 2010).

The context of the therapeutic relationship

Can the therapeutic relationship only occur in a confidential and boundaried dyad or does it exist within a team, with its overarching adherence to NHS and social services policy and statutory and legal frameworks? This issue is similar in any service for complex cases.

Supervisors need to be aware of the many different ways in which this context affects the role of the therapist working with intellectual disability. Whereas supervisees working in intellectual disability may have extensive experience of participating in multi-agency reviews, including discussions about capacity, and carrying out duties under the Safeguarding Vulnerable Groups Act (2006), a supervisor working in private practice or primary care may have little. Such a supervisor might, for example, be against opening e-mails or taking phone calls from the police and social services and reading or writing reports, believing these would breach the boundaries of therapy. The supervisee might experience such a supervisor as controlling, and respond by being anxiously or crossly compliant, or covertly defiant. Doing complex work may mean a duty of care to protect the client and also others who may pose a risk to them or be at risk from them. This may also mean informing clients about possible legal charges they could face, aiming to help them understand the potential implications of certain actions.

Conversely a supervisor may need to help the supervisee stay connected with the client in the therapy. If a therapist prefers working with staff, who have fewer communication problems and appear more attractive than clients, the client gets overlooked.

Making reasonable adjustments

Managing risk

Supervisors need to be particularly aware of the risks which therapists deal with regularly in intellectual disability work which are less common in adult mental health, such as those caused by having limited intellectual capacity to understand

and cope with complex, sophisticated and technological societal demands. For example, one of my clients got into debt through using internet dating and being exploited by scams for money and therefore needed to be directed towards internet dating sites for people with learning disabilities which are moderated to keep out criminals.

Acknowledging histories of abuse

One of the striking features in intellectual disability work is that services may turn a blind eye to abuse, whereas if someone gave a history of abuse in mental health services there would be greater emphasis on the abuse. This is because abuse is such a common feature in the history of clients in intellectual disability services that therapists might not notice it as unusual. Supervisors need to make a point of enquiring about a history of physical, emotional and sexual abuse as well as neglect. This may lead supervisees to engage in a time-consuming and active process, for example, by investigating history contained in records, rather than just asking clients, who may not know how to describe what happened. Furthermore, information is usually distributed across various separate agencies in many different and archived files, so the 'system' can be a weak and dissociated historian.

Consent, referral and assessment

This is particularly pertinent to intellectual disability services as clients rarely refer themselves to psychological therapy. One of the main questions here is who is the client? Is the client really the staff team who wish the therapist to be able to remove behaviour they find aversive? Supervisors can helpfully enquire about the reciprocal roles within the referral such as *'misunderstanding and misinterpreting'* in relation to being *'misunderstood and unheard'*. What is the client's problem and what is a problem for other people? For example, the client may be referred for screaming, but states in therapy that nobody listens to her. At assessment, asking clients what they see as the problem may produce bewilderment (they do not know why they are here), defensiveness (they presume they are being told off for something), a wish for a new friend (they do not know what therapy is and assume the therapist is a new support worker,) or they repeat statements such as 'I want to be more independent' which come over as more of a quote from their annual care review than something for which they have sought therapy. For these reasons, it is common for the assessment to take six or more sessions to enable the client to gain a more informed idea about what consenting to therapy means.

Power imbalance

Social exclusion and a lack of self-agency can lead to the development or reinforcement of problematic procedures which may be enacted in the therapy relationship. A supervisor can explore and acknowledge variations of the *able* to *disabled* reciprocal role procedure in the therapy relationship (e.g. *powerful* to *powerless, controlling* to *controlled* or *benignly patronising* to *disempowered*). In intellectual disability services, the therapist is seen as having far more agency, power, intellectual ability, academic attainment, job and social status than their clients, even though in practice their power to change a situation may be limited.

Directiveness

The supervisor may come to see work in intellectual disability services as less collaborative than CAT with other clients. Sometimes collaborative working is difficult, owing to clients' suggestibility and their tendency to acquiesce or give desirable responses to challenges or questions. Supervisors need to be aware that being directive is often a feature of therapy with people with intellectual disabilities. Therapy may involve specific skills development that contrasts with the incidental learning the therapist might expect to emerge in therapy. Work may include more concrete and specific formulations, that focus on developing an alternative more helpful strategy, rather than exploring the origins of problems. For example, a therapist may encourage a client, who makes up stories in order to be liked (but ends up getting ignored as he is not very credible), to join appropriate social clubs, rather than explore the roots of his fabricating. CAT does incorporate the use of behavioural techniques, but through doing new things *with* the person rather than doing *to* the person.

The presence of the support worker in the room

The decision about whether the support worker is in the therapy room cannot be made via hard and fast rules but depends on circumstances. These include the worker's relationship with the client, the purpose of accompanying the client in therapy (e.g. to help with processing and remembering the session or to be a chaperone) and the need to encourage independence and autonomy by offering therapy unaccompanied. Often a compromise is reached where a support worker leaves the therapy room after the first five minutes or comes in at the end. Supervision includes discussing the involvement of the client's support worker in therapy sessions, as this can be contentious when client and staff have different agendas. Sometimes a support worker may consider that the client just needs to be informed about what behaviour is acceptable (i.e. therapist as Lecturer or Policeman) as they do not understand therapy is a dialogical process. Getting a reasonable balance between the support worker being helpful or intrusive is a delicate task that cannot be pre-judged.

Missed sessions

Supervisors need to be aware of particular issues affecting attendance at therapy sessions by people with intellectual disability. A missed session requires investigation via the carers, not just asking the client. All of us working in intellectual disability services have had experience of carers not bringing clients because no staff were available, the appointment was omitted in the diary, or staff unilaterally decided not to bring them as a way of either punishing clients for 'bad' behaviour or protecting them if they were upset the previous time. Keeping clients away from the final sessions is particularly common, as if they will not notice the absence of therapy if they do not say goodbye. None of these events may relate to the client's wishes. *Controlling* to *controlled* is a common reciprocal role enacted by the 'system'. Additionally, making sessions accessible if clients cannot cope with sitting and talking for prolonged periods means offering shorter sessions, which in turn means the number offered will be greater. Follow-up periods may also need to be extended, especially when this includes working with the staff team and carers.

Communication and use of tools

Therapists and supervisors need to discuss which therapy tools to use and adapt in the context of the client's zone of proximal development and cognitive functioning. How these tools are used may be different; for example, only small sections of an assessment tool may be useful.

Supervisors need to encourage creative approaches to adapt letters and diagrams using accessible pictures (see Figure 18.1 and also Lloyd and Clayton 2013 for examples.) Although this approach to developing and using creative materials is great fun, the supervisor may need to encourage therapists who believe they cannot draw. Many members of the CAT Intellectual Disability group view themselves as unskilled, clumsy artists; but a healthy viewpoint sees this as the therapeutically horizontal or levelling moment when therapists are less likely to outshine or overwhelm their clients. Therapists model being OK with their 'disabilities', and their lack of artistic sophistication becomes a relational bond. The same could be said of not always knowing what to say to the client.

Being open-minded about supervising consultative work as well as therapy

Consultation with paid and unpaid carers is a main focus for many health professionals working with people with intellectual disabilities. For those who cannot participate in individual therapy, the approach is only via staff teams or unpaid carers, whilst for others a time-limited therapy may be insufficient, so in fact, most therapeutic interventions include a systemic component. In learning disability work, supervisors should supervise contextual staff team work, not just individual cases, because so much work is done systemically.

Carers and staff teams have a central role in the lives of people with complex needs and can respond in helpful or limiting ways; for example, they can see beyond provocations or respond in kind to abusive invitations. They can be nurturing or neglectful of people who do not or cannot care for themselves. Care

242 Julie Lloyd

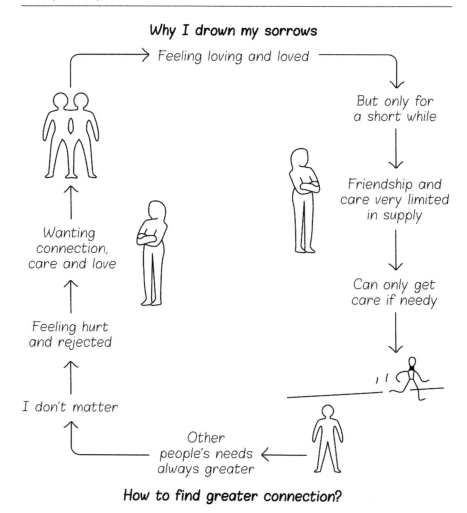

Figure 18.1 CAT diagram using accessible images

staff are often untrained, or they may be trained in intellectual disability but not in relational thinking, yet they are expected to be on the front line dealing in physical reality and actual events. This is a huge contrast with encounters in the therapy room, where clients are removed from their normal everyday life. A discussion in therapy about a time when the client lost their temper is very different from having to deal with it when it occurs. The staff team and the therapist may end up split because the staff team have to deal with client aggression, whereas, in therapy, that aggressive incident has usually been dealt with and instead a reflective discussion occurs. A client's poorly integrated functioning may well temporarily lead to a lower level of integration in staff members (see Chapter 2), so it is not surprising that there is often neglect and abuse of clients by staff and carers. The supervisor's aim is to facilitate the therapist's awareness of how clients and staff teams get 'stuck' in unhelpful patterns, often similar to the ones the therapist has experienced when working with the client.

Supervision can be particularly helpful for therapists when 'challenging behaviour' splits teams as people take on different reciprocal roles in relation to the client. Typically, consultations with staff teams open up a lot of subtle or more obvious conflict within teams. For example, one group of staff may consider the priority for their role is to be especially caring. They will try to be ever-attentive, and encourage the client's right to choose. Another group may consider their role requires setting secure limits, staying aware of the client's 'manipulation', and helping the client face up to consequences. The first group are likely to see the others as rejecting, depriving and controlling, whereas the others may view the first group of staff as over-indulgent. A third set of staff may say that the client does not bother them i.e. deny there is a problem. Any of these groups may be contemptuous and perhaps envious of the therapist. This means the supervisor needs to encourage the therapist to find out:

- what each member of the group thinks and feels about the consultation process (what role they are in; what they might feel if this is pointed out, or questioned).
- how the therapist feels (e.g. scared of confrontation; slightly superior to these 'unreflecting' colleagues).
- what each team member hopes to gain or to avoid from working with the therapist and other members of the client's team.

Supervision offers an opportunity to think through systemic formulations, and includes discussions about what adjustments to a client's environment / world are reasonable. Supervision can also support the therapist to offer staff training on attachment and relational issues and on-going reflective sessions that help staff manage their relationships with the client. Sometimes a therapist can work with a client to present some feedback from the therapy jointly to the staff team.

Supervision offers a lifeline when therapists feel they are the only ones in a service engaging in a different type of relationship with clients; otherwise therapists can feel extremely isolated. Therapists can be invited to believe, and indeed encourage such a belief themselves, that they are solely responsible for 'curing' the client. It is helpful to support the therapist to develop a dialogue with the team. If staff teams work with the therapist to develop a formulation, then therapeutic ideas become more understandable, accurate and attractive for the people who have been involved in discussions to develop them. This can reduce the risk that the staff team believes that 'therapy' is someone else's responsibility without their relationship with the client needing to change. CAT's mapping of interprofessional relationships attracts many intellectual disability workers to CAT and training days on working with staff teams are increasingly popular. (For more discussion of supervising consultation, see Chapter 16.)

Mutual learning in a mixed supervision group

An advantage for members of a mixed supervision group (in which supervisees work in different areas) is that some skills in working with intellectual disability transfer easily to other populations, such as those with acquired brain injury or acute psychosis. Working with severe personality disorder, especially borderline personality disorder, overlaps with intellectual disability work because for both groups, thinking skills are hard to access. The content of the therapy may be adjusted, but the process remains the same recognisable process as in any other therapy. Our experience in mixed supervision groups is that clients become seen as the people they are.

Jackie Drohan, clinical nurse specialist in intellectual disability and CAT practitioner, illustrates these themes, describing her experiences of being in a mixed supervision group with a supervisor who did not have an intellectual disability background:

> *Initially the main difficulties I experienced were the differing pace I was taking in producing the reformulation letter, and then in adapting the monitoring sheets to make them accessible to the individual (part of the course requirements). The difficulties were around the supervisor having limited knowledge of clients with intellectual disabilities and the other group members also having no experience. It was as though we were all initially 'disabled' when discussing adaptations. This whole process helped me reflect on the daily struggles my clients have, thus mirroring their experiences.*
>
> *The views in the group began to change from believing people had to be of a certain intellectual ability to use talking therapies. We all became actively involved in identifying the reciprocal roles, traps, snags and dilemmas, and the client's label of an intellectual disability was soon forgotten. We thought about the client as an individual who had experienced painful traumas. These traumas are frequently dismissed with people working in intellectual disability services as we tend to become desensitised to the abuse our clients experience. In the same breath, our clients have also become void of any feeling when talking about their lives and often maintain a happy face, when describing such horrors e.g. sexual and physical abuse, bullying, being ignored. Being supervised by a non-disability group helped me normalise these appalling experiences and to really think about the impact they had on the individual and on their relationships. Coming from a behavioural background where 'I did to', the non-disability group helped me to 'be with'.*
>
> *I was surprised how similar patterns emerged for all our clients within the supervision group and my visual aids and pictures became useful for others, who were struggling to name emotions and gain a shared understanding. Seeing the person and their life story beyond the label has become my mantra now.*

What do supervisors from intellectual disability services need to hold in mind when supervising in adult mental health?

On the whole it may be easier for supervisors who have predominantly intellectual disability experience to supervise in adult mental health than the other way round. However, they too may find themselves in a dilemma:

> Either feeling that adult mental health work will be overwhelming or that it simply requires a bit of common sense.

The power of this dilemma may be reduced by knowing what new issues supervisors need to hold in mind.

Risk

Suicide is extremely rare in learning disabilities services but sadly common in mental health services. This means the intellectual disability supervisor needs to be aware of this risk, able to recognise the hopeless and helpless reciprocal role, and know how to handle it. Supervisors also need to support and understand anxious supervisees as well as make sure they follow the service's suicide prevention protocols.

Difference in some mental health conditions

Supervisors need to be aware that some conditions present differently in mental health services. For example, the presentation of obsessive compulsive disorder is different because a person of average intelligence often experiences cognitive dissonance about their behaviour, whereas in intellectual disability services, most clients are perfectly happy going about their obsession and it is other people who worry and complain. Anorexia is extremely rare in intellectual disability services and many supervisors from such services would never have worked with someone with anorexia.

Power differentials

In mental health services a therapist may experience a patient as powerful, for example, if the patient competes with the therapist or compares their current therapist with a previous one, in order to dismiss what the therapist says.

Communication

The amount of verbal material may seem overwhelming for supervisors from intellectual disability services. Whereas in intellectual disability work the therapist uses countertransference to understand the material that the client does not have words to say, in adult mental health the therapist and supervisor may also need to recognise a client's forbidden emotions by spotting, amidst lots of words, what the client is censoring.

In addition, patients may intellectualise, which means that they use reasoning and words to distance themselves from feelings, whilst in intellectual disability services the client may simply change the subject.

Expression of feelings may be more subtle and muted and body language may be more constrained. In intellectual disability services what you see is what you get, but in mental health services, some patients may be adept at adapting their presentation of themselves to fit their perception of the therapist's requirements. Clinicians, who are experienced in working with people who prefer simple and direct speech, may come over as rather blunt when working with more neurotypical people, who say things in a delicate or vague way and allude to, rather than state, what they want to talk about. There may be a parallel process in supervision, when topics are brought up in a more roundabout and tactful manner than supervisors are used to.

Reciprocal role procedures (RRPs) in the therapy relationship

While many of the same reciprocal roles are enacted in both intellectual disability and mental health services, some may be different, for example, trying to please, bottling up feelings and being polite may be more common in adult mental health services than RRPs often seen in intellectual disability services, such as giving and receiving controlling care, or 'I can only get care if I seem needy'.

In intellectual disability services, the therapist may be seen as the loving parent, the client's best friend or someone brought in to tell the client off. However, in mental health services, the relationship may also include sexual attraction. Unless the therapist brings it explicitly to supervision, the disability experienced supervisor could miss this, because being attracted to clients would not occur to them, if they are more used to coping with feelings of distancing and even repulsion.

Cultural issues

Cultural issues may have less weight in intellectual disability services than in mental health services, partly because having an intellectual disability is often used to overshadow everything else. The intellectual disability supervisor may be more used to thinking about behavioural phenotypes (for example, the relational repertoire commonly seen in someone with Down's Syndrome) than thinking about their culture.

Conclusion

Although the idea of supervising clinical work in an unfamiliar setting might be daunting, such anxiety respects the challenge ahead. Once this challenge is grasped, as this chapter describes, the experience is often enriching and rewarding.

Much depends on how open-minded the supervisor can be in recognising what they can learn from their supervisees (and by extension, the supervisee's clients) as well as how the supervisor can focus on all the relational issues including the wider team around the client, the relationship in the therapy room and in the supervision room.

References

Beinart, H. (2003) 'Models of the supervisory relationship and their evidence base', in I. Fleming and L. Steen (eds) *Supervision and Clinical Psychology*, Chichester: Brunner-Routledge.

Bender, M. (1993) 'The unoffered chair: The history of therapeutic disdain towards people with a learning difficulty', *Clinical Psychology Forum*, 54: 7–12.

Emerson, E. and Baines, S. (2010) 'Health inequalities and people with learning disabilities in the UK', *Improving Health and Lives*, Department of Health. Online. Available HTTP <https://www.improvinghealthandlives.org.uk/uploads/doc/vid_7479_IHaL2010-3HealthInequality2010.pdf> (accessed 30 July 2015).

Equality Act. (2010). Online. Available HTTP: <http://www.legislation.gov.uk/ukpga/2010/15/section/6> (accessed 30 July 2015).

Greenhill, B. (2011) 'They have behaviour; we have relationships? Using CAT to understand why the "un-offered Chair" remains un-offered to people with learning disabilities', *Reformulation*, 37: 18–24.

Hinshelwood, R.D. (1999) 'Countertransference', *International Journal of Psychoanalysis*, 80: 797–818.

Hirons, A. and Velleman, R. (1993) 'Factors which might contribute to effective supervision', *Clinical Psychology Forum*, 57: 11–13.

Lloyd, J. and Clayton, P. (2013) *Cognitive Analytic Therapy and People with Intellectual Disabilities and Carers*, London: Jessica Kingsley.

Psaila, C.L. and Crowley, V. (2006) 'Cognitive analytic therapy in people with learning disabilities: An investigation into the common reciprocal roles found within this client group', *Reformulation*, 27: 5–11.

Safeguarding Vulnerable Groups Act. (2006) Online. Available HTTP: <https://www.legislation.gov.uk/ukpga/2006/47/contents> (accessed 30 July 2015).

Sinason, V. (2010) *Mental Handicap and the Human Condition: An Analytic Approach to Intellectual Disability*, London: Free Association Books.

Swartz, D. (1974) 'Similarities and differences of internal and external consultants', *Journal of European Industrial Training*, 4, 5: 258–262.

Chapter 19

CAT supervision in forensic practice

Working with complexity and risk

Karen Shannon

Introduction

Provision of therapy in forensic services involves working in diverse settings (community, in-patient, prison settings) with complex and challenging clients who have a high likelihood of boundary breaches, pose multiple risks and are managed by multiple agencies (e.g. probation, police, health, and voluntary services). Therapists are also subject to wider systemic pressures of judicial and public scrutiny. These high demands raise frequent moral and ethical issues and systemic re-enactments that impact on therapeutic work. Effective, systematic clinical supervision for those working in forensic settings is a recognised necessity for the positive well-being of the therapist and 'healthy' team, and service functioning (Davies 2015) and is ultimately beneficial for the client and therefore safeguards any potential future victims.

This chapter will discuss and illustrate with case examples and specific methods how CAT supervision can support therapists to work relationally and effectively with the challenges of 'hard to help', risky clients in the forensic system. In particular, it will show how supervision can support the therapist with: dual role of client care and public protection, confidentiality in forensic settings, therapists' management of colleagues' expectations, safeguarding risk/distress for therapist, disentangling ambivalence, threats to the therapeutic alliance, boundary breaches and unethical behaviour, understanding and accountability for offending behaviour, transitions and endings and CAT risk assessment.

The value of the CAT model in forensic settings

The utility of CAT as a therapy has become increasingly recognised across the full range of forensic settings and security levels. This owes much to the development of innovative, diverse practice in CAT across disorders, offence types (Pollock and Belshaw 1998, Shannon et al. 2006) and age ranges, involving adaptations for different formats (Duignan and Mitzman 1994) and cognitive limitations (Lloyd and Clayton 2013).

Using key CAT concepts, in particular the multiple self-states model (MSSM) (Ryle 1997), the CAT supervisor can support supervisees to recognise the extent of damage and deficit common in complex presentations. The MSSM describes the narrow range of distorted, rigid, unrevised reciprocal roles, experienced as dissociated states, which impede clients' self-reflective ability. It helps the therapist to understand the reasons for clients' abrupt, disproportionate, affective and behavioural changes and how the client experiences the self as fragmented and discontinuous. This helps therapists in forensic services to have realistic expectations of the tasks of therapy, the process and pace of engagement and change, and to recognise what may appear to be small achievements as important, not least engagement in therapy itself (Azar 2000).

Dual role of therapist: Responsibility to the public and the client

A common task for forensic supervisors is to assist supervisees to manage the tension in their dual role of ensuring effective public protection and addressing the client's needs via therapeutic care. Invariably, given the client's risk potential, the needs of the public take priority over the needs of the client (observable by incarceration or being placed in the community with restrictions). Historically interventions have focused on criminogenic needs and risk reduction, as opposed to addressing the relational needs of the individual (Shannon 2009).

The tension of this dual role introduces barriers for the therapist engaging with the client from the outset. Unless it is addressed, clients can experience offence-focused interventions as 'done to' them with little, if any, input regarding choice of focus or type of therapy. Often clients' return to community living or reduced levels of security are contingent on successful engagement in offence-focused work. It is therefore not uncommon for clients to engage superficially in therapies, apparently demonstrating change by repeating psychological jargon but not necessarily addressing issues sufficiently to reduce and sustain non-recidivism in the longer term.

Supervisors can encourage supervisees to establish clear expectations with the client from the outset, by discussing their dual role of care for the client and responsibility for public protection. Supervisees need to feel confident to anticipate, name and negotiate difficulties such as power differences (e.g. the therapist's liberty and choice versus the client's detention and restriction).

Confidentiality

Issues around confidentiality of therapy are common and the supervisor needs to provide clear guidance to assist the supervisee, particularly regarding safe versus incriminating disclosure by the client of current or past harm to self and others.

Confidentiality of CAT tools (the psychotherapy file and reformulation letters) is particularly important in forensic settings, where transparency is expected and routine paperwork can become evidence within the judicial system. The therapist can experience pressure to disseminate the full content of the therapy, enacting unhelpful reciprocal roles such as *imposing, exposing* to *powerlessly exposed,* which threaten the therapeutic alliance. Supervisors can encourage supervisees to explain to colleagues before the start of CAT therapy, that CAT tools are jointly created mediators of the therapy and are therefore not part of the official paperwork of the forensic system (see Brown 2010). Therapists should seek to allay suspicion or concerns from colleagues by establishing that summaries of pertinent risk-related information will be shared with the team and wider multi-agencies (Shannon 2009), but that the therapy tools and non-risk related information will remain within the therapy.

Managing expectations and enactments in the forensic system

The expectations and enactments of other professionals both in the service and in the wider system should be a focus of supervision when considering delivery of therapy. Potential enactments the therapist may experience include idealisation, i.e. placing the therapist in the responsible, rescuing role of 'fixing' the client, or denigration, i.e. viewing the therapist as naïve and manipulable for developing a collaborative therapeutic alliance. Particularly within secure in-patient units or prison settings, the supervisor should aid the supervisee to consider potential organisational enactments (intended or otherwise) that can have a detrimental impact on therapy, e.g. unplanned transfer to another prison or cancellation of sessions because there are insufficient staff to escort the client to therapy. The therapist should be encouraged to offer information about the ethos and aims of CAT and negotiate requirements for consistent and continuous provision of therapy, e.g. use of 'medical hold' in prison to prevent transfer mid-therapy or agreement to maintain and not change a client's neuroleptic medication.

Safeguarding therapists and therapy in forensic services

Therapists working within the forensic environment are often exposed to clients' narratives of distress, survival and harm of others, which can provoke difficult emotions, and may elicit vicarious trauma (Kadambi and Truscott 2003). The provision of the safe, containing space of supervision, where supervisees can normalise their countertransference feelings and actively reflect on them, is key to limiting the experience of distress or isolation. This helps the supervisee to anticipate enactments, powerful pulls into the role of victim, abuser, neglectful parent or rescuing carer in therapy. With containment from the supervisor, supervisees are more able to be authentic, active and exposed and use the alliance as a vehicle for change. In turn, this can assist the client to reflect on feelings elicited in the therapist, and therefore in others. This is important in enhancing the client's theory of mind skills and may help the client to reflect on their victims' experiences – a key need within forensic services.

A crucial issue within forensic services is to ensure that minor changes to a therapist's usual practice do not slip into 'unethical blindness' (Peternelj-Taylor and Yonge 2003) and collusive, damaging patterns of relating. The supervisor should, therefore, be alert to supervisees' omission or concealment of risk-related client information and boundary breaches, e.g. sharing personal information or creating a special therapist-client relationship by giving preferential treatment. These unhelpful practices have all too frequently and destructively been enacted in forensic services, perpetuating harm to client, therapist and teams and resulting in numerous national inquiries (e.g. Fallon inquiry, Department of Health 1999).

In forensic services, the intensity and duration of client contact varies by profession. Those with least training often have most contact with clients (Moore 2012) and are more likely to slip into boundary breaching behaviour or to engage in ways of relating with clients that inadvertently contradict or undermine psychological interventions provided by colleagues. Regular reflective practice for all staff and a relational and shared understanding of clients, preferably enhanced by CAT-informed training for staff, is therefore arguably a necessity.

Making therapeutic alliances and disentangling themes around ambivalence to engage

Therapists know that the therapeutic alliance is the single best predictor of positive outcome in psychotherapy (Martin et al. 2000). Forensic clients have often experienced profound loss and deprivation, multiple traumas and disrupted attachments (Aiyegbusi 2004). Therefore they experience greater problems in making and maintaining therapeutic alliances. Wierzbicki and Pekarik's (1993) meta-analysis of forensic psychotherapy found the mean non-completion rate was 47%. Non-completion can lead to reduced client and therapist morale, increased recidivism and limited effectiveness of future therapy. The forensic client's ambivalent engagement and high-risk potential can make building an alliance particularly challenging and therapy can easily become confrontational or an imposition resulting in ruptures or superficial engagement. The supervisor's role within a forensic context is, therefore, to help the supervisee recognise and avoid common iatrogenic dynamics in the provision of therapy, such as being *powerfully accusatory, imposing and controlling* in relation to an *imposed upon, judged and powerless* client (Aiyegbusi 2004). Instead the aim is to assist the supervisee to engage with the client collaboratively and ensure non-reciprocation of harmful reciprocal roles. It is essential to avoid any sense of imposition or coercion of the client in the process of change and to discuss and agree the client's expectations of therapy and therapeutic boundaries (Evershed 2010).

Using CAT's approach of beginning where the client is, the supervisor can assist the supervisee to provide 'pre-CAT work', i.e. time-limited sessions to reflect on the client's engagement and motivation. This allows discussion of 'what's in it for the client', the actual or perceived desirability of therapy, the assumed cost of change for a client and a client's strengths and psychological, social, and environmental needs (e.g. Ward and Laws 2010). The supervisor should encourage the supervisee to use CAT flexibly; this might mean initially contracting for a reformulation only, in order to increase a client's curiosity about their patterns of relating without addressing the need for change. The latter can be negotiated at the reformulation stage when an alliance has been established, the client has been socialised into the nature of therapy and can see the origins and repeating, unrevised nature of their patterns. The supervisor should also ensure the supervisee negotiates with the client and team at the contracting stage of therapy regarding the management of potential escalating risks within and between sessions. This helps the client to take some responsibility for recognising, and beginning to tolerate and modulate, difficult emotional responses and seeking or accepting appropriate support where necessary.

Unsurprisingly, ambivalence or poor motivation for engagement in therapy is a common experience. Complex clients often reject the therapeutic care they need, or are unable to make use of it. For example, clients can be contemptuously hostile towards the therapist or, alternatively, dependent and needy, passively waiting for rescue, but not taking responsibility for change. This elicits countertransference feelings of frustration, apathy and rejection in the therapist. The supervisor's role here is to provide containment, to encourage reflection and disentanglement of the sources of both the client's and the supervisee's feelings and to assist the therapist to share responsibility for engagement and change with the client.

Without attention in supervision, the client's ambivalence about change may become evident only when the therapy becomes stuck or ineffectual. The supervisor needs to aid the supervisee to sensitively establish whether the client needs further support to engage in change or whether they are not actually seeking change. Making the distinction between 'can't change' (but may change with more support) versus 'won't change' leaves the decision-making and choice with the client and enables the therapist to be transparent about engagement in therapy and to either adapt the therapy to aid engagement or help the client to disengage (see example below). Where the client chooses to disengage and has been supported to take responsibility for this choice, a process of growing psychological discomfort can arise, which may lead the client to review their motivation for, and investment in, change and to re-engage more fully.

The supervisee described how her client Tina either arrived for therapy sessions late, claiming she had attended (non-urgent) physical health appointments, or was fixated on discussing her minor physical health problems. She had a long history of offending (fraud, theft and handling) and poor engagement with multiple services.

The supervisee described working hard to help Tina to make links between her physical symptoms and psychological distress, but she was left feeling frustrated, stuck, and not good enough. The supervisor supported the supervisee to express her countertransference feelings and to recognise the enactment of the reciprocal role of 'withholding, dismissing' (client) to 'invalidated and dismissed' (therapist). She was encouraged to help Tina explore her feelings about engaging in therapy, in particular to think whether therapeutic change was a struggle for her and how therapy might be adapted to support her, or, alternatively, whether Tina did not want to engage in change. The supervisee felt this differentiation empowered her to help Tina to share responsibility for the choice about whether to engage in therapy.

Tina subsequently chose to prioritise her physical health and withdrew from therapy. Tina was thereby neglecting her psychological well-being, and preventing reduction of her risk of re-offending, and this was explicitly discussed. However, the therapist communicated her respect for Tina's decision because, in doing so, she was making an informed choice. The therapist recognised that she had exited from the collusive pattern of anxiously striving to give care in response to Tina's dismissal of her psychological needs (and limping through an unsatisfactory therapy).

The supervisor has a key role in aiding the therapist's recognition of countertransference enactments where they may contribute to client ambivalence and poor engagement. For example, the ambivalent client may elicit striving and rescuing feelings in the therapist. The more the therapist strives to provide care, the more the client withdraws, externalising responsibility back to the therapist and the surrounding system. Such enactments are familiar in forensic services and are reinforced by the public and judicial pressures on practitioners, making them feel responsible for risk reduction and public protection and therefore under pressure to impose therapy.

Facilitating understanding of, and accountability for, offending behaviour

Clients' lack of accountability for their offending behaviour – their denial, minimisation, or silence – can conceal feelings of guilt, judgement, shame or trauma about their offence. The supervisor should therefore assist the supervisee to be sensitive and skilful in dialogue with the client about their offences. By conceptualising the reciprocal role as a continuum of severity, the therapist can work within the client's zone of proximal development (ZPD) on what the client can acknowledge about their role in their offending potential as a starting point (see Figure 19.1):

A Continuum of Reciprocal Role enactments: to encourage acknowledgement and insight of offending behaviour and feelings elicited in the victim, and child-derived experiences of abuse and poor care

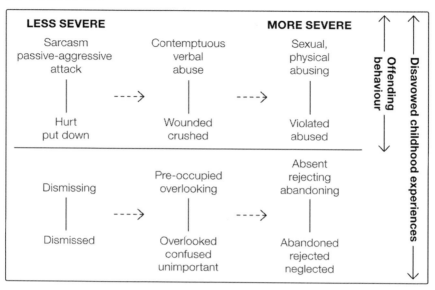

Figure 19.1 Continuum of reciprocal role enactments

The supervisor should encourage the supervisee to listen carefully throughout therapy for descriptions of current examples of more severe re-enactments and assist the client's recognition of, and accountability for, them.

The supervisor can guide the therapist to make tentative links with the client between early experiences and their offending behaviour, using Figure 19.1 and to help them recognise and internalise the painful meaning of their early experience. When the client is helped to uncover the target problem and target problem procedure (TPP), the relational nature of their offending pattern, its repeating unrevised nature and the link with their chronic emotional pain, the realisation of these links- the 'aha' moment in therapy – can powerfully galvanise the client's motivation to change. The needs of the client and the need for public protection, i.e. the client's and society's goals for therapy then coincide, perhaps for the first time. Importantly recognition and change of the core TPP underlying the offending or risky behaviour reduces the likelihood of symptom replacement, diversification of offending behaviour and/or time-limited change. This is an innovative approach compared to the historical forensic service intervention where focus is solely on the medical symptoms or offending behaviour, which may seem irrelevant to the client.

Where exploration of historical offending patterns is outside the client's ZPD or the therapeutic timing is inappropriate (e.g. if exploration of childhood trauma could lead to increased vulnerability and potential for victimisation within a prison setting), the supervisor can encourage the therapist to adjust the focus of therapy to the recognition and revision of patterns in relationships with self and others (including the therapeutic alliance) in the 'here and now'.

'Poor me' versus 'bad me'

Clients' expression of distress or remorse for their offences can be a promising indicator of change, which can be seductive for the therapist. However, the supervisor needs to alert the supervisee to attend closely to the client's narrative and the supervisee's elicited countertransference feelings, to ascertain the true nature of the client's underlying feelings. In differentiating between the entrenched and unrevised states of '*poor me*' and '*bad me*' (Wessler and Wessler 1980) the therapist recognises that, in the former, the client presents as self-pitying, aggrieved, wrongly treated by others and has fewer self-negative views and lower levels of depression. In contrast, in the latter the client expresses feelings of deserved punishment for perceived badness and self-loathing, lower self-esteem and high levels of depression and anxiety. On the surface, both individuals can sound sorrowful and remorseful, but the therapist's countertransference will differ for each presentation, e.g. irritation in relation to the 'poor me' and sadness in relation to the 'bad me'.

CAT and transitions and endings

Forensic clients have usually experienced repeated episodes of inconsistent care with multiple breakdowns of foster placements or care homes and/or loss of a parent (via death or repeated 'absences' e.g. custodial sentences, habitual drug abuse, mental health problems). Forensic services commonly re-enact these unpredictable, difficult endings by failing to recognise either the necessity of planning service provision or the need to communicate with clients about endings or transitions (e.g. between teams, wards, types of therapies). With unplanned 'mini-endings' (e.g. staff cancellation, holiday, change of key worker) or transitions (e.g. change of ward) services unknowingly evoke feelings of loss and anxiety in clients. This reinforces clients' intolerance of perceived loss and difficulty in forming healthy alliances with staff. It also contributes to increased risk, as clients escalate their behaviour in response to perceived or actual re-abandonment or neglect by enacting rejecting, clinging, contemptuous or self-harming responses.

As the duration of therapy and its ending can be unclear in forensic settings (because of on-going 'contact' between the client and therapist after therapy has finished when provided in secure/in-patient settings, or abrupt prison transfer, recall to prison, sentencing to custody or unplanned release via mental health tribunal from secure settings), it is vital for a supervisor to ensure that the therapist discusses the ending of therapy and other potential endings, at the point of contracting with the client and throughout therapy. Unresolved feelings of loss and abandonment are commonly at the core of clients' offences, providing further reasons for the need to address endings in therapy. The therapist (and care team) need to plan and co-ordinate therapy and the multidisciplinary pathway of care realistically to ensure predictability, stability and security for the therapy.

John was in a secure unit (under section 37) following conviction for sexual abuse of a young boy. He was having CAT with a trainee therapist, who told her supervisor she felt unconvinced about the significance of the ending of the therapy for John, because she was scheduled to do group work with him in the near future.

The supervisor reminded her that John's index offence had been triggered by being let down by a partner and encouraged her to suspend her uncertainty and to explore the issue of ending with him. The supervisor subsequently raised the ending at every supervision session, modelling for the supervisee what she needed to do with John.

John was initially dismissive and avoidant about ending therapy. The therapist explored with John how he would feel about her visiting the unit and seeing other clients post therapy. John was unsure but then disclosed that four weeks previously he had been overwhelmed and desperate to see the therapist, and was distraught when she was not available. She explored these feelings with him.

During session 22 (in the 24 session therapy), the supervisee experienced John as pressurising her, emphasising how both he and his mum did not think the break between therapies was a good idea, he just wanted to 'get on with it'. However, he also told the therapist that he had felt low for the past few days when thinking of the loss of a very supportive friend, someone he had valued. The therapist helped John to reflect on the possible relevance of these feelings to the ending of individual therapy. This allowed John to express his feelings about the difficulty of trusting someone else in the future and his fear of being let down again.

In session 23 as the therapist read the goodbye letter out, John became anxious but signalled for her to continue. He said it was very difficult to hear, that he wanted to take the letter away and read it again when he felt less anxious. He did this and in session 24 his anxiety about the ending reduced a little. He said he felt sad about therapy ending and asked how their therapeutic relationship in the group would be different.

The supervisee subsequently reflected that supervision had helped her to stay longer with the opportunities for John to experience his emotions. She realised if she had not explored these fully she would have enacted neglect towards John (mirroring earlier experiences) and maintained his sense of danger around issues of loss which would have maintained or increased his risk potential.

Use of CAT in forensic risk assessment and collaborative management

Assessment, formulation and management of risk are at the heart of forensic practice (Shannon 2009, Withers 2010). However, risk assessments are usually completed without any meaningful input from the client for reasons such as external pressures or staff anxiety and uncertainty. The reason for a client's poor engagement in risk assessment is often seen as located in the client, who is perceived to be controlling, withholding or manipulating the therapist and the surrounding team (Shannon 2009). This is despite guidance from the Department of Health (DOH 2007) that recommends that risk assessments and management are conducted in the spirit of collaboration, based on a trusting relationship with the client and recognition of the client's strengths.

Using CAT's understanding of the damage and deficit experienced by forensic clients, in particular their poor self-reflective ability, discontinuous sense of self and lack of accountability (Shannon 2009), the supervisor can remind the supervisee that clients do not necessarily have a formulated understanding of the nature and context of their offending and their state of mind at the time of the offence (Pollock et al. 2006). Initially therefore they are unable to contribute to risk assessment in a meaningful way (Shannon 2009).

The CAT supervisor can support the therapist to work within the ZPD of the client to develop a relational formulation of the client's offending behaviour, the offender-victim relationship and future risk potential (Pollock et al. 2006). Insight into the intolerable states of mind (reciprocal roles where the risky behaviour is more likely) and integration of emotions, memories, thoughts, behaviours and motivation enables clients to take responsibility for the offending pattern and awareness of both victim and offender roles.

Historically, information from psychotherapy and psychological interventions has been seen as distinct and separate from formalised risk assessment and therefore, unfortunately, has not been harnessed and incorporated (Shannon 2009). Supervisors can help supervisees to work collaboratively with clients to discuss the relevance of their risk related TPP(s) and their integration into risk assessments. The supervisor can also help the supervisee to understand reciprocal role enactments of seemingly minor boundary pushing or unhelpful behaviours as offence paralleling behaviours (Jones 2004). This means that interpersonal patterns on the ward or the prison landing, or a client's description of their behaviour or fantasies, may be understood as patterns that parallel past or potential future offending. This information is invaluable in informing detailed relational risk assessment as well as decision-making about appropriate levels of relational, procedural and physical security (Crichton 2009), care pathways and release or discharge plans. CAT reformulation provides a detailed relational understanding for risk assessment, which is a valuable contribution to scenario planning in structured professional judgement risk assessments (for example, see *Risk for Sexual Violence Protocol,* Hart et al. 2003). This collaborative, relational approach also helps the development of relapse prevention plans with the client, equipping the offender with portable tools to think, understand and act in a manner that helps in real-time situations (Pollock et al. 2006).

Relational risk management plans are especially useful where clients are unable or unwilling to engage in therapy. The supervisor can support the supervisee to develop skills to use CAT risk reformulation in contextual working with teams and services surrounding the client (Shannon 2009), to inform interventions between clients and families or within offence focused group work programmes.

Conclusion

The supervisor has an important role in containing the supervisee in the, at times, toxic environment of the forensic system and to protect the supervisee from enactment of collusive and harmful patterns which cause ethically unsound or risky behaviour. This chapter shows that CAT methods and understanding can address common issues in forensic services such as ambivalent client engagement, risk assessment and management and unhelpful systemic enactments, to ensure non-collusive collaborative working with the client, care team and multiple services surrounding the client.

References

Aiyegbusi, A. (2004) 'Forensic mental health nursing: care with security in mind', in F. Pfäfflin and G. Adshead (eds) *A Matter of Security: The Application of Attachment Theory to Forensic Psychiatry and Psychotherapy*, London: Jessica Kingsley.

Azar, S.T. (2000) 'Preventing burnout in professionals and paraprofessionals who work with child abuse and neglect cases: A cognitive behavioural approach to supervision', *Journal of Child Psychology*, 56, 6: 643–663.

Brown, H. (2010) 'Confidentiality and good record keeping in CAT therapy – A discussion paper', *Reformulation*, Summer, 34: 10–12.

Crichton, J.H.M. (2009) 'Defining high, medium, and low security in forensic mental healthcare: The development of the matrix of security in Scotland', *Journal of Forensic Psychiatry and Psychology*, 20, 3: 333–353.

Davies, J. (2015) *Supervision for Forensic Practitioners*, London: Routledge.

Department of Health. (1999) *Committee of Inquiry into the Personality Disorder Unit*, Ashworth Special Hospital (Fallon Inquiry), Department of Health.

Department of Health. (2007) *Best Practice for Managing Risk*, London: Department of Health.

Duignan, I. and Mitzman, S. (1994) 'Change in patients receiving time-limited cognitive analytic group therapy', *International Journal of Short-Term Psychotherapy*, 9, 2–3: 151–160.

Evershed, S. (2010) 'The grey area of boundary issues when working with forensic patients who have personality disorder', in P. Wilmot and N. Gordon (eds) *Working Positively with Personality Disorder in Secure Settings*, Oxford: Wiley.

Hart, S.D., Kropp, R. and Laws, D.R. with Klaver, J., Logan, C. and Watt, K.A. (2003) *The Risk for Sexual Violence Protocol (RSVP)*, Burnaby, BC: Mental Health, Law and Policy Institute, Simon Fraser University.

Jones, L. (2004) 'Offence paralleling behaviour (OPB) as a framework for assessment and intervention with offenders', in A. Needs and G. Towl (eds) *Applying Psychology to Forensic Practice*, Oxford: Blackwell.

Kadambi, M.A. and Truscott, D. (2003) 'An investigation of vicarious traumatisation among therapists working with sex offenders', *Traumatology*, 9, 4: 216–230.

Lloyd, J. and Clayton, P. (2013) *Cognitive Analytic Therapy for People with Intellectual Disabilities and Their Carers*, London: Jessica Kingsley.

Martin, D., Garske, J.P. and Davis, M.K. (2000) 'Relation of the therapeutic alliance with outcome and other variables: A meta-analytic review', *Journal of Consulting and Clinical Psychology*, 68: 438–450.

Moore, E. (2012) 'Personality disorder: Its impact on staff and the role of supervision', *Advances in Psychiatric Treatment*, 18, 1: 44–55.

Peternelj-Taylor, C.A. and Yonge, O. (2003) 'Exploring boundaries in the nurse-client relationship: Professional roles and responsibilities', *Perspectives in Psychiatric Care*, 39, 2: 55–66.

Pollock, P. and Belshaw, T. (1998) 'Cognitive analytic therapy for offenders', *Journal of Forensic Psychiatry*, 9, 3: 629–642.

Pollock, P.H., Stowell-Smith, M. and Gopfert, M. (eds) (2006) *Cognitive Analytic Therapy for Offenders: A New Approach to Forensic Psychotherapy*, New York: Routledge.

Ryle, A. (1997) *Cognitive Analytic Therapy and Borderline Personality Disorder: The Model and the Method*, Chichester: Wiley.

Shannon, K. (2009) 'Using what we know: Cognitive analytic therapy contribution to risk assessment', *Reformulation*, 33: 16–21.

Shannon, K.L., Willis, A. and Potter, S. (2006) 'Fragile states and fixed identities: using CAT to understand aggressive men in relational and societal terms', in P.H. Pollock, M. Stowell-Smith and M. Gopfert (eds) *Cognitive Analytic Therapy for Offender: A New Approach to Forensic Psychotherapy*, New York: Routledge.

Ward, T. and Laws, D.R. (2010) 'Desistance from sex offending: Motivating change, enriching practice', *International Journal of Forensic Mental Health*, 9:11–23.

Wessler, R.A. and Wessler, R.L. (1980) *The Principles and Practice of Rational Emotive Therapy*, San Francisco: Jossey Bass.

Wierzbicki, M. and Pekarik, G. (1993) 'A meta-analysis of psychotherapy drop out', *Professional Psychology Research and Practice*, 24: 190–195.

Withers, J. (2010) 'Cognitive analytic therapy (CAT): a treatment approach for treating people with severe personality disorder', in A. Tennant and K. Howells (eds) *Using Time, Not Doing Time: Practitioner Perspectives on Personality Disorder and Risk*, Oxford: Wiley.

Appendix 1

Resources

The website of the Association for Cognitive Analytic Therapy (ACAT) www.acat.me.uk has much information about CAT, the association, training, research and events. Additional website resources are available to members of ACAT and Friends of ACAT. People who have an interest in CAT and the aims and objectives of ACAT but who are not trained or qualified in CAT can become Friends of ACAT for an annual fee. These additional resources include copies of *Reformulation* (the ACAT magazine) and its predecessor, *ACAT News*, therapy tools, and documents directly relevant to supervision e.g. ACAT Code of Ethics and Practice for Training and Supervision, the Competence in CAT measure (CCAT), ACAT Supervision Requirements and Supervisor Training Guidelines.

Appendix 2
ACAT Code of Ethics and Practice for Training and Supervision

Revised and amended, and approved at ACAT AGM on 11 July 2014.

Introduction

The purpose of the Code is to establish and maintain standards for trainers and supervisors who are members of ACAT and to inform and protect therapists seeking CAT supervision and training.

All members of this Association are required to abide by the main Code of Ethics governing the relationship between therapist and client. This Code of Ethics and Practice for Training and Supervision should be read as an extension (covering the conduct of supervisors and trainers) of the underlying principles already set out there. Whilst this Code is not definitive, it aims to provide guidelines for good practice and has application, in particular, to supervisors and trainers recognised by ACAT.

1 Purpose of CAT training and supervision

Training is a means of establishing and maintaining the understanding of, and competence in, the principles and practice of Cognitive Analytic Therapy. Any particular element of training exists within a range of educational purposes and qualifications and the trainer should ensure a clear account is given to trainees of the level, application of and limitations to the training provided. A clear written account of the aims and objectives, methods and where appropriate, means of assessment and examination, should be made available to, and discussed with, both prospective and actual participants to any training.

Supervision is a formal and mutually agreed arrangement for CAT practitioners and psychotherapists to discuss their work regularly with someone who is an experienced and competent CAT therapist and familiar with the principles and practice of supervision and training. The task is to ensure and develop the efficacy of the supervisee's CAT practice. Supervision provides supervisees with the opportunity on a regular basis to discuss and monitor their work with clients. It should take account of the setting in which the supervisee practices.

The supervisory relationship has areas in common with, as well as differences from, the therapeutic relationship. The supervisor shares in common with the supervisee a central concern for the well being of his/her client. Supervision is intended to ensure that the needs of clients are being addressed and to monitor the effectiveness of therapeutic interventions. However, the focus of the supervisor's attention is on the professional competence and development of the supervisee, for it is through the work with the supervisee that the client's well-being is protected.

Supervision is a formal collaborative process intended to help supervisees maintain ethical and professional standards of practice and to enhance their effectiveness and creativity as therapists and practitioners. It is essential that the supervisor and supervisee are able to work together constructively as supervision includes both supportive and challenging elements.

2 Breaches of the code

The trainer/supervisor has an obligation to be acquainted with, and to act in, accordance with these principles. Where a breach of this Code is perceived by a supervisee, trainee or a fellow member of ACAT, the Association has a Concerns and Complaints Procedure in order to investigate such a breach and to take appropriate action should it be found that a breach has occurred.

3 Terminology and definitions

Training is the term that will be used throughout this Code and refers to all aspects and levels of training and education in Cognitive Analytic Therapy including introductory courses, skills courses, practitioner and psychotherapy training and continuing professional development.

Trainer refers to both established and trainee trainers.

The word **"trainee"** stands for all kinds of participants in training whether taking part in a formally assessed course, an introductory course or post qualifying training.

Supervision is the term that will be used throughout this Code and refers to supervision in Cognitive Analytic Therapy. It is also known as consultative support, clinical supervision or non-managerial supervision. It is an essential part of good practice for CAT therapy. It is different from training, personal development and line management accountability though it may contain elements of each. Appropriate management of these issues should be observed.

The word **"client"** stands for both patient and client.

The **supervisor** should normally be a practising and experienced CAT practitioner or psychotherapist – for supervisors of trainee practitioners or trainee psychotherapists please refer to the ACAT document; "Supervision Requirements across ACAT".

4 Non-exploitative and anti-discriminatory practice

Trainers/supervisors are expected to treat trainees/supervisees with integrity, impartiality and respect. They must recognise and work in ways that respect the values and dignity of supervisees and their clients with due regard to issues such as status, race, gender, age, beliefs, sexual orientation and disability.

a   The trainer/supervisor has a responsibility to be aware of his/her own issues of prejudice and stereotyping and particularly to consider ways in which these may be affecting the training/supervisory relationship. The trainer/supervisor has a responsibility to make such issues explicit where appropriate.
b   The trainer/supervisor needs to be alert to any prejudices and assumptions that supervisees reveal in their work and to raise awareness of these so that the needs of clients may be met with sensitive recognition and appreciation of difference.
c   The supervisor must not exploit his/her supervisee sexually, financially, emotionally or in any other way.

5 Boundaries of supervision

It is essential to be aware of the boundaries of supervision:

a   The supervisor and supervisees should take all reasonable steps to ensure that any personal or social contact between them does not adversely influence the effectiveness of CAT supervision.
b   The supervisor must not give supervision and a personal CAT therapy with the same supervisee over the same period of time.
c   Former clients should not be taken on as supervisees and former supervisees should not be taken on as clients. If a deviation from this is being considered then a supervisor should be consulted first.
d   It is unethical for the supervisor to enter into a sexual relationship with his/her supervisee during a supervisory contract.
e   The supervisor has a responsibility to enquire about relationships outside the therapeutic contract between supervisees and their clients to ensure that these do not impair the objectivity and professional judgement of supervisees.
f   The supervisor working with trainee CAT practitioners or therapists must clarify the boundaries of their responsibility and their accountability to their supervisee and to the training course and any agency or placement involved. This should include any formal assessment required.
g   The supervisor is responsible for setting and maintaining the boundaries between the supervision relationship and other professional relationships, e.g. training and management.

h   Where a supervisee works in an organisation or agency, the supervisor must clarify with the supervisee that the lines of accountability and responsibility are clearly defined in respect of: supervisee/client; supervisor/supervisee; supervisor/client; organisation/supervisor; organisation/supervisee; organisation/client.
i   The supervisor who becomes aware of a conflict between an obligation to a supervisee and an obligation to an employing agency must make explicit to the supervisee the nature of the loyalties and responsibilities involved.
j   A supervisor must make a clear distinction between line management supervision and CAT supervision. The best practice is that the same person should not act as both line manager and supervisor to the same supervisee.

6 Conduct of training

6.1 The trainer must be an experienced CAT practitioner.
6.2 Training should take place in an appropriately confidential and conducive setting and any client or personal details discussed should be done with respect for confidentiality and in accordance with the main Code of Ethics and Practice.
6.3 Whilst training may not have the same level of involvement as supervision and personal therapy, it is essential that both trainers and trainees are able to work together constructively in an atmosphere of personal learning and exploration. Trainers should have some familiarity with and responsibility for both educational and group processes in the pursuit of training.
6.4 The trainer is responsible for setting and maintaining the boundaries between the training role and other professional relationships such as supervision and management.
6.5 A trainer and or trainee should take all reasonable steps to ensure that any personal or social contact between them does not adversely influence the effectiveness of training for all parties involved. It is unethical for a trainer to enter into a sexual relationship with someone whilst they are a trainee with them.

7 Contractual arrangements

7.1 **The trainer** should ensure as far as is possible that trainees are aware of the contractual boundaries of the training activity.

   a   The training status of trainees continues until graduation (or completion of training where no qualification is offered) and/or formal withdrawal from training.
   b   The trainer should make known to trainees, and act in accordance with, clear procedures for the presentation, submission, assessment and examination of work associated with training and qualification in the principles

and practice of CAT. This includes general arrangements such as timing, length, spacing and location of training, the nature and level of the qualification and its professional standing and limitations in relevant settings. Training should take place within surroundings that provide privacy and comfort.

c   Where the training is linked to qualification or accreditation, clear consideration should be given to the recruitment of trainees with appropriate experience, qualifications, standards and aptitudes to be able to make professional use of the training.

d   The trainer is responsible for making clear and keeping to any contractual arrangements regarding appropriate setting and environment, fees, relating to employers, professional bodies and writing references. The trainer must satisfy him/herself that s/he is covered by indemnity arrangements against claims for damages from alleged negligence or accidental injury in respect of any training work or materials s/he offers or provides.

7.2 The supervisor should ensure as far as is possible that the supervisee is aware of the contractual boundaries of the relationship.

a   This includes, day and times of meetings, arrangements for holidays, method of termination of supervision. Financial arrangements need to be clearly established.

b   The supervisor is responsible, together with his/her supervisees, for ensuring that the best use is made of supervision time, in order to address the needs of clients.

c   The supervisor and supervisees must make explicit the expectations and requirements they have of each other. This should include the manner in which any formal assessment of the supervisee's work will be conducted. Each party should assess the value of working with the other, and review this regularly.

d   The supervisor is responsible for helping supervisees to reflect critically upon their work but clinical responsibility remains with the therapist.

e   Before formalising a supervision contract, the supervisor should ascertain what personal therapy the supervisee is having or has had.

f   The supervisor must ensure that together with his/her supervisee they consider their respective contractual obligation to each other, to the employing or training organisation if any, and to clients.

g   Where the supervisor and supervisees work for the same agency or organisation, the supervisor is responsible for clarifying all contractual obligations.

h   The supervisor must inform his/her supervisee about his/her policy regarding giving references and any fees that may be charged for this or for any other work done outside supervision time.

8 Confidentiality

The supervisory relationship is one in which the supervisee should feel confident that the content of the meeting is private and confidential. As a general principle, the supervisor must not reveal confidential material concerning the supervisee or their clients to any other person without the express consent of all parties concerned. Exceptions to this general principle are contained below:

a   The supervisor may speak about his/her supervisee's work with those on whom the supervisor relies for supervision or consultancy. The same general rules of confidentiality apply to this communication.
b   The disclosure of confidential information relating to supervisees and their clients is permissible when relevant to the following situations:

- Discussion concerning supervisees for professional purposes, e.g. references, assessments and in regard to the supervisee's training.
- Pursuit of disciplinary action involving supervisees in matters pertaining to standards of ethics and practice.
- When the supervisor considers it necessary to prevent serious emotional or physical damage to the client, the supervisee or a third party. In such circumstances the supervisee's consent to a change in the agreement about confidentiality should be sought, unless there are good grounds for believing that the supervisee is no longer able to take responsibility for his/her own actions or there is serious concern about the safety or interests of others who may be threatened by the client's behaviour. Whenever possible, the decision to break confidentiality in any circumstance should be made after consultation with another experienced supervisor.
- In the case of the latter two situations, any breaking of confidentiality should be minimised by conveying only information pertinent to the immediate situation on a need-to-know basis.

The ethical considerations needing to be taken into account are:

- the supervisor's responsibility to the client and to the wider community
- enabling the supervisee to take responsibility for his/her actions
- maintaining the best interests of the supervisee.

c   Information about work with a supervisee may be used for publication or in teaching only with the supervisee's permission and with anonymity preserved unless the supervisee wishes his/her identity to be known.

9 Limitations on effectiveness

The supervisor should be aware of the limitations of the supervisee and his/her own ability to offer an effective service.

a   The supervisor is responsible for helping the supervisee recognise when his/her functioning as a therapist is impaired due to personal or emotional difficulties, any condition that affects judgement, such as illness, the influence of alcohol or drugs, or for any other reason, and for ensuring that appropriate action is taken.
b   If, in the course of CAT supervision, it appears that personal therapy may be necessary for the supervisee to be able to continue working effectively, the supervisor should raise this issue with the supervisee.
c   The supervisor must monitor regularly how the supervisee engages in self-assessment and the self-evaluation of his/her work.
d   The supervisor must ensure that the supervisee acknowledges his/her individual responsibility for ongoing professional development and for participating in further training programmes.
e   Where the supervisor has concerns about or disagreements with the supervisee's work which cannot be resolved by discussion between supervisor and supervisee, the supervisor should consult with a fellow professional and, if appropriate, recommend that the supervisee be referred to another supervisor.
f   The supervisor is responsible for seeking ways to further his or her own professional development and for making arrangements for his or her own supervision in order to support supervision work and to help evaluate own competence. S/he is responsible for monitoring and working within the limits of his/her competence.
g   The supervisor is responsible for withdrawing from supervision work either temporarily or permanently when his/her functioning is impaired due to personal or emotional difficulties, illness, the influence of alcohol or drugs, or for any other reason.

10 Appropriate environment

The supervisor has a responsibility to ensure that s/he is working within an appropriate environment. Supervisees should be seen in appropriate surroundings providing privacy, security and comfort. The supervisor must satisfy him/herself that s/he is covered by indemnity arrangements against claims for damages from alleged negligence or accidental injury whether in his/her private practice or in the work which s/he undertakes for an employer.

11 Obligations to the association and the profession

The supervisor

The supervisor has an obligation to act in accordance with an awareness of the standing of his/her profession. The supervisor is responsible for taking action if s/he is aware that his/her supervisee's practice is not in accordance with the main ACAT Code of Ethics and Practice.

The trainer

Whilst the trainer does not have the same formal responsibility as a supervisor for the professional practice of trainees s/he should work with reference to the best interests of clients, of the professional and ethical aims of ACAT in particular and the professional standing and effectiveness of psychotherapy in general.

The trainer is responsible for withdrawing from training either temporarily or permanently when his/her functioning is impaired due to personal or emotional difficulties, ill health or for any other reason.

The trainer must regularly monitor the effectiveness of his/her work, take into account routine evaluation and seek to maintain a high personal standard of continuing professional development. The trainer should put in place procedures for peer review of the effectiveness of his/her training and seek appropriate consultation in respect of any difficulties s/he may encounter whilst doing training. The trainer is responsible for working within the limits of his/her competence and should not make inappropriate claims regarding CAT or other models of psychotherapy.

12 Risk

Therapists, supervisors and trainers need to work within the risk management and safeguarding frameworks of the law, ACAT, their employers, local authorities and other regulatory and professional bodies that define the context in which they are practising. There is a duty to act to protect clients and to safeguard others.

Trainers and Supervisors should work with trainees and therapists to consider the appropriate course of action to manage issues of risk of harm to self and others and safeguarding concerns.

There can be a need to balance the duty to act against the duty of confidentiality and further advice from employers or professional bodies should be sought where there is doubt about the appropriate course of action. The trainer or supervisor should ensure that the trainee or supervisee has carried through actions that have been agreed in the context of supervision and consultation. There are times when the trainer or supervisor may need to act to ensure risk is being communicated and acted upon. Any such action should be with the agreement of the trainee or supervisee where they can be reached.

ACAT offers the following guidance in these areas:

- Safeguarding Vulnerable Adults and Children 2010
- Equality and Diversity Policy 2010
- Supervision Requirements across ACAT (revised March 2014)

Appendix 3

The CCAT – A measure of competence in Cognitive Analytic Therapy (CAT)

Dawn Bennett and Glenys Parry

1 Instructions for use of the CCAT measure
2 Overview of the 10 domains of the CCAT
3 Domains 1–10

Acknowledgements

This research was funded by the Mental Health Foundation and Department of Health NHS R&D programme.

We are grateful to the therapists who offered audio-tapes of their therapy and members of the expert panels for their contribution during the stages of measure development: Gill Aitken, Brigitta Bende, Gill Bloxham, Kate Cahill, Phil Clayton, Sarah Cluley, Louise Cooke, David Crossley, Mark Evans, Kate Freshwater, Deborah Gamsu, Yvonne Harris, Anna Jellema, Sarah Littlejohn, Carol Lomax, Judy Merchant, Sue Pethen, Debby Pickvance, Rachel Pollard, and Lawrence Welch. We should also like to thank Mark Evans and Sarah Littlejohn CCAT raters for inter-rater reliability and validity tests of the CCAT. We thank Tony Ryle for his support and contribution to this work.

© Dr Dawn Bennett & Professor Glenys Parry
Reproduced with permission of Dr Dawn Bennett and Professor Glenys Parry

Instructions for use of the CCAT measure

This scale contains 77 elements of therapist competence in Cognitive Analytic Therapy (CAT) across 10 domains of therapeutic practice. For two of the domains of competence (1 and 3), the section you rate depends on the stage of therapy, a) for early sessions, b) for later ones. For these two, please rate *either* section a *or* section b, but not both.

Some of the domains of competence are highly CAT specific (e.g. CAT specific tools & techniques) whilst others reflect generic competencies (e.g. common factors: basic supportive good practice).

The scale is designed for use with audiotapes of whole CAT therapy sessions in which the therapist's competence in each of the domains of practice is rated for **the session as a whole**. For each tape you will receive contextual information relevant to the current stage of the therapy.

Part A

Work through the 10 domains, look at each element of competence and decide if it was **present or absent** in the session.

> If the competence was **present** you will be asked to rate how well it was demonstrated.
> If the competence was **absent** you will be asked whether this constitutes a therapist error, in which case, consider the following points:

1. Sometimes it is *inappropriate* for a particular competence to be demonstrated. For example, if the therapeutic alliance were intact, the therapist would not need to identify and work with threats to the alliance (competence 9.4) or it may be too early in therapy to focus on change (competence 3.12). Code this **XI**.
2. An in-session event may make it *difficult* for the therapist to show the competence. For example, it is difficult to focus on specific formulation work when the client uses the session to discuss a current major life event. Code this **XD**.
3. The competence should have happened and didn't – the therapist failed to respond to a cue and there was a *missed opportunity*. Code this **XM**.
4. If the competence was absent for some other reason, please specify.

Ratings

Rate each element of competence in the following way

Present/observed: √+ well demonstrated
√- observed but with missed opportunities and/or not good enough

Absent/not observed: **XI** it was inappropriate to practise the competence
XD it was difficult to practise the competence
XM missed opportunity(ies) to practise the competence
XO absent for other reason, please specify

Part B

For each of the ten domains please make a general rating of competence on a scale of 0–4. Do this after you have scored the individual elements. This rating summarises competence in the whole domain and takes the individual items into account but is not derived directly on them. It is based on your overall judgement of the therapist's work in that particular session. A score of 4 represents highly competent practice and 0 represents completely incompetent practice. The scale is anchored and contains descriptions of competent and incompetent performance. For any session that you rate using the CCAT be aware of the whole range of possible competencies e.g. the worst session possible versus an expert therapist working with a highly responsive client. Use

X if you are unable to rate a cluster (e.g. if the competency domain was not observed in this session)

Overview of the CCAT measure

The 10 domains of competency are:

1   Phase Specific Therapeutic Tasks

    1a   Early engagement, induction and remoralisation
    1b   Review and evaluation of process and outcome

Section (1a) concerns competencies specific to early sessions and includes the therapist engaging the client in identifying the areas for work, raising hope about the possibility of change, establishing the client's commitment to therapy and generally establishing the therapeutic roles.

Section (1b) concerns competencies more specific to the middle or later phases of therapy and includes reviewing progress and the ability of the therapist and the client to engage in the work.

2   Theory – Practice Links

This section is concerned with the therapist's application of theory to practise and includes the use of a theoretical model to plan and structure the work and make sense of the client's material.

3   CAT Specific Tools & Techniques

    3a   CAT specific tools & techniques (reformulation)
    3b   CAT specific tools & techniques (post reformulation)

Section (3a) concerns competencies specific to early sessions (pre-reformulation and reformulation phase) and includes the therapist's competence in identifying TPs, TPPs and developing the CAT tools.

Section (3b) concerns competencies more specific to the middle or later phases of therapy (post reformulation phase) and includes the therapist facilitating the client in their use of the CAT tools to recognise and revise procedures within and outside sessions.

4   Establishing and Maintaining the External Framework

This section concerns the boundaries to the therapy and the therapeutic relationship.

5   Common Factors: Basic Supportive Good Practice

This section concerns basic factors common to all therapies, and includes support and attentiveness to the client's stage of readiness for the work.

6 Respect, Collaboration & Mutuality

This section includes establishing a mutual, collaborative, respectful and authentic therapeutic relationship.

7 Assimilation of Warded-off, Problematic States and Emotions

This section includes the therapist's capacity to experience, stay with and tolerate painful affect and to facilitate assimilation and integration of these experiences.

8 Making Links and Hypotheses (between therapy and client's past and client's other relationships so facilitating awareness of procedures that are operating)

This section includes the therapist's ability to offer links and hypotheses in an appropriate and timely way.

9 Identifying and Managing Threats to the Therapeutic Alliance

This section concerns the therapist's competence in identifying and managing in-session reciprocal role enactments that represent obstacles to the therapy and/or threats to the alliance.

10 Therapist's Awareness and Management of Own Reactions and Emotions

This section concerns the therapist's ability to appropriately reflect, express and manage their own feelings and reactions.

I Phase specific therapeutic tasks

Section (1a) concerns competencies specific to early sessions and section (1b) concerns competencies more specific to the middle or later phases of therapy.

Please use the section most appropriate to the phase of therapy represented by your tape. As a general rule, 1a would be used for sessions 1–5 and 1b for sessions from session 6 onwards.

Ia Early engagement, induction and remoralisation rating

1.1 An assessment is made of the client's capacity for and commitment to therapeutic work
1.2 One or more potential area of work is identified with the client without premature focusing or imposition of the therapist's own model
1.3 The client's assumptions are reviewed and/or agreement reached on the nature of the working relationship

1.4 A preliminary formulation of presenting problem is offered in a way that makes sense to the client and implies the possibility of change
1.5 Assessment is concluded in a way that ensures the client's identified goals have been addressed and that suggests the possibility of change
1.6 The client is assisted in deciding whether or not to make use of the proposed approach to therapy (for example, the therapist presents alternatives, appraises risks and benefits and elicits informed consent)
1.7 The details of the immediate next action are checked with the client and implemented by the therapist

1a Early engagement, induction and remoralisation

Make an overall rating of the therapist's competence in this domain.

1b Review and evaluation of process and outcome rating

1.8 The appropriateness of styles and methods of intervention are assessed in relation to the client and to the experience of working together
1.9 The therapist's capacity to engage with the particular client is reviewed (if appropriate)
1.10 Changes in the focus or nature of the therapeutic work are discussed or agreed
1.11 The usefulness of the current therapeutic approach is monitored and where necessary, modified
1.12 Progress is assessed against statements of change within the CAT model (for example, using rating sheets, TP/TPP list, exits on SDR/SSSD)
1.13 The client's use of interventions is monitored in terms of their appropriateness and usefulness
1.14 The therapist evaluates the extent of change the client has made and maintained relative to the TPs, TPPs and/or RRPs

1b Review and evaluation of process and outcome

Make an overall rating of the therapist's competence in this domain

very competent   good   satisfactory   unsatisfactory   incompetent   unable to rate

4	3	2	1	0	X

←more competent   less competent→

Therapist reviews and evaluates process of therapy, appropriateness and effectiveness of methods, extent of client change and focus on client's desired change

Therapist fails to review or evaluate process or outcome of therapy, does not 'stand back' and ensure it is serving the interests of the client

2 Theory – Practice links rating

This section concerns both explicit references to theory by the therapist and implicit use of theory by the therapist.

The theoretical base is used to

2.1 Assist in understanding the client's narratives (e.g. offering preliminary hypotheses)
2.2 Review the presenting problems in the light of the hypotheses
2.3 Offer tentative formulations of the client's situation
2.4 Plan and structure the session (e.g. use of a therapeutic framework)
2.5 Assist the therapist in reflecting on and/or exploring their contribution to the therapeutic process
2.6 Assist the therapist to progress the therapeutic work (e.g. inform decision-making)
2.7 The therapist's application of their knowledge base is timely, relevant and appropriate to the client

2 Theory – Practice links

Make an overall rating of the therapist's competence in this domain

very competent   good   satisfactory   unsatisfactory   incompetent   unable to rate

4	3	2	1	0	X

←**more competent**   **less competent**→

Therapist refers to theory (in understanding client, deriving hypotheses, planning therapy) in timely, relevant, appropriate ways

Therapist does not derive practice from any coherent theoretical framework. Interventions are purely pragmatic, responsive to cues or drawn inconsistently from a hodge-podge of concepts

3 CAT specific tools & techniques

Section (3a) concerns competencies specific to early sessions (pre-reformulation and reformulation phase) and section (3b) concerns competencies more specific to the middle or later phases of therapy (post reformulation phase).

Please use the section most appropriate to the phase of therapy represented by your tape. As a general rule, 3a would be used for sessions 1–5 and 3b for sessions from session 6 onwards.

3a CAT specific tools & techniques (reformulation) rating

3.1 The therapist explores and expands the initial formulation collaboratively with the client by reflecting on all the material the client brings to the session
3.2 The therapist identifies Target Problems with the client
3.3 The therapist identifies Target Problem Procedures with the client
3.4 The therapist writes a reformulation that conveys an understanding of the links between early experience, current experience and the therapy experience
3.5 The therapist collaboratively draws a diagrammatic reformulation of the client's current difficulties
3.6 The therapist uses assessment tools (e.g. psychotherapy file, dyad grid)

3a CAT specific tools & techniques (reformulation)

Make an overall rating of the therapist's competence in this domain

very competent good satisfactory unsatisfactory incompetent unable to rate

4	3	2	1	0	X

←more competent   less competent→

Therapist reformulates   CAT-specific tools for
client's presenting difficulty   reformulation are not used,
using CAT-specific tools; TP &   used inaccurately and
TPP list, prose reformulation,   incompetently SDR/SSSD etc.

3b CAT specific tools & techniques (post reformulation) rating

3.7 The therapist facilitates the client's awareness of their thoughts, feelings and behaviour, including that occurring in-session, by collaboratively formulating reciprocal role and target problem procedures
3.8 The therapist encourages/facilitates the client's capacity to use the jointly created tools both within and outside sessions (so promoting self-observation and reflective capacities)
3.9 The therapist identifies TPPs and/or RRPs *within* the session and encourages the client to monitor enactments
3.10 The therapist identifies TPPs and/or RRPs *outside* the session and encourages the client to monitor enactments
3.11 The therapist builds on the SDR/SSSD to describe different states of self and shifts between them in the client's life and/or in the session with the therapist, where appropriate

3.12 The therapist helps the client to explore alternatives or exits to current TPPs and RRPs

3.13 The therapist suggests and describes relevant work between sessions in recognising and revising TPPs

3b CAT specific tools & techniques (post reformulation)

Make an overall rating of the therapist's competence in this domain

very competent   good   satisfactory   unsatisfactory   incompetent   unable to rate

4	3	2	1	0	X

←more competent   less competent→

Therapist uses CAT-specific tools appropriately and fosters their use by client: TPPs and RRPs are identified in narrative, diary and in-session and linked to prose reformulation and SDR/SSSD

Therapist fails to link narrative, diary and session to reformulation and SDR/SSSD. Tools are not used, homework is not set or if set, therapist fails to follow it up

4 Establishing and maintaining external framework rating

4.1 A safe environment is maintained in which work can take place

4.2 The need to keep to the time constraints of sessions is clarified

4.3 The boundaries and nature of the therapeutic relationship are negotiated

4.4 The boundaries in the therapeutic relationship are maintained and lapses in the boundaries are reviewed

4.5 Ways of working and accepted behaviours within the therapeutic sessions are reviewed and/or agreed

4.6 The nature of any contact outside the therapeutic sessions is reviewed

4.7 The nature and effect of any personal, organisational or statutory constraints upon the therapeutic contract are reviewed

4 Establishing and maintaining external framework

Make an overall rating of the therapist's competence in this domain

very competent	good	satisfactory	unsatisfactory	incompetent	unable to rate
4	3	2	1	0	X

←more competent less competent→

Therapist establishes & maintains the external framework for therapy: a safe environment, clear boundaries, time limits, appropriate behaviours etc

Therapist violates or colludes with violation of external framework: time limits are not established or are disregarded, inappropriate behaviours are observed, environment is not safe or protected

5 Common factors: Basic supportive good practice rating

5.1 The common factors necessary to the working relationship are maintained and modelled where appropriate
5.2 Consistent commitment to the client is demonstrated which transcends negative and positive comments or changes of attitude on the part of the client
5.3 Indications of possible separations and endings in the working relationship are identified and reviewed with clients
5.4 The therapist demonstrates the capacity to make professional use of the therapeutic process by entering into, staying alongside reflecting upon and using the therapeutic relationship
5.5 The two-way nature of the process is established
5.6 Positive changes and growth in clients are acknowledged where appropriate
5.7 Therapist acknowledges or suggests awareness of areas where client is ready to make changes

5 Common factors: Basic supportive good practice

Make an overall rating of the therapist's competence in this domain

very competent	good	satisfactory	unsatisfactory	incompetent	unable to rate
4	3	2	1	0	X

←more competent less competent→

Therapist shows basic good supportive relationship skills: commitment to client, awareness of client's pace, responsiveness to client's level of anxiety and readiness to change, breaks or endings are handled in advance

Therapist fails to provide support and basic good practice: e.g. commitment to client is reduced by negative comments, pace of intervention disregards client readiness, gives insufficient attention to impact of breaks or endings

6 Respect, collaboration & mutuality rating

6.1 The therapist sensitively shares the CAT tools (e.g. reformulation letter) with the client, demonstrating the capacity to alter understanding where they are inaccurate and identifies where further work needs to be done in order to enhance the client's understanding

6.2 The therapist demonstrates a reflective awareness of the strengths or weaknesses of these tools (e.g. as general therapeutic interventions and/or as a valid intervention for this specific client)

6.3 The therapist appropriately handles agreement and disagreement over the content of the written and/or diagrammatic reformulations

6.4 The working relationship is conducted in a manner which ensures a reciprocal process including the opportunity for the client to ask questions, express doubts and/or assess the therapist

6.5 A mutually acceptable use of language and other modes of communication are arrived at which assist the client's and therapist's understanding of the relationship

6.6 The client's aims and expectations of the relationship are updated and re-focused in the light of reviews

6.7 The therapist demonstrates sensitivity to and respect for issues of difference in the therapeutic relationship (race, gender, class, sexual preference, cultural differences)

6 Respect, collaboration & mutuality

Make an overall rating of the therapist's competence in this domain

very competent   good   satisfactory   unsatisfactory   incompetent   unable to rate

4	3	2	1	0	X

←more competent

less competent→

Therapist's style fosters respect, mutuality, collaboration, uses shared language, explores working relationship, allows doubt & disagreement to be expressed

Therapist style is dogmatic defensive, non-collaborative and not mutual. Doubts or disagreements interpreted as "resistance". Therapist does not allow exploration of working relationship

7 Assimilation of warded-off, problematic states and emotions rating

7.1 The therapist focuses on and reflects the client's emotional experience

7.2 The therapist shows the client that they have the capacity to experience, acknowledge and think about the working relationship

7.3 The therapist's willingness to stay with and tolerate impasses and strong feelings is demonstrated in a way which remains in the service of the client
7.4 The therapist demonstrates a willingness to explore feelings which are difficult to recognise, attribute and make sense of
7.5 The therapist helps the client to explore ways of working through emotions which are acknowledged as difficult/repressed
7.6 The therapist facilitates integration of conflicting experiences and/or self states

7 Assimilation of warded-off, problematic states and emotions

Make an overall rating of the therapist's competence in this domain

very competent   good   satisfactory   unsatisfactory   incompetent   unable to rate

4	3	2	1	0	X

←more competent   less competent→

Therapist enables client to assimilate painful, warded-off or problematic emotions and to integrate confusing or conflicting states of mind

Therapist does not foster assimilation and integration: e.g. does not reflect on or contain clients emotional expression, is unwilling to stay with strong feelings or explore feelings, fails to reflect on confusing or conflicting states

8 Making links and hypotheses (between therapy and client's rating past and client's other relationships so facilitating awareness of procedures that are operating)

8.1 The relationship between areas of greatest psychological pain, limitation or inhibition and key aspects of presenting problems is established
8.2 Emerging patterns and themes in the client's life are identified and related to the client's present situation
8.3 The therapist tests hypothesised links between current material and childhood experience by sharing these with the client in a tentative form
8.4 Links are made between the therapist-client relationship and the client's past and present relationships
8.5 Changes in the client are related to aspects of the therapeutic relationship
8.6 Timely interpretations and links are offered to increase the client's awareness of the procedures operating (which can include defensive/avoidant procedures)

8.7 Hypotheses are formulated and offered to the client in an appropriate and useful form

8 Making links and hypotheses (between therapy and client's past, client's other relationships so facilitating awareness of procedures that are operating)

Make an overall rating of the therapist's competence in this domain

very competent   good   satisfactory   unsatisfactory   incompetent   unable to rate

4	3	2	1	0	X

←**more competent**

Therapist makes links and offers hypotheses about relationship, for example, between therapy and past relationships, current material and childhood, therapy relationship and change in clients, unconscious behaviour and conscious awareness

less competent→

Therapist fails to make any links, or offers vague or over-general interpretations, or makes over-concrete and rigid interpretations

9 Identifying and managing 'threats' to the therapeutic alliance

This domain is not specific to particular phases of therapy and should be rated for all sessions, although, therapists would not be able to use fully developed CAT tools to assist in their management of threats to the therapeutic alliance prior to their development in the early sessions. However, the therapist would be able to use provisional understandings and emerging joint tools (e.g. TPPs and psychotherapy file). Ratings should therefore be made in reference to the tools emerging between therapist and client.

Threats to the therapeutic alliance are understood to reflect the emergence within the therapeutic relationship of the client's TPPs and RRPs. At times these TPP or RRP enactments may not be considered to amount to an actual 'threat' to the alliance but would reduce the collaborative nature of the therapeutic process. This section is therefore intended to refer to the therapist's competence in identifying and managing all such in-session enactments.

Rating

9.1 Opportunities to review and/or reflect upon the relationship are offered at appropriate moments
9.2 Potential obstacles to the working relationship are monitored and/or explored with the client
9.3 The therapist shows that they have an awareness of the possibility of invitations by the client to enact their anticipated reciprocal role, and the desirability of avoiding this
9.4 Threats to and breaches in the therapeutic alliance are named as TPP and RRP enactments within the session
9.5 These TPP and RRP enactments are identified and responded to in a non-collusive manner
9.6 These TPP and RRP enactments are linked to/located on the SDR/SSSD

9 Identifying and managing threats to the therapeutic alliance

Make an overall rating of the therapist's competence in this domain

very competent good satisfactory unsatisfactory incompetent unable to rate

4	3	2	1	0	X

←more competent   less competent→

Therapist identifies potential or actual threats to alliance, RRP enactments and negative therapeutic reactions and links them to formulation to enhance mutual understanding of processes

Therapist fails to recognise breaches or threats to alliance or else retaliates in enacting negative RRPs without reflecting on the link to reformulation

10 Therapist's awareness and management of own reactions rating and emotions

10.1 The therapist makes an appropriate expression of his or her own reactions within the therapeutic relationship
10.2 The therapist demonstrates awareness of his or her own responses and images of the client and reflects upon them, in order to develop understanding of the therapeutic process
10.3 The therapist's own feelings and anxieties aroused by the therapeutic relationship are contained and managed

10 Therapist's awareness and management of own reactions and emotions

Make an overall rating of the therapist's competence in this domain

very competent good satisfactory unsatisfactory incompetent unable to rate

4	3	2	1	0	X

←**more competent**   **less competent**→

Therapist is aware of own responses, emotions and anxieties in the relationship and reflects on, contains or expresses these appropriately

Therapist is unaware of own emotional responses or fails to contain them, or expresses them inappropriately

Index

Note: Pages in *italics* indicate figures, boxes and tables.

Note for readers unfamiliar with CAT: Procedure, problem procedure, role procedure, reciprocal role procedure (RRP) and target problem procedure (TPP) have very similar meanings and are used almost interchangeably.

accountability: for offending behaviour in therapy in forensic services 253–5; in supervision 188
activity theory 4, 10
aim *see* exit
alliance rupture: in consultancy work 211, 213; in supervision 6, 14, 16, 41, 59, 62, 74, 78, 79; in therapy 42, 62, 83, 91, 92, 93, 149, 169, 232, 251
Altman, N. 9
ambivalence of forensic clients 251–3
American Psychiatric Association (APA) *see* Diagnostic and Statistical Manual of Mental Disorders (DSM-III); Diagnostic and Statistical Manual of Mental Disorders (DSM-5)
anxiety: in cross-modality supervision 207; in supervisees 12, 63; in training context 187, 189, 190, 192, 193, 194, 195, 196
appraisals 135, 193–5; group or individual 135
Aron, A. 8
attachment 251; figures 13; history 80; pattern 61; in relationship with supervisor 61; secure 20, 34; theory 33, 61
attunement 25, 33, 34, 36, 99
Atwood, G.E. 8, 9

Bakhtin, M. 4, 40, 44, 49, 86, 116, 117, 174–6, 196
Beinart, H. 61
Bender, M. 235
Benjamin, J. 9
Bennett, D. 42, 74, 92, 149, 151, 210, 211, 213, 214, 216, 271
Bernard, J.M. 54
Bion, W. 9, 179
Blavatsky, Madame 176
blind spots 32, 33, 141
borderline personality disorder 20, 95; CAT for 83–93; DSM-5 description 83–4, 85, 89
boundaries of supervision 265–6
boundary breach 43, 248, 251
Boundary Seesaw model 217–19, *217*
breach of ethical code 264
Bromberg, P. 9, 138, 144
Brown, H. 109, 112
Bruch, H. 194
Bruner, J. 23
Buddhism 163, 165, 169
Buirski, P. 9
Burkitt, I. 114

cage diagram 104–5, *105*
Callahan, J.L. 55
Carradice, A. 210, 211, 212, 213, 214, 216, 219
Casement, P. 45, 46, 179, 187, 188, 189, 195, 205, 210
CAT: development of 4, 10; effectiveness with people with personality disorders 84; introduction to model 19–23, 37–41; as lens for examining culture 113; as a

286 Index

relational therapy 4; as a time-limited model 39
categories of intervention in supervision (Heron) 27–9, *28*
CAT supervision: early days of 4–5; interpersonal learning in 38; as a relational model 5–7; Ryle's approach to 4–5; use of self in 6
CAT supervision group 88, 125–36; as carrier of CAT culture 136; development of 127–8; frequency of 134; joint reflection in 41, 44, 45, 49, 75; mutual learning in mixed 33, 244; negotiation of time and boundaries 64, 135, 190; relationships within 41–2; setting up new 42–4; similarity and difference within 127, 128–30; size of 134; time allocation 64, 135
CAT with young people 222–33; adapting CAT tools for 229–30; ending therapy in 232; inclusion of others in therapy with 231–2; playfulness in therapy with 230
CCAT *see* Competence in CAT measure
Chanen, A. 84, 150, 223
Charura, D. 3
checking-in in supervision 44
Clarke, S. 84, 150
Clinical Hexagon 130, *131*
COAL: Curious, Open, Accepting and Loving (Siegel) 43
code of ethics 71
Code of Ethics and Practice for Training and Supervision (ACAT) 263–70
collaboration in supervision 5, 11, 12, 27, 41, 45, 57, 61, 62, 65, 73, 74, 115, 129, 149, 170, 192, 194, 195, 202, 204, 230
Competence in CAT measure (CCAT) 149, 271–84; description 151; implications for supervision 152–4; methodological issues 156–8; rating guide 155–6; supervisees' perspective 158–62; use in supervision 149–62
competency *versus* adherence 150
competency *versus* effectiveness 150
confidentiality in therapy in forensic services 249–50
confidentiality of supervision 268, 270
conflict in supervision 41, 60, 62, 65, 74, 75, 132, 133, 207
consultancy 198, 201, 202; CAT framework for 216–17, *216*; CAT supervision for 209–20; CAT templates for 219–20, *219, 220*; challenges 210

consultation in intellectual disability work 241–3; supervision of 241–4
consultative supervision 201
context: impact on therapy with people with intellectual disabilities 236, 237, 238
contextual diagram: use in supervisory impasse 134
contextual reformulation 214–16, *215*, 217, 232; in forensic work 257; in intellectual disability work 241
continuum of reciprocal role enactments 253–5, *254*
contract for supervision 12, 43, 203, 267
core pain 98, 141, 165, 167, 170, 171, 193
countertransference xvii, 6, 10, 37, 47, 49, 73, 86, 129, 133, 141, 145, 200, 205, 236; in borderline personality disorder work 83; elicited 6, 79, 167, 191, 255; in forensic work 250, 252, 253, 255; identifying xvii, 205; in intellectual disabilities work 245; learning to notice and use 189, 205; and parallel process 15, 205; personal 6, 7, 42, 167, 191; and reciprocal roles 146, 190; reciprocating xvii, 205; sexualised 77; supervisee's 11, 13, 191, 207, 252, 255; supervisor's 11, 12, 13, 24, 25, 79, 130, 175
cross-cultural: settings 110, 112; therapy 116; *see also* intercultural supervision
cross-modal supervision *see* supervision, of non-CAT therapists
cultural: context of the self 175; differences 7, 50, 79, 109–12, 114; differences between client, therapist and supervisor 76; differences in supervision group 50, 79, 109, 111, 114, 126, 129; differences, respect for client's 280; expectations 115; formation of mind 37; history 125, 175; identities 113; influences on the self 7, 175; intergenerational conflict *119*; layer of supervision process 199; meanings 125, 126; norms 117; notions 111; transgenerational patterns 125, 177
cultural issues in intellectual disability work 246
cultures, supervision across *see* intercultural supervision
curiosity, curious enquiry 13, 43, 45, 73, 79, 87, *87*, 91, 107, 108, 112, 114, 146, 149, 158, 194, 204, 230, 236; and mindfulness 169, 170, 171, 172, 173

Daniels, J. 62
Darongkamas, J. 27, 202
deaf spots (Ekstein) 33
dependence 42, 107
Diagnostic and Statistical Manual of Mental Disorders (DSM-III) 100
Diagnostic and Statistical Manual of Mental Disorders (DSM-5) 83, 91, 96, 99
diagrammatic reformulation 143, 199; supervision of 142
diagrams 20, 40, *40*, 42, 47, 137; adapting for intellectual disabilities 241, *242*; adapting for young people 229–30; in borderline personality disorder 88, 89; cage 104–5, *104*; in consultancy 213–14, *213*, 219–20, *219*, *220*; contextual 134, 214–16, *215*; evolution of 5; of narcissistic dynamic 104, *104*; with 'observing eye' 48, 168; of patterns in supervision 16, 47; provisional nature of 46; self states sequential 89; split egg 104; universal *22*, 30; use of in supervision 47, 149, 192, 193, 228; *see also* diagrammatic reformulation; mapping; sequential diagrammatic reformulation
dialogic complexity 175–6
dialogic, dialogical 8, 37, 49, 113, 125, 126, 136, 147, 138, 166, 174, 188, 196, 240
dialogical sequence analysis (Leiman) 178
dialogical stance 38, 49, 187
dialogical understanding 125
difference: curiosity about 236; gender 224; naming 112; power, in forensic work 249; recognition of client's 265; *see also* cultural, differences
difficulties in supervision 12, 29, 44, 60, 62–3, 71–82, 194, 195, 199, 244
dilemma xvii, 39, 114, 142, 234
dilemmas in supervision in intellectual disability services 234–47
directive role of supervisor 132–3
distance supervision 50
diversity: of supervisees in group 126, 129; *see also* cultural, differences; difference
dumb spots (Ekstein) 32, 33, 107
dynamic administration 126–7

Efstation, J.F. 56, 57, 60
Ekstein, R. 32
Ellis, M.V. 53, 54, 59

emotion regulation systems (Gilbert) 104
enactments 11, 154, 191, 213, 214, 219, 224, 225, 232; countertransference 253; in forensic settings 250, 251, 253, 255, 257; intersubjective theory of 9; organisational in forensic services 248, 250; and parallel process 15; in supervision 11, 74, 78; in therapy with borderline patients 93; threatening therapeutic alliance 145, 154; use of SDR in describing and addressing 40; value of mapping 144–5; *see also* continuum of reciprocal role enactments; reciprocal role; recruitment
ending supervision relationship 131–2
ending therapy 41, 48, 193; with borderline patients 93; dealing with 279; in forensic settings 255–7; premature 77; with young people 223, 232–3
ethical dilemmas 72, 75, 76
ethical principles 71, 72, 79
Evans, K. 3, 12, 13, 201
exit xvii, 144, 167, 168
external supervision 203

Fairbairn, R. 4, 10
feedback: from supervisees to each other 33, 43, 44, 46, 107, 132, 155; from supervisees to supervisor 6, 33, 43, 149; from supervisor to supervisees 13, 31, 41, 42, 43, 44, 62, 64, 154, 157, 193, 194, 230; from therapy clients (use in supervision) 64
flexibility: of CAT model 198, 201, 222; of supervision in intellectual disability work 237; of supervisor 188, 195
focussed thinking 165
forensic services 248–58; accountability for offending behaviour 253–5, *254*; boundary breaches 248, 251; confidentiality 249–50; endings and transitions 255–6; expectations and enactments by professionals 250; pre-CAT work 252; public protection role of therapist 248, 249, 253, 254; therapeutic alliance 251–3; using CAT in risk assessment 256–8
formative *see* functions of supervision
Foster, J.T. 61
Foulkes, S. 125, 127
Frawley-O'Dea, M.G. 11, 15
frequency of supervision 55, 61, 134

Friedlander, M.L. 59, 60, 61
functions of supervision (normative, formative restorative) 210

Germer, C. 164, 168
Gilbert, M.C. 3, 12, 13, 201
Gilbert, P. 105
goodbye letter xvii, 5, 41, 44, 48, 93, 175, 193, 256
'good enough': care by teams 218; CAT 154, 192; mother 10, 32; supervisor 25, 34, 35–6, 93, 160; therapist 10, 228; therapy ending 223
Goodyear, R.K. 54
Gray, L.A. 59, 60
Greenberg, J.R. 8
group: manifest level 127; primary level 127
group analysis 125, 126
group dynamics 127; impact of departure and arrival on 131
group supervision *see* CAT supervision group
Guntrip, H. 10

Hamilton, L. 217
Harris, A. 8
Hasenkamp, W. 165
Hawkins, P. 4, 25, 26, 27, 32, 54, 188, 189, 193, 195
healthy self-state *97*, 98, 100; weakness in narcissism 96, 100
healthy supervisor 19–36
helicopter ability 25, 27, 35
helpful and unhelpful supervision events *58*
Helpful Aspects of Supervision scale (HAS) 56, 57
helpfulness in supervision 19, 56–60
hermeticism 176
Heron, J. 27, 28, *28,* 29, 30, 35
Hicks, D. 42
Hirsch, I. 9
human rights 110, 112, 120

inclusion, Buber's idea of 12
independence 74, 107, 240
Inskipp, F. 202, 203, 210
institutional policies impact on supervision 133
insula 165
integration 21, 23, 30, 32, 33, 34, 35, 243, 257; and fragmentation 24; river of (Siegel) 34
integrative relational supervision 12–13

intellectual disabilities 234–47; acknowledging abuse history 239; in the client-therapist-supervisor triad 237–8, 241; communication 241; consent 239; consultation with team 241–4; context of therapeutic relationship 238; cultural issues 246; diagram with images *242*; differences from adult mental health 245–6; dilemma for supervisors outside the field 234–6; directiveness of therapist 240; managing risk 238–9; missed sessions 240–1; mutual learning in mixed supervision group 244; power imbalance 239–40; presence of support worker 240; reciprocal role procedures in therapy relationship 246
intercultural supervision 109–21; positioning of supervisor in 112–13; principles of 120
interdependence 42
internal consultancy 209
internalisation 38; of external voices and dialogues 37, 38, 50; of joint activity 38, 195; of reciprocal roles xviii, 4, 20, 23, 37, 98, 106, 107, 126, 140, 177; of skills and processes 44, 130; of social roles and values 113; of therapist's voice and tools 38, 39
interpersonal neurobiology 33
intersubjective space 3, 12
intersubjectivity 8–10, 11
intuition 151, 178–9

Jones, L. 257
Jung, C.G. 178

Kabat-Zinn, J. 165, 166
Kerr, I. 16, 104, 125, 191, 192, 205

Ladany, N. 41, 53, 54, 61, 63, 73, 75
Langs, R. 43
language: body or non-verbal 50, 99, 178, 246; as carrier of culture 115; primary 110, 116
Lawson, C.J. 56
learning disabilities *see* intellectual disabilities
learning in interpersonal context 6, 38
Lehrman-Waterman, D.E. 63
Leiman, M. 113, 175, 178
level 1, level 2, level 3 procedures 21, 23, 24, 27, 29, 30, 32

levels of damage or disturbance 89; *see also* level 1, level 2, level 3 procedures
levels of work in consultancy 213–16, *213*

mapping 137–47; in consultancy work 214, *215*; supervision group *227*; supervisor's style 146–7; tools 140
'mapping the moment' in supervision 145–6
Marx, R. 3, 6, 38, 41, 199
McLeod, I. 194
McNeill, B.W. 60
Mehr, K.E. 63
metaprocedures 21, 25
metashifts 21, 22, 23; *see also* universal diagram
microcosm: in CAT supervision 174–84; and macrocosm 176–7
microsupervision 78
Miller, L. 14, 15
Milne, D.L. 54
mindfulness 163–73; and CAT 167–8; definition 163; origins 163; practice 166–7; in relational supervision of cognitive therapy 14; research 165; in supervision 168–73
mindsight (Siegel) 33
mistakes: by supervisee 62, 73, 107, 197, 230; by supervisor 23, 59, 108
Mitchell, S.A. 8
moment of meeting (Stern et al.) 9
Msebele, N. 109, 112
multiple self-states model (MSSM) 248–9
Muran, J.C. 14, 60

narcissism 95–108; dimensions 99–101; 'healthy' 98; key dilemmas in 97; modifications to standard CAT 101, 103–5; naming of 105; procedures in supervision 106–8; relational factors in childhood of 98–9; as a syndrome 99–101; in therapists 75, 106–8; twin self-states 96, *96*, 98, 99, 100, 102, 104, 106
narcissistic personality disorder 96
National Institute for Health and Care (NICE) 211; guidelines for borderline personality disorder 85; guidelines for personality disorders 83, 84
Nehmad, A. 23, 96, 102, 103
Nelson, M.L. 59, 60, 62
neurobiology 33, 35
neuroscience 33, 165

non-disclosure by supervisee 63, 75; *see also* withholding information in supervision
normative *see* functions of supervision
note-keeping 48–9
now moment (Stern et al.) 9

observing eye 40, 44, 48, 86, 138, 179, 188; development of 89; supervisor's 86
'observing us' 27, 33, 35, 202, 204, 205
offence paralleling behaviour 257
Ogden, T. 9
optimal conflict (Kegan) 41

parallel process 14–16, 31, 35, 106, 107, 146, 153, 199; asymmetric 15; CAT understanding of 15–16, 31, 199, 246; in consultancy supervision 211–12; contemporary relational view of 15; origin of concept 14; symmetric 14, 15
Parry, G.D. 42, 149, 151, 271
Paul, S. 3
performance issues in supervisees 73, 74, 75, 80–1, 155, 157, 195
Pilling, S. 54, 61
Plant, R. 130
Pollock, P. 257
power dynamics: in society 114; in supervision 49
PPND (people with a predominantly narcissistic dynamic) *see* narcissism
pregnant therapist 80
presence 34, 36, 163, 167; Siegel's definition 34
problem procedure xvii, 171, 228, 239; exacerbated by systemic pressures 118; exacerbated by therapist 225; in health service staff 81; mapping of 138; mindfulness increasing awareness of one's 167; narcissistic 95, 99, 101, 102, 103; in psychotherapy file 39; in reformulation xviii; self-harm 117; in sequential diagrammatic reformulation 40; as serving useful purpose in past or present 112; in teams 210, 214, 217; transgenerational 177; *see also* dilemma; reciprocal role procedure; snag; target problem procedure; trap
procedure or procedural sequence xvii, 39, 142, 231; *see also* level 1, level 2, level 3 procedures; problem procedure; reciprocal role procedure
Proctor, B. 127, 194, 202, 203, 210

psychoanalysis in the UK 10
psychotherapy file xvii, 39, 99, 102, 249

reciprocal role (RR) xviii, *19*, 37, 46, 110, 138, 199; in childhood of people with predominantly narcissistic dynamic 98–9; cultural 112, 114; internalisation of 4, 19–20, 23, 107; and parallel process 32; power, status and social factors and 112–13, 114; recruitment into 23, 31, 46; in self-state xviii, 46; in sequential diagrammatic reformulation xviii, 40, *40,* 140, 142, 143; in state of mind xviii; in supervision 31, 33, 41, 42, 44, 132, 133, 134; supervisor's 7, 11, 23, 32; and target problem procedure xviii; and transference xix; *see also* mapping; problem procedure; repertoire of reciprocal roles and reciprocal role procedures; self-state; sequential diagrammatic reformulation; state (state of mind)
reciprocal role procedure (RRP) xviii, 5, 7, 19–21, 24, 37, 140, 196, 202; in countertransference xvii; enacted in supervision 41, 73, 74–5, 78, 106–8, 204; enacted in therapy 38, 41, 47, 77, 79, 81, 91, 147, 187, 195, 240, 246; enactments at end of therapy 48, 93; exit from xvii, 144, 167; internalisation of 140; in parallel process 15–16, 31, 199; self-to-self 16, 37, 81, 195; therapist's unresolved 41, 49, 153; in use of CCAT in supervision 158–62, *159*; *see also* enactments; level 1, level 2, level 3 procedures; mapping; problem procedure; reciprocal role; recognition and revision of target problem procedures; reformulation; reformulation letter; sequential diagrammatic reformulation; target problem procedure
reciprocating countertransference xvii, 205
recognition and revision of target problem procedures 39, 47–8, 192, 255
recruitment 40, 106; of supervisor by supervisee 31; of therapist by client 31, 102
reformulation xviii, 89, 191, 199; in consultancy work 214–16; supervision of 44–7
reformulation letter 33, 39, 45, 48, 89, 91, 103, 192, 229, 244, 249

relational models of psychotherapy 3
relational models of supervision 3, 4
relational psychoanalysis 8
relational psychoanalytic supervision 8–12
relational psychodynamic supervision model (Frawley-O'Dea and Sarnat) 11
relational supervision of cognitive therapy 13–14; experiential nature of 14; relational context of 14
relational turn in psychoanalysis 8
remorse of forensic clients 255
repertoire of reciprocal roles and reciprocal role procedures xviii, 20, 21, 24, 25, 26, 29, 32, 74, 91, 113, 126, 168, 246; in borderline personality disorder 87, 89
research on supervision 53–65; critique 53
resonance 34, 36
restorative *see* functions of supervision
review of supervision 44
risk 245, 270; to client 72, 77; in forensic practice 249–56; in intellectual disability work 239–40; to other 72, 75; to therapist 72, 79
role ambiguity 61
role conflict 61
role play 14, 46, 152, 155, 160, 189, 193, 214
Roth, A. 54, 55, 61
RR *see* reciprocal role
RRP *see* reciprocal role procedure
rupture *see* alliance rupture
rupture-inducing competency assessment *159*
Ryle, A. 37, 38, 41, 44, 114, 139, 147, 189, 192, 205, 209, 214, 228, 232, 233, 248; approach to supervision 4–5, 6, 125, 191; on borderline patients 83, 84, 85, 88, 89; development of CAT model 4, 10, 37; on flexibility in therapy 45; on level 1, 2, 3 procedures and disturbance 21, 89; on parallel process 16; on split egg diagram 104

safeguarding 72, 75, 76
Safran, J.D. 13–14, 44, 60, 145, 169
Salzberger-Wittenberg, I. 191
Samuels, A. 10
Sarnat, J.E. 11, 15
scaffolding xviii, 10, 23, 39; in supervision 6, 16, 31–2, 43, 110, 150, 155, 160, *161*, 189, 190, 192, 200, 202, 204, 205; *see also* zone of proximal development

Schore, A. 9
SDR *see* sequential diagrammatic reformulation
Searles, H. 14
self: CAT view of 125, 175; use of in supervision 6
self-care: of supervisee 210; of supervisor 50
self-disclosure by supervisor 13, 63–4, 65
self-state xviii, 19, 20, 22, 30, 88, 89, 96, *97*; twin in narcissism 96, *96*, 98, 99, 106, 100, 104; *see also* healthy self-state; reciprocal role
sequential diagrammatic reformulation (SDR) xviii, 40, *40*, 47, 89; *see also* diagrammatic reformulation
seven-eyed model of supervision (Shohet and Hawkins) 4, 25, *26*, 27, 35
Shanfield, S.B. 59
Shaw, E. 74
Shohet, R. 4, 25, 26, 27, 32, 54, 188, 193, 195
Siegel, D. 33, 34, 36, 43
signs, joint creation of 38
Six Category Intervention Analysis (Heron) 27–9, *28*
Skjerve, J. 64
Smith, M. 130
snag xvii, xviii, 39, 112, 114, 120, 165, 168
social formation of mind 38
stance of curious enquiry *see* curiosity, curious enquiry
state (state of mind) xviii, 9, 23, 28, 31, 34, 43, 88–9, 91, 102, 111, 138, 158, 167, 202, 249, 255, 257
state shift (or switch) 19, 20, 21, 88, 89
Stern, D. 9
Stiles, W. 125, 188
Stolorow, R.D. 8, 9
stuckness in supervision group dynamic 133–4
Sturm, D.E.R. 169
suffering 163, 167
Sullivan, S. 109, 112
super-addressee 117
supervision: of CAT trainees 187–97; definitions 54, 264; excellent 59; of experienced therapists 49; impact on client outcomes 54–6; making best use of 64; of non-CAT therapists 198–207; poor or harmful 59, 60, 65; strategies in intercultural context 112; *see also* difficulties in supervision

supervision goals 203, 204
supervision group *see* CAT supervision group
supervisor-led co-supervision 126, 131–2
supervisory alliance 5, 14, 41, 61, 65, 73, 74, 78, 79, 204; *see also* alliance rupture; supervisory dialogue; supervisory relationship; working alliance
supervisory challenges 71–81
supervisory dialogue 63–4
supervisory relationship: and attachment pattern of supervisee 61; breakdown 79, 236; as central in helpful supervision 60; conflictual 60; negative impact of 60; *see also* alliance rupture; collaboration in supervision; supervisory dialogue
Supervisory Working Alliance Inventory (SWAI) 56, 57, 61

Tanner, C. 43, 191
target problem (TP) xviii, 38, 39, 89, 91, 228; in reformulation letter 45, 46
target problem procedure (TPP) xviii, 39, 140, 254; in reformulation letter 45; *see also* dilemma; reciprocal role procedure; reformulation; reformulation letter; sequential diagrammatic reformulation; snag; trap
therapeutic alliance: with forensic clients 251, 252; impact of power differences on 113; *see also* alliance rupture
Thich Nhat Hanh 166
threat to therapy boundary 77
time allocation *see* CAT supervision group
tools of CAT 39, 47, 199; adapting for intellectual disabilities work 241
TP *see* target problem
TPP *see* target problem procedure
training course: supervisor's relationship to 193–5
training of CAT supervisors 27
transference xix, 10, 11, 196; diagram or to understand 40, 47, 139, 141, 145; eroticised 72, 77; and parallel process 15; and reciprocal role procedures 37, 47, 146, 172, 190
transgenerational communication of trauma 177
transgressive behaviour 78
trap xvii, xix, 39, 112, 114, 115, 168
Trevarthen, C. 9
Twomey, J.E. 14, 15

universal diagram *22*; *see also* metashifts
unoffered chair 235

victim blaming 117–20
Vygotsky, L.S. 4, 6, 23, 38, 92, 147, 195, 200

Wallin, D.J. 9
Welwood, J. 163
Wessler, R.A. 255
Wessler, R.L. 255
Winnicott, D. 4, 10, 32

withholding information in supervision 194
working alliance: in consultancy between supervisor and team 211; scale to measure 60; in supervision 12, 60, 63; *see also* therapeutic alliance
Worthen, V. 60

Yerushalmi, H. 11

zone of proximal development (ZPD) xix, 23, 30, 31, 38, 102, 150, 191, 200, 229, 253; *see also* scaffolding